Edwin and Willa Muir

Edwin and Willa Muir

A Literary Marriage

MARGERY PALMER MCCULLOCH

Great Clarendon Street, Oxford, OX2 6DP,
United Kingdom

Oxford University Press is a department of the University of Oxford.
It furthers the University's objective of excellence in research, scholarship,
and education by publishing worldwide. Oxford is a registered trade mark of
Oxford University Press in the UK and in certain other countries

© Ian McCulloch 2023
Editorial material © Oxford University Press 2023

The moral rights of the author have been asserted

All rights reserved. No part of this publication may be reproduced, stored in
a retrieval system, or transmitted, in any form or by any means, without the
prior permission in writing of Oxford University Press, or as expressly permitted
by law, by licence or under terms agreed with the appropriate reprographics
rights organization. Enquiries concerning reproduction outside the scope of the
above should be sent to the Rights Department, Oxford University Press, at the
address above

You must not circulate this work in any other form
and you must impose this same condition on any acquirer

Published in the United States of America by Oxford University Press
198 Madison Avenue, New York, NY 10016, United States of America

British Library Cataloguing in Publication Data
Data available

Library of Congress Control Number: 2022945375

ISBN 978–0–19–285804–7

DOI: 10.1093/oso/9780192858047.001.0001

Printed and bound by
CPI Group (UK) Ltd, Croydon, CR0 4YY

Links to third party websites are provided by Oxford in good faith and
for information only. Oxford disclaims any responsibility for the materials
contained in any third party website referenced in this work.

In Memoriam
Margery Palmer McCulloch
1935–2019

Foreword

Margery Palmer McCulloch was an Honorary Senior Research Fellow at the University of Glasgow. She published widely on Scottish literature in the twentieth century, with special interests in the rise of modernism in Scottish writing and the work of Scottish women writers in the interwar years and the modern period. Her monographs include *The Novels of Neil M. Gunn* (1987), *Edwin Muir: Poet, Critic and Novelist* (1993), and *Scottish Modernism and its Contexts 1918–1959* (2009). Dr McCulloch edited *Modernism and Nationalism: Literature and Society in Scotland* (2004), and co-edited the *Edinburgh Companion to Hugh MacDiarmid* and *Scottish and International Modernisms* (both 2011) along with the *Scottish Literary Review* from 2005 to 2013. She had just completed the first draft of a major biography of the marriage between Edwin and Willa Muir when, at the age of 84, in the early months of 2019, she suffered a serious and ultimately fatal stroke. Her typescript was not yet ready for publication and the task of revising and editing the computer files was taken up by Professor Roderick Watson at the request of Margery's husband Ian McCulloch. His introduction to the book sets the stage for the study to follow.

Acknowledgements

Special thanks must go to the Leverhulme Emeritus Fellowship, awarded in 2013, which allowed Dr McCulloch to travel all over Europe in pursuit of the Muirs, and special thanks must go to the invaluable support of the Muir estate, the late Ethel Ross, and especially Kenneth Ross for permission to use the material in this study. Thanks also go to Professor Ritchie Robertson for access to his 1981 thesis 'Edwin Muir's contact with German Literature and its influence on his thought and poetry'; and to Dr Kirsty Allen, for access to her unpublished 1997 PhD *The Life and Work of Willa Muir, 1890–1955* (PhD research repository, University of St Andrews). This study would not have been possible without the support of the librarians and the keepers of manuscript collections in the following libraries: The Holms/Kingsmill collection and the Schiff papers in The British Library; the Muir correspondence, the Peter Butter papers, and the Soukup papers in the National Library of Scotland; the Muir collections in Special Collections at St Andrews University Library; Muir material at the Orkney Library and Archive at Kirkwall, including the Mary Bosdet papers (Edwin and Willa Muir), and the Ernest Walker Marwick papers; the Routledge Archive and the Hogarth/Chatto & Windus archive at the University of Reading Special Collections; the Muir and George Barker correspondence held by the Reference and Research Services at the Harry Ransom Center at the University of Texas at Austin; the University of Edinburgh Centre for Research Collections; the Scottish Theatre Archive in Archives and Special Collections at the University of Glasgow Library; correspondence from the Newman/Cairns collection by permission of Edward Newman and the Master and Fellows of St John's College, Cambridge. Extracts from *Collected Poems* by Edwin Muir are reprinted by permission of Faber and Faber Ltd. Extracts from the typescript for the BBC talk on Edwin Muir (Sp Coll STA Kc7/6) are reprinted by permission of University of Glasgow Library, Archives & Special Collections. A final acknowledgement must go to the work originally done in this field by Professor Peter Butter and to the personal support given by the late Professor Alexander Scott and Professor Aniela Korzeniowska, Head of the Department of Applied Linguistics and Translation at the University of Warsaw.

Contents

List of Illustrations	x
Introduction	1
1. Coming Together 1918–1921	10

PART I. ADVENTURING IN EUROPE

2. Prague and a New Czech Republic 1921–1922	29
3. Elbflorenz 1922–1923	41
4. North and South 1923–1924	54
5. Fête du Citron 1924–1926	68

PART II. PUTTING DOWN ROOTS

6. Early Writings	85
7. Willa and Womanhood 1927–1929	99
8. Crowborough and Literary Life 1929–1931	112

PART III. THE POLITICAL THIRTIES

9. Changing Worlds and a Hampstead Idyll 1930–1933	129
10. Scottish Journeys 1933–1935	146
11. Scotland and Europe 1935–1939	159
12. Translating for a Living	175

PART IV. A SINGLE, DISUNITED WORLD

13. The Second World War in St Andrews 1939–1942	193
14. Edinburgh and a New Poetry 1942–1945	206

15. The Cold War and Prague 1945–1948	218
16. Roman Interlude 1948–1950	243
17. Newbattle Abbey 1950–1955	255

PART V. A NEW WORLD

18. American Adventure 1955–1956	277
19. Swaffham Prior 1956–1959	290
20. Willa Alone 1959–1963	302
21. Last Years 1963–1970	319
Appendix	336
Bibliography	339
Index	343

List of Illustrations

0.1. Willa Muir in 1944. Portrait by Nigel McIsaac *Source*: National Galleries of Scotland. © The McIsaac Family	xi
0.2. Edwin Muir in 1955 *Source*: From Willa Muir, *Belonging. A Memoir* (London: The Hogarth Press, 1968)	xii
1.1. Wilhelmina Anderson at St Andrews 1910 *Source*: From Willa Muir, *Belonging. A Memoir* (London: The Hogarth Press, 1968)	13
1.2. Edwin Muir in the 1920s *Source*: Orkney Library and Archive	14
2.1. Prague, The Powder Tower *Source*: https://libreshot.com/powder-tower-in-prague/	30
4.1. Francis George Scott *Source*: https://www.open.edu/openlearncreate/mod/oucontent/view.php?id=147713&section=4	57
12.1. Hermann Broch *Source*: https://medium.com/@mjcantinho/hermann-broch-da-poesia-como-absoluto-edd06ac320e	184
15.1. Refugees. 'On a pilgrimage from nowhere to nowhere' *Source*: dpa picture alliance / Alamy Stock Photo	219
15.2. 'The towns in ruins.' Prague after the American bombing *Source*: https://albumwar2.com/prague-after-the-american-mass-bombardment/	219
17.1. Newbattle Abbey *Source*: National Galleries of Scotland. Collection of Mrs Catherine Clark, gifted by her sons Sandy, David and Peter in her memory, 2008	256
17.2. George Mackay Brown *Source*: Orkney Library and Archive	261
21.1. Willa Muir in 1967 *Source*: Orkney Library and Archive	327

Introduction

This is the story of a literary marriage. It tells of the partnership between two intellectuals from small-town Scottish backgrounds and their discovery of Europe in the years after the First and Second World Wars. It tells us a lot about the cultural, social, and political issues of those dynamic and difficult years and much else, in intimate detail, about their own personal struggles to make a living. Edwin and Willa Muir never wavered in their commitment to the arts, to the place of the spirit, and the value of lyric poetry in a world of social inequality, dispossession, and suffering. Their experience tells of intellectual emancipation in circles at home that often seemed narrow and constrained, and it testifies to their lifelong vision of the importance of European culture. When Hugh MacDiarmid was insisting on a European dimension for the renaissance of modern Scottish writing, the Muirs were actually travelling and living in Europe, engaging with European culture, translating German literature, and moving beyond Scotland to Czechoslovakia, Germany, Austria, Italy, France, and the United States.

Edwin and Willa became a well-known couple in literary circles both at home and abroad. They were an important part of the Scottish literary renaissance, though they saw themselves more as socialists than nationalists, and when they moved to London, they made friends with Catherine and Donald Carswell, Helen Cruickshank, T. S. Eliot, A. S. Neill, and Kathleen Raine. Willa was the better linguist of the two, but Edwin's early interest in Heine and the philosophy of Nietzsche led them to translate many German authors, notably Lion Feuchtwanger, Gerhard Hauptmann, Hermann Broch, and most famously Franz Kafka. It is a notable fact that the English-speaking world's first contact with *The Castle*, *The Trial*, and *Metamorphosis* was entirely due to the work of these two Scots: one brought up in Orkney and the other in the small east-coast town of Montrose. Their time together in Prague, in both the 1920s and the 1940s, may have given them special insight into Kafka's writing, and their exposure to the terrible aftermath of the Second World War in Europe has been memorably caught in poems by Edwin such as 'The Good Town', 'The Interrogation', and 'The Refugees' whose lines still speak to us today: 'We saw our houses falling / Wall after wall behind us. [...] This is our punishment. We came / Here without blame, yet with blame.'[1] In fact, Edwin Muir's engagement with the realities and the trauma of post-war

---

[1] 'The Refugees' from *The Narrow Place* (1943), in *The Complete Poems of Edwin Muir*, ed. by Peter Butter (Aberdeen: The Association for Scottish Literary Studies, 1991), p. 99.

European experience in the twentieth century is still insufficiently acknowledged in our accounts of modern poetry in English.

This is not a critical study of the writings of Edwin and Willa Muir as such, although it does trace the issues that engaged them in fascinating detail, with telling insights into their key publications, their interests, and also their anxieties during a long and devoted partnership. Peter Butter's critical biography *Edwin Muir: Man and Poet* from 1966 was long the standard account of Edwin's life and work, followed by Dr McCulloch's *Edwin Muir: Poet, Critic and Novelist* (1993). Later scholars with new information have added to our critical and biographical knowledge, and this new study makes especially clear the extent to which the Scottish poet's career was made possible by the unstinting support of his wife. Edwin's poetry has been widely analysed and appreciated. Willa's writing, on the other hand, has had rather less attention, although the last twenty years have seen a welcome revival of interest in her work, including a critical study of her writing by Aileen Christianson and significant biographical research by Kirsty Allen.[2] In fact, Willa's first novel has been rediscovered as a milestone in the contemporary revaluation of twentieth-century Scottish women writers and their contribution to the literary renaissance. *Imagined Corners* (1931) is a memorably searing analysis of modern society, via the pettiness of small-town Scottish life, but it also offers a challenging account of the sexual and psychological differences between women and men, as its two leading female characters, Elise Mütze and Elizabeth Shand, court social scandal and disgrace by overthrowing their traditional roles and striking out for sexual and social independence.

We already have the benefit of the Muirs' own accounts of their own lives, for they both wrote autobiographies, with *Belonging* from Willa in 1968 and Edwin's *The Story and the Fable* from 1940, later revised and expanded as *An Autobiography* in 1954. But in bringing them together for the first time, Dr McCulloch uses each to supplement the other, noting the points of difference or disagreement—as well as the sometimes rather telling omissions in their mutual memoirs. This study also draws extensively from less accessible sources including Edwin's diaries, Willa's unpublished journals, as well as correspondence from friends, family, and publishers, along with radio broadcasts, and the personal recollections of friends and colleagues, such as Morley Jamieson, Jumir Soukup, Violet Schiff, Joseph Chiari, Kathleen Raine, Pat Swale, Edwin's brother, and the Marwick family in Orkney. Dr McCulloch's study also offers many additional insights into the literary world and the cultural, social, and political circumstances of the first half of the twentieth century, often in strikingly immediate and domestic detail. The

---

[2] Kirsty Allen did groundbreaking work on *The Life and Work of Willa Muir, 1890–1955* (PhD research repository, University of St Andrews, 1997); and this was followed by Aileen Christianson, *Moving in Circles: Willa Muir's Writings* (Edinburgh: Word Power Books, 2007). A special issue of the literary journal *Chapman*, edited by Joy Hendry, produced the memoirs and essays in *Peerie Willa Muir* (1993), and see also Willa Muir's selected fiction and prose writings published as *Imagined Selves*, edited and introduced by Kirsty Allen (Edinburgh: Canongate Books, 1996).

story of Edwin and Willa is the moving tale of a unique, if complicated creative partnership in difficult circumstances, but it is never less than a love story, too.

Our couple's story begins, as this study does, with a party in Glasgow in September 1918. These two were not an obvious match, but the attraction must have been strong, for they were married by June the following year. Edwin was a budding literary critic and essayist. As a convinced socialist, fascinated by the iconoclasm of Nietzsche, he was making a reputation for himself with contributions to A. R. Orage's influential London periodical *The New Age*. Born in Orkney on 15 May 1887, Muir was largely self-educated and rather shy in social company. He was working as a shipping clerk in Glasgow when he met Willa, and had entered the literary scene with a series of 209 self-consciously radical and high-toned aphorisms published in 1918 as *We Moderns*.[3] Born in Montrose on 13 March 1890, Willa had a much better formal education than Edwin. A strong-minded Classics graduate of St Andrews University, with an interest in psychology and educational psychology, she had just been appointed as vice principal at Gipsy Hill Teachers' Training College in London when they met. Three years younger than Edwin, her own writing life did not begin until 1925 with *Women: An Enquiry*, published by the Hogarth Press. Its proto-feminist ambitions are somewhat weakened to modern eyes by linking woman's creativity to fertility and her role as a wife, but Willa's interest in the value of strong feeling and the importance of love as a positive source must have chimed with the section on 'Creative Love' in Edwin's first book. Even so, she had plenty cause to be radical about the experience of women, for according to the protocols of the time she had to give up teaching when she married, and was discriminated against by a college principal who disapproved of the 'atheism' in her husband's new book. As a gifted university graduate in the years immediately after the First World War, she found professional employment elusive, as so many women did at the time, nor was it always easy for her to be cast as 'the poet's wife' in literary circles.

When Willa did find her own *métier* it was because her training as a classicist gave her a linguist's precision when she began to translate modern German literature. This started—like Edwin's role as book reviewer—as a matter of necessity when the couple had to make a living in London. Their names usually appeared together on the works they translated, but it has become clear to modern researchers that Willa's superior linguistic skills, were fundamental and indispensible to the success of these projects, which included more than thirty books and plays translated from German, along with many other shorter pieces.[4] There were times when the burden of this work seemed particularly heavy, and Willa's middle years were marked by recurrent ill health, but her achievement stands as an

---

[3] Edward Moore, *We Moderns: Enigmas and Guesses* (London: George Allen & Unwin, 1918).
[4] See Appendix. A further critical account of Willa's writing can be found in Aileen Christianson, *Moving in Circles: Willa Muir's Writings* (Edinburgh: Word Power Books, 2007).

important contribution to the dissemination of modern German literature in the English-speaking world. Nor should her authorial skills be underestimated. *Imagined Corners* remains her most significant achievement, but as Dr McCulloch argues, Willa's autobiography, along with her diaries, letters, and occasional essays, show a lively and humorous mind at work, no less alert to the ironies of her perceived role as 'the poet's wife'. The closing chapters of this study show us a woman living on her own, still possessed of a caustic wit, newly determined to be given proper credit for her work as a translator, committed to write the book on the Scottish Ballads that her husband never started (*Living with Ballads*, 1965), and fully determined to make sense of their time together. 'Belonging', the title of her autobiography, published only two years before she died, says much about a spirit that sought to ground itself and find itself, wherever she was, during a long and devoted marriage and a much-travelled life.

The focus of this study is on the changing dynamics of the relationship between Edwin and Willa, from the moment they formed the partnership that powered their time together, along with all the successes, pains, and setbacks they encountered along the way. But before that journey begins, it makes sense to offer a brief introduction to their earlier selves, before they met at that party in Glasgow.

Mr Muir and Miss Anderson had very different upbringings, but they soon discovered that they had common roots in the culture of the northern isles. Willa's parents, Peter and Betty Anderson, came from Unst in the Shetlands but chose to move to the Scottish mainland, probably for economic reasons. It was there that they met each other, married (she was a dressmaker), and set up a successful draper's store in Montrose. This was a small town of rigidly Presbyterian values, lowland Scottish bourgeois prosperity, and narrow-mindedness, all of which, along with the national psyche, was vividly excoriated in Willa's study *Mrs Grundy in Scotland* (1936)[5] and revisited under the fictional name of 'Calderwick' in *Imagined Corners*, her first novel. In such a milieu Willa came to value what she thought of as her Shetland roots, and the sense of difference it gave her, referring to herself in Shetland dialect as 'peerie' Willa (little Willa) in her relationship with Edwin. He would have been more than familiar with her use of dialect for he had been born and brought up in the Orkney Islands, which have their own highly distinctive linguistic and cultural character.

Willa's early years were comfortable, and the success of the Anderson drapery shop meant that she could be sent to a small private school in Montrose. But Peter Anderson's death when Willa was only 9, threw the family into straitened circumstances and the young girl's sense of her own difference, both socially, intellectually, and in terms of her family's origins, was brought home to her when she

---

[5] See Willa Muir, *Imagined Selves*, ed. by Kirsty Allen (Edinburgh: Canongate Classics, 1996). Introduced by Kirsty Allen, this anthology contains *Imagined Corners*, *Mrs Ritchie*, *Mrs Grundy in Scotland*, *Women: An Inquiry*, and 'Women in Scotland'.

had to transfer to larger classrooms in the local school system. She was a bright student, however, and a scholarship took her to Montrose Academy where her love for the classics was encouraged and she flourished intellectually, despite the local snobberies that saw her as a 'bursary' pupil. It was here that she met her friend Emily Stobo, whose mother was to introduce her to Edwin Muir. 'Mam' Stobo's lively social occasions at home, in Montrose and later in Glasgow, were a new and welcome experience for Willa, whose relationship with her own mother—hard-pressed to maintain the family business—was not always easy.[6] Willa thrived at Montrose Academy, taking medals in Greek, Latin, and English and gaining entrance (along with Emily Stobo) to the University of St Andrews, where she was to do even better, graduating with first-class honours in Greek and Humanities in 1911, followed by English and History, winning various prizes and the Class Medal along the way, together with a Fellowship that allowed her to study for another year. It was during this time that a love affair with a particularly handsome but wayward rugby player ended with a broken engagement in 1912 and the need to leave St Andrews, where Willa had been so happy and successful, to turn south and seek employment with various teaching roles elsewhere.

In London, helped by a Carnegie scholarship, Willa pursued a special interest in educational psychology and experimental child psychology at Bedford College, now part of the University of London. Caught up by the need to make a living during the difficult wartime years, she never completed her thesis, and a post teaching factory girls followed, and then a post as a lecturer and vice principal at Gypsy Hill Training College. This was the job she later had to leave because of what the principal of the college took to be her husband's 'atheism'. Her own interest in psychology was equally challenging to polite society at the time, and she rather enjoyed taking a racy psychoanalytical line on issues under discussion, to the occasional alarm of friends and colleagues. Unsettled in wartime London, she would take holiday breaks in St Andrews whenever she could, which led to her meeting with the man she would marry.

Edwin's life was very different. He was the youngest of six children born on a farm in the Orkney Islands. His early childhood was spent on the island of Wyre in a small God-fearing community with a strong oral tradition rich with song, folklore, and local tales of witches and shipwrecks. As he later put it, this was a place 'where there was no great distinction between the ordinary and the fabulous'.[7] Indeed the original title of his autobiography in 1940—*The Story and the Fable*—speaks directly to his later sense that mythic experience was only ever just beneath the surface of the everyday. Poems from his first collection in 1925 reimagine tales

---

[6] I am indebted to Kirsty Allen for information about Willa's early life. See *The Life and Work of Willa Muir, 1890–1955* (PhD research repository, University of St Andrews, 1997). https://research-repository.st-andrews.ac.uk/handle/10023/9073

[7] Edwin Muir, *The Story and the Fable. An Autobiography* (London: George Harrop & Co, 1940), p. 12.

from the Bible and the Greek myths (themes he was to return to again and again) fused with his sense of a timeless childhood spent in a remote and beautiful part of the world, entirely disengaged from modernity, whose tensions can only rumble like distant rumours beyond the horizon. The first two chapters of Muir's autobiography, almost half the book in length, are a brilliantly moving account of these formative years, along with deeply reflective thinking about whether we can know ourselves at all, and what it might be to write about one's life, given the mysteries and problems of time and identity.

The family moved to another farm on the Orkney mainland near to Kirkwall when Edwin was 8, and he attended school there. But the land was poor, the landlord was intransigent, and living had become especially hard after the three older sons left home to try their luck in Central Scotland. James Muir finally gave up the struggle in 1901 and decided to move the household to join Johnnie and Jimmy in Glasgow. Edwin was 14 years old, and the change was traumatic. Remembering the experience in an extract from his diaries, published in *The Story and the Fable*, he had this to say:

> I was born before the Industrial Revolution, and am now about two hundred years old. But I have skipped a hundred and fifty of them. I was really born in 1737, and till I was fourteen no time-accidents happened to me. Then in 1751 I set out from Orkney for Glasgow. When I arrived I found that it was not 1751, but 1901, and that a hundred and fifty years had been burned up in my two days' journey. But I myself was still in 1751, and remained there for a long time. All my life I have been trying to overhaul that invisible leeway. No wonder I am obsessed with Time.
>
> Every summer, during my two weeks' holiday, I travelled back that hundred and fifty years again. What a relief it was to get back to the pre-industrial world, and how much better everything was arranged there![8]

Muir's poetry is indeed haunted by a sense of time and the timeless, for the patterns and structures of myth are always present for him, just beneath the surface of human experience and history. In terms of technique, he was no modernist, and he was never tempted to follow his friend Eliot's example. (In fact, he did not much care for *The Waste Land*.) His own poetry preferred more conventional structures and references, not without a spiritual dimension, often speaking in symbolic terms. His work in prose fiction on the other hand (he wrote three novels) did not shy from the horrors of history and the present day, most especially in his last and best novel, *Poor Tom* (1932), which drew on his grim urban experiences in Glasgow.

---

[8] 'Extracts from a Diary', in *The Story and the Fable*, p. 263.

That was not a happy time. Within a year of arriving in Scotland's largest industrial city, father James Muir had a fatal heart attack and Edwin's second brother Willie died of tuberculosis. Four years later, his third brother Johnnie died of a brain tumour, followed by his mother Elizabeth, who died three months after Johnnie. At 19 years old Edwin was thrown onto his own resources. Alone in Glasgow, he sought work as an office boy in various firms throughout the city. At one time he was a clerk in a bone factory, where rotting bones were rendered down to fat, leaving a stench and a vision of decay he was never to forget. Edwin's health was not strong, and during the First World War—judged unfit for the army—he worked in the offices of a shipyard. Looking for meaning in these years, he did not find it in the religious revivals that were then sweeping the city, but his sense of poverty and social injustice in the 'grimy desolation' of the city took him instead to socialism and the Independent Labour Party. Making friends in these circles and reading widely, Edwin sought insight and hope for the future in Shaw, Ibsen, Whitman, and what he saw as the 'ironical paganism' of Heine, leading eventually to his own literary ambitions, and the cultural criticism and radical philosophies of Friedrich Nietzsche.

From such beginnings Edwin went on to become a well-respected reviewer and essayist. T. S. Eliot, his editor and friend (a year and a half younger than Muir), regarded him as one of the best critics of his day and Muir's essays were collected in *Latitudes* (1924), *Transition: Essays on Contemporary Literature* (1926), and *Essays on Literature and Society* (1949). He came to poetry relatively late. Edwin was 38 when his first collection was published and his work shows a sense of spiritual longing and unease born of the dislocation he experienced in industrial Glasgow, in terrible contrast to what seemed to him to be the primal and Edenic state of his childhood in Orkney. In the aftermath of his family trauma, Edwin underwent psychoanalysis when he was with Willa in London. He kept a dream notebook and dreams and dream-like images feature in many of the poems he now began to write.

Muir's engagement with mythic timelessness is characteristic of his contribution to the poetry of the twentieth-century Scottish literary renaissance, and in this respect he stands as a kind of counterpart to Christopher Grieve, the major poet of that movement, best known by the pen name (soon to become his whole identity) of 'Hugh MacDiarmid'. He and Muir were both socialists, but MacDiarmid's communism and nationalism took him along much more radical paths, while Edwin's time in post-war Prague gave him a very different opinion of communism in practice. They share a strong sense of the spiritual dimension in human affairs, but MacDiarmid's engagement with the material world of politics and science—especially in his later poetry—is very different from Muir's fascination with symbolic thinking and the recurrence of mythical patterns. Edwin's roots in Orkney made him particularly sympathetic to George Mackay Brown, who became a student of his at Newbattle Abbey in the 1950s. Influenced by his

Catholic faith, Mackay Brown's poems evoke a vision of Orkney as a land, steeped in seasonal rhythms, whose history goes back to the time of the Vikings. Nevertheless, and notwithstanding his own fascination with the timelessness of 'fable', Edwin's extensive engagement with modern German literature and especially his experience of living in Europe after the two World Wars means that his art has also spoken strongly about the 'story' of modern history. Seamus Heaney recognized this in an essay first published in *Verse* in 1989:

> [Muir's] metaphysical habit of mind and mythological disposition had kept him out of the political swim of 'Thirties' English poetry. There seemed to be nothing up to date about him. But in the Forties, and especially in this 1949 volume, [*The Labyrinth*] we can watch the gratifying spectacle of a solitary poetic endeavour attaining representative status; or to put it another way, by then Muir's subject was everybody's subject. His stand-off with modernity had preceded the general post-war dismay at human destructiveness and a new recognition of human frailty in the atomic age. His experiences in Austria and Czechoslovakia that had kept him at a slight remove from English literary culture in the pre-war years now gave him a unique personal perspective and enabled him to write a poetry recognizably akin to that being written by the tragic ironists and parablists in post-war Eastern Europe.[9]

This is a timely recognition of Muir's sometimes underestimated quality as a modern poet. He was at odds with the buzz of modernism, and with MacDiarmid's enthusiasm for the dynamic use of colloquial Scots, but more than most of his generation, he confronted the spiritual vacuum at the heart of the twentieth century, by seeking understanding and some hope, too, with a more timeless perspective on the recurring cycles of human history, failure, decency, and endeavour. The closing page of the first draft of his autobiography had this to say:

> I leave my fragmentary record at this point, the point at which, by imaginatively understanding my own life as a human being, I begin to understand human life not as a life of routine and machinery, but as a fable extending far beyond the experience given to us by our senses and our practical reason. My road to that realization was not, I feel, a typical one; perhaps, indeed, it was fantastically abnormal; but there must be countless roads to it, and this was mine.[10]

It remains to be said that much of the power of Edwin Muir's work is the legacy of two key factors in his life: his childhood in Orkney, and his marriage to Willa Anderson, 'the most fortunate event in my life'. It was Willa Anderson who gave

---

[9] 'Edwin Muir' in Seamus Heaney, *Finders Keepers. Selected Prose 1971–2001* (London: Faber and Faber, 2002), pp. 254–5.
[10] *The Story and the Fable*, p. 236.

him the stability he needed as a creative artist, even at the cost of her own ambitions, during all their travels and travails together. 'How European we were', they used to reflect fondly, having travelled so far from their roots in Orkney and Montrose. Margery McCulloch's major study is the record of their remarkable journey together.

Roderick Watson

1
Coming Together 1918–1921

> We both went down to London without a job between us, with very little money, and with hopes over which our sensible friends shook their heads.
>
> Edwin Muir, *The Story and the Fable* (1940)

Edwin Muir and Wilhelmina Anderson first met at a mutual friend's home in Glasgow in September 1918. Willa, as she later called herself, had graduated with First Class Honours from the University of St Andrews in 1911, and was now vice principal and lecturer in a training college for teachers in London. Edwin was a clerk in a shipping office in Renfrew, just outside Glasgow. The friend who organized this introductory meeting was Mrs Stobo, generally known as 'Mam', the mother of Emily who had been Willa's best friend at Montrose Academy and at St Andrews University. Although the friends and Mam had fallen out as a result of a young man at the university showing a clear preference for the company of Willa as opposed to Emily, over time this breach in their friendship had largely healed. The Stobos were now resident in Glasgow and Mam's dinner parties were as popular in that city as they had been in east-coast Montrose. On this particular occasion she was anxious to introduce Willa to one of her more recent regular visitors, a young man of promise. This was Edwin Muir, who as 'Edward Moore' had published *We Moderns*, a collection of Nietzschean essays that had first appeared as a series in *The New Age* magazine. Mrs Stobo presented Willa with the book as soon as she arrived on the afternoon of the dinner party, and Willa found herself both irritated and intrigued by the nature of its style and contents and what her hostess saw in it.

Willa would later write, 'What Mam asked from life and from the books she read was material that could be turned into amusing stories. She was concerned with appearances, with show business, and cared little for truth.' But this book by her new protégé appeared to be written 'by a young man trying to lift himself up by his boot-straps beyond his ledgers into a world he accepted as noble and true, inhabited by figures he thought noble and true, such as Goethe and Ibsen and Nietzsche'. Willa was puzzled; because 'Edward Moore' appeared to be exactly the kind of young man that Mam would have found 'boring'. Yet there was something in his ideas and writing that she herself responded to, a feeling she had of 'belonging to the Universe'. Was Edward Moore's insistence that 'To love one is to love all' in the section 'Love and Innocence' the same as her own sense of 'overflowing feeling'? Nevertheless, she would neither give in to Mrs Stobo's urging nor say how much she liked the book, telling herself that these epigrams were 'Nietzschean' and determined to say nothing that 'would add to the size of the fish in Mam's net'.[1]

When he arrived at the flat, the 'fish' was not at all as expected. Edwin Muir's brow was that of an intellectual, 'disproportionately wide and high' but his eyes were 'dreamy-looking, sea-blue, with a hint of distance in them, and his mouth was well cut, with full sensitive lips'. His body, on the other hand, was 'meagre', and she noticed that 'one of his thin shoulders, the left, as if cramped with too much leaning on an elbow, was held stiffly above the level of the other'. But when he laughed, 'two blue flashes shot from his eyes' and the cramped shoulder was forgotten. 'His voice, too, was pleasantly soft and gentle.'[2] Neither he nor Mam mentioned the book, and Willa followed suit. Instead, as his voice reminded her that he was Orkney-born, she told him that her own people had originally come from Unst in Shetland; and they began to discuss Orkney and Shetland words and phrases and the similarities and differences in their island ways of life. When Mam suggested that she might sing some of the student songs she and Emily used to sing around the piano, Willa—who admitted that she had no real 'singing voice'—decided instead to croon some Gaelic songs she had heard sung by Patuffa Kennedy Fraser, daughter of the musician and song-collector Marjorie Kennedy Fraser. Edwin appeared to enjoy the songs but left the party shortly afterwards, much to his hostess's chagrin, since she had wanted his book to be the centre of discussion. She insisted, however, that Willa must write to him when she got back to London, to say how much she had enjoyed his book.

But it was Edwin who wrote to Willa first, about six weeks after the dinner party, apologizing for writing what he called a 'career-y' letter, and asking her opinion about his chances of finding more congenial work in London. Willa, with her postgraduate interest in psychology, was struck by his very small, neat, compressed handwriting—very difficult to read, as if its author might be a man who was used to hiding his inner thoughts and self. She thought he seemed to be in 'a state of quiet desperation, although he had tried hard to suppress it'.[3] Willa answered warmly, and, being an optimist about London, she assured him that there were plenty of opportunities in the capital for the development of diverse interests. They exchanged several letters more before arranging to meet one evening in Glasgow when Willa came north for Christmas.

The meeting took place in Miss Craig's 'High Tea' restaurant, where they exchanged information about their jobs. Willa told about the factory girls she had taught in wartime London and the difficulties she had getting them off the escalators at Liverpool station where they 'abandoned themselves to the ecstasy

---

[1] *Belonging* (London: Hogarth Press, 1968), pp. 13, 14, 15.
[2] Ibid., p.15.
[3] Ibid., pp. 16–17.

of rushing up the Down and down the Up'. Edwin described his shipbuilding office—'more easy going than any others he had been in'—where the large number of clerks meant that they 'had a daily rota for escaping to the lavatory, where each man smoked a cigarette or two and read for about twenty minutes'. Edwin took a volume of Nietzsche with him when it was his turn. By the end of their high tea, they realized that their several months of correspondence since their first encounter had developed into a friendship, and they arranged to meet again at Easter. Edwin was involved with the Glasgow Guilds movement and Willa had a friend from her St Andrews student days who was also a member and was planning an Easter dance to which Willa had been invited. Edwin would be there too, and Willa wrote that 'despite Edward Moore's disdain for the "camaraderie of the sexes"' in *We Moderns*, they were now 'on Christian-name terms'.[4]

The Guilds Easter dance would prove to be a key event in the development of their relationship. When Willa arrived to stay at her cousin's home in Glasgow shortly before the evening of the dance, she discovered that the members of the Glasgow Guilds group were planning a 'crusade to save Edwin Muir from being swallowed alive by Mam'. They told Willa that he was in Mam's house every night and how unaware he appeared to be of his danger. Willa's first response was that Edwin might not be so helpless as the group feared; and in any case why should he not spend his evenings in Mam's house where he would be 'made welcome and given a good supper'. Later, however, the wild student part of her nature led her to say 'bet you a bob' to her cousin that she, Willa, could detach Edwin from Mam's ministrations and set at rest the Guilds' fears. She won her bet, but on the evening of the dance, Edwin arrived with Mam's daughter, Emily, and so it was some time before he and Willa were free to dance together. Given her surmises about his handwriting during their previous correspondence, she was surprised to find that when they danced 'our steps matched so well that we floated rather than danced around the hall. I had never had so light-footed a partner.' They spent the rest of the evening dancing and went off together at the end, with Edwin quite forgetting that he should have seen Emily home again. Instead, he steered Willa into a park near the university, which Willa suspected he may have been accustomed to use as a 'trysting place', where they 'sat on a park bench for hours', being disturbed only by a policeman who shone his lantern on them and enquired 'Is this love or lunacy? It was both we answered him.'[5] Before Willa set off for Montrose to see her mother, they arranged to join a small party of Willa's cousins and friends in a long weekend at a hotel in St Andrews. And it was there that they decided to marry in London at Whitsun when Edwin would be at the National Guilds League conference.

This was something of a whirlwind courtship, and despite their growing intimacy and their shared Orkney and Shetlandic roots, they really knew very little

[4] Ibid., pp. 17–18, p. 20.
[5] Ibid., pp. 21–2.

about each other. Behind Willa's confident, dramatic, exterior personality was the clever little girl who had found herself a scholarship pupil in Montrose and St Andrews. But it was not easy, for when her father died when she was still in primary school, she had had to exchange her early private schooling for the town school and the taunts of its playground activities. Later, she had to endure the snobbery that existed in both Montrose Academy and St Andrews University, where bursary scholars were looked down upon by their wealthier fellows. As her future writings would show, Willa maintained a deep-rooted antagonism towards her childhood Montrose, and this was closely related to her relationship with her mother, who appeared to favour her two sons while ignoring her daughter's achievements. So Willa had learned to use her cleverness and her capacity for inventive and dramatic activity to draw fellow students towards her at St Andrews, where she shone in the university's clubs and societies. She was a member of the Classical Society, the Women Students' Debating Society, of which she was president in the 1910–11 session; she was vice president of the Women Students Suffrage Society, and became a regularly contributing committee member of the *College Echoes* magazine (Figure 1.1).

Figure 1.1 Wilhelmina Anderson at St Andrews 1910

Source: From Willa Muir, *Belonging. A Memoir* (London: The Hogarth Press, 1968)

In June 1911 Willa graduated with First Class Honours in Classics and Humanities and the award of the Berry Scholarship enabled her to continue her studies for a further year. But she turned down the possibility of a research scholarship to the British School at Rome when she fell in love with a rugby-playing medical student and became engaged to him despite his reputation as a philanderer. Perhaps the rejected little girl still within her had wanted the emotional success of being loved for her female self rather than for the academic achievements that came so easily to her. Whatever lay behind her hasty action, the engagement proved to be a disaster. In order to support herself financially after her final year at university, Willa had obtained a post as Classics Mistress at a Rectory School in the north of England, and in her absence her new fiancé had divided his time between his medical studies and a series of romantic affairs, which he appeared to take some delight in recounting to her when she returned to St Andrews. The engagement ended when she threw her diamond and sapphire engagement ring off the town pier and into the sea, telling her faithless lover to 'Watch this!'[6] So there were two Willas within the young woman who had agreed, on a short acquaintance, to marry Edwin Muir in June 1919. And there was more than one Edwin Muir in her new fiancé (Figure 1.2).

Figure 1.2 Edwin Muir in the 1920s
Source: Orkney Library and Archive

[6] Ibid., p. 26.

Before their decision to marry in London when he came south for his Guilds meeting, Edwin had made what seemed to be an attempt to cut off their relationship before it went any further, saying to Willa as they sat in the sun on the St Andrews sand dunes towards the end of their long weekend—'You know, this isn't going to do.' 'What isn't?' Willa had responded in some puzzlement. 'You and I' was his reply. Willa wrote later that this struck her as such an absurd statement that she began to laugh. And as she continued to laugh, Edwin joined in and nothing more was said about it. Instead, as they spent their last evening together before returning to Glasgow and London, it was Edwin who suggested that they get together in London when he came for the Guilds League conference. This time it was Willa who surprised herself by thinking 'this isn't going to do', telling Edwin that if they had any children, then she wouldn't 'like them to be bastards'. Later she would say that she could not remember who first used the word 'marry', but a Whitsun wedding was somehow agreed and Willa undertook to post the banns in London so that they could marry in a register office when Edwin came south. It was only later, once they were wed, that Edwin told her that his comment about 'this isn't going to do' had been his customary way of bringing to an end an affair that was in danger of becoming too serious and he felt that his own independence was under threat. If the girl in question wept, then he would weep with her before they parted. Willa had broken this pattern by laughing at him instead, and he could not help laughing too.[7]

Independence was important to Edwin as a young man working as a clerk in Glasgow, a city he detested. Reading Nietzsche and hoping to make his way in the literary world, he had joined socialist movements such as the National Guilds and the Clarion Scouts, making new friends and seeking new horizons, he was determined to make a better life for himself. Among these new friends were Hugh Kingsmill (or 'Lunn', the family name he still used at that time) and John Holms, who had met each other in Karlsruhe prison camp in Germany during the Great War. Kingsmill was close to Edwin in age, having been born in 1889 to Edwin's 1887; Holms was ten years younger, born in 1897. Kingsmill had doorstepped Edwin in March 1919 during a visit to Glasgow from his family's hotel in Bridge of Allan and later described the encounter to Holms, who was still waiting impatiently for his own demobilization from the army.

> I had a really first rate day in Glasgow on Monday, went in more or less on business, and, my uncle having turned home, I called on Edward Moore, who wrote that article on Dostoieffsky in the New Age. A very pleasant fellow here, called Wilton, had given me Moore's address (I discovered later that Wilton had only met him for the first time two days before).[8]

---

[7] Ibid., pp. 23–4, 25.
[8] Hugh Kingsmill, letter to John Holms, 26 March 1919, London, British Library, Add MS 85335, vol. xiii.

Edwin may have been a little taken aback by Kingsmill, whom he had never met before, while Kingsmill described him to Holms as 'a quiet reserved Scotchman' and said he had initially found the situation 'a little trying' before they eventually 'set off for dinner, and had a great evening'. 'You would like him immensely,' he told his friend, and went on to give a portrait of the Dostoieffsky author, bringing out character qualities he appeared to share with Holms. For Kingsmill, his new acquaintance had 'really remarkable intelligence, and is absolutely unaffected, and his laugh bursts through the intervening obstacles like, in a more subdued key, your own'. He continued to describe his new friend:

> Since fourteen (he is now thirty-one) he has worked as a clerk in a shipping firm in Glasgow. He was as reserved as yourself, but these details came out one by one. He has never been able to learn languages, except French to read. Not even German, though he worships Goethe, and of course not Greek or Latin. He goes to work at 8.15 and returns at 6.30, with hardly any vitality to spare. He takes no interest in his work, and this for seventeen years—just think of it. His book *We Moderns* was completed last April. It's only about 45000 words, but the strain led to a nervous breakdown. He can't, as you or I could, get a more or less easy teaching job, because he's never been able to get a degree. His book has sold 460 copies, and he doesn't see a cent till it gets above 500.

Their social backgrounds were clearly different. 'His digs. Were pervaded with the smell of cooking—you know the kind,'[9] but Kingsmill seems to have formed a genuine liking and respect for Edwin and tells his friend that 'of course I wouldn't write so freely except to you, because I feel it's hardly fair. But it is pretty ghastly, and he looks tired out.' He wishes that Holms could meet Edwin, saying 'I have seldom liked any one so much, and he is really first rate critically. I think if he can free himself he will write great criticism.'[10] He also tells Holms that Edwin is trying to get to London as a journalist, and that Orage of the *New Age* is helping him. Orage was certainly supporting Edwin in the sense of giving him space as a contributor to his journal, and he was also keeping his eyes open for possible suitable positions for him, although as yet without success. In the meantime, Kingsmill urges Holms to buy Edwin's book and to tell other friends to buy it, in the hope of sales reaching the necessary figure for the payment of royalties. And he invites Edwin to spend the weekend with him in Bridge of Allan.

Edwin enjoyed his visit to Bridge of Allan and a friendly exchange of letters between him and Kingsmill was soon underway. This new and unexpected friendship with someone who shared his literary interests and appreciated his work would appear to have given Edwin more confidence about finding a congenial

[9] Ibid.
[10] Ibid.

position in which to further his own writing. In mid-April he approached G. K. Chesterton, who had written 'very generously more than once' about *We Moderns*, asking him for advice about finding a journalism position in London, adding that Orage is also looking out for him. Kingsmill, too, was enquiring among London contacts, while Edwin in turn approached Glasgow connections such as William Power, literary editor of the *Glasgow Herald*, about possible reviews of Kingsmill's recently published first book *The Will to Love*. And in a letter of 7 May he tells Kingsmill of his recent introduction to the Frenchman Denis Saurat, a lecturer in French at Glasgow University as well as a philosophical writer who appears to have inspired Edwin to engage in 'a sort of philosophical poem'—'Heaven knows whether it will be good or bad'. He advises his new friend that he will be going down to London 'in 4 weeks time for my holiday, and to have a look round'[11] but he makes no mention of a Whitsun marriage with Willa.

Willa, meanwhile, was making preparations. She wrote to her mother, saying she was going to marry a man called Edwin Muir—an intimation which her mother ignored for some time, not taking this as a serious statement of intent. She advised the principal of her training college of her intended marriage and she appeared to respond sympathetically. The principal herself had recently married, and Willa did not expect difficulties in her own case. She gave her a copy of *We Moderns* by her prospective husband and went happily back to her lodgings. A few days later, however, she was summoned to a special meeting with the principal and the patroness of the College, a wealthy elderly lady named Miss Belle. Both women had shocked expressions on their faces and Miss Belle, picking up Willa's copy of *We Moderns* with distaste, asked the bride-to-be if she realized that the man she proposed to marry did not believe in God. It was made clear to Willa that if she persisted in going through with marriage to a godless man, then there could be no place for her as lecturer and vice principal in their teacher training college. Willa rescued her copy of the godless *We Moderns*, resigned from her post, and left the meeting. Although now without the prospect of a job, she continued with her plans for the wedding, taking up the offer of the loan of a flat over Whitsun which would enable her to marry Edwin at St Pancras Register Office, filling out the necessary forms for the marriage, and booking two good seats for a performance of Diaghileff's ballet *La Boutique Fantasque* for the evening of the wedding.

Edwin arrived as promised for his tryst in London, they were married at St Pancras, and he was captivated by the Diaghileff. He had never seen a ballet before, and now he wished he could have been a ballet dancer. Willa reported that they 'were both drunk with sheer elation' when they went back to the borrowed flat in Hunter Street, adding that in bed together they were as well matched as they had

---

[11] Edwin Muir, letter to Hugh Kingsmill, 7 May 1919, BL, Add MS 95330.

previously been on the Glasgow dance floor. Next day, however, Willa lost a little of that elation when she heard her new husband deliver his speech at the Guilds conference. She had never heard Edwin speak publicly before, and being herself an excellent public performer, she had not given any thought as to how her new husband might fare. Now his hesitant style of speaking, with its stops and starts joined together with many 'eh's, caused her cheeks to burn, although Edwin himself seemed not too bothered, saying only that he had been 'a bit nervous'.[12] Willa privately made up her mind to take him in hand so far as public speaking was concerned.

After the conference they went to the seaside. One of Willa's friends had given them the present of three days in a hotel in Sherringham beside the sea, where they duly bathed and lay in the sun. Edwin could not swim, so he lay on the beach longer than Willa and became somewhat sunburned. This did not appear to cause him much discomfort, but he was disturbed to discover that Willa would lose her teaching job at the end of the session, despite her confidence about finding another post. At the end of their short honeymoon Edwin went back to Glasgow to resign from his clerking post and work his notice, while Willa remained in London to complete the session at her teacher training college and furnish the half-maisonette she had agreed to rent for their residence in London. She had been fortunate in this, for a fellow member of the Club she belonged to, the 1917 Club, had taken an option on part of a house in Guilford Street, on the edge of Bloomsbury and near Russell Square. The area had become rundown, but was being rehabilitated with houses repointed and freshly painted and divided into upper and lower maisonettes. Willa's acquaintance was Barbara Low, one of the first British psychoanalysts, whose parents had emigrated from Hungary to Britain. She was also the aunt of Ivy Low, friend of D. H. Lawrence and the Scottish writer Catherine Carswell. In 1916, Ivy had married the Russian Maxim Litvinov, later Stalin's Foreign Minister and Russian Ambassador to the United States during the Second World War, but in 1919, while arranging to join Barbara at the Guilford Street house, Willa had no idea of her co-tenant's interesting background and connections. She knew only that Barbara was a Freudian psychoanalyst. They did not always get on together, however, and she and Edwin later came to think of her as 'an unhappy old woman'.[13]

Barbara Low had the two upper rooms in the renovated maisonette and Willa and Edwin the two lower ones, with upstairs bathroom and basement kitchen shared between them. With housing in London so scarce at the end of the war, Willa felt she was lucky to have the chance of this accommodation and that Barbara Low herself had probably succeeded in renting it because it was No. 13 Guilford Square, with thirteen considered by many to be an unlucky number.

[12] *Belonging*, p. 28.
[13] Ibid., p. 29.

Having found the flat, which cost her forty-five pounds annually, Willa set out to furnish it. One of her uncles, leaving for the United States, presented the newlyweds with an old wheel-back armchair which was hand-carved, and two small chairs to match it; she had a Morris armchair and two blue pouffes from her college sitting room, and the new sitting room itself had an Adam chimneypiece, so it had an impressive air when furnished. The small bedroom at the back of the house had a paved area outside it, which Willa decorated with a border of African marigolds. Satisfied with her housing achievements, and finished with her exam marking, she boarded the Glasgow train at Euston and went north to meet Edwin.

One of Edwin's friends had lent Edwin his flat while he himself was on holiday so that the newlyweds had somewhere in Glasgow to live until they joined Willa's mother in Montrose. Willa was surprised to find a large coal range in the kitchen, which she had no idea how to use, and was relieved to notice that there was also a gas ring, a kettle, and a frying pan which would suffice for the few days before they left for Montrose. She was even more surprised when Edwin, looking embarrassed and on the defensive, confessed that he had not yet submitted his week's notice to his office. She reminded him that he had said that he did not want to be a clerk in an office all his life and wanted to get out of Glasgow for something more congenial. To this he could only reply that here in Glasgow he was earning 'three pounds seventeen and six a *week*', stressing the *week*, as if this was too much to give up in order to move to London. Willa tried to reassure him that together they would earn much more than that, although the recent loss of her teaching position must have weakened her case. She realized that there was much that she did not know about her new husband, and felt slightly fearful when she remembered his stories of how he could cut off personal relationships when his own independence became threatened. Tired after her long journey, Willa suggested that they should 'sleep on it' and take any decisions in the morning.

When morning came, Edwin still seemed undecided and departed for his office in Renfrew, leaving Willa to look around their borrowed kitchen, the workings of which seemed to her as incomprehensible as her new husband. She went out to do some shopping, got lost, but eventually managed to find her way back to the flat. She decided to take a tram to the country and the hills that Edwin claimed were so close at hand. But she did not understand the destinations of the trams, and instead of being taken into the country she found herself deeper and deeper in suburbia. She did not know where she was, and when she eventually regained their borrowed flat, she could only sit down and cry. When Edwin returned, however, she amused him with her blunders, getting on the wrong trams and losing her way in the wrong streets. Willa was always able to make an entertaining drama out of difficulties, and she soon had Edwin laughing at her geographical muddles. Then she asked him if they might go and visit some of the friends he had talked to her about, the musician Francis George Scott, for example, or his new acquaintance the French lecturer Denis Saurat.[14] But both were on holiday in early summer, as were Willa's own Glasgow cousins. It dawned on Edwin that the city of Glasgow and its hinterland was largely foreign territory to Willa, despite her visits to Mrs Stobo and her cousins, so he suggested that he should play truant from the office and take her to Strathblane and the surrounding hills. Edwin being Edwin, he would do this not the next day, but the next again, so that he could get ahead with his office work before taking time off.

On the chosen day, Willa telephoned Edwin's office in what she hoped was a suitable Glasgow accent, pretending to be Edwin's landlady, and communicating that Mr Muir had a very bad cold and could not come to work. They took off for the hills and spent the day like children launching leaf boats in the burns and recapturing the excited exchange of Orkney and Shetlandic terms which had brought them together at Mam's dinner party. Edwin seemed much happier when they returned to the flat in high spirits, his obligations to his office quite forgotten. But another problem arose. As Willa looked at Edwin, she found herself exclaiming, half laughing, half in dismay—'Thu's freckled like a troot!'[15] Edwin, whose fair skin had burned easily in the south of England sunshine, was now covered in freckles after his day on the Scottish hills. Clearly a return to the office from a bed of sickness was no longer viable, and he had to play truant for a second day, this time keeping well out of the sun. This escapade finally convinced Edwin to give the shipbuilding office a week's notice, and he was duly provided with a reference as to his efficiency as a costing-clerk and his trustworthiness in relation to cash. The next hurdle was their meeting with Willa's mother, but it went off well and ended, in Willa's view, with her mother favouring Edwin more than she did her daughter. 'He would never have a button on his shirts', her mother told him, 'or on his trousers, or a pair of whole socks to put on his feet, poor Edwin.'[16]

In contrast to Willa's dismay when confronted with the Glasgow flat, Edwin was delighted when he entered the Guilford Street home early in September. They began to apply the adjective 'peerie' to their surroundings and to themselves. 'Peerie' is an Orkney term meaning 'small' with affectionate overtones, as in Edwin's mother's name for her son when he was a boy—'Peerie breeks'—'Wee breeches or trousers'. 'Peedie' is a similar term in the Shetland language, but 'peerie' was also used there, so Edwin and Willa became 'Peerie Willa' and 'Peerie Breeks'. Willa's wedding ring was too large for her, so they had it shrunk to fit, delighted to gain fourteen shillings for the gold that had been taken out of it. They raised more money by selling wedding presents for which they had no use, such as a claret jug

---

[14] Saurat, like F. G. Scott, was an influential figure in the early years of the modern Scottish literary renaissance. In fact, he is credited with using the term 'renaissance' in writing about the new poets of the 1920s.
[15] Ibid., p. 33.
[16] Ibid.

of green glass, two feet high, with an ornate silver lid, and a pair of silver entrée dishes. Willa became 'gaily expert' at withdrawing a shilling or two from the gas meter in the basement.[17]

Among the first visitors to their new flat were Hugh Kingsmill and John Holms. Edwin had finally met John when Holms was in barracks in Hamilton awaiting demobilization in July 1919. The meeting went well, as Edwin wrote to Kingsmill on 16 July:

> The walk with Holmes [sic] was a great success. I haven't enjoyed such a good philosophical set-to for a long time, and neither, so he said, has Holmes. We lay about in hay fields for indefinite periods discussing the Absolute, and recognising each other's positions is the only thing that really sincere discussion comes to in the end.

He added, 'I think Holmes is decidedly exceptional—his mind is one of that rare kind which concerns itself with real things instead of mere abstractions. When he is talking it is difficult to remember he is only 21.'[18] He also wrote confidently to Kingsmill about his recent visit to London in June and his interaction with various newspaper editors to whom he had been given introductions by the editor of the *Glasgow Herald*. He tells Kingsmill that he is thinking of reworking the draft of a novel he had previously attempted but put aside, and that after he has 'expunged the worst crudities', he may hand it over for his 'mature judgement'.[19] It is not clear whether he mentioned his marriage when he and Holms were lying about in hayfields discussing the Absolute, nor does he mention it in the body of his letter to Kingsmill, adding only at the top left-hand corner of the letter that he expects his wife to be in Glasgow the next week and giving Kingsmill a contact address for the friend's flat they have temporarily borrowed.

As far as Willa was concerned, the arrival of the previously unknown Kingsmill and Holms (still in his army uniform) at 13 Guilford Street must have seemed something of an intrusion into her happy new relationship with Edwin, at a time when neither of them had found employment. In her future memoirs, she would tell how she felt excluded from the talk of the three men, particularly, she believed, on the part of Holms, who appeared to want to re-establish the intellectual conversational relationship he had achieved with Edwin when they first met in Glasgow. In her later accounts of this visit, Willa would congratulate herself for putting the men in their place by ostentatiously and ironically pulling out a work basket and beginning to darn, with exaggerated movements, the thickest sock she could find, thus becoming 'what I should have been all along, an undemanding bit of background, a proper wife darning a sock'. She reported that the men, duly

---

[17] Ibid., p. 35.
[18] Edwin Muir, letter to Hugh Kingsmill, 16 July 1919, BL, Add MS 85330.
[19] Ibid.

reassured, had apparently lost their embarrassment and awkwardness and 'began to quote Shakespeare, interrupting each other freely', while 'Holms started a long monologue.'[20] This is an amusing story, when told in retrospect by Willa, but it is prescient of her life-long inability to recognize that even happily married men and women might need to have their own 'space' within that marriage in order to pursue their individual interests and meet friends with whom they had interests that were not necessarily shared by their marriage partner. While Willa would always be willing to give Edwin the space he needed for his own writing, without attempting to interfere, she was unable to show the same openness in regard to personal matters. Marriage to her would always mean 'belonging', and 'belonging' meant sharing friends who were appreciated by both partners, and by whom both partners were appreciated. With his 'Muir remoteness', on the other hand, Edwin needed to go his own way in regard to intellectual friendships, and his long-lasting friendship with Holms would continue to be an irritant, even if a minor one, in his marriage to Willa.

Shortly after the visit from Kingsmill and Holms, and about two weeks after their own arrival in London, the newlyweds each found employment on the same day. Edwin was taken on as a clerk in an engraver's office and Willa obtained a post in a 'cramming institution' teaching précis-writing.[21] These were not the longer-term positions they had hoped for, but provided just enough money to live on until something better came along. Edwin's post in the engraver's office seemed to consist mainly of packing engraving blocks for delivery—a parcelling skill which lasted for the rest of his life. What caused him more anxiety was that he had to find his way around London on his own when going to and from the office. Previously, he and Willa had explored together, and as Willa was already familiar with the city this had been an enjoyable activity. Now, without Willa, and without the familiar routine of his Glasgow occupation, Edwin began to fear the big city, afraid that the high buildings would topple on him, troubled by the crowds of people who surged past him as if he did not exist. Accustomed to the streets of Glasgow, he found the Londoner's impersonal glance unsettling. Willa realized that he was having difficulties and took him to visit her London friends, while Edwin's contacts with Orage at *The New Age* also began to help him settle.

At Christmas they both fell ill with the Spanish flu. This pandemic had been sweeping across Europe in the post-war years, eventually killing more people than died in the war. The age group most affected appeared to be those between 15 and 40, and a quarter of the British population was infected, leading to over 220,000 deaths. Willa and Edwin struggled to nurse each other, and Willa managed to make contact with a Russian friend she met when he was studying medicine at St Andrews. Alexis Gregorievitch Chodak had fled from Russia after becoming

---

[20] *Belonging*, p. 38.
[21] Ibid., p. 35.

involved as a student in the 1905 revolution and he and his wife were now doctors with a practice in Bloomsbury. Willa had renewed their acquaintance when she came to live in Guilford Street, and the Muirs would later say that he saved their lives. Once they had sufficiently recovered, Chodak paid for them to convalesce in a hotel he knew of in Crowborough. Here they gradually extended their walks into the countryside and the Ashdown Forest, and Willa taught Edwin the names of the various forest trees. Trees had never been a part of his childhood in the bare Orkney landscape.

Shortly after their return to London, Orage invited Edwin to become his assistant in the *New Age* office. He could work there for three days a week and would be paid three pounds a week. This was not a large salary, but at three days compared to five and a half days in Glasgow, he would have time to develop his own writing, and even more important were the literary contacts he could make in his new post. The *New Age's* weekly conferences were held in the Kardomah Café in Chancery Lane, and here he met many of the writers associated with the magazine such as AE and Ezra Pound, as well as the Yugoslavian Janko Lavrin, who became a good friend and would much later, in the mid-1930s, join with Edwin in the editing of the new *European Quarterly* magazine. There was also an exotic Serbian, Dmitri Mitrinović, a friend of Orage, who would regularly visit the Guilford Street flat, bringing two large quart bottles of beer which, when empty, Edwin and Willa would exchange for coppers at the local pub.

As Orage's assistant, Edwin would also at times be behind the editorial desk, and in this capacity he met Aldous Huxley, and also the Sitwells, who were on a mission to challenge Orage in relation to comments he had made about them in a recent article. Edwin, who was not a combatant, invited them to sit down and succeeded in calming them. Orage encouraged him to approach Middleton Murry, who agreed to send him books to review in the *Athenaeum*. It was at Murry's Hampstead home that he first met Katherine Mansfield, telling Willa that, 'a fairy-like creature' opened Murry's door, and when he addressed her as 'Mrs Murry?' she 'pirouetted on one leg to respond—"I'm not Mrs Murray. I'm Katherine Mansfield".[22] Edwin's circle of contacts in the London literary scene was becoming wider, and he no longer felt himself to be an unknown outsider. He also gained a post as drama critic for the *Scotsman* newspaper, which added to his earnings and provided opportunities for theatre-going while also keeping a small contact with Scotland. Things were moving.

Willa's employment situation was less stable than Edwin's. Around the same time as he joined *The New Age*, Willa had been offered the post of headmistress in a Day Continuation School for female workers in London's West End drapery stores. This was a new venture which had been organized by three young Oxford University graduates whom Willa had helped to train as teachers for just such

[22] Ibid., p. 42.

day-release education. They had met during the war in Canning Town when Willa was working with a Mansfield House project to educate packers from a soap factory and a match factory. Having encouraged a group of West End drapery proprietors to start up the school, the young women persuaded them to appoint Willa as the head of the Continuation School at a salary of £400 a year. This was a sizeable addition to the Muirs' finances, and Willa was only too happy to take up the post, entering into it with enthusiasm. She planned a curriculum around textile materials, teaching the girls about the great Silk Road from China and the waulking of Harris tweed from the Scottish Isles, as well as Indian muslins and Australian wools, all of which would lead them into history and geography. English literature would be taught through the reading of poetry and dramatic love stories, which she believed would take her charges 'easily into Shakespeare'.[23] She added practical items such as fashion drawing and colouring, and the remainder of the timetable was given over to eurhythmics, dancing, and singing. There was even a class for the 18-year-old girls on general psychology, taught by Willa herself.

In Willa's view, these classes went well and the girls enjoyed them. The employers, however, were not so certain that her curriculum was best suited to working in a department store. There were significant differences of social class between the girls. The young ladies from the showrooms who would interact with well-off customers looked down on the girls from the workshops, who were kept out of the public eye; and then there were the more educated girls who did the clerical work, who were less well-dressed than the showroom employees. It could not have been an easy group to educate together, especially with the forward-thinking curriculum designed by Willa, and complaints began to filter through from visiting forewomen from the various departments of the stores. The welfare workers on the staff also disapproved of Willa's constant smoking at her desk and her lack of censure in relation to unpunctuality. After what Willa believed to have been an enjoyable and profitable year, she was asked to resign and was given a sum of money in compensation. A new headmistress was appointed, but the school eventually closed, in part at least because Parliament had not passed the expected law to make such Day Continuation study compulsory.

Willa's compensation from the Drapery Stores management allowed her to spend some time at home, time that she spent learning how to cook before once again entering teaching, this time lecturing to London County Council evening classes, which was a better match, perhaps, to her own educational background and interests. In the meantime, their life was becoming increasingly busy, with invitations to the homes of new acquaintances as well as old and new friends regularly dropping by. Edwin could be at the theatre several times a week for his *Scotsman* reviews, only to find a sitting room full of visitors when he got home. Time for the development of personal essays, or other such writings, was in almost

---

[23] Ibid., p. 50.

as short supply as when he was a clerk in Glasgow. But he was becoming more assured in himself.

Orage had sensed something of Edwin's insecurity when he first arrived at the *New Age*, and suggested that he might meet with a psychiatrist friend to talk over his worries. This analysis resulted in Edwin having strange, troublesome dreams and eventually exhilarating but also frightening moments of waking mythical visions that he seemed able to turn on and off at will. The psychiatrist became concerned about such waking visions and told Edwin he must not encourage them. After a time, these sessions began to peter out, and when another psychiatrist took over, Edwin's visits ceased entirely. It was, nevertheless, a disturbing period for him and Willa, whose own interests in psychology led her to discuss these waking visions with her husband as well. Nevertheless, psychoanalysis seemed to give Edwin a degree of self-knowledge and emotional security, although the visions he experienced were to reappear later when he first seriously began to attempt to write poetry.

One positive aspect of Willa's adventure with London's West End drapery stores was that it had enabled her to buy some good, fashionable clothes, including an elegant cloak that she wore when she and Edwin went north at Easter in 1921. This garment led some members of the Glasgow Guilds Group to suggest that the Muirs, and Willa especially, were getting a bit above themselves when they referred to 'Mrs Muir's *clowk*'[24] in what they intended to be an Anglicized accent. Willa met Edwin's older brother Jimmie and his sister Lizzie for the first time during this visit. Edwin would say nothing in his later autobiographical writings about how he came to regain contact with surviving members of his family in Glasgow, although some contact had clearly been made. Willa was introduced to Jimmie at his workplace, where he was in charge of a department in a Glasgow furnishing warehouse. In her later memoir, she would describe how she and Edwin 'went up in a goods hoist to a large barn-like room where the three of us presently stood in a corner, Jimmie leaning against one wall, Edwin at right angles to him leaning against another, and I in the open between them'. The brothers were not unfriendly towards each other, but there was clearly some kind of barrier between them, perhaps because of their age difference, or perhaps, as Willa speculated, because of an innate reticence that she had already encountered in her husband. There was no eye contact between them as they made remarks to each other, and Willa was not included in the conversation. When she referred to the meeting later, Edwin merely laughed and said that, being twelve years older than himself, Jimmie was only distantly related to him. And he told her, 'Wait till you see Lizzie', adding 'She's even farther away from this world.' Lizzie was six years older than Edwin, and when they met, Willa found her to be 'small, spare, gentle, and reticent, with a face very like Edwin's except for the brow'. Unlike Jimmie, Lizzie 'laughed easily', but Willa was

[24] Ibid., p. 52.

also aware that she was not the kind of person to be patronized by strangers, 'even when relaxed she still had the same quiet, withdrawn dignity'. Willa decided that remoteness was clearly a Muir family characteristic 'a built-in power of withdrawing into some inner fastness of their own'. And compared to his sister and brother, she decided that Edwin might even pass as 'an extravert'. He told her, however, that as a young woman Lizzie had been very ambitious, while Jimmie as a young man had been 'a great lad for the girls'. But the family's emigration from Orkney to Glasgow had made life as difficult for them as it had for Edwin. Lizzie had had a hard life, Edwin said, and he thought that Jimmie 'had been more or less conditioned into respectability by his wife'.[25] Willa could not imagine ever trying to condition Edwin into respectability and hoped he would never feel the need to retreat from her.

Remoteness would have been difficult in the midst of their increasingly busy London life, and then, unexpectedly, a new opportunity presented itself. Although Edwin was moving away from his previous commitment to Nietzsche, his *We Moderns*, with a strongly supportive introduction by H. L. Mencken, had been published by Knopf in the United States in the early months of the previous year. In the wake of this American publication, Van Wyck Brooks, the literary editor of a new American weekly, *The Freeman*, asked Edwin to contribute one or two articles a month at a fee of sixty dollars per article. This invitation seemed to offer both a large sum of money and an opportunity to try something different. Neither Edwin nor Willa had ever travelled beyond Britain and they had heard, from the many young painters they met through Janko Lavrin, that everyday living in Europe was cheap. Could they also try adventuring in Europe? They judged that they could live abroad on the *Freeman* money, and expand it if necessary with contributions to other journals as well. They asked Janko Lavrin for his advice and he suggested that they should try Prague. It was in the very centre of Europe and, he added, it had the best ham in Europe and the best beer. At this point, to both Edwin and Willa, Europe was 'an imaginary region, a never-never land, for our knowledge of it was gathered from books, except for newspaper reports of fighting during the war'.[26] Janko was persuasive. They began to make preparations for their departure and arranged to leave the Guilford Street home at the end of the quarter in June 1921. Furniture they wanted to keep was given to friends who promised to look after it until they returned, and what they did not want was given to friends who were in need of it. Willa's mother agreed to keep their books and their cat, and having deposited these with her and made arrangements with their bank to transfer any remaining money to Prague, they embarked in August at the port of Leith en route for Hamburg, and then onwards to the new Czechoslovakia.

[25] Ibid., pp. 52–3.
[26] Ibid., p. 54.

PART I
ADVENTURING IN EUROPE

2
Prague and a New Czech Republic 1921–1922

> We decided to go to Prague, knowing nothing about the Czechs and Slovaks except that they had got a country for themselves out of the Great War.
>
> Willa Muir, *Belonging* (1968)

In August 1921 the Muirs sailed from Leith, just outside Edinburgh, to Hamburg in Germany. Edwin wrote that the passage was a rough one and that everyone on board was sick until 'on the second morning the cliffs of Heligoland, rising and falling, plunged past, and we were sailing between the flat green fields on either side of the Elbe estuary.' From Hamburg they travelled on to Berlin where their 'inadequate' German language resulted in them being assigned to a rather expensive hotel room 'with a dais, as if we were royalty', but being tired and intending to stay for one night only, they decided to accept it. They hired a droshky to drive along Unter den Linden, and the next day they left Berlin by train on their journey to Prague.[1] Writing later to his sister Lizzie and her husband in Glasgow, Edwin spoke of his surprise at the atmosphere they found in Germany, 'where things are supposed to be so bad'. He continued, 'I was absolutely astonished at the difference between Berlin and London. In Berlin there was a feeling of cheerfulness, of comfort, of contentment, especially of hope for the future, that came like a breath of fresh air after London.' The train journey from Berlin to Prague also brought its surprises:

> Germany as I saw it from the train is the most clean, neat, orderly and efficient nation that one could imagine. Everything looks as if a hose had just been turned upon it: There are the most delightful little villages, and especially in the south, between Dresden and the borders of Czechoslovakia the scenery is very romantic and beautiful. It was a lovely autumn afternoon when we saw it first from the train, which runs along the banks of the Elbe, by this time quite a small river, for two or three hours.

[1] *The Story and the Fable*, p. 218.

As they continued their journey into Czechoslovakia, the old Bohemia, this too appeared 'beautiful in the north, but incredibly dry and dusty; the train which in Germany seemed to be running on a vacuum-cleaned carpet, immediately began to raise whirlwinds of dust as soon as it got into Czechoslovakia'. Prague itself, however, was 'a very clean town', (Figure 2.1) and one that, visually at least, reminded Edwin of Edinburgh—'Its situation is somewhat like Edinburgh's, with a castle on the top of a rock standing by itself; only where the Princes Street Gardens are in Edinburgh there is a fine river in Prague, the Vltava (or Moldau), crossed by about a dozen of stylish bridges, one very old one dating from the 14th century.'[2]

Neither Edwin nor Willa knew much about the city of Prague, except that it was now the capital of the new Czechoslovakian Republic which had come into being as a result of the Treaty of Versailles at the end of the 1914–18 war. And of course Janko Lavrin had promised them the best ham and the best beer in Europe. Prague, however, was to present them with less familiar experiences. An immediate difficulty was the Czech language. Both Muirs had a smattering of German, but Czech was completely unfamiliar and linguistically much more challenging. Arriving in the large railway station with the stairways marked 'Vchod' and 'Vychod', they found that the best course of action was to follow the crowd, which

Figure 2.1 Prague, The Powder Tower
Source: https://libreshot.com/powder-tower-in-prague/

[2] Edwin Muir, letter to Lizzie and George Thorburn, 8 February 1922 (mistakenly dated 1921), Edinburgh, National Library of Scotland, MS Acc. 13226.

eventually resulted in them reaching open air. The problem of finding accommodation was solved in an unexpected way. By chance they arrived in Prague at the same time as a Trade Fair was being held in the city, and the driver of one of the horse-drawn open carriages parked outside the station, saw they were foreigners, and took them to a Büro that had been set up to organize accommodation for Trade Fair visitors. This resulted in a hotel room in the heart of the Staré Město, the old city, close by the medieval Powder Tower. As in Berlin, the hotel room appeared to them to be 'very grand indeed', with Willa commenting that they came 'to take it for granted that hotel rooms in Czechoslovakia should be lofty, with large double doors, well-spaced tall windows and still taller porcelain stoves'. When they later travelled in Austria, they discovered that 'this style of room was typically Austrian', and still later they discovered that '"typically Austrian" buildings took their inspiration from Italy.' Although they did not realize it at the time, they were in the process of discovering Central Europe and the shared cultural influences of the former Austro-Hungarian Empire.[3] Exploring the streets of Prague, they became aware of what Willa called 'the lively "feel" of the air' in a city that seemed to her to be 'sizzling with hope and experiment and enthusiasm'. Edwin found that 'the life of Prague had a somewhat improvised air; this was inevitable, since it was new and not yet properly organized; but the very improvisation gave it extraordinary vigour.'[4] The fact that they 'had no clue at all to the Czech language', however, meant that they could not identify what they were eating in restaurants and cafés, or buy a tram ticket, or 'order tea with lemon or rum'. And they soon had to find more permanent and affordable accommodation than their rather grand hotel room. They also had to deal with the Czech banking and postal system so that they could receive Edwin's regular cheques from the American *Freeman* magazine.

Dealing with the bank was difficult. About a week after their arrival in Prague they found themselves in need of money and set off to the local bank in accordance with arrangements made before leaving Britain. No trace could be found, however, of any account in the name of 'Edwin Muir'. Eventually, with help from the British Consul in the city (who was stunned to discover that their lost bank account came to no more that thirteen pounds sterling), the mystery was solved. 'Muir' was a name unknown to the Czech bank clerks who had changed it to the more German-spelling 'Meier', and had lodged the money under that name. But their problems did not end there. Being quite ignorant of Czech pronunciation, they sat waiting for Edwin's name to be called until the bank was empty, only to discover that the impatient call for 'Pan Mooeersh' which had been echoing at intervals while they waited, had been directed at him. Yes, 'Pan Mooersh' was indeed Edwin. Another financial problem at this time, lay at the door of the postal services in relation to the non-arrival of cheques sent by the *Freeman*. It seemed

---

[3] *Belonging*, pp. 56, 57.
[4] *Belonging*, p. 56; *The Story and the Fable*, p. 226.

that an illicit practice had developed in the Czech postal office, by which mail sent from Czechs in America to their relatives at home was frequently opened, and the dollars enclosed (intended to help the home-based family) duly extracted. In their early days in the city, the Muirs' mail from the United States seems to have become caught up in this activity, with two out of three letters failing to arrive, and the enclosed cheques presumably destroyed when found to be useless to the thieves. Gossip suggested that the Czechs had been accustomed to cheating the Austrians for so long that the habit was simply continued under the new Republic. By the time they left Prague, however, the post office had brought stronger controls into the system and the indispensable *Freeman* cheques were arriving regularly.

After some false starts in the old town (due to bedbugs and tram and train noise pollution), their accommodation was settled when they found lodgings on the quieter Mala Strana side of the Vltava River in a house on Nábřeži Legii (today renamed Janáčkovo Nábřeži in honour of the Czech composer), which is a tree-lined road running alongside the higher reaches of the river. Their windows looked out over the river to a water tower erected by the Bohemian general from the Thirty Years War, Albrecht von Wallenstein, whose monumental palace and walled garden lay further up the hillside, below the Hradčany, the area of Prague Castle and its related buildings. The waters of the sluice opposite their windows reverberated softly in the late summer, and more violently when the ice broke up after a hard winter. Their landlady was called Pani Mala, described by Edwin as a 'kind, handsome, and charming woman' who lived there with her daughter, elderly mother, housemaid Marie, and a 'very fat poodle'. In Edwin's view, it was 'a pleasant, kind, and good house, in which everyone, from Marie to the old mother, seemed to be happy'.[5] As they settled in to their new lodgings and became more familiar with the city and its layout and customs on both sides of the river, they found the courage to make use of their letters of introduction. They had been given these before leaving London by Paul Selver, an English writer and translator of Slavonic literature who also had associations with Orage's *New Age*. And in this way they made contact with the playwright Karel Čapek and his painter brother Josef and, through the Čapeks, with the theatre and cultural community in Prague.

Karel and Josef Čapek were at the centre of Prague cultural life both in the pre-1918 period and the interwar period. Karel in particular had a wide international reputation as essayist, novelist, and playwright, with his plays being almost immediately translated into English and produced in theatres in London and New York. In the 1920s he was probably the best-known Czech writer internationally and, through his writings and his association with Czechoslovakia's first president, T. G. Masaryk, he contributed significantly to the building up of the new republic. Things were to change, however, in the uncertain political climate of the late 1930s. Then, Čapek's writings were banned by the Nazis for their

---

[5] *The Story and the Fable*, pp. 219, 220.

anti-fascist themes, and in the years after the Second World War they were banned by Soviet-dominated governments in Czechoslovakia because of their writer's previous refusal to endorse communist ideology. Karel Čapek died in 1938, shortly after the Munich Agreement and the Allies' abandonment of his country. The Nazis looked for him in vain after their invasion of Czechoslovakia in the spring of 1939. They found his painter brother Josef, however, who died in Bergen-Belsen concentration camp in 1945.

The Muirs were fortunate to meet the Čapek brothers in the optimistic days of the young republic. Karel had recently been appointed *regisseur*, or director, of the Vinohrady Theatre in the Vinohrady district of Prague, and Willa credited him with being 'a focus for much of the heady excitement in the city'. Both Muirs were particularly struck by the vigour and modernity of the theatre, which, in Edwin's view, had probably the most brilliant producers and actors in Central Europe, and this was only just over two years after the end of the war. There were two principal theatres in Prague, the flamboyant Vinohrady, built in 1907, with its decorative mixture of art nouveau and neo-Baroque elements; and the National Theatre, overlooking the Vltava River and situated at the bottom of the busy Národní Street which, decades later in 1989, would see the start of the 'Velvet Revolution' in Prague. In 1921 Karel was also an adviser in the National Theatre, and during their stay in the city Edwin and Willa saw plays by Ibsen, Strindberg, and Chekhov, as well as Sophocles, Shakespeare, Racine, and Molière. It was in Prague also that they first encountered the composer Schoenberg's music in a performance of *Pierrot Lunaire*. Encouraged by Karel, Edwin and Willa both took lessons in Czech, with Willa progressing sufficiently to read his *Insects* play in Czech—an achievement he rewarded by promptly presenting her with another one. Edwin, on the other hand, gave up when, in his own words, he had sufficient language to buy a few items from a shop. Both found the language difficult to pronounce, however, with too many consonants and too few vowels to encourage fluent speaking. By a lucky chance, the Čapek brothers also happened to live on the Mala Strana side of the river 'in a rambling old house with a large garden hidden behind it' and so were only 'a few minutes' walk' from where the Muirs had found their comfortable lodgings.[6] Willa described their first meeting in her short essay 'The Brothers Čapek at Home':

> It is an old street, quiet and blind-looking, with big double wooden doors. We push open the door of No.11 and walk along a stone passage into a paved court where a cheerful Czech woman is doing a large washing. A stair of shallow wooden steps leads up to the left, and, twisting leisurely, brings us out on a small landing overlooking the court. On one side there is a door marked 'Josef Čapek', and in front of us, on a kind of wooden grill barring the way to a narrow balcony, a

[6] *Belonging*, p. 58; *The Story and the Fable*, pp. 226, 228.

visiting card tacked up announces 'Dr Karel Čapek'. We peer inquiringly through the bars, and somebody who has heard us appears from a curtained door opening on the balcony and comes forward to let us in. It is Karel Čapek.[7]

Their meeting could not have been altogether easy since although Karel Čapek understood English to some extent, Willa noted that he 'speaks it with difficulty'. The Muirs' knowledge of Czech was at this point 'negligible' and their German still 'painfully inadequate'. Willa wrote later that they always felt welcome in the Čapek's house, 'although our conversation had to be carried on in a wild farrago of French, German, Czech, English and gesturing.' Language exchange in this first meeting would have been similarly polyphonic, yet it appears that they were soon at ease with each other, helped by the regular exchange of cigarettes. They talked about Karel's plays—'You think too much of R.U.R. I don't like it very much myself as a play', he tells them. 'I much prefer an earlier play of mine, the first I ever wrote, called *The Robbers*.' R.U.R. is the short title for *Rossum's Universal Robots*, the play that gave the word *robot* to the world. Written in 1920, it was first performed in the National Theatre of Prague in January 1921, and in London at St Martin's Theatre in April 1923. It was immensely popular in both cities, and although the English translation was not published until 1923, there had already been more than two hundred performances of the play in the New York theatre season of 1922. In England, its popularity apparently resulted in a spate of new businesses making toy robots for sale, while in Prague children 'played robots' for months afterwards. Karel Čapek later admitted, in a newspaper article in 1933, that it was actually his painter brother Josef, not himself, who had invented the word that is now a fixture in our dictionaries and increasingly in our factories, perhaps soon in our homes. When speculating on a new idea for a play while his brother was busy 'splashing the canvas with paint', Karel had lamented '"But I don't know what to call those artificial workers […] I'd call them laborators, but it seems to me somewhat stilted". "Call them robots then", murmured the painter with a brush in his mouth and proceeded with his painting. And that was the way the word "robot" was born.'[8] Although *R.U.R.* had not yet been performed in London when the Muirs set sail for the continent in the autumn of 1921, they had heard all about it from Paul Selver who, with Nigel Playfair, made the first English translation for performance. So it is not surprising that it became a talking point at their first meeting with its author. Willa also noted the paintings in the house. She writes that Karel's room is 'full of pictures, mainly by Václav Špála and Jan Zrzavy, two Czech artists belonging to

---

[7] Willa Muir, 'The Brothers Čapek at Home', unpublished essay, Willa Muir deposit, University of St Andrews, MS 39466, 1/16.

[8] Karel Čapek, 'About the Word Robot', *The People's Paper*, 24 December 1933, collected in Šarka Tobrmanová-Kühnová (ed. and transl.), *Believe in People: The Essential Karel Čapek* (London: Faber, 2010), p. 103.

the same group as his brother Josef. There are also sketches by Josef.'[9] And then they were taken into the next room to meet Josef himself.

Willa's account of this first meeting with the Čapeks was probably written after she and Edwin had become more familiar with the brothers and their working relationship in regard to their theatre productions. She writes,

> Karel is perhaps responsible more for the writing of the plays, and Josef for their artistic setting; but they are so perfectly complementary to each other that once a play has passed through the minds of both it can be described only as the work of the brothers Čapek—like the Insect play.[10]

Karel Čapek always made it clear that *R.U.R.* was a play about human beings and their frailties as opposed to science fiction robots. *From the Life of the Insects*, which followed *R.U.R.*, was also primarily about the lives of human beings, although it appears to have been inspired by the entomological studies *La vie des insects* and *Souvenirs entomologiques* of Jean Henri Fabre (1823–1915). Čapek's play is itself subtitled *An Entomological Review in Three Acts, a Prologue and an Epilogue*. An important factor in Karel's political and social thinking in the 1920s was his commitment to the new state of Czechoslovakia and to President T. G. Masaryk, about whom he wrote a well-received biographical study *Conversations with T. Masaryk*. This positive involvement with his country and its future featured in his journalism, his creative writing, and his social critiques. The same focus is found in his *Insects* play, as a participatory voice often given to the Tramp who, like the Chorus in Greek drama, at times comments on the action and at others enters into it. It is also a play where the participation of Josef in the visual realization of the various insects on stage must have been crucial to its dramatic success with its audiences; and like *R.U.R.* it was immensely successful at home and abroad. In Willa's view, 'Any production of a Čapek play in a foreign country which leaves out of account the costumes and stage-scenery designed by Josef presents but a mutilated version of the original conception.'[11]

Willa's account of their first meeting with the Čapeks ends with Karel having to go off to rehearsal at the theatre, and as their own lodgings in Nábřeži Legii lay in the direction of the Most Legii, the Legion Bridge that would take him across the river to the National Theatre, he suggested that they should walk part of the way with him. Edwin was especially impressed by the fact that Karel Čapek 'seemed to be known and loved by everyone, and when we walked along the street with him every second or third passer-by would shout out in a delighted voice, "Oh Karličku", the equivalent of "Hullo, Charley!" as if the mere sight of him filled them

---

[9] 'The Brothers Čapek at Home, UStA, MS 39466, 1/16.
[10] Ibid.
[11] Ibid.

with pleasure'. For Edwin at that time in the new Prague, there appeared to be 'a feeling of nationality and a feeling of equality, and the two things went together'. It seemed to him that the 'warm, easygoing contact' they had witnessed 'could only have been possible in a comparatively small town, and it was the first thing that made me wish that Edinburgh might become a similar place and that Scotland might become a nation again'.[12] Interestingly, this comment about Scotland becoming a nation again was omitted from the revised and extended version of *The Story and the Fable*, which was published as *An Autobiography* in 1954.

Despite their enthusiasm for what they saw as the early days of a new Czechoslovakian self-determination, the Muirs' difficulty with the Czech language and their limited understanding of Czech history concealed from them that there was in Prague another social grouping about which they knew nothing. Given that they were later to become the first English translators of the German-language fiction of Franz Kafka, it does seem surprising that they knew nothing about Kafka and heard nothing about Kafka, even from the Čapeks, during that first stay in Prague—a period which saw both the beginning and abandonment of Kafka's novel *Das Schloss*, *The Castle*, which they would themselves translate into English in 1930. Willa would later draw attention to this strange absence when she referred to the hostility she thought she had encountered initially in Prague when she tried to make up for her lack of Czech language by asking for directions in German. She writes in *Belonging*—

> I had long ago picked up a few scraps of German, enough to ask my way politely in a street, and the first time I approached a kindly-looking Czech and asked if he could direct me to the Post Office I got a shock. His smile vanished, his face stiffened, his eyes narrowed, he shot out a couple of Czech sentences and spat on the pavement at my feet. I now know that he said 'I don't understand German, I don't speak German', and that it was probably a lie, since all Czechs had been technically Austrians until not so long before.

She continues—

> We were so busily involved in Czech doings, private parties as well as public shows, that we never knew about the German life still going on in pockets here and there in Prague. We never got even a hint that Kafka or his friends had ever existed in the city. An invisible but unyielding barrier cut off German-speakers from Czech-speakers, and it was only the Czech-speakers that we came to know.[13]

After the enthusiastic letter about Prague to his Glasgow relatives in February 1922, Edwin's first formal accounts of the Czech capital were communicated in

---

[12] *The Story and the Fable*, p. 228.
[13] *Belonging*, p. 62.

three articles he wrote for the American *Freeman* journal, published in the issues of 10 May, 9 August, and 11 October 1922: the first two were titled 'Impressions of Prague', followed by 'Impressions of a People'. Edwin was contracted to write two pieces per month for the *Freeman*, together with one for the *New Age*. His early contributions to the *Freeman*, from before his departure for Europe in June 1921, continued with the kind of Nietzschean topic and style that had characterized his *New Age* writing, with articles such as 'In Defence of New Truths', 'Against Optimism and Pessimism', and 'Beyond the Absolute'. It is not until the issue of May 1922, with its first 'Impressions of Prague', that this thematic approach is broken. Yet Edwin seems to be struggling, not only to come to terms with his unfamiliar physical and cultural environment, but also to find a new and more personal way of writing about it. The Prague found initially in the *Freeman* is not the 'sizzling' and challenging city described in the early letter to his sister and their later recollections, but reads like the somewhat laboured product of a conscientious student. This May essay (for it seems more like an essay than a lively descriptive article) begins—

> When one emerges from the Wilson station in Prague, with memories of Berlin still fresh in one's mind, one is immediately struck with the quietness of the town, the slowness of its *tempo*. The droshky takes one through deserted streets, pleasant and roomy in the dusty afternoon heat, and one suddenly crosses a main thoroughfare where electric cars rattle and clang and crowds jostle with the unceremonious determination of Continental peoples. But the flurry is on such a small scale and is so much more an affair of effervescence than of business necessity that one is not deceived for a moment. Prague is a country town, a big country town, dignified, even distinguished, but still a country town. From the moment one set foot in it one would not think of calling it a metropolis.[14]

As they themselves readily admitted, Europe was an unknown continent to both Muirs when they set off in the late summer of 1921. Yet Edwin strives here to give the somewhat blasé impression of one long familiar with its ways, with phrases such as 'the unceremonious determination of Continental peoples' and 'The paradox of Prague is that it is the antithesis of its own spirit.' He seems more comfortable when he moves into an historical mode and tells the story of Jan Hus and Bohemia's religious struggles. Yet even here artificiality intrudes, as in his comment, 'If I were a Czech I think I should regard Prague with a sort of melancholy pride as a beautiful daughter who had sold herself again and again, and in doing so had become infinitely rich in foreign allurements and exotic memories,

---

[14] Edwin Muir, 'Impressions of Prague, *Freeman*, 10 May 1922, p. 204.

achieving a unique synthesis of harmonious and contradictory charms.' Until a moment of reality—and honesty—briefly intrudes with the additional comment 'But very likely I should not feel like that at all.'[15]

The second *Freeman* article from August was in later years transposed, with some light editing and sizeable sections of the final October article, into Edwin's 1940 autobiography *The Story and the Fable*. He did this because he considered that these contemporaneously written pages were more vivid than his later recollections, and so would better communicate his first impressions. While the uncertainty of his early responses are to some extent still present in the second article, together with a romanticized portrait of the 'magnificent old women' he sees on a boat trip, and often in the markets 'carrying immense burdens with a careless air', these articles, and especially the final October one, point to a less constrained observer. Here we find a more politically acute writer, perhaps influenced by his interaction with the Čapeks and his invitation, through this connection, to the Hradčany to meet with President Masaryk, where he points to the benefits of a republic where 'one can change one's president, work for or against him, and discuss with him with more freedom than one can one's next door neighbour. A republic becomes a part of one's activities in a more concrete sense than a monarchy.'[16] Edwin was socialist in his politics, after all, and an active member of socialist organizations in his Glasgow years. In his final 'Impressions' article, he seems to have found a voice to interpret and communicate more freely what he notices in the streets of the city, perceptions that fit more readily with Willa's memories of a 'sizzling' atmosphere. After the opening sentiments of the October article, Edwin continues in a similar vein—

> One becomes aware of the vitality of the republican idea in Prague as soon as one enters the city. Whether one walks the streets or sits in the cafés, one hears a political din; it seems as if the whole people, old and young, after being denied all their life any voice in their political fate, had resolved at last to enjoy an orgy of self-government. They discuss politics, interests, grievances, new acts, with measureless delight; they enjoy their very difficulties because of the freedom with which they can discuss them. Their political passion bursts out everywhere: in the cabarets, where no evening passes without the singing of half-a-dozen patriotic songs in which every line ends with '*Cesky*' that does not end with '*Republiky*'.

There is also a greater understanding of the contemporary problems facing the new Republic, such as the 'the large block of Germans still left in Bohemia as an unlucky reminder of the old Government'; and also, the 'trouble with Slovakia, which considers that it is not being treated on an equality with Bohemia'. And in a comment that has some relationship, perhaps, to his own difficulties with the

---

[15] Ibid., p. 205.
[16] *The Story and the Fable*, p. 221.

banking and postal services, he adds 'It has an ocean of muddle left by the old Empire, and a new and inexperienced class of Czech officials who, like amateur Columbuses, are attempting to circumnavigate it; for all the Imperial officials were Germans.'[17]

Looking back to their residence in Prague in *The Story and the Fable*, Edwin credits the experience with its helping to free his imagination, and the evidence of his *Freeman* articles would appear to confirm this. Remembering their time in Prague, he realized that he and Willa had 'a great deal of leisure', and his two articles a month for the *Freeman* and a weekly piece for the *New Age* enabled them to live comfortably, because living was so cheap. He continues, 'It was the first time since fourteen that I had known what it was to have time for thinking and daydreaming. I was in a foreign town where everything—the people, the houses, the very shop-signs—was different; I began to learn the visible world all over again.'[18] In Glasgow, in contrast, 'the ugliness of everything—the walks through the slums, the uncongenial work—had turned me in upon myself, so that I no longer saw things, but was merely aware of them in an indirect way. In Prague everything seemed to be asking me to notice it.'[19] While this, and their association with the Čapeks, must certainly have played a large part in helping them feel at home in the city, they also met up with Prague's 'English colony' in the winter, some of whom 'were giving English lessons, some studying Czech; the others were mainly concerned with business concerns or the Embassy'. Edwin writes of a dancing class where 'the Czechs and the English met twice a week'. He and Willa joined and 'heard all the gossip which flies through a foreign colony, the members of which are slightly suspicious of one another for living out of England'. No doubt they themselves became a target for gossip when they received a visit from John Holms, Edwin's colourful friend from his Glasgow days who arrived 'enveloped in an enormous long brown overcoat, in which, with his red hair and red beard, he looked Russian'. Apparently he made a strong impression on the English colony, 'who kept trooping to our lodgings to have a look at him'. Another visitor was an aspiring young novelist from the Midlands, described by Edwin as 'a cross between Aubrey Beardsley and Samuel Smiles', who came 'carrying a copy of *Ulysses*, which had just come out'. The English colony apparently 'did not know what to make of him' either. Edwin does not say what he thinks they made of Willa and himself.[20]

Winter in Prague had its downside. The Vltava was frozen solid by November, and in March the ice was only beginning to break up. Willa developed bronchitis, and despite assurances from friends that Prague would be beautiful with blossom in the spring, that spring seemed far off. When Willa recovered, they decided to go for a weekend to Dresden—only a moderate train journey—'to see what it was

---

[17] Ibid., pp. 224–5.
[18] Ibid., p. 229.
[19] Ibid.
[20] Ibid., pp. 231–2.

like'.[21] They liked it so well that they decided to come back to live there. Spring had already reached Dresden. Back in Prague the river ice on the river had broken, but still it 'was coming down in irregular blocks, some of them as big as a dancing-floor'. They packed their suitcases, 'said goodbye to everyone we knew and vanished into Germany'.[22]

---

[21] *Belonging*, p. 65.
[22] *The Story and the Fable*, p. 233; *Belonging*, p. 66.

3
Elbflorenz 1922–1923

> In Dresden during that hot, idle summer I seemed at last to recover from the long illness that had seized me when, at fourteen, I came to Glasgow.
>
> Edwin Muir, *The Story and the Fable* (1940)

The Muirs left Prague for Dresden at the end of March 1922, and loved 'the fine, spacious city'. Edwin's choice of phrase speaks of the freedom and relaxation they felt after the circuitous streets of the old town of Prague, and the involved, and at times hectic life they had been leading in the Czech city. Willa wrote that Dresden gave 'plenty of elbow-room', and that what lingered most in her memory of their early months in this former capital of Saxony was 'the fragrance from avenues of blossoming lime trees which went to our heads as we sat in the open eating ices in mindless peace'.[1] After staying for a week in a small hotel while they made themselves familiar with their new environment, they found lodgings just inside Dresden Neustadt, the new town of Dresden, in a flat on the top floor of a building situated on a quiet square near the river. The flat belonged to the family of the official caretaker of the insurance company building and they were able to rent two large rooms that looked over the treetops to the Elbe beyond. The caretaker's conditions of employment forbade the letting of rooms and so the visitors were asked to pass themselves off as cousins from Scotland, something they were willing to do for their spacious accommodation, 'furnished in high style with leather armchairs, an enormous flat desk at which we could both sit, and in the bedroom a Himmel-Bett adorned with cherubs'.[2] At this point, Dresden seemed far removed from the privations of the recent war, a city aiming to live its comfortable life as in the past. Only their landlady's half-humorous insistence that they must find her teenage daughter a British or American husband might have signalled an uneasiness beneath the apparently settled surface of life.

The Muirs soon settled in. As summer approached, they spent hours on the Neustadt shores of the Elbe among other sunbathers, while the pleasure steamers, as captured by Canaletto in his paintings of Dresden and its riverside, plied their trade from the opposite Altstadt banks below the famous Brühl Terrace, called by Goethe 'the balcony of Europe'. Willa describes how on their first visit to the

---
[1] *The Story and the Fable*, p. 233; *Belonging*, p. 67.
[2] *Belonging*, p. 68.

river, Edwin, a non-swimmer, went off to buy swimming trunks, while she picked her way 'among recumbent monsters, fat men like walruses in drab loin-cloths, with sausage-rolls at the back of their necks, tanned a deep mahogany colour that made them look like bronze images, replicas, say, of the Chinese God of Prosperity'. When the 'monsters' suddenly began to stir and even sit up, she also looked up to see 'a streak of moonlight flickering past the bronzes and coming my way, an incredibly slim, incredibly white-skinned figure in daffodil-yellow trunks, Edwin, stepping jauntily among the walruses'[3]—not at all the kind of image more usually associated with this future poet. They had plenty of free time once Edwin had written his articles for the *Freeman*—and Dresden, often called *Elbflorenz*—Florence on the Elbe—had much to offer besides its sunbathing opportunities. They enjoyed the city's fine baroque buildings, with art galleries and museums such as the Zwinger and the Albertinum, and the Frauenkirche, the Opera House and the Concert Hall, all within reasonable walking or tram distance from their lodgings. They set themselves to learning German more fully and attended concerts and cabarets, often accompanied by John Holms and his companion Dorothy Jennings who had also come to the city.

Holms had found it difficult to settle in London after his demobilization from the army and was now, like Edwin and Willa, travelling in Europe. He wrote to his friend Hugh Kingsmill in April 1922 that he was living in Dresden for at least three weeks and that the Muirs were in the city also, planning to stay for two or three months. He added, 'The rooms are delightful, a fine town and *incredibly* cheap—15/- a week means luxurious living—and such a nice lot too, although uninspiring to look at'. He had not realized 'how bitterly thread-bare tired' he had been in London and he was now 'aching' to get settled and to work. After Dresden, while waiting for Dorothy to join him, he was planning to move on to Munich where he thinks he will be able to work, for although he finds it 'quite pleasant round here', he feels the need 'to see mountains'.[4] By early June, however, Holms decided to return to Dresden, telling Kingsmill that Edwin has sent him advertisements for rooms in the city, saying 'I know what it's like and that I can work there'. Holms was obviously in an unsettled frame of mind, but an additional problem was the difficulty in obtaining permission from the authorities to stay for any length of time in Germany in this early post-1918 period. He told Kingsmill that the authorities 'won't give one more than a month now, owing to the flooding of Germany with Americans'. He himself is against the 'tourists', for they are the ones 'who put up the prices', but he clearly does not consider himself—or the Muirs—to be in the tourist category. They are in the category of 'needy artists' and have work to do. Neither Edwin nor Willa would mention any such permissions problems in their future memoirs, but Holms writes that in fact Edwin 'was flatly refused an extension,

---

[3] Ibid., pp. 68–9.
[4] Letter from John Holms to Hugh Kingsmill, April 1922, BL, Add MS 85338 vol. xvi.

and only got it through the help of a common friend of ours there, and then only on the ground of writing political etc. articles on the state of Germany.'[5] Edwin was indeed writing monthly articles for the American *Freeman*, many of which concerned his current travels in Europe, although they were literary and cultural as opposed to political. But these essays, along with those for *The New Age*, seem to have been enough to extend his stay in Dresden.

Among the qualities that attracted Edwin to John Holms was his capacity to talk enthusiastically and with knowledge about so many different subjects; and Edwin's quality as a quiet but interested and intelligent listener was no doubt equally attractive to Holms. Writing about these Dresden days, Edwin would recall discussions with Holms over pots of beer as to 'whether Wagner compared with Beethoven could be called a great man, and whether love satisfied or love unfulfilled was the better inspiration for the artist, Wagner standing for the first and Beethoven for the second'.[6] Edwin was beginning to write poems, but was not yet convinced of their success. Holms was an encouraging supporter, writing to Kingsmill in July that 'Muir is developing in an extraordinary way—half pathetic and half remarkable— he's writing a lot of poetry—one in particular, in spite of very bad patches, is really damned good.'[7] Willa, on the other hand, was still unable to welcome Holms after her first encounter with him and Hugh Kingsmill in her Guilford Street flat, and she did not appreciate his tendency to speak exclusively to Edwin when they met in the evenings. One such discussion seemed to involve Holms's idea for a long poem 'on the metamorphoses of the animals, in which the various species would be shown emerging pictorially in the course of a long magical process, by an enormous speeding up and simplification of time'. Willa associated this with the story of the biblical flood, and influenced by her love of theatre and her connections with the Čapeks in Prague, she sketched out a scenario for a play that would dramatize, in modern terms, the story of Noah and his family after the floods had receded and life had to begin all over again. When she told Edwin of her idea, however, it was immediately rejected as an unsuitable use of the biblical story, although he himself would later use the theme in a more traditional form in his poem 'Ballad of the Flood'. Holms, despite his enthusiasm for the metamorphosis idea, did not succeed in taking his long poem further than his usual animated discussion.

Holms seems to have been unable to settle for long in any one place nor do the work he often spoke of longing to do, suffering from what Edwin described as 'the lethargy which weighed upon him'.[8] Nowadays his condition would most probably be diagnosed as traumatic stress disorder resulting from the war experiences for which Holms was awarded the military cross. Perhaps Edwin's own

---

[5] Letter from Holms to Kingsmill, June 1922, BL, Add MS 85338 vol. xvi.
[6] Edwin Muir, *An Autobiography* (London: Methuen & Co Ltd, University Paperbacks, 1968), p. 198.
[7] Holms, letter to Kingsmill about Edwin's poetry, July 1922, BL, Add MS 85338 vol. xvi.
[8] *An Autobiography*, p. 199.

illnesses and the psychological distress of his Glasgow years led him to recognize the vulnerability below the voluble and dominant personality that so irritated Willa. At the same time, Holms's wide-ranging talk opened up worlds that Edwin's own limited education had left unexplored. In the closing chapter of *The Story and the Fable*, Edwin would write that 'in Dresden during that hot, idle summer I seemed at last to recover from the long illness that had seized me when, at fourteen, I came to Glasgow. I realized that I must live over again the years which I had lived wrongly, and that every one should live his life twice, for the first attempt is always blind.' In the 'resting space' that Dresden provided, he had come to know himself, 'or rather struck up a first acquaintance with myself.' And he continues—

> I had been existing, to use Holms's phrase, merely as something which consisted of 'the words with which one tries to explain it'; so that when at last I looked back at that life which, whatever I might think of it, was the life I knew best it seemed to me that I was not seeing my own life merely, but all human life, and I became conscious of it as a strange and unique process.

Looking back on that new consciousness from the standpoint of 1940 when the first version of his autobiography was published, he turned to Proust's *Le Temps Retrouvé* for his image of 'a moment liberated from the order of time', adding 'How much this revolution was due to Willa and how much to Holms I do not know.'[9]

Edwin and Willa's leisurely life in Dresden took an unexpected turn when they met the Scottish educationalist A. S. Neill, an old friend from Willa's university days, at a tram stop in the city. 'What on earth are *you* doing here?' they greeted each other. Edwin had had little if any previous acquaintanceship with Neill, and Willa had not seen him since her teaching days in London when Neill was teaching at King Alfred School in Hampstead. Now he was involved with what he called self-regulatory education where pupils would learn at their own pace and according to their own interests and inclinations, as opposed to the traditional system of compulsory subjects, exam timetables, and imposed discipline. He was living in Hellerau, a small village close to Dresden, where he had established an International School which would eventually transfer to England and become the Summerhill School for which he is now best known.

Hellerau, advertised for tourists today as *die erste deutsche Gartenstadt*, the first German Garden City, was created in 1909 as a result of new movements in architecture, applied arts, and creative and performing activities such as music and dance, together with social concerns about the need to create a new community that would allow people to live in harmony with their natural environment, in contrast to the industrialization and alienation of a fast-changing modern world. Jacques-Dalcroze established his experimental Eurythmics dance school in

---

[9] *The Story and the Fable*, pp. 234, 235.

Hellerau where he put into practice his theoretical ideas about restoring harmony to the lives of modern people through rhythmic movement. A special educational building—Die Bildungsanstalt Jacques-Dalcroze—was designed for his school by the architect Heinrich Tessenow, and its Festspielhaus was considered a pioneering building not only for its hosting of Dalcroze's dance innovations and summer festivals, but also for its own architectural design qualities. The First World War inevitably interrupted such cultural and social developments, but in the early 1920s a rhythmic dance school returned to Dalcroze's Bildungsanstalt under the name of Die Neue Schule für Rhythmic, Musik und Körperbildung. In 1921 Neill had arrived in Hellerau to stay with his friends Dr Otto Neustätter and his wife, and when the Dalcroze School learned that he was looking for a building where he could introduce his new theories, it was suggested that the Dalcroze School should be turned into an International School where its existing rhythmic and musical practices could be accompanied by Neill's educational innovations. After some thought and encouragement from Frau Doktor Neustätter, an Australian whom he had met during the war when she had brought her son to be educated at the King Alfred School, Neil agreed to become involved in the Hellerau project. He was looking for additional teachers to join him in the more traditional areas of education, so that his School could be accepted by the German Inspectorate, when he encountered Willa and Edwin at the Dresden tram stop quite by chance.

Aware of Willa's strong educational achievements and teaching experience, Neill proposed that she should join him in his Hellerau venture. This was an unexpected turn in their affairs, but without making firm promises Willa and Edwin took the tram to Hellerau the next day and liked what they saw there. 'Both of us at once liked the look and the feel of Hellerau, a village planned for craftsmen and artists, the original model for places like Letchworth, with pleasant houses set irregularly on the slopes of a sandy hill among pinewoods and hedged in everywhere by fragrant sweetbriar.'[10] They were welcomed by Frau Doktor Neustätter, who offered them lodgings and board very cheaply in her own house, if Willa would come as a teacher. Edwin would be free to write his articles and could become involved with the life of the community or stay apart from it, just as he wished. Both liked the idea of an international school, and finding Hellerau and the Neustätter accommodation attractive, they moved to Neill's School in the summer of 1922.

In her later memoir *Belonging*, Willa described the Hellerau community as 'a European international enclave', with every European country represented except Italy, Spain, and Russia. The eurhythmic students—young women from the age of 17 to about 23 years, many of whom wanted to become professional dancers—came from various European countries, while three of Neill's International School students, two young brothers and a girl in her early teens, were

[10] *Belonging*, pp. 73, 74.

English. The Eurhythmic School occupied the central section of the original Dalcroze Bildungsanstalt, with its theatre—the Festspielhaus—and its practice rooms and sun terraces. Neill's International School was situated in one of the two large wings, the other of which housed a German school for village children. A separate building, named the Schulheim, provided both a residence for Neill and his own pupils and the dining room where all staff and pupils met together for their midday meal. Frau Doktor Neustätter had taken upon herself the role of housekeeper and matron for the Schulheim, and was known to everyone as Frau Doktor. German became the language of teaching in the Schools and in general conversation around the Schulheim dining table. Willa said that both she and Edwin 'soon became fluent in German since every word we learned was on active service'. Edwin was more cautious, writing to his Glasgow relatives in December 1922 that he had 'made some progress in German' while 'Minnie speaks the language almost like a native.'[11] (Muir's family knew Willa as 'Minnie'.) They settled well, patronizing the village bars with other staff members in the evenings, or visiting Hellerau residents with whom they had become friendly. Dresden was still close enough for visits to the concert hall and theatre, and on two occasions they spent a weekend in Berlin at the invitation of an American journalist based in the city who had come to Hellerau specially to meet them. On the second weekend visit to Berlin they were fortunate to see a performance of Karel Čapek's *Insects* play, which Willa had translated into English when they were living in Prague and which she now found very well produced in German. They did not much enjoy the cabarets to which their hosts took them, finding them, according to Willa, 'brittle, smart and strikingly immoral to our unsophisticated minds'. Visual art Constructivists such as Lissitsky fared better, although 'the bits and pieces of their *collages*, tram tickets and match-box tops and rusty wire springs, spoke to us of past stringencies rather than of the future.' While admitting that 'what we brought back from Berlin were personal impressions of likes and dislikes but no understanding of that feverish city,' Willa concluded that 'Germany did not mean Berlin to Edwin and me; it meant Dresden, and Hellerau where by this time we knew every man, woman, child, cat and dog in the village.' As for Edwin, she believed that he 'had never been so carefree in his life.'[12]

Apart from sharing lunch times, evening activities, and various countryside excursions, Edwin was very much left to his own devices in Hellerau. His principal task was providing the *Freeman* with monthly articles, sometimes divided into three contributions in the same month, such as his 'North and South' of November 1922, or an article followed by a shorter item in the same month. He continued to contribute to the *New Age*, and in November 1922 began a new series,

[11] Ibid., p. 74; *Selected Letters of Edwin Muir*, ed. by P. H. Butter (London: The Hogarth Press, 1974), p. 26.
[12] *Belonging*, p. 77.

'*Causerie de Jeudi*', similar to his earlier 'We Moderns', but less aphoristic in their manner of writing. This series continued until August 1923 and in its later stages often took the form of literary reviews. In June 1922, around the time of their move to Hellerau, his poem 'Rebirth' (later retitled 'Ballad of Rebirth') appeared in the *New Age*. This was Edwin's first poem and his first British publication under his own name as opposed to his *New Age* pseudonym 'Edward Moore'. It was followed in July by 'Ballad of Eternal Life', later revised and published in his *First Poems* as 'Ballad of the Soul'. Both poems seem to be related to the waking dreams he experienced as a result of his psychoanalysis in London. John Holms wrote to Hugh Kingsmill about Edwin's new poetry, and in one of his July letters he sent him part of 'Ballad of Eternal Life', saying that it had 'some really excellent things in it too' and that it had its roots in a dream. Holms realized that 'all these dreams occurred long ago when he was being psycho-analysed—so in his case psycho-analysis is to a certain extent justified by its fruits.' He added, 'Still it seems rather a precarious source of inspiration—precarious though perfectly genuine—it's a damned interesting subject for speculation, isn't it? What do you think of it?' In a letter of 24 July, he enclosed a copy of the 'Ballad of Eternal Life' taken from the July issue of *The New Age*, recommending that Kingsmill 'try and read it as though printed in 4 line stanzas as Ancient Mariner.' Orage had apparently printed the poem without verse divisions, earning Holms's rebuke that 'Orage is a fool', since this lack of division 'halves the effect as it is', and he asks Kingsmill to 'let me have it back a soon as possible—it's the only copy he's got.'[13]

In Hellerau, Edwin found sources of inspiration beyond his early dream visions. While Willa was involved with her teaching duties, he was developing a friendship with an impoverished aristocrat, Iwar von Lücken, now separated from his family and very much down on his luck as a result of the recent war and his own difficulties in fitting into a conventional lifestyle. In his autobiography, Edwin would describe Lücken as living in a small basement room in the Hellerau Schulheim, having 'lost all he had in the inflation'; and giving Spanish lessons to students who paid him 'at his own request, in parcels of food, pounds of rice, pats of butter'. He refused to let anyone enter his room, probably, Edwin thought, because of its lack of furnishings, and although he and Willa tried to persuade him to have a meal with them, he very rarely agreed, and if he did 'as a point of private honour, would eat very little.'[14] Despite his reticence, Iwar von Lücken provided the gateway to Edwin's discovery of currently influential German-language poets such as the recently republished early Romantic period Hölderlin and the later Hugo von Hofmannsthal, Stefan George, and Georg Trakl. Edwin had for long felt an affinity with German writers whose work he had read in English translation as a young man in Glasgow. Nietzsche was the philosopher to whom he had turned when

---

[13] Letter from John Holms to Hugh Kingsmill, 24 July 1922, BL, Add MS85338 vol. xvi.
[14] *An Autobiography*, p. 204.

trying to understand his own sense of personal dislocation in the industrialized city, and he had found 'a sickly, graveyard strain' in the poetry of Heinrich Heine which lay alongside its 'exquisite wit'. This was the unlikely combination that had sustained him when he was employed as a clerk in a foul-smelling bone factory in Greenock. The *Sehnsucht*, the sense of longing in a poem such as Goethe's 'Kennst du das Land' from *Wilhelm Meisters Lehrjahre* was another important psychological influence in those Glasgow years. Now, in his new leisure in Hellerau, and under the influence of his talks with Lücken, these earlier influences were reawakened, but this time in their native German-language context, along with German writers who were considered to be important by contemporary Germans interested in poetry.[15]

Lücken was familiar with most living German poets, and had written poetry himself, with a modest publication record. Although the Muirs do not seem to have been fully aware of his previous contacts with artistic communities in Germany, later researches by the German scholar Howard Gaskill suggest that Lücken may have been a quiet member of a group of artists including the painter Oskar Kokoschka, who was resident in Dresden between 1917 and 1924. Kokoschka made a lithograph portrait of Lücken, which featured in a collection of his poems published in Berlin in 1928, and he appears as one of the 'friends' in Kokoschka's Dresden-period painting 'Die Freunde' of 1917 (which includes the painter himself). On the canvas Lücken is seen engaged in conversation with a Dr Fritz Neuberger, who was involved in rescuing artists and poets from the First World War, and who is believed to have rescued Kokoschka at Dresden railway station on his way back to the Front. Lücken would appear to have been a member of Dr Neuberger's refugee group in Dresden before his move to Hellerau, and it seems possible that he too might have been rescued by Neuberger from the accident-prone war service he later described to Edwin. Whatever the precise details of his history, his knowledge of and commitment to German poetry, and his willingness to share this, were of immense importance to Edwin at this critical point in his own creative life, when he was attempting, seriously, to write poetry and when he now had sufficient understanding of German to meet with the new poets introduced to him by Lücken. Of all the poets whose work he knew and admired, Hölderlin was the one closest to Lücken's heart, and before long Hölderlin and his gods also became increasingly important to Edwin.[16]

Edwin's three-part article 'The Meaning of Romanticism', published in the *Freeman* in December 1923 and January 1924, grew out of his talks with Lücken and the German poetry he read, and the poetry he was inspired to attempt himself. In his Romanticism article he argued that unlike Classicism, which belongs to the

---

[15] Ibid., p. 144.
[16] Information about von Lücken from P. H. Gaskill, 'Edwin Muir's Friend in Hellerau: Iwar von Lücken, *German Life and Letters*, vol. 32, issue 2, January 1979, pp. 135–47.

past and whose literature does not speak to us with the urgency of contemporary literature, the Romantic movement was a continuum of the human spirit which could encompass both awareness of the need for change and hopes for a more fulfilling future. Its literature and its aspirations were still alive in the present as opposed to existing only in their own past, as he believed was true of classical literature. Similarly, he found in Hölderlin a poet whose imagistic vision of the gods was not one divorced from human life but one where gods and humans could interact fruitfully with each other.

Hölderlin had only recently been rediscovered in Germany through the reissue of his work in an edition by Norbert von Hellingrath towards the end of the First World War, and his influence can be seen in Edwin's writing. 'A Note on Friedrich Hölderlin' appeared in the *Freeman* on 1 August 1923 (and so must have been written during his stay in Hellerau). It was also published, with some additional material, in Hugh MacDiarmid's *The Scottish Nation* in the same year and was followed by 'The Poetry of Hölderlin' in *The Saturday Review of Literature* in January 1925 and by 'Friedrich Hölderlin' in the *Adelphi* of 1926. For Edwin, Hölderlin's work was 'metaphysical', a quality he found absent in previous German poetry. And this metaphysical poetry was also 'in a sane way mystical'. It was a mysticism grounded in the human world, which 'worked, not by depriving the world of any of its reality, but by deepening that reality rather, until it gave a final satisfaction'. What seemed especially important was that in this poetry Hölderlin 'did not abolish the gods, he humanized them, regarding them as real and natural essences, as they must have been perceived by those who saw them for the first time'. In the case of the Christian god—'He did not interpret Christ; he met him in imagination on the shores of Galilee and recorded his impressions. He imagined Christ in the flesh, and not as, twisted by the thoughts of men, He was later to become.'

For Edwin, then, Hölderlin's poetry, like his view of Romanticism, was a continuing positive motivating force in human life, something particularly important in Germany in the wake of the First World War. He wrote, 'To the generation of moral and spiritual misery which followed the War he showed the foundations of human dignity and freedom.' In particular, younger Germans 'found in him a profound and radical thinker who never was disruptive, a poet not in the modern spirit, but one rather to decide for them what would be modern'. For Edwin himself, 'he was an innovator, but in going forward to the bounds of experience he went back also to its sources.'[17] Edwin saw Hölderlin as a poet who could speak to modern times after a disastrous war but also in the context of his own traumatic transplantation from the Orkney of his childhood to industrialized Glasgow at the turn of the century. The German poet's bringing together the world of Nature with the world of human childhood was something that especially caught his imagination, as in the

---

[17] Edwin Muir, 'The Poetry of Hölderlin', *The Saturday Review of Literature*, 3 January 1925, p. 434.

poem 'Da ich ein Knabe war'—'Da spielt ich sicher und gut / Mit den Blumen des Hains / Und die Lüftchen des Himme / Spielten mit mir' ('There I played safely and well / with the flowers of the thicket / and the little breezes of heaven / played with me'). These lines may well have echoed Edwin's own memories of an Orkney childhood in a world where 'the sky fitted the earth and the earth the sky.'[18] Thinking back later to his own attempts to write poetry in these Dresden and Hellerau days, Edwin wrote—

> I must have been influenced by something, since we all are, but when I try to find out what it was that influenced me, I can only think of the years of childhood which I spent on my father's farm in the little island of Wyre in Orkney, and the beauty I apprehended then, before I knew there was beauty. These years had come alive, after being forgotten for so long, and when I wrote about horses, they were my father's plough-horses as I saw them when I was four or five. [...] The bare landscape of the little island became, without my knowing it, a universal landscape.[19]

In his Hellerau reading with Lücken, Edwin's imagination was also captured by the metaphysical use of landscape imagery in the early lyrical poetry of Hugo von Hofmannsthal, and his essay on Hofmannsthal was published in the *Freeman* in October 1923, shortly after the one on Hölderlin. Despite Edwin's excited response, however, Hofmannsthal is a very different poet from his Romantic-period predecessor. Instead of communicating the unity and protectiveness of the nature imagery found in Hölderlin's 'Da ich ein Knabe war', Hofmannsthal's nature imagery, in a poem such as 'Ballade des äusseren Lebens' ('Ballad of external life'), creates specific yet also metaphorical scenarios where the world of nature offers no hope and no possibility of understanding to the young person on the bridge between childhood and adulthood: 'Und Kinder wachsen auf mit tiefen Augen, / Die von nichts wissen, wachsen auf and sterben / Und alle Menschen gehen ihre Wege'. ('And children grow up with deep eyes, / which know nothing, grow up and die, / and all human beings go on their course.') In his essay Edwin does not dwell on this apparently resigned and fatalistic outlook, so different to Hölderlin's positive vision, which he had endorsed so strongly in his earlier *Freeman* and later *Saturday Review of Literature* essays. Instead, he seems caught by Hofmannsthal's perception 'that so and so things happen, that children grow up, become something different, and die, that some men are born to glory and others to poverty; above all, that all things pass, and having passed, can never be recaptured.'[20] These lyrics may well have aroused memories of Edwin's own struggle to make sense

---

[18] Friedrich Hölderlin, 'Da ich ein Knabe War', *Harrap Anthology of German Poetry*, ed. by August Closs (London: Harrap, 1957), p. 272; *An Autobiography*, p. 33.
[19] *An Autobiography*, p. 206.
[20] See Edwin Muir, 'Hugo von Hofmannstal', *The Freeman*, October 1923, pp. 152-4.

of human existence as a teenager in Glasgow, separated from the security of his Orkney childhood, bereft of his parents and the brothers who had not survived life in the city. Although he does not acknowledge Hofmannsthal's poetry as a direct influence, such memories in this vein would become a persistent theme in his own early poetry and in the fiction he wrote in the late 1920s and early 1930s.

Another positive influence on Edwin's poetry during his stay in Hellerau was his friendship with one of the young eurhythmics students, Gerda Krapp. There would appear to have been good relationships between the various teaching staff members and the eurhythmics students—frequently meeting together in the Schulheim or in the evenings in the village pub, and making group excursions in the surrounding countryside and woods in their free time. Gerda was one of the students who took part in these events, but she also had a keen interest in poetry and translated several of Edwin's Hellerau poems into German, confirming that these verses were indeed written during that new creative period in his life. Among the poems translated by Gerda was 'Childhood', which was published in its original English-language form in *Living Age* in December 1923 and in the *Dial* in February 1924 before being included in Edwin's *First Poems* collection published by Hogarth Press in 1925. She also translated an early version of the long poem 'Chorus of the Newly Dead', a poem which preoccupied Edwin over many years and various versions. He published an early version of this poem—perhaps the version translated by Gerda—in MacDiarmid's *Scottish Chapbook* of August 1923, and in December 1925 sections of it appeared in a short-lived British journal *The Calendar of Modern Letters*. The *Scottish Chapbook* publication and Gerda's translation confirm that the poem was being worked on during his year in Hellerau as opposed to Neill's school in its new Sonntagberg location in 1924, as Edwin later claimed in his autobiography. Other poems translated into German by Gerda were 'Ballad of Eternal Life', published in the *New Age* in July 1922, and one that seems to have had similarities with 'The Lost Land', published later in the *Dial* in February 1925 before its inclusion in *First Poems* in the same year.[21]

What these translations and the periodical publication of his poems confirms is the commitment with which Edwin worked at his new poetry during his year in Hellerau, marking a significant development from the dream-inspired ballads mentioned by John Holms in his correspondence with Hugh Kingsmill, to poems such as 'Childhood' translated by Gerda, and 'Horses', published in the *Nation* in May 1924. Holms stayed in touch with Edwin regularly during the Hellerau year and kept Kingsmill up to date with his progress and his determined attempts to have a collection of these new poems published. Writing to Kingsmill on Christmas Day 1922 from the Hellerau address of 'Am Sand' where he and Dorothy had obtained lodgings, Holms reported that Muir's poems 'though patchy

---

[21] For information about Gerda Krapp, see Howard Gaskill, 'Edwin Muir in Hellerau', *Scottish Literary Journal*, vol. 11, no. 1, May 1984, pp. 45–56.

(they become less so) are really astoundingly good and as original as anything I have read—I mean when they are good. He's just got them back from Heinemann who wouldn't take them. He sent them to Elkin Matthews too—not heard yet'. Holms was not a man to pretend an interest where he felt none, and he was not altogether in sympathy with what he called Hellerau's 'barren heartiness'. But his comments to Kingsmill confirm his sincere belief in Edwin's progress. He writes that if the poems are sent back from Matthews, 'I wonder if, when you're back in London, you could take them to Chapman?' And he continues—'Anyway, I'd like you to read the lot and hear what you think of them—especially, though not as good as bits of the others, of the ballad ones. They have more of the ballad spirit than any imitations I have read—in his case the form is entirely natural—he writes in ballad form far more quickly and easily than in any other. A pure question of race'.[22]

At this time Edwin himself was not such a conscientious correspondent with his Glasgow relations as he appears to have been with potential publishers, but in a Christmas letter to his sister Lizzie and her husband from Hellerau dated 15 December 1922 (his first letter to them since leaving Prague in the spring), he wrote that he had been—

> writing a lot of poetry again, two samples of which you might have seen in 'The New Age'. I have collected 12 of my poems, three in Scotch, and have sent them to Heinemann in London for publication, but have received no reply yet. I am in negotiation for the publication of a volume of essays in America (they have appeared already in the American 'Freeman', a very good journal) and I am preparing a volume of aphorisms which I intend to try my luck with in London in the next few weeks.

He adds, 'If any or all of these projects come off, I may reap a little fame from them, especially the poems, which are easily the best things I have yet written.'[23] Edwin goes on to tell Lizzie and George about his liking for Germany and the German people and for Dresden itself—'a very pretty, but a very bourgeois town' with its fine art gallery, opera house, and a 'state theatre where the acting is intensely bad'— a change from the Čapek's theatre activities in Prague that had so excited him and Willa despite their language difficulties. He describes Hellerau with its 'Eurhythmics School for teaching dancing, in which there are girls from all the nations in Europe', the 'free school' in which Willa now teaches, and 'the usual complement of Communists, vegetarians, simple-lifers and so on'. He tells them of the Wander Vogel movement of young people who live simply and go walking in the woods every weekend, singing German songs and sleeping at nights under the trees. For Edwin, however, 'they are a bit too serious, reject smoking, drinking, the cinema

---

[22] John Holms, letter to Hugh Kingsmill, 25 December 1922, BL, Add MS85338 vol. xvi.
[23] Edwin Muir, letter to Lizzie and George Thorburn, 15 December 1922, *Selected Letters*, pp. 24–6.

and foxtrotting as inventions of the devil'. The cheapness of living in Germany is stressed in the letter, with 'a pint of beer less than a penny', 'good Rhein wine' costing 3 pence a bottle, and 'good Virginia cigarettes, better than "Gold Flake" for 12 a penny'. There is not yet—at least in this correspondence with his relatives— any expectation of the political and financial crises in Germany that would in the next few months drive them to leave Dresden and Hellerau for the Italian south.

Evidence of the still unresolved political crises in Europe emanating from the Treaty of Versailles penetrated the seemingly secure world of Hellerau and its International School in the early days of 1923. Germany had been instructed by the Treaty to pay reparations in the form of coal and timber to the French, but had been slow to fulfil these obligations. On 11 January, the French government led by Poincaré decided to take the matter into its own hands and collect the coal and timber itself by sending troops to occupy the Ruhr basin and seize the coal mines. Historians record that the result was passive resistance on the part of the Germans, an attitude supported almost universally in Germany. One American observer is said to have remarked that only two people had been able to bring about German unity, these being Bismarck and Poincaré.[24]

The bitterness resulting from the invasion was compounded by the fact that the French had sent Algerian troops into the Ruhr, and in her memories of that time Willa describes how their friends in Hellerau were 'forlorn and cast down', especially since they felt it as 'a deliberately planned humiliation that the occupying troops were Algerians—black men, they said bitterly'. Then the currency began rapidly to fall in value. The Muirs remained comfortable since they were living on the dollars and pounds that came from Edwin's journal contributions, but their Hellerau friends were badly affected. Initially, Edwin and Willa 'began taking people into Dresden by the half-dozen, to the best restaurant, the Königsdiele, knowing that whatever they ordered, let them begin with champagne cocktails and finish with *omelette surprise*, the bill would not amount to more than ninepence a head'. Prices were soaring in the Dresden market-place—'A man would cram his week's wages into a suitcase and run full tilt to the market-place, hoping that he might still have enough to buy a dinner for his family. Elderly people stood there holding out for sale bits and bobs of family possessions, since even old junk was becoming more valuable than paper money.'[25] Eventually the Muirs decided that matters were beyond their control. Neill had lost his money, having invested it in the Hellerau venture, changing it into marks, and the future of the International School was uncertain. John Holms and Dorothy had rented for the summer a lodge-house by the sea close to Forte dei Marmi in Italy, and they were short of money to pay for it. They asked Edwin and Willa to join them and share their costs, and 'feeling like cowards we decided to run away.'[26]

[24] James Joll, *Europe since 1870* (Harmondsworth: Pelican Books, 1985), p. 284.
[25] *Belonging*, p. 79.
[26] Ibid.

4
North and South 1923–1924

> There has always been in Northern Europe a poignant longing for the South as for a home from which men were exiled and to which they could never return […] a sense of mystery and of loss as strong as that which religious men feel when they dream of a lost Paradise, as hopeless as that which poets cherish for their vanished childhood.
> Edwin Muir, 'North and South', *The Freeman* (1922)

The Muirs were now on their way to the idealized South Edwin had written about in *The Freeman*, but its satisfactions proved to be as elusive as his article had envisaged. Edwin says nothing about the manner of their departure from Hellerau in his later autobiography, but Willa describes how they were escorted to the station in a high state of emotion by students from the Eurhythmic School, with Gerda hanging on Edwin's arm and Nushi, a popular young Jewish student who would later die in a gas chamber in Auschwitz, clinging to Willa. A third student from Finland kept telling them to visit her in Helsinki—just ask for her father's sugar factory which everyone knew. The train south was hot and both Edwin and Willa were exhausted, with Edwin complaining of a headache that became worse as the day moved on. At Riva on Lake Garda he did not want to travel further, and they booked into a hotel close to the station and the lake. During the four days they spent in Riva neither Edwin's headache nor his apparent depressive state of mind—what Willa often called his Muir family remoteness—seemed to lift. They walked together and drove down each bank of the lake in a carozza. They took the paddle steamer to the Sirmione of Catullus, which Willa with her Classics background had always wanted to visit, but nothing ameliorated the atmosphere of unhappiness, or indeed the 'waves of silent hostility' emanating from Edwin. Then, after a direct question from Willa, the reason for the trouble emerged. 'On the way to the station Gerda had confessed that she loved him and he wanted to go back to Hellerau, to Gerda. A man couldn't just abruptly go away and leave a woman who said she loved him; it wasn't a thing anyone should do. He must go back to Gerda.' Willa later wrote of the 'storm of rage and grief' that rose up in her at this announcement, describing how she ran to the lakeside and roared over its 'unheeding waters' at the fact that 'Edwin couldn't leave Gerda, but he could leave *me*', adding 'I had not roared like that since I was fourteen.' Yet her characteristic capacity for coping with emergencies and her instinct for emotional involvement and impulsive volubility came to her rescue. She returned to Edwin and told him that they had not made their marriage to be a 'cage' for either of them, and that 'if he wanted to go back to Gerda he should go.' But first he would have to give her money, since she would have to 'find a British Consul and get a passport'. Perhaps it was that mundane but essential request that brought Edwin to his senses, for 'the Edwin I knew' came back to ask her forgiveness.[1]

In her later memoir Willa claimed that they never again referred to Gerda or the episode on Lake Garda. This, however, is not actually the case, for in the journal she kept during the early 1950s, when they were living at Newbattle Abbey just outside Edinburgh, Willa writes about how she raised the episode concerning Gerda when Edwin was working on the enlarged version of his autobiography, asking him if he intended to include a reference to it. Edwin, not surprisingly, said he had no intention of mentioning it, which distressed Willa and unleashed a current of emotions and detailed memories of what she called 'that terrible time'.[2] She would have been more distressed had she known the full story of the Gerda episode. For Edwin had written to Gerda, offering to return to her if that was what she wanted, and his letter, which arrived in Hellerau about two weeks after the Muirs' departure, must have been written or at least posted from Forte dei Marmi when they were staying with John Holms and Dorothy. Gerda was unprepared for her poet's response. She was clearly very fond of Edwin and had worked closely with him, in the translation of his poems in Hellerau; but she liked Willa also, and had not intended to break up their marriage by her impulsive declaration of love. She consulted Frau Doktor Neustätter, who advised her to write to Edwin, thanking him for his offer to return, but saying that she thought they should leave things as they were. And this she did.[3] Willa would appear to have known nothing of this exchange, but could see that Edwin was 'on bad terms with himself' and that both were for a time 'inclined to be diffident with each other'.[4] Living with the Holmses, as Willa called them, did not help the situation. Willa still resented John and had been less than enthusiastic about the plan to join him and Dorothy in Forte dei Marmi. Edwin, on the other hand, was in favour of the move. On the positive side, the southern sunshine and the beach, where they lay most of the day, 'bathing and dreaming by turns', was a kind of compensation. Willa taught Edwin to swim, and remembered him 'floating on his back, paddling gently and gazing into the sky'. In her estimation 'In the Tyrrhenian sea he began to recover his inner peace'.[5]

Edwin's own account of his first encounter with Italy is less conciliatory. He wrote that 'coming for the first time to the South, I was repelled by the violence of

---

[1] *Belonging*, pp. 81, 82, 83.
[2] Willa Muir, Journal for January 1951–September 1953, UStA, MS 38466 Box5/7.
[3] Howard Gaskell, 'Edwin Muir in Hellerau', *Scottish Literary Journal*, vol. 2 no. 1, May 1984, pp. 45–56.
[4] *Belonging*, pp. 87, 84.
[5] Ibid., p. 89.

the colours, the sea like a solid lake of blue paint, the purple sky, the bright brown earth: to my unaccustomed eyes the contrasts seemed crude and without mystery.' In addition, the insects 'a different race from any I had known before, troubled me by the intensity of their life, and I found myself watching them with the attraction I had felt as a child in Orkney, staring at a worm writhing in the heart of a dandelion'. Unusually for Edwin, he began to feel a certain irritation in John Holms's company.

> I think we should have come to know Italy better had it not been for Holms. He had been in Italy before; we were newcomers, and he could not resist the temptation of acting as a benevolent Virgilian guide and making us see everything with his more expert eyes. His tone at these moments was indulgently authoritative, and I still hear him, as he gazed at a particular effect of light one calm evening, saying pensively, while he plucked at his beard: 'It's pure Leonardo da Vinci'.

For Edwin, Holms's 'pre-digested Italy, of whose authority he never had a doubt, came between us and the Italy we wished to see for ourselves'.[6] Another reason for Edwin's discontent may have been the suspicion that Holms knew about the Gerda affair. This seems possible because in writing to Kingsmill about the publication of Edwin's *First Poems*, three years later, Holms refers to the poem 'An Ancient Song' with its lines 'Lost Love which flies aghast it knows not where, / And finds no foothold but the dreadful air', and notes 'Oddly enough it was written before the German business, at least before he was in the least conscious of being in love.'[7] This comment seems to confirm that Holms knew of Edwin's dilemma while they were all at Forte dei Marmi. Perhaps a break was needed. So it was that in August, when the beach close to their rented lodge-house was becoming 'crowded with upper-class Italian families, and fat men stood in the lukewarm sea without moving for hours, with parasols held over their heads,'[8] Edwin suggested that he and Willa should make a visit to Florence, after which she could return to Forte dei Marmi while he went north to Salzburg to meet with his old Glasgow friend the composer Francis George Scott, who was attending the Chamber Music Festival in Salzburg (Figure 4.1). Willa was happy to agree, and so they left for Florence.

Italy's Florence, however, turned out to be very different from the Elbflorenz that had so charmed them in the north. If anything, it increased their sense of alienation, at least as far as Edwin was concerned. For each of the four nights that they spent in their hotel—an ancient fourteenth-century building—Edwin was persecuted by the same violent dream in which he saw himself as a young man, dressed in a black-coloured renaissance type of costume, waiting in the shadow of a dark archway for the approach of a man he intended to kill. When footsteps came near, he sprang out, plunging a dagger into the man's breast, causing the blood to spurt

---

[6] *An Autobiography*, pp. 210, 211.
[7] Letter from Holms to Kingsmill, 22 June 1925, BL, Add MS 85338 vol. xvi.
[8] *An Autobiography*, p. 211.

Figure 4.1 Francis George Scott
https://www.open.edu/openlearncreate/mod/
oucontent/view.php?id=147713&section=4

all over his own hands—and this spurting of the warm blood in his dream life wakened him to real life. The dream followed exactly the same pattern each night, and his awakening each night came with the same spurt of the blood over his hands. With her interest in psychoanalysis, Willa wondered if this strange and frightening experience might be some kind of therapeutic dream, acting as a catalyst for the expulsion of repressed anger or hatred—whether of himself, or her, or someone else she could not tell, but did not think it wise to ask. When they left the hotel, they seemed to leave the dream behind them. Edwin made his way north to Salzburg to see F. G. Scott, and Willa returned to Forte dei Marmi and the Holmses.

Salzburg made a strong impression on Edwin, and he published two articles on the Austrian town within a short space of his visit. 'At Salzburg' appeared in the *New Age* on 23 August 1923, and again in the *Freeman* on 19 September; and 'Edwin Muir and Francis George Scott: A Conversation', was published in the *Freeman* on 19 December of the same year. The first article dealt specifically with the music festival, a new topic for Edwin, but a partial return to the artificially knowledgeable and aphoristic style of his early *New Age* contributions about Prague. The Salzburg Festival was of very recent origin, although Edwin writes as if he had had a long acquaintanceship with it. It began in 1920 with open-air performances of Hugo von Hofmannsthal's play *Jedermann* staged on the large square in front of Salzburg Cathedral. The play was so successful that it became part of the festival's identity and was performed each subsequent year in that same location. In 1921, concerts were added to the programme, and in 1922 Richard Strauss—for whose operas Hofmannsthal had written several libretti and who had worked with Hofmannsthal towards the founding of the festival—brought opera to the stage by performing four works by the Salzburg-born Mozart, including *Le Nozze di Figaro* and *Die Entführung aus dem Serail*. Strauss was a conductor and general manager at the Vienna State Opera in these years, and once opera became a regular part of the Salzburg Festival it was often characterized as the summer residence of the Vienna State Opera Company. Edwin does not appear to have known this, calling it the 'Chamber Music Festival'.

To be fair, there were no opera performances in 1923, the year of his visit, probably because of the worsening economic conditions, and in fact the festival was suspended the following year as a result of the crisis in Austria. Edwin had mixed feelings about the event, writing that the 'Chamber Music Festival at Salzburg this year has been a very business-like affair', with—

> a striking absence of any extraneous grace calculated to please the camp-followers of music. There have been no great figures pleased to recognize and be recognized. The composers themselves have stayed away with a self-control which one must admire. They have had their reward; for if it was disappointing to miss the Festival, it might have been still more disappointing not to miss it.

He goes on to make a comparison with contemporary poetry. 'The keynote of the whole affair at Salzburg, indeed, has been carefulness; a carefulness in music almost as extreme as that of Mr T. S. Eliot in poetry.'[9] At this time Edwin admired Eliot's criticism, but he was no great fan of his poetry. As for music, there are very few references to music, especially contemporary music, in Edwin's autobiographical and other prose writings, nor is his poetry, even his later mature work, characterized by the musicality of its rhythmic movement. Perhaps his return to the artificial knowledgeability of his older *New Age* writing style suggests that his Salzburg article was constructed from programme notes and newspaper reviews with some input from F. G. Scott. In fact, there is a strong French musical presence in the discussion, a primary interest of 'F.G.' (as he was known to his friends) when Edwin notes that 'the French musicians were selected by their Government, and paid by them to represent French musical technique and taste at Salzburg', adding 'Even in the matter of culture France does not wish to appear foolish in the eyes of foreign nations.'[10]

---

[9] Edwin Muir, 'At Salzburg', *The Freeman*, 19 September 1923, pp. 39, 40.
[10] Ibid., p. 40.

Edwin's second Salzburg contribution, published in the *Freeman* of 19 December 1923, takes the form of a lengthy conversation in which Muir speaks for German and Scott for French culture. Scott begins with reservations about the Schönberg song cycle they had heard the previous evening, but this develops into a cultural debate. According to Scott, who prized Flaubert's *Madame Bovary*, the French 'know that art is *artificiel*, a word that in French, and quite rightly, has a far more respectable meaning than our "artificial."' He argues that the French 'are aware that art is one thing and life is another, and they do not try to crush into art *das Ganze, das Geheimnis, die Seele, der Zeitgeist*, and on top of all that a *Weltanschaung*.'[11] Edwin makes a plucky defence of his German poets and their attempts 'to find answers to questions that the French, and the classical peoples generally, have never been much concerned with. I mean such questions as, Why should a man wish to create a work of art at all? Why, if it is merely a personal satisfaction for him, should it give pleasure to other people? What is beauty, an affirmation or a denial of life?'[12] In Edwin's support for the German side of the artistic question, one can hear the young man who struggled in his early days in Glasgow, after the seemingly meaningless deaths of his parents and brothers, to make some kind of sense of human life through translations of Nietzsche, Goethe, and Heine. Following his earlier 'North and South' article, Edwin goes on to claim that 'all the great literatures of Europe have been written by Northern races when they have encountered in one form or another the shock of the South.' Although 'the North can not do without the South in some form', it is nevertheless 'the Northern people who have been the productive agents' in the history of literature while 'the Southern races have been the passive element.' F. G. Scott had a reputation among his Scottish acquaintances for fighting to the end and for winning complex arguments, but in this case he appears to have given up trying to bring Edwin over to the classical French side, replying briefly to his final argument on behalf of the North—'I really do not know. Your theory requires a great deal of evidence, and we have none. Perhaps there is something in it.'[13]

Edwin's fortnight of concert-going and feisty discussions with his old Glasgow friend appears to have had a restorative effect on his mind and emotions, for he returned to Forte dei Marmi very nearly himself again and seemed as glad to see Willa as she was to see him after her time alone with the Holmses. Edwin suggested that the two of them should 'have a look around Tuscany' before leaving Forte dei Marmi for Salzburg in the autumn. They visited Lucca in September during the Annual Feast of the Black Christ, where the day of celebration included not

---

[11] Edwin Muir, 'Edwin Muir and Francis George Scott: A Conversation', *The Freeman*, 19 December 1923. Quoted from Maurice Lindsay, *Francis George Scott and the Scottish Renaissance* (Edinburgh: Paul Harris Publishing, 1980), Appendix B, 'Edwin Muir and Francis George Scott: A Conversation', pp. 166, 165.
[12] Ibid., p. 167.
[13] Ibid., p. 172.

only religious processions and services but also circuses and fun fairs, something that Willa contrasted with the 'narrowness of Scottish Sabbatarianism' in which both she and Edwin had been brought up. She found it 'a revelation of how the whole fullness of life can be taken as pleasing to God, deep religious devotion being entirely compatible with high enjoyment on swings and roundabouts'. Edwin also found the fair—'in full swing, with booths displaying giants and dwarfs, clowns and conjurors'—in no way 'incongruous' with the earlier solemn religious procession before the image of the Black Christ, which was 'a day of sorrow for the death of God and of reassurance for the year to come'.[14] They returned briefly to Forte dei Marmi, and early in October they left the Holmses there and returned north to Salzburg alone.

In Salzburg, as in Prague and Dresden, they again found themselves in a city with a river flowing through it, this time the Salzach, along whose banks they could stroll on mild October evenings with the trees still in their autumn colours. Looking around her, Willa realized that many of the buildings they had seen in Prague had been Austrian in their style—something she had not been aware of in their early days of travel in the new Czechoslovakian Republic. Salzburg was also Mozart's birthplace, and although he had not been treated as he deserved to be by the aristocratic and church sources of patronage, the town itself and its buildings seemed in harmony with his music. Their own accommodation was rather less elegant, for their lodgings had no bathroom and they had to go to the municipal baths if they wanted a comprehensive wash. Willa described their surprise at the nature of these city baths, observing that they would have provided an 'ideal rendezvous' for the 'amorous couples' in turn-of-the-century plays by the Viennese dramatist Arthur Schnitzler.

> No one asked us to prove that we were married; we were passed at once into a large room in which a spacious bath was sunk, a warm little swimming-pool edged with marble; beside it a sofa and two armchairs stood waiting round a coffee table. We had only to ring for coffee or beer or cigarettes, wrapped in huge towels as we lounged, a most comfortable arrangement which we naturally decided was 'very Austrian'.[15]

The municipal theatre also provided enjoyable experiences, with audiences much less solemn than those to be encountered in Dresden. They went to see the widely advertised Rudolf Steiner dancers—

> There was no choreography. Each girl leaped and gestured and mimed as seemed good to her. One ought to have been pleased by so much spontaneity, but the

---

[14] *Belonging*, pp. 91, 92; *An Autobiography*, p. 213.
[15] *Belonging*, p. 94.

spectacle grew wilder and funnier, and Frau Steiner's voice sounded more and more bogus. Not only Edwin and I but everyone around us began to giggle until uncontrollable laughter rocked the whole house.[16]

There was, however, a dark underside to that seemingly free and welcoming Salzburg.

Edwin noticed in a café a local paper titled *Der Eiserne Besen*, the Iron Broom, which seemed full of what seemed to him to be libellous charges against the local Jewish community. They met 'seemingly intelligent Austrians' who argued that Ramsay Macdonald and Bernard Shaw were Jews, a view they supported by their opinion that politician and writer were both 'subverters of society'. Edwin found that his friendly discourse with a bookshop owner changed suddenly when he asked for the poems of the Austrian Jewish writer Hugo von Hofmannsthal, to be told abruptly that the bookshop did not stock them. It was only later that it occurred to him that the bookseller must have believed it 'presumptuous' for a Jewish writer to write in German. Equally troubling was his thought that the 'boisterous' son of their landlady 'would have laughed heartily over the stories in *Der Eiserne Besen*'.[17] Another unsettling aspect of Austrian society came to their attention when they visited a former acquaintance of Willa, a young woman who had taught German in a school where Willa had once taught Classics. This person was now married with two young sons and living in the spa town of Bad Gastein in the mountains south of Salzburg. The Muirs visited in early December when the hot baths of the town were officially closed until the new season, but special arrangements were made for the visitors to sample them, and Willa remembered how 'Edwin and I wallowed in bubbling, streaky green water and came out feeling exhilarated'. She also remembered with pleasure not only the welcome given by her friend but also the many greetings of 'Grüss Gott' which met them as they made their way through the town over newly fallen snow. Less welcome was their introduction to the Austrian tradition of the Krampuses where before Christmas a male member of the community dressed as Santa Claus would visit groups of neighbours accompanied by two 'Krampuses', attendant 'devils' with blackened faces, antlers on their heads, and heavy chains around their waists and in their hands which clanked as they rattled them. The job of the Krampuses was to frighten children who behaved badly or did not do their school lessons well, while Santa Claus was there to prevent them harming the children whose parents confirmed that they had been very good, not naughty. Both Muirs felt uneasy, seeing this strange haunting as something with roots in an older age of demonology. Yet their Austrian

---

[16] Ibid., p. 95.
[17] *An Autobiography*, pp. 215, 214.

hosts laughed at their fears, saying that the children knew there was no danger in these strange visitors and that Santa Claus would bring their Christmas presents.[18]

Another insight into the tensions beneath the surface of an Austrian culture that had so charmed them lay in wait when they moved from Salzburg to Vienna. Both had wanted to be in Vienna for Christmas, and with no experience of the city, Willa wrote to A. S. Neill, who had friends there, asking if he could recommend an inexpensive hotel. As a result, they found themselves in what, unknown to them, was the Jewish Quarter, set apart by the Donaukanal, the Danube canal which had to be crossed via a bridge for access to the main part of the city. Edwin remembered breakfasting in the little enclosed veranda of their hotel on the Saturday morning after their arrival. The street was strangely empty, the shops were shut, and little groups of people, 'old men with long ritual curls and dressed in caftans' stood talking quietly. They realized that it was the Sabbath and they were in the Jewish quarter of the city, struck by 'how cut off was the life of that populous but restricted quarter and how different from the rest of Vienna.'[19] Yet they still did not fully understand what it must mean to be permanent outsiders, the ones who could not belong, who were not allowed to belong, as Edwin had seen when the Salzburg bookshop owner refused to stock Hofmannsthal's poems. Later, when they moved their lodgings and settled into the main life of the city, they met intelligent and professional people who seemed to believe that the Jews were the source of subversion in society, and had made themselves rich by speculating on the stock exchange while ordinary Viennese people were losing all their money as a result of inflation. Edwin later admitted that they 'were without knowledge of Jewry and felt at a loss when involved in Antisemite discussions'. They could see that the Viennese were indeed suffering under inflation, and their troubles were showing more publicly than had been the case in Dresden. Edwin remembered how, when he and Willa were walking along the Ringstrasse—the 1860s boulevard that encircled the inner city and followed the line of the old city walls—they encountered a man 'half-sitting, half-lying on the wet pavement with his back against the wall of a great block of offices', shaking continually and mumbling to himself. Passers-by gave him a glance, but none stopped to speak or attempted to help him. Edwin and Willa discovered that he was trying to get home after having been in hospital to have an old war wound on his head treated. With no money for a tram, he had attempted to walk home, and now could walk no further. They asked where he lived, hailed a taxi and gave him some money, but the incident told of a darker side to the characteristically lively cultural life of the city. Edwin quoted a story, current at the time, that 'while in Berlin people were saying: "The position is serious but not critical", the Viennese struck a lighter note with "The position is critical but not

---

[18] *Belonging*, pp. 96–7.
[19] *An Autobiography*, p. 218.

serious"'. The visiting Muirs recognized a kind of forced gaiety in this response, a 'needy caricature' of the old Viennese spirit.[20]

Edwin wrote his customary Christmas letter to his sister Lizzie and her husband in Glasgow on 20 December 1923, shortly after they arrived in Vienna, wishing 'a Happy Christmas to you all from us both, or as the Germans say 'glückliche Weihnacht!' As in his previous letters from Prague and Dresden/Hellerau, there is a much more relaxed, spontaneous, and amusing persona to be found in these family letters than in Edwin's correspondence with fellow writers or even to other friends. Here there was no talking-down from a European traveller to stay-at-home relatives, but an inclusive, involved account of the new places he had visited with Willa, or 'Minnie', as he often calls her in these family letters. He says he found 'little mosaic brooches' in Florence on the Ponte Vecchio during their visit in the autumn 'bought with an eye on Ethel and Irene [his young nieces] and here they are'. And he adds (somewhat surprisingly in view of the young age of the recipients) 'We collected the comic matchboxes at Salzburg on the way here with the same idea. May much enjoyment arise therefrom!' The girls' parents will receive 'a volume of W. H. Davies' latest poetry in a separate parcel' for their own enjoyment, and in the New Year a copy of Edwin's collection of essays, *Latitudes*, to be published by Huebsch in New York. He mentions also that he is still trying to find a publisher for his poems, but so far without success. He is enthusiastic about the city, which he calls by its Austrian name 'Wien (pronounced Veen)', describing it as 'a lovely town, laid out spaciously, and, although it has about 2 ½ million inhabitants, you can see the surrounding hills from the very middle of it'. He is much taken with the 'splendid buildings everywhere, a relic of the Hapsburgs, who must have been an able lot. They bossed everything, and only allowed whole streets to be built in the style they wanted. No muddle, congestion or jerry building was permitted by them.' And in a comparison that would resonate with his Glasgow relatives he continues 'in one whole street they compelled the builders to build huge colonnades in front of the houses, to protect passers-by from the rain, with a pavement about as broad as Great Western Road'—the spacious street where Glasgow West-enders strolled on Sunday afternoons in their weekend finery. He also draws attention to Vienna's culturally *risqué* reputation, saying that 'the town is as gay and immoral as it has the reputation of being, with chambres separées publicly advertised in some of the restaurants: that is, rooms where a young Wiener can take a young Wienerin for supper, and lock the door if he wants to make love intimately.'[21] The downside of what Vienna has to offer is that 'it's extremely dear', but 'we're going to find a cheaper way of living locally' and he seems confident that 'we shall manage nicely when we've learnt the ropes.' Another problem, hopefully temporary, relates to Willa who 'in some way caught a bad dose of the eczema, which quickly spread

[20] Ibid., p. 219.
[21] Edwin Muir Correspondence, Edinburgh, NLS, MS 13226.

over her body, and she had to see the doctor, who gave her a salve which she had to plaster all over'. And he adds 'She's had a bad time of it, poor lassie, lying in bed and being prostrate, but the eczema is much better now and I hope she will be up in a few days. It was hard lines, coming just at Christmas too; but we'll have a good time when she's better.'[22]

Willa had had a bad time of it in more ways than one since they left Hellerau in the late spring of 1923, and regular travelling and changes of lodgings may have combined with her unsettled emotions in regard to Edwin to bring on an eczema attack. She seemed to recover reasonably quickly, however, and by January they had found suitable accommodation in a boarding house which also provided lodging for young American doctors working or training in the several large hospitals and clinics for which Vienna was then famous. They came to know a number of American writers living in the city, and congregated with these new friends for lunch at a regular table in a nearby restaurant in the Alser-Strasse. They visited the Volks-Oper where they experienced the whole of Wagner's Ring Cycle for the first time in their lives—although, according to Willa, they did not particularly enjoy it, much preferring the works of their familiar Mozart and Schubert. They heard Mozart performed at the principal opera house, and on two occasions they attended gala evenings there, attended by Viennese high society. Willa remembered 'a ball in the Redouten-Saale [which] provided an evening of sheer delight; waltzing through the rococo suites under crystal chandeliers we decided that Vienna was more civilized than Berlin, where we had seen people dancing the Black Bottom in cellar night-clubs'. And she adds in parenthesis '(Haben Sie je ge-Black Bottómed, gnädige Frau?' I was asked in Berlin—surely a remarkable word coinage.)'[23] She does not say how two literary gypsies, adventuring in Europe with as little luggage as possible, could have obtained sufficiently upmarket garments to go to such a ball. No doubt Austrian inflation played a part.

In the spring their Viennese lifestyle was suddenly and unexpectedly brought to an end by a letter from *The Freeman* intimating a decision to cease publication with the issue of 5 March 1924. *The Freeman* had started four years earlier, on 17 March 1920, in the context of a mood for regeneration and fresh enquiry into American life and culture in the wake of the First World War. The same spirit had inspired other significant journals such as *The New Republic*, *The Nation*, and *The Dial*. Now its financial supporters, Francis Neilson and his heiress wife Francis Swift Neilson, were ready to move in new directions, perhaps aided by the fact that *The Freeman*, although highly regarded, was also highly loss making. Its founding editors Albert Jay Nock and Van Wyck Brooks and its publisher Benjamin W. Huebsch were themselves exhausted by the demands of the journal, and it was decided that it should cease at the highest point of its achievement

---

[22] Ibid.
[23] *Belonging*, pp. 98–9.

and circulation.[24] It may also have been that the growing European political and financial problems, currently being witnessed by the Muirs in Austria, were beginning to affect decision-making in the New World. For Edwin and Willa, the loss of the *Freeman* income was a disaster. They could no longer afford to live in Vienna, and more seriously, they did not have the financial reserves to travel back to Britain. What was to be done? Willa's thoughts immediately turned to Neill, whose experimental school was now re-established on the Austrian Sonntagberg, the Sunday Mountain, but without the Eurhythmic School, so she asked Edwin if she could write to Neill to see if they could join him once more. Edwin had a keen eye in relation to financial matters and agreed. Neill duly replied that he would take them in, and they left Vienna and its sophisticated lifestyle for a school on Sunday Mountain.

In her later memoir of this period in their lives, Willa would write that 'a less suitable place for a "free" school could not have been chosen, as we were to discover, but our first impressions delighted us.'[25] The school was housed in a former monastery situated at the top of the Sonntagberg and reached by a climb of about two and a half hours up a winding road from the little town of Rosenau which lay at the foot of the mountain. The situation high above the clouds was spectacular. 'Neither Edwin nor I had ever been so high up before and this was our first gods' eye view of the earth.' Edwin was especially affected, or 'liberated' as Willa described it, by this proximity to the 'gods', for he returned with enthusiasm to the series of poems he had begun in Hellerau, called 'Chorus of the Newly Dead'. These were the poems that Gerda had translated into German, some of which appeared in English in MacDiarmid's *Scottish Chapbook* of August 1923. Edwin himself would appear to have misremembered the origins of these poems which preoccupied him for so long, even after he left Austria, for in the enlarged edition of his autobiography he credits the Sonntagberg as their inspiring spirit. He writes that walking in the woods he felt the stirrings of a long poem, 'a chorus in which the dead were to look back at the life they had left and contemplate it from their new station'. In his 1950s, as a mature poet, Edwin acknowledged that although the idea of the project 'moved' him, his 'imaginative excitement never managed to communicate itself, or at best now and then, to the poem; the old disability which I had struggled with in Hellerau, a simple lack of skill, still held me up'. He concluded, 'In any case the theme was far too great for my powers.'[26] *Chorus of the Newly Dead* was published by Leonard Woolf at Hogarth Press in 1926, after endless discussions of it by Edwin in letters to a new acquaintance, the writer Sydney Schiff. Woolf regarded it highly, but Edwin left it out of his later *Collected Poems*. It is intriguing, however, that the poem's actual origins in Hellerau,

---

[24] Information about the *Freeman* from Charles H. Hamilton, 'The Freeman, 1920–1924', *Modern Age*, Winter 1987, pp. 52–9.
[25] *Belonging*, p. 102.
[26] *An Autobiography*, p. 223.

its publication in MacDiarmid's *Scottish Chapbook*, and the translation of the early version into German by Gerda should appear to have been so fully excised from his memory. There are also intriguing hints as to Edwin's state of mind in these earlier 'adventuring in Europe' days as he thinks back to them in the 1950 version of his autobiography and quotes to himself some of the lines from *Chorus of the Newly Dead* which he says 'bring back the days I walked in the pine-woods on the Sonntagberg, and the difference between what I thought myself then and what I think myself now'. He finds that 'one of the disconcerting accidents of a writer's life is that if he reads again what he wrote, say thirty years before, as I have just been doing, he may appear quite strange to himself'. After quoting some lines from the poem he continues—

> These three lines seem so strange to me that I almost feel it was someone else who wrote them; yet that someone was myself. I fancy we all have sometimes this sense of strangeness, or of estrangement, when we look back, perhaps at some moment in our childhood, or at a boy waiting for a girl he loved or thought he loved—both gone and almost forgotten, never in any case to be recovered—or at a young man loitering in a summer dream beside a river which flows now into a different sea. Time wakens a longing more poignant than all the longings caused by the division of lovers in space, for there is no road back into its country.[27]

Perhaps Edwin's unconscious mind decided it was less disconcerting to place the origins of *The Chorus* in the phenomenal gods-scape of the Sonntagberg as opposed to the more emotionally unsettling human world of Hellerau and his association with Gerda and her translation of his poem.

Willa was less involved with Neill's school at the Sonntagberg than she had been in Hellerau since Neill had already engaged an English-speaking assistant teacher. She and Edwin therefore had more free time together to explore their new environment. It was springtime and the mountain slopes were covered with primulas and blue gentians as the couple made their way down the regular road to Rosenau at the foot of the mountain, or over the rocky footpath to the south of the mountain to Waidhofen, a little town that Willa considered more 'civilized' than Rosenau because of its menus of 'fresh trout with melted butter and great bowls of wild strawberries'.[28] Then they had a stroke of luck in the form of a cable from Huebsch in America, which asked if they would be willing to translate into English blank verse three plays by Gerhardt Hauptman at a fee of 100 dollars a play. They replied immediately in two words which was, as Willa said, all they could afford—'Yes, Muir'. This windfall would allow them to pay their debts to Neill and eventually secure their return to Britain. Willa wondered if Huebsch's offer was the

---

[27] *An Autobiography*, p. 224.
[28] *Belonging*, p. 105.

result of her chance meeting in a street in Vienna with the poet Louis Untermeyer, who had connections with Huebsch, on the day that they had received the news of the cessation of *The Freeman*. Huebsch was about to bring out Edwin's *Latitudes* essay collection and the poet's review essay 'Hauptmann's Song of Songs' had appeared in the *Freeman* in February 1924. Being aware of Edwin's interest in German poetry and their current presence in German-speaking Europe, he may have been persuaded by Untermeyer that the Muirs would be suitable candidates for the Hauptmann translation. Whatever inspired the request, this Hauptmann commission was the beginning of a new career in translation that lasted until the outbreak of the Second World War. Willa in particular looked on the venture with pleasure, for she felt that this was something she could do, and wondered why she had never before thought of translation as a way of earning money. The years she had spent translating Latin and Greek as a student had given her a sense of confidence and competence. She knew she was well trained in accuracy—a good thing, she now thought as they worked on the Hauptmann—for in her view Edwin's interpretations 'tended to be wild and gay'.[29]

Eventually it became clear to Neill that the Sonntagberg was not a suitable place for a Free School. At Easter the strong religious identity of the area had come to the fore, when groups of pilgrims and their brass bands arrived for religious ceremonies in the church, with many ascending the church steps on their knees. The chanting and band-playing began about five o'clock in the morning, there was feasting and drinking in the local inns, and at night those who could not afford to sleep in the inn, slept on mattresses placed behind hedges. These pilgrims, along with the deeply conservative local people, considered the Sonntagberg to be a holy mountain, and they were beginning to look on Neill's school and its inmates—both young people and teaching staff—as foreigners and most probably heretics. They also disapproved of the seemingly 'free' nature of the conduct of the school, and local gossip and insinuations eventually resulted in the arrival of a gendarme and an order for Neill to complete an official questionnaire about the nature of the education being offered in his establishment. Neill decided to move his school to England, and Willa and Edwin, who could now afford to travel home from their continental adventuring, decided to leave with him. They arrived back in Britain in July 1924.

---

[29] Ibid., p. 106.

5
Fête du Citron 1924–1926

> We loved Mentone. Our turreted half-villa was as if made for us to be happy in. […] I never picked a fresh lemon from the tree at our door without feeling as if I were in the Garden of Eden.
>
> Willa Muir, *Belonging* (1968)

After their long absence on the Continent, both Muirs were anxious to return to Scotland as soon as possible to see relatives and friends, and no doubt to measure their new European sense of self against their previous identities. When Edwin left London for Prague in 1921 he was known to a small circle of readers as 'Edward Moore'. Now he had a much higher publishing profile in his own name with essays in *The Freeman*, a continuing presence in *The New Age*, and a developing reputation as a perceptive book reviewer in *The Nation*. Several of his new poems had been published in *The Nation* as well as in *The Dial*, and 'Horses', which appeared in *The Nation* in May 1924, would be included in the anthology *Best Poems of 1924*, to be published the following year. 'Horses' evokes the poet's boyhood vision of his father's great plough horses as sublime and terrifying creatures in the timeless landscape of the Orkney fields, a landscape that was to haunt many of his early poems. Edwin was much more confident and at ease with himself than he had been during his previous residence in London, not to mention his Glasgow years. Willa had always been more enterprising than Edwin, but she too had changed during their years on the Continent and was returning with a commission to translate Gerhart Hauptmann. This was something she knew she could carry out successfully. She would be making her own contribution to their finances, as opposed to feeling like a 'kept woman', an insight that came to her in Forte dei Marmi when, feeling critical of Holms's companion Dorothy, she realized that she was herself wholly dependent on Edwin.

Edwin was unwilling to contemplate living permanently in London and was anxious to move to Scotland. First of all, however, they arranged to spend a couple of days with Denis Saurat. His old Glasgow friend was now Director of the French Institute in London, and when they arrived at the Institute they found an invitation from Sydney and Violet Schiff to spend two days with them at their home in Chesham. Sydney Schiff was a very recent acquaintance, although he and his wife Violet were well known in London literary circles, and Edwin's connection with him had come about in an unusual and amusing way. In his work with *The Freeman*, Edwin had been sent for review the novel *Prince Hempseed* by an author named Stephen Hudson. He had been greatly taken with the book, although he had not previously heard of its author, whom he assumed to be a young writer beginning to make a reputation. He wrote in the review, which was published in the last issue of *The Freeman* on 5 March 1924, that he considered Stephen Hudson to have a promising future. This amused and intrigued the older, experienced, and well-known Schiff who, as the actual author of the book in question, had been sent a cutting of Edwin's review by a friend. Schiff wrote to Edwin, and their correspondence, which began when Edwin was living at Neill's school on the Sonntagberg, continued regularly into the 1930s and then less frequently up to the outbreak of war in 1939. In admitting his dual identity, Schiff told Edwin that he had learned from two sources, one of whom was Janko Lavrin, that his reviewer, Edwin Muir, was none other than the 'Edward Moore' of the *New Age* who had written *We Moderns*. 'I had, so to say, my eyes on you', he tells Edwin as he confirmed his interest in that earlier work and the fact that he had frequently discussed 'Moore' with like-minded acquaintances.

Schiff's confessions produced a similar response in Edwin, who told him about his family's misguided emigration to Glasgow, his own unhappiness growing to adulthood in the city, and the marriage to Willa that had changed the course of his life. 'Fortunately I met my wife, but for whom I might still be in that melancholy circle. She shook me out of my unavailing struggle, and gave me the courage to come down to London and tempt fate on, I think, between us, £13.'[1] Schiff's account of his own psychological (although not impecunious) difficulties as a young man, in books such as *Prince Hempseed* and *Tony*, which he had sent to Edwin along with his initial letter, would appear to have spoken, in their turn, to Edwin's sense of his own younger and still evolving self. There developed between them an open and wide-ranging correspondence about contemporary life and literature in which Edwin in particular spoke of what he was trying to achieve in his writing, alongside his awareness of how far he still was from his goals. Both Schiff and Edwin—and Willa also—looked forward to bringing this on-paper acquaintanceship into an actual physical meeting of minds when they met in London before moving north.

Both the reunion with Saurat and the first meeting with the Schiffs were highly successful. Willa described Edwin's enjoyment in 'meeting his old friend Denis in the familiar Saurat tilting-yard where we were at once assailed with reproaches for having gone to Europe without visiting France'. And, as in Salzburg with Francis George Scott, Edwin for his part argued that 'Germany had more potentiality in it and was more interesting.'[2] Their visit to the Schiffs was 'more than pleasant'. Willa's first thought was how 'highly finished they were, compared to us, in

---

[1] Edwin Muir, letter to Sydney Schiff, 7 May 1924, Schiff Papers, BL, Add MS 52920.
[2] *Belonging*, p. 112.

dress, manner, sophistication and experience'. She also noticed how Edwin and Sydney 'lit each other up', and 'marvelled at the passion driving each of them as they discussed the making of works of art, the transmutation of experience into structures which they saw as crystalline and immortal'. Both men were agreed on the need for the writer or artist to detach himself from emotion, but Willa could not agree, since 'I could never detach myself from my emotions and rise into their immortal world of art'. Nevertheless, she was excited by the 'invisible fireworks' the men were setting off, even as she was 'calmed and steadied by Violet, a poised and beautiful woman with far-seeing eyes'. The Schiffs gave their Scottish visitors 'our first glimpse of a world we had never encountered'—perhaps not even in the ballrooms of Vienna—and tried to persuade them to remain in London or at least rent a cottage somewhere in the country within reach of the city, which they would be willing to help them find. But the Muirs were determined to go north to Scotland. In Edwin's words 'We thirst for it, and that probably means that we need it.'[3] They left London with the promise that they might later rent a cottage in the English countryside, and the Schiffs promised to help when they felt ready. They could not have met more supportive and well-connected friends than Sydney and Violet Schiff. Sydney was an established writer who subsidized the briefly influential periodical *Art and Letters* (1918–1920) and knew most of the key literary figures of the day, including Aldous Huxley, T. S. Eliot, Wyndham Lewis, and Katherine Mansfield. Schiff's own novels (as 'Stephen Hudson') in the '20s and the '30s spoke of their times with a strongly autobiographical element, he was a translator of Hesse and Proust, and by the 1940s he had become something of a patron and supporter of all that was new in the arts.

Alas, the reality of Scotland did not suit the Muirs. About two weeks after their arrival in Montrose, Edwin wrote to Schiff, 'Scotland has been a sad disappointment to us after all the longing we had for it, so shut in, unresponsive, acridly resolved not to open out and live. For our own sake we shall not live here for long, not more than two months I think, if we can help it.' Then he added 'But this sounds worse than I had intended. We love the landscape here, and the lingering twilight, if not the people, and we shall get a solid amount of work done.'[4] Willa was less despondent; she was, after all, returning to her childhood home, although she realized that Edwin's Scottish compass always pointed to Orkney, and Montrose was not Orkney. She also felt that they could get good work done while staying with her mother. As things turned out, Montrose was their temporary home for longer than two months, and they did not move south until the turn of the year. Without distractions, Montrose proved to be a good base for the growing amount of literary work—both commissioned and prospective—that came their way. Willa was principally occupied with the Hauptman translations commissioned by Huebsch,

[3] *Belonging*, pp. 112–13; Edwin Muir, letter to Schiff, 7 May 1924, Schiff Papers, BL, Add MS 52920.
[4] Edwin Muir, letter to Schiff from Montrose 2 August 1924, in *Selected Letters*, p. 41.

but was also beginning to think about an essay on the subject of the differences between men and women in their approach to creative work, speculations that were to result in the publication of her Hogarth Press essay *Women: An Inquiry* in 1925. Edwin continued with the essays that would eventually appear as the critical collection *Transition*, published by Hogarth Press in 1926, in which he explored the *Zeitgeist* behind a period of literary and cultural change by examining the work of several prominent writers of the time. This was a topic that had first come into his mind on the Sonntagberg and had been a subject of discussion in his early letters with Schiff. Now, from Montrose, he continued to refine his responses to his chosen writers in his correspondence, while producing a growing number of commissioned reviews for journals such as *The Nation*. In September he was delighted to hear from Leonard Woolf that Hogarth Press wished to bring out his first collection of poems in the coming year. He wrote to Schiff 'This is great news. I do most sincerely attach more importance to them than to anything else I have written; they are nearer my heart.'[5]

Shortly after arriving in Montrose, the Muirs met up with Christopher Grieve and his wife Peggy, who was expecting their first child in September. Working as a journalist for the *Montrose Review*, Grieve was determined to make his mark on the literary scene. Between 1920 and 1922 he produced three anthologies called *Northern Numbers* to offer a 'representative selection' of work from the 'Scottish poets of today—and tomorrow!'[6] This was followed in 1922 with a monthly *The Scottish Chapbook*, whose aim was 'to bring Scottish Literature into closer touch with current European tendencies in technique and ideation'[7]. The fourteen numbers of this journal and its editor's 'Theory of Scottish Letters' were enormously influential in promoting what became known as the modern Scottish Literary Renaissance. It also featured some of the first poems in Scots by Grieve himself, under the pseudonym 'Hugh M'Diarmid' (latterly 'MacDiarmid') whose first collections of poetry in Scots in the mid-twenties were to prove equally influential. By 1923 Grieve was also producing the weekly *Scottish Nation* (thirty-four numbers) which made a passionate case for the revival of Scottish identity in political and social terms. F. G. Scott had persuaded Edwin to send some of his poems and essays to these magazines in order to lend support to the movement. Grieve himself admired the position Edwin had achieved in current literary criticism and would later refer to him in his own essays for the *Scottish Educational Journal* as 'a critic incontestably in the first flight of contemporary critics of welt-literatur.'[8]

The Muirs and the Grieves met amicably in Montrose, although Willa would later be somewhat patronizing in her description of their 'living in a council

---

[5] Edwin's letter to Schiff, 25 September 1924, Schiff Papers, BL, Add MS 52920.
[6] C. M. Grieve, 'Foreword', *Northern Numbers* (London & Edinburgh: T. N. Foulis, 1920), p. 9.
[7] 'The Chapbook Programme', *Scottish Chapbook* 1,1, August 1922.
[8] Christopher Grieve, 'Edwin Muir', *Contemporary Scottish Studies* (London: Leonard Parsons, 1926), p. 108.

house on the fringe of the town, where Peggy cooked the meals and washed and ironed Christopher's shirts', calling her 'an embodiment of the "wee wifie" loved by Scotsmen'.[9] Edwin himself would later write supportively of Christopher's new poetry in a revitalized literary Scots language in the collections *Sangschaw* (1925) and *Penny Wheep* (1926) and in his long dramatic monologue *A Drunk Man Looks at the Thistle* (1926). Yet their positions in regard to literary language and politics were essentially different, as would become clear in the 1930s. For Edwin, despite his wish that Scotland might become a nation again in the spirit of Čapek's republican Prague, socialism still had to come before nationalism, and as an Orkneyman he was not particularly committed to a revival of the lowland Scots language for literary purposes, preferring to write in English. Furthermore, Edwin and Christopher had very different temperaments. By late 1924 the two households found that they had only a limited number of interests in common, and in the autumn the Muirs were ready to move south again. Sydney Schiff had organized the let of a country cottage in the village of Penn in Buckinghamshire, and at the end of December they left Montrose, first of all for a short stay with A. S. Neill at his school in Lyme Regis, then onwards to their cottage in Penn.

Unlike Peggy Grieve, good housewifery never appeared to be among Willa's accomplishments, and after years of living in Europe 'with attendance' and eating out regularly in restaurants, together with her mother's more recent cooking and housekeeping hospitality in Montrose, the prospect of being sole mistress of an old rural cottage in Penn must have been a daunting one. Before leaving Montrose, Willa had told the Schiffs of the need to employ someone to clean the cottage before they moved in. She had also raised her uncertainty about some of the conditions of the lease, which she feared might prevent her from putting in an oil stove in place of a coal range for cooking. She had never used a coal range and was fearful of this and the possible costs involved. Her fears were prescient, for they found themselves in an area of the village that had neither sewerage, gas, nor electricity. Their cottage was the only one in a lane of cottages that had piped water, but it had no damp course and the open fireplace smoked. On the positive side, the previous resident, who had lived and died in the cottage, had been the village smith, and they found that his large, empty smithy made a good study once they managed to find a way to heat it. They employed a girl from the village to keep the house clean, and found that their proximity to London and to old and new friends was a compensation for difficult winter living conditions.

Springtime brought bluebells, carpeting the earth in the fresh green beech woods, followed by a hot, dry summer. In addition to seeing friends in London, summer in Penn brought visitors from London to their country cottage, with regular tea parties and discussions under the shade of a large tree. The smithy proved to be a fine summer study where they could write with the doors wide open and the

---

[9] *Belonging*, p. 116.

sunlight filtering in, and they had plenty of literary work to keep them busy. They were delighted that Willa's essay on women would be published by Hogarth Press in its Hogarth Essays series, thus following in the footsteps of Virginia Woolf's *Mr Bennet and Mrs Brown* in the previous year; and Leonard Woolf had accepted Edwin's long-gestated *Chorus of the Newly Dead*, to be published in 1926. They had much to feel contented about in that hot, sunny summer, although by late August they felt the need of a break from playing host to summer visitors, and escaped for a week or two to Neill's Summerhill School in Lyme Regis. By late autumn, however, the deficiencies of their cottage began to show themselves again, and they remembered the chilly dampness and heating difficulties of their early months in Penn. Some friends—including the Scottish artist William McCance and his wife Agnes Millar Parker who were now living and working in London—had told them of an unspoilt fishing village called St Tropez in the south of France, and they began to think of moving to the Continent again. First of all, however, Edwin was anxious to finish off the final essays for the forthcoming *Transition* book, so they decided to return temporarily to Willa's mother's house in Montrose.

As before, however, their second trip to Montrose lasted longer than they planned. Both were laid up with colds on their arrival, and Willa in particular was feeling generally unwell without being able to pinpoint the cause. Then in early December she had a miscarriage. Edwin wrote to Sydney Schiff on 10 December.

> We have had a really bad time since coming here. The last thing to happen is that on Tuesday Willa had a miscarriage. Evidently she was right in guessing that she was on the way to having a child—poor thing, she has suffered enough these few days. There was nothing she did which could account for the miscarriage; but evidently, according to the doctor, such things happen often to women in the ordinary blundering way of nature. When she is better the doctor is going to try to find out what caused this painful business to happen.[10]

Willa herself was more dramatic and self-ironic about the occurrence when she wrote at the end of January to Florence McNeill, bringing together her miscarriage and her discussion of women as mothers in her Hogarth Press essay. She wrote to 'My dear Floss'—

> You are a dear: you have lifted a weight off my mind. I have not been able to write to anybody for some time, & I had visions of wrathful friends. We have had a trying time—you will understand why, when I tell you that shortly after I came home I proceeded to have a bad miscarriage—think of it! I had no idea that I was pregnant (I thought I had got a chill, & when I was sick I thought it was caused by lumbago) and then we were worried by a debt which suddenly cropped

[10] Edwin Muir, letter to Schiff 10 December 1925, Schiff Papers, BL, Add MS 52920.

up—very worried—and then I had the miscarriage, to my own shock & surprise. No wonder I was brooding over the bearing of children!

And she added at the end of her letter—

My old essay has fallen very flat. [...] *The Nation* said it was as unexciting as boiled rice. *Time & Tide* has not reviewed it at all! I thought women's societies & associations would have been interested. However—I shall launch bombs next time![11]

It was Edwin who first knew Florence Marian McNeill, who was an old schoolfriend from their Orkney days and an active campaigner for equality and women's suffrage during the war. In Edinburgh she came to work for the Scottish National Dictionary and became a founder-member of the Scottish National Party. Better known as 'F. Marian McNeill', she produced *The Scots Kitchen* in 1929, a best-selling compendium of traditional dishes, followed in the 1950s by *The Silver Bough*, a four-volume study of Scottish folk lore and seasonal festivals. Edwin addresses her as 'Dear Flossie' and, as a more recent acquaintance, Willa urged her 'Of course address me as Willa. I don't like formalities.' From August 1925 Willa's correspondence with McNeill reveals that Florence had in fact already suggested an appointment with a gynaecologist of her acquaintance, a Dr Louise McIlroy who practised in the Royal Free Hospital, London. Willa confesses to being 'half feared and half pleased' at the news, saying in her next letter that she had 'taken the plunge and written to Dr McIlroy. When she asks me to come in, I should love to see you. I may need to have my hand held.'[12] Dr McIlroy responded to Willa in late October, suggesting that she come in to the hospital for a week for investigations, but by that time the Muirs had decided to escape the winter in Penn by leaving for the comfort of Willa's mother's house in Montrose where, utterly unexpectedly, she suffered her miscarriage. The letters to McNeill show that Willa had been concerned about her inability to conceive and, now in her mid-30s, had decided that it was time to investigate possible reasons for this. She writes 'The doctor said it was a two months foetus, or thereabouts. However, it is established that there is no displacement, & I may live in hope that it may be all right next time. Why I have had no conceptions until now neither he nor anyone can tell me. It is so far good that it encourages me to believe in a "next time".'[13] Hopes of a 'next time' did not, however, dissuade them from their plans to return to Europe. After Willa recovered her strength, and Edwin had recovered from his own (perhaps empathetic) attack of threatened appendicitis which took place almost immediately after Willa's

---

[11] Willa Muir, letter to Florence McNeill, 26 January [1926], NLS, MS 26194.
[12] Willa Muir, letters to Florence McNeill, 9 July 1925, 25 October 1925, NLS, MS 26194.
[13] Willa Muir, letter to Florence McNeil, 26 January [1926], NLS, MS 26194.

miscarriage, they set off for St Tropez in the early spring of 1926 with a new translation commission from Secker. This was to translate *Jüd Süss*, a novel by Lion Feuchtwanger written in 1920 and published in 1925. They also hoped to begin some fiction work of their own.

In their initial conversations with the McCances and Sydney Schiff about their plans to go to St Tropez, it was suggested that they might be able to rent a flat there belonging to the art critic Roger Fry. Whether it was unavailable in the end, or perhaps too expensive, Willa's first postcards from St Tropez give the 'Hotel Fernand' as their address 'for a week or so'. The local Syndicat d'Initiative told them of a villa owned by an elderly English couple who had to return to England for a period, and they rented this for the sum of 'thirteen shillings and fourpence a week'. The villa, called 'La Vétille', was situated about a quarter of a mile outside the village of St Tropez, which, outside the summer months, was still free of the tourism that would later transform the Mediterranean coast. The villa had 'four rooms and a kitchen fully furnished, a wide stretch of maquis outside, including a private path to a rocky beach, eight almond trees, a rosemary hedge and a green bank covered with bright mesembryanthemums'.[14] Like the warm-scented air and the birdsong that greeted them on their first evening in St Tropez, as they sat looking out to the sea and the harbour, La Vétille was a far cry from Penn and Montrose.

Once they were settled, their first task was 'to polish off *Jew Süss*', as Willa put it. She would appear to have been the principal translator, since she had begun the task in Montrose when Edwin was completing his *Transition* essays, and she described her approach as being 'to tailor the style to what I felt would better suit an English public'.[15] Based on historical fact, Feuchtwanger's novel tells of the rise and fall of Joseph Süss Oppenheimer, a Jewish businessman at the court of Duke Alexander of Württemberg in the eighteenth century. Caught up in a web of corruption, jealousy, and violence, the protagonist is cast in a sympathetic light as he meets an unjust end. (In 1940, the same tale was perverted and retold as a violently anti-Semitic film under the orders of Joseph Goebbels.) Published in November 1926, the Muirs' translation was a popular success, but since they had not negotiated a royalty on sales, Willa complained that they had to settle for a single fee of £250 despite the 'thousands' acquired by the publisher.[16]

Their main work in St Tropez, however, was to develop the ideas they each had for novels of their own. The *Jew Süss* translation was completed by the end of May, and after taking time off to enjoy their new surroundings, they made a start on their own writing. In her later memoir of this period in France, Willa would contrast her own approach to creative writing with Edwin's, saying that while he communicated his themes in a more impersonal way through symbols,

---

[14] *Belonging*, p. 123.
[15] Ibid., pp. 125–6.
[16] Ibid., pp. 125–6.

she relied 'on the empathy of personal feelings and memories'. She hoped that even if she could not detach herself from her emotions, she might be able to use them to 'present a story in a Montrose setting, imagining what might have happened had I married my Rugby champion and gone to live there'.[17] The challenge was to use life-writing in an emotionally distanced way to explore and understand her younger self, while at the same time producing an artistically satisfying composition. As far as Edwin was concerned, he had abandoned the idea of a short Glasgow novel titled 'Saturday', as discussed in his correspondence with Sydney Schiff, but he was less ready to discuss his new idea with Willa, except to say that she might find it peculiar since it dealt with 'an idiot boy falling in love with a wooden marionette and that he was setting it in Salzburg'. In *Belonging*, Willa was to say that both her own and Edwin's proposed scenarios were 'treating the same theme; that is to say, having found the right kind of love we were now both writing about the wrong kind; but Edwin's handling of it was more detached than mine'.[18] This view reflects the leitmotif of belonging to each other that runs throughout Willa's memoir of their marriage. In fact, Edwin's novel, *The Marionette*—which was published by Hogarth Press in May 1927—is a much more philosophically and psychologically far-reaching work than Willa acknowledges. (Indeed, the same could be said of her own Montrose-situated novel when it eventually achieved publication in 1931.) In his correspondence with Sydney Schiff, Edwin describes his own book as having 'a philosophical background but no philosophical dialogue'; and to its American publisher Huebsch he said it was 'less a novel than a sort of metaphysical or symbolical tragedy'.[19]

As the height of the summer season approached, so did the number of tourists in St Tropez increase, and with them, to Willa's irritation, came the Holmses, who found cheap lodgings in one of the houses close to the harbour. Tired by her translation work and still shaken, perhaps, by her miscarriage, Willa was not pleased to see them. She complained that they had to dine with John and Dorothy every night, and were forced to move from the *Place*, their customary restaurant to the much cheaper *Café du Commerce* on the harbour front where the Holmses usually 'bagged the bench facing the harbour'. As before, John monopolized Edwin while Willa was left to talk with Dorothy. She found Dorothy 'looking the worse for wear; her face was both peaked and flabby, her ankles had swollen and her hair had lost its radiance. Trailing up and down the Riviera with Holms was apparently taking the heart out of her.' She had nothing but contempt for Holms himself. He had written nothing since they last met him despite all his 'interminable monologues'. She wondered if it was his 'vanity' that continually compelled him 'to finger his own feelings, because he wanted to make sure that they would make great poems?

[17] Ibid., pp. 126, 125.
[18] Ibid., p. 126.
[19] Edwin Muir, letter to B. W. Huebsch, 10 November 1926, *Selected Letters*, p. 58; Letter to Sydney Schiff, 10 November 1926, Schiff papers, BL, Add MS 52920.

For he wished to be not merely a poet, his will was set on being a Great Poet.'[20] She was temporarily relieved by the arrival of Francis George Scott, on his way to the Music Festival at Salzburg, and by Mary Litchfield at whose London flat they had occasionally stayed when living in Penn. Mary was an old acquaintance from Willa's teaching days in London, and by chance a previous girlfriend of Edwin's when he was in Glasgow. Willa commented that she was both 'startled and amused to discover that Mary's seven years in London had turned her into a siren capable of annexing at once any man she wanted, and still more startled to observe her effect upon Scott'. She then added in a somewhat self-congratulatory way that 'Edwin was quite immune to her magnetic power, and I realized that she actually respected me for having succeeded in marrying him.'[21]

The arrival of these two visitors whose 'Scottish temperaments got free rein on holiday' soon came to an end, but they did not reduce Willa's inability to share Edwin. He, on the other hand, insisted that Holms 'was in great difficulties and needed him'. Willa was less convinced, and when she remembered Holms saying that Menton was the 'last place on earth he would ever be found in', she suggested they make the move. Their lease of La Vétille was in any case about to come to an end, and so they duly travelled east, some eighty miles along the Riviera coast. They were immediately charmed by what they saw of the Old and New Town of Menton and, away from St Tropez, Willa unburdened herself of the extreme dislike she felt for Holms and her reasons for it. Nothing is known about Edwin's response except for Willa's comment 'We never had so painful a disagreement again.'[22]

It is intriguing that in the enlarged version of his autobiography, Edwin makes no mention of the Holmses presence in St Tropez and writes only of the transfer to Menton. He does, on the other hand, make what might seem a somewhat excessive condemnation of what he calls 'the cult of untrammelled freedom [which] had become an established fashion among some of the intellectuals and artists' who frequented St Tropez to whom 'life, under its assumed carelessness, was joyless and without flavour.' He continues—'their brief love affairs resembled those of children who had acquired the knowledge and the desires of mature men and women, and in their conduct, perhaps even in their thoughts, remained children.'[23] Such judgmental thoughts are at odds with his previously amused and seemingly tolerant comments in his letters to his Glasgow relatives about the 'chambres séparées' advertised in some Vienna restaurants.

Writing to Schiff from St. Tropez, and then from their new home in Menton, Edwin has more to say about how literary life on the Côte d'Azur had begun to lose its charm. 'We had far too much of the society of artists and literary people in St Tropez, all of them tenth rate, and on the top of that the constant companionship

---

[20] *Belonging*, pp. 126–7.
[21] Ibid., p. 128.
[22] Ibid., p. 130.
[23] *An Autobiography*, p. 229.

of Holms and his wife; and we are glad to be here in almost solitude for a while.' And talking of Holms, whose presence he mentions frequently, he adds, 'Holms I think is still looking out for a house in some other town. I like him very much, I hope he may justify himself some day.' Such comments in Edwin's correspondence of the time may give a more accurate impression of their sojourn in the south of France than does the severity of his 1950s autobiographical account, which was coloured, perhaps, by unresolved emotional responses and the memory of Willa's strong feelings about the incident with Gerda in Hellerau. He never did, on the other hand, lose sympathy with John Holms. They saw less of each other in the later 1920s, however, when Holms parted from Dorothy and eloped with the American heiress Peggy Guggenheim, who had come to St Tropez with her husband and family. Unlike Willa, but like Edwin, Peggy Guggenheim seemed to recognize the war-engendered trauma that lay behind Holms's incapacity for action, while, again like Edwin, she was captured by his knowledge and eloquence, writing in her memoirs that 'he talked like Socrates' and 'held people spellbound for hours'.[24]

Edwin's *Autobiography* was to testify at length to his fascination with Holms, 'the most remarkable man I ever met', auburn haired, sensual, tall, and commanding, with a pointed goatee beard he liked to stroke. Edwin's words explain a lot about Willa's reservations about this extraordinary man's influence over her husband:

> His mind had power, clarity and order, and, turned on any subject, was like a spell which made things assume their true shapes and appear in their original relation to one another, as on the first day. [...] His talk had an extraordinary solidity which made even the best serious talk seem flimsy or commonplace. [...] His knowledge of his genius and its frustration made him wretched and sometimes sardonically critical when he saw the second-rate acclaimed.[25]

Peggy Guggenheim (who thought he looked like Jesus Christ) found Holms equally enthralling, as did his friend Hugh Kingsmill and many others in the literary circles of the time, including Djuna Barnes and Evelyn's brother Alec Waugh. But in the course of a peripatetic life Holms wrote little more than some unfinished poems, one short story, and some essays. Edwin later observed, 'Though his sole ambition was to be a writer, the mere act of writing was an enormous obstacle to him: it was as if the technique of action were beyond his grasp, a simple, banal, but incomprehensible mystery.'[26] Hugh Kingsmill was an equally brilliant talker, marked, like Holms by his wartime experiences in the field and in captivity, but in

---

[24] Peggy Guggenheim, *Out of this Century. Confessions of an Art Addict* (London: Deutsch, 1979), p. 79.
[25] *An Autobiography*, pp. 178, 179.
[26] Ibid., pp. 177–8.

the 1930s and 1940s he went on to become a much respected journalist, author, critic, biographer, anthologist, and editor with over thirty books to his name. Holms remains a charismatic and influential figure in Edwin's life, equally commanding in the literary circles of the time, but whether his creative gifts were stifled by his own despairs, or indeed were there in the first place, remains something of a mystery.[27]

The old-fashioned elegance of Menton (so despised by Holms) suited the Muirs better than the fashionable modernity of St Tropez in summertime. During their brief explorative visit, they had arranged to rent the upper floor of a villa situated en route to a hilly area named 'Les Ciappes'. The villa was called 'Villa Soleil' and was approached by the Rue Pietra Scritta, a road not far from the railway station leading up into the higher countryside. Willa described how they immediately fell in love with the villa—

> partly because of the turret, in which Edwin fancied himself installed, while I was fascinated by the views from either end, one towards the sea [...] and the other up the valley towards Mont Agel, a rampart that helped to keep the north winds from Mentone. The front door faced the hill, with a marble table beside it, a lemon tree and a mimosa tree. We scarcely bothered to look inside, although we did climb a corkscrew iron staircase into the turret. It was ours, at about twenty-five shillings a week.[28]

Their attachment to Menton continued when they took up the lease at the end of September. Edwin wrote to his sister Lizzie and her husband in Glasgow on 21 November adding yet another perspective on his response to St Tropez.

> We have only been in this place, two miles from the Italian border, since the beginning of October. It used to be called Mentone in the geography books. Before that we were living in a little fishing village called St Tropez; a rather primitive, but pretty place, where most of the inhabitants, I believe, are Communists. It was very hot in summer, and we could not have supported it, except by bathing in the sea, which was so warm that you could stay in for a long time.

And he continued—

> There were two huge snakes in the grounds of the house we rented at 13/- shillings a week; and Minnie killed two scorpions which the kitten was playing with. Figs grew along all the roads; there were grapes everywhere; but the heat, for us,

---

[27] See Jonathan Law, 'John Ferrar Holms: The Greatest Writer Never to Have Actually Written Anything', in *The Dabbler* blog, http://thedabbler.co.uk/2015/05/john-ferrar-holmes-the-greatest-writer-never-to-have-actually-written-anything/

[28] *Belonging*, pp. 130–1.

was sometimes unspeakable. Menton is a much more civilised place, and we are enjoying the change, although now it has been raining for about a month solid.[29]

In this letter Edwin also refers to the political and economic problems being experienced currently in Scotland, for 1926 was the year of the General Strike. His brother-in-law George was a strong socialist and Edwin expressed his own commitment to Socialism as well as his uneasiness about doing nothing for the cause. 'But one can't do two things, and it is better to try to become a good writer than to be a bad writer and a bad Socialist.'[30]

In *Belonging*, Willa would always refer to Menton by its Italian name of Mentone, while Edwin uses the French name Menton. The town, situated on the border with Italy, became part of France after a plebiscite in 1860 confirmed its official transfer to France. Menton's pleasant and mild climate during the months from autumn to late spring had attracted, throughout the nineteenth century, a class of winter visitors known as *hivernants*, a leisured class of *rentiers* who lived on unearned income. There were others who came to the town for health reasons, such as Robert Louis Stevenson in the late nineteenth century and Katherine Mansfield in the early twentieth. The First World War changed everything, for few people could now afford to spend the winter months idling on the coast, and the German, Austrian, and Russian regulars were no longer present in the town. Its reputation as a health resort, however, and its numerous hotels with English names such as the *Astoria, Bristol, Balmoral,* and *Royal Westminster,* proved especially popular with English visitors and American tourists in the post-war years.

The Muirs arrived in the early summer of 1926, pleased to find the town more conservative than the Côte d'Azur resorts such as Nice, Cannes, and Juan-les-Pins. Willa commented that they avoided English compatriots in Menton whose presence could be seen in institutions such as the English Church, English tea rooms, and an English library, as well as in newspaper advertisements for their activities. They made friends instead with Americans who were also transients, such as Mary and Arthur Mason, with whom they dined regularly in the evening, and with whom they continued to correspond after leaving Menton. They do not appear to have made much contact with the Mentonnais residents themselves, although Willa briefly mentions a young French bank clerk who brought the writer Norman Douglas to meet them one evening in the hotel where they usually dined. They also attended concerts in what Willa calls the 'Casino'—not the present-day casino, built only in the 1930s, but probably the Kurstall, which is now the Palais de l'Europe. Here they heard the fine French pianist Cortot play and the black American Paul Robeson sing, and they regularly visited Monaco to see the Monte Carlo ballet company perform. They did have to deal with local political tensions, however, for Benvenuto Mussolini, who became prime minister of Italy in autumn

---

[29] Edwin Muir, letter to Lizzie and George Thorburn, 25 November 1926, *Selected Letters*, pp. 59–60.
[30] Ibid.

1922, considered Menton to be part of Italy. In Mussolini's view, Nice and Menton as well as Corsica, Tunisia, and Malta were *'terres irredentes'* (unliberated territories), a term which reprised a nationalist doctrine from the 1870s claiming such places as part of the kingdom of Italy. There would appear to have been a considerable amount of activity on the part of Mussolini's fascists against Menton in 1926, the year the Muirs arrived, and they were warned not to stray over the unmarked border when walking in the hills above the town. They heeded the warning and kept their excursions well away from the Italian border.

Most importantly, Menton and Villa Soleil, with its relatively isolated position on the higher edges of the town, proved to be a good place to get on with their writing undisturbed. Apart from his continuing review work, Edwin's principal preoccupation was with his novel *The Marionette*, the progress of which, including his own assessment of his growing narrative skill, was regularly discussed in his correspondence with Sydney Schiff. Despite Willa's 'scunner' at Holms, Edwin kept in contact with him, at times in Menton itself, and especially in relation to the progress of his novel. *The Marionette* tells the story of a mentally retarded, perhaps autistic boy, whose mother died giving birth to him, who has grown up in isolation from the world and also his father, whose own grief separated him from his son. Both are brought to a new relationship with each other, and to some acceptance of their place in the world beyond them, through involvement with a marionette theatre operator and his inanimate performers.

Edwin sent John Holms a typescript of the finished work around the same time as he sent one to the publisher Huebsch, who professed himself 'delighted' with it. Both Violet and Sydney Schiff liked the finished story. Sydney commented on 'some immaturity of technique in the composition' but reaffirmed his view that Edwin was 'a poet' and that *The Marionette* was 'essentially poetry, not prose'.[31] Unfortunately Holms—on whose critical opinion at this time Edwin still relied— was less impressed. According to Edwin, Holms was 'very severe on the second half', justifiably as he now thought, and he told Schiff that he had decided to take Holms's advice and rewrite that part of the work. This meant that he had to ask Huebsch to delay publication until the second half was redrafted. Holms wrote to Hugh Kingsmill about *The Marionette* and its problems as he perceived them, saying that 'the first half had a good deal of merit, with some really fine things, whereas the second half was so bad, almost from any point of view, that I am surprised the publisher took it', adding that [Edwin's] 'incapacity for self-criticism is extraordinary, coupled with his immediate recognition of faults when they are pointed out'. Holms was happier with the revised version, although 'even now I don't think it's successful really as a whole; but it's very remarkable and clearly written by someone with genius'.[32] The book had favourable reviews, but it did not sell well, and

---

[31] Letter from Sydney Schiff to Edwin Muir, 25 November 1926, Schiff papers, BL, Add MS 52920.
[32] Letter from John Holms to Hugh Kingsmill, 3 January 1927, BL, Kingsmill Papers, 85338, vol. xvi.

in later years Edwin was dismissive of the work that had occupied so much of his time in the south of France. It is not, however, a book to be dismissed but remains imaginatively provocative and emotionally moving to the reader, as well as being a significant landmark in its author's own creative and psychological development. Without the original draft to compare with its published version, however, it is not possible to say whether Holms's criticisms improved or misdirected its author's original intentions.

Willa was less fortunate with the progress of her 'Montrose' novel, for her work on it was interrupted by a request to translate an additional three plays by Hauptmann, which was an offer from a financial perspective that they could not refuse. And when the translation work was completed, and the novel resumed, it was interrupted once again by the Menton carnival, which took place each March to mark the ending of winter. Both Muirs were ready for some fun after their months of writing. Willa describes how they danced in the streets, 'dressed up as Pierrots in yellow suits with black ruffs and buttons, pelted our friends with flowers and sang the absurd little carnival song Coucou, coucou, / Coucou, soulève ton loup' (Cuckoo, cuckoo, lift your [carnival] mask). Such carnival festivity had an unexpected outcome in that their son Gavin was conceived during this 'Fête du Citron', as the Menton Carnival was in later years to be renamed. In Willa's view, Gavin 'could not have had a more carefree origin.'[33]

Inevitably, Willa's pregnancy led to a change in their living plans. Previously they had thought to escape the summer heat, from which Menton was not immune, by going north to the Tyrol before returning in the autumn. However, a friend's warning that if their baby turned out to be a boy he might in the future be liable for French military service, made them think again. So it was that at the end of May, they left Menton and Villa Soleil with its lemon tree, in order to return to Britain. Willa kept repeating to herself the names of the coastal places they had come to know and love—Cap Martin, Roquebrune, Villefranche—as their train journeyed westwards to Marseilles and the boat for England. Yet she realized that although they felt that they 'belonged to Mentone, our Mentone did not belong to anything but a dream-world', and that, in time, that dream world's lack of connection, 'which so far had been good for us, might have made us eat each other's hearts out'. It was probably the right time to leave. 'We were ready and braced for the discipline of living under the pressure of public opinion and public feeling in our own country.'[34]

---

[33] *Belonging*, p. 134.
[34] *Belonging*, p. 135.

PART II
PUTTING DOWN ROOTS

6
Early Writings

Art is for me the only way of growing, of becoming myself more purely.
Edwin Muir, Letter to Sydney Schiff (1925)

Although neither Willa nor Edwin was quite ready to recognize it when their train left Menton in the early summer of 1927, it was probably time to put down roots and build on the creative and personal maturity they had gained during their European travels. As well as the need to prepare a stable home for the birth of Willa's baby in the late autumn, Edwin in particular needed to be able to interact more readily with the literary scene in London. He now had a strong reputation as a perceptive fiction reviewer and essayist, with Leonard Woolf remarking that Edwin's reviews for the *Nation* were the best the journal received. These essays, along with the translation work in which Willa would continue to be the more active partner, would provide an essential part of their income in the interwar years. In addition, Edwin's residence in Dresden and Hellerau had released his creative imagination and enabled him to explore in poetry aspects of his early life that had previously remained locked up inside him. By 1927 he had two collections of poems published by Hogarth Press—*First Poems* in 1925, and *Chorus of the Newly Dead* in 1926, and although *The Marionette* had been published by Hogarth around the time of their return to England, he believed that poetry was now his principal creative activity, a belief endorsed by Sydney Schiff's comment that *The Marionette* was 'essentially poetry, not prose'.[1] Willa's progress with her Montrose novel was slower than she had planned because of her translation commitments and her unexpected pregnancy, but for her, too, the years of travel in Europe had encouraged a new confidence in essay writing, creative fiction and her translation skills. This chapter will look more closely at the Muirs' early writing, beginning with the more established and comprehensive work of Edwin at this period.

Edwin's *New Age* prose-writing and *We Moderns*, published as a book in 1918 with an American edition in 1920, undoubtedly led to the *Freeman* contract and the journey to Europe. As 'Edward Moore' or 'E. M.', he had also published several poems in the *New Age* between 1913 and 1916, and these were in a Heine-influenced form of *jeu d'esprits* on contemporary topics such as 'Address to the Wage Slaves', 'A Question to my Love', 'Utopia'. His true beginning as poet, however, took place in Dresden and Hellerau. As John Holms recognized, Edwin's first

---

[1] Sydney Schiff, letter to Edwin Muir, 25 October 1926, Schiff papers, BL, Add MS 52920.

serious attempts at poetry came from the waking dreams he had experienced in London as a result of a period of psychoanalysis, and were written in ballad form, or a modification of it. Holms had written to Kingsmill in July 1922 and again in December of that year about what he considered to be the importance of Edwin's approach, with 'more of the ballad spirit than any imitations I have read—in his case the form is entirely natural—he writes in ballad form far more quickly and easily than in any other. A pure question of race'.[2] What is surprising in relation to these early poems and Holms's notion of 'race'—which in Edwin's case would be the Scottish ballad tradition—is that Edwin's best ballad poem was never collected. This is 'The Ballad of the Black Douglas', published in the *Scottish Chapbook* in July 1923—a splendid authentic Scottish ballad, written in traditional Scots language (as opposed to MacDiarmid's modernist literary use of Scots) with all the qualities one expects to find in a ballad, spoken dialogue, visual imagery, anticipation and retrospection, suspense, the seeking of a positive goal yet the sense of tragedy which awaits the seeker. And the poem 'sings'.

> The king lay on his dowie bed,
>   The may was on the tree:
> 'O ride ye for the Black Douglas,
>   For I maun swiftly dee'... .
> They rade a' night, and wan at last
>   The Douglas castle wa',
> They've brought him in the morning mirk
>   Into the royal ha'.
> 'O what is this that lies sae white?
>   Is it may plucked frae the tree?'
> 'It's the king's body that's covered a',
>   Wi' the white leprosy.'

The Black Douglas pledges the dying king that he will take his heart to the 'winding braes' of the Jerusalem he has always longed for, and sets out 'wi' his gude men' to the Holy Land in the attempt to fulfil his pledge. But—

> He never saw Jerusalem's
>   Green shaws and flowery braes,
> His king and he lie side by side
>   In a far lanely place.[3]

It is difficult to believe that Edwin forgot about this poem, for in January 1923 he had published his essay 'A Note on the Scottish Ballads' in the *Freeman*, and

---

[2] John Holms, letter to Hugh Kingsmill, 25 December 1922, Holms/Kingsmill correspondence, BL, Add MS 85337 vol. xv.

[3] 'The Black Douglas' is included in *Complete Poems*, Appendix 1 'Uncollected Poems', pp. 280–2.

this was included in his *Latitudes* collection of 1924, a year before the publication of his *First Poems* to which 'The Ballad of the Black Douglas' would have made a positive contribution. Even more relevant is that the *Scottish Chapbook* issue of July 1923 in which the Black Douglas ballad appeared also contained two further ballads by Edwin, 'The Ballad of the Flood' and 'The Ballad of the Monk', both of which did feature in *First Poems*. While both are satisfactory poems in the ballad form, neither is as striking or as closely linked to the Scottish tradition as 'The Black Douglas' poem. Many years later, in 1950, discussing a proposed anthology of Scottish verse, Edwin would write to the poet Douglas Young that the 'most Scottish poem' he himself had ever written was the 'Ballad of the Flood'; and in 1958, when his *Collected Poems* was under preparation with Faber, he wrote to T. S. Eliot about the poem's inclusion in the collection 'I hope you will like "Ballad of the Flood" in ballad Scots, which is so different from that of Burns.'[4] He does not mention the 'Ballad of the Black Douglas' and perhaps by 1958 he really had forgotten about the poem. On the other hand, its omission from *First Poems* in 1925 may have to do with his strong wish to make a name for himself in the London market. He had written to Sydney Schiff from Montrose in August 1924 'I want particularly to be published and recognised in some form in England, and at the earliest opportunity.'[5] His reviews of MacDiarmid's new poetry in *A Drunk Man Looks at the Thistle* (1926) and the collections of lyrics *Sangschaw* (1925) and *Penny Wheep* (1926) show his awareness of the potential of Scots in a modern literary context in the hands of a poet like MacDiarmid, but in his hopes for recognition in the London literary scene he may have felt that strongly Scottish themes were best avoided. Both 'The Ballad of the Monk' and especially the well-known biblical story of Noah's Ark in 'Ballad of the Flood' have wider religious associations, and their use of Scots is much less rich than in 'The Black Douglas'—more easily accommodated, perhaps, to the non-Scottish themes of *First Poems* as a whole. By 1936, with the publication of his book *Scott and Scotland*, Edwin had become much more sceptical about the possibility of Scottish writers making a living from their work by remaining in Scotland or writing in Scots.

First Poems is a highly eclectic collection where Edwin can be seen to be trying out various forms of expression in an attempt to find his own voice. He would comment later about his beginning to write poetry at the age of 35 instead of in his 20s.

> I had no training; I was too old to submit myself to contemporary influences and I had acquired in Scotland a deference towards ideas which made my entrance into poetry difficult. Though my imagination had begun to work I had no technique

---

[4] Edwin Muir, letter to Douglas Young, 15 July 1950, *Selected Letters*, pp. 156–7; letter to T. S. Eliot, 10 September 1958, *Selected Letters*, pp. 208–9.
[5] Edwin Muir, letter to Sydney Schiff, 2 August 1924, Schiff Papers, BL, Add MS 52920.

by which I could give expression to it. There were the rhythms of English poetry on the one hand, the images in my mind on the other. All I could do at the start was to force the one, creaking and complaining, into the mould of the other.[6]

Two of the most successful poems in the collection are 'Childhood', first published in the *Nation* in October 1923, and 'Horses' of May 1924 was chosen for an anthology of the best poems of 1924. Both seem to have developed from Edwin's attempt to recapture his childhood in Orkney. In 'Horses', the sight of horses in a field takes the speaker of the poem back to his father's plough horses returning to their stable at dusk 'with steaming nostrils' and appearing 'gigantic in the gloam' to the watching child. 'Childhood' calls up his young self lying on a grassy hillside in close proximity to the family farmhouse, looking over the still sea, the 'sound' that separated the group of islands that were his home, wondering what lay beyond them but untroubled by that strangeness, content with what is within his present awareness. There is a wonderful sense of stillness, of secure at-homeness, in the poem, complemented by its regular rhyming and quiet verse movement, and endorsed by the simplicity of its final line 'And from the house his mother called his name'. Edwin had for long been interested in Wordsworth's poetry, with its own capture of childhood experience, its nature imagery and reflective themes, and in Hellerau Iwar von Lücken had added the poetry of the German Romantic-period Hölderlin to his group of favourite poets. Unlike Wordsworth, Hölderlin's poetry did not offer new ways forward stylistically for the apprentice Edwin, but the German poet's belief in integration answered his philosophical need at this time. Hölderlin's 'Da ich ein Knabe war' is close to Edwin's 'Childhood' poem and his description of his home island of Wyre as a world where 'the sky fitted the earth and the earth the sky'.

Not all the evocations of childhood and island life in this first collection are of this integrated kind. Although his friendship in Hellerau with von Lücken was largely responsible for developing Edwin's interest in contemporary German poetry, in his previous life in Glasgow Edwin had turned to translations of older poets such as Goethe and Heine in an attempt to make some kind of sense out of human life. Heine taught him to treat suffering with a synthetic witty cruelty, as in his 1913 *New Age* poem 'A Question to my Love' where the speaker asks 'How dost thou win repose's balm, / When I must toss on life's wide sea?', and suggests 'Is it wisdom makes thee calm, / Or, dearest, mere stupidity?'[7] In contrast, Goethe's lines from *Wilhelm Meisters Lehrjahre* had real meaning for Edwin in these pre-Europe days 'Nur wer die Sehnsucht kennt / Weiss, was ich leide! / Allein und abgetrennt / Von aller Freude'. ('Only someone who experiences

---

[6] *The Story and the Fable*, p. 235, *An Autobiography*, p. 205.
[7] *The New Age* XIV, No.7, 18 December 1913, p. 197; Johann Wolfgang von Goethe, 'Nur wer die Sehnsucht kennt', *Harrap Anthology*, p. 220 (my translation).

longing, knows what I suffer! / Alone and separated from all happiness.') Yet the Sehnsucht in Goethe as communicated in Mignon's song, 'Kennst du das Land', also from *Wilhelm Meister*, has the compensating richness of a memoried world absent from Edwin's early poems of longing such as 'The Lost Land' from *First Poems*. In Mignon's song, the idealized vision of her lost home is vitally brought to the reader's imagination 'die Zitronen blühn, / Im dunkeln Laub die Goldorangen glühn'; 'es glänzt der Saal, es schimmert das Gemach' ('the lemons blossom / the golden oranges glow in the dark foliage; the hall gleams, the room shimmers with light'). By comparison, everything in 'The Lost Land', even the object of the speaker's longing, is nebulous and unreliable as a dream—'The houses waver towards me, melt and run'. And when the longed-for landscape eventually comes into focus, it shows a deserted scene 'the doors wide open where the wind comes in'; 'the still church standing lonely on the mound'. Then the dream vision becomes not only a deserted place, but something alien 'I look again. Alas! I do not know / This place, and alien people come and go [...] this is not my haven'. In contrast to Goethe's poem, the homeland here is not only lost through exile, but the fact that it ever existed is brought into doubt. Although Edwin was not familiar with Rilke's poetry at this point in his life, the psychological situation presented in many of these early poems is close to Rilke's definition of Sehnsucht 'Das ist die Sehnsucht: wohnen im Gewoge / Und keine Heimat haben in der Zeit' ('That is what longing is: to dwell in a state of flux / And to have no homeland in the world of Time'). Similarly, in the poem titled 'Houses', there is potential menace even in the midst of the memory of a previous secure existence. In this poem's dream vision, the land is 'the green estranging land'; rooms are 'closed'; the child in the poem is 'half-afraid', and 'those distant houses shine with grief and mirth'. Not only are such dream visions in Edwin's early poems at the opposite pole of longing from Goethe's expression of Sehnsucht in Mignon's song, but they also seem at odds with the integrative vision of Hölderlin to which he had been introduced in Hellerau, and more attuned (although less expertly expressed) to the view of human life communicated in Hugo von Hofmannsthal's 'Ballade des äusseren Lebens', a poet whose work he had also first encountered in Hellerau through his friendship with Lücken.

> Und Kinder wachsen auf mit tiefen Augen
> Die von nichts wissen, wachsen auf und sterben
> Und alle Menschen gehen ihre Wege.
> (And children grow up with deep eyes
> Understanding nothing, grow up and die
> And all people go on their course.)[8]

---

[8] Goethe, 'Kennst du das Land', *Harrap Anthology*, pp. 219-20; Edwin Muir, 'The Lost Land' and 'Houses', *Complete Poems*, pp. 4, 6, 7; Rainer Maria Rilke, 'Das ist die Sehnsucht', *Harrap Anthology*, p. 498; Hugo von Hofmannsthal, 'Ballade des äusseren Lebens', *Harrap Anthology*, p. 493 (my translations).

Poems in this first collection, although simply expressed, do show Edwin's growing confidence in poetic expression, moving on from his earlier obsession with the lost land of his childhood. These include 'October at Hellbrunn', published in the *Nation* in February 1924, and so written either during his stay with Willa in Salzburg or shortly afterwards; 'Salzburg—November', probably written before they moved on to Vienna (Hofmannsthal's home town) at Christmas 1923; and 'Autumn in Prague', which must have been written some time after their stay in the Czech capital, since the beginning of Edwin's new poetry did not take place until their stay in Dresden and Hellerau. And then there is 'An Ancient Song', whose lines 'Lost Love which flies aghast it knows not where, / And finds no foothold but the dreadful air'[9] so intrigued John Holms and Hugh Kingsmill in relation to Edwin's difficulties over his relationship with Gerda in Hellerau.

First Poems was published by Hogarth Press in April 1925, with an American edition published in New York by Huebsch, but the collection did not take London's literary world by storm. Holms wrote to Kingsmill in June 1925 that 'his reviews have been fatuous; no one I know thinks anything of his poetry.' Holms himself was on the whole appreciative, since he had witnessed Edwin's development as poet from its beginnings, although he was also critical when he felt it necessary. He was glad, however that Edwin's poems gave Kingsmill 'such pleasure', and gives his view in his letter that 'The Chorus of the Newly Dead', now completed, is 'mixed but has some even finer poetry than the first, I think. Purely mystical some, and some much richer and more human.' He quotes a verse that gave him 'great also very peculiar pleasure'.

> And that ghostly eternity,
> Cut by the bridge where journeys Christ,
> On endless arcs pacing the sea,
> Time turning towards his solar tryst.[10]

Chorus of the Newly Dead, dedicated to John Holms, was hand-printed by Leonard and Virginia Woolf at the Hogarth Press in 1926 and was similar in appearance to their single volume edition of T. S. Eliot's *The Waste Land* in 1922. Edwin sent Schiff a copy from St Tropez in July 1926, saying that July was a very bad time of year for its publication but that he himself was happy to see it in print. He wrote—

Perhaps I get a far more intense impression from this poem than anybody else will, but in my own eyes at any rate I can congratulate myself that I have written it; it is to me the best thing I have ever written; there is more of myself in it. I

---

[9] Edwin Muir, 'An Ancient Song', *Complete Poems*, p. 12.
[10] John Holms, letter to Hugh Kingsmill, 22 June 1925, Holms/Kingsmill correspondence, BL, MS 85338, vol. xvi. *Chorus of the Newly Dead, Complete Poems*, p. 47.

know its faults pretty well, but they are unavoidable, for they are my own faults, not due to carelessness or lack of effort, but to limitation. I hope you will like it, but if you do not please do not hesitate to tell me so, for that, I am sure, is the most friendly thing to do.[11]

Although Edwin comments here that the poem has more of himself in it, he probably means this in terms of its ideas rather than in any more biographical sense. He had previously sent Schiff a long letter from the Sonntagberg, when the poem was at an earlier stage of development, saying that his aim was 'to get a certain pathos of distance in contemplating human life'. He wanted to do this through 'types like the Saint, the Beggar, the Idiot, the Hero, the Mother, the Rebel, the Poet, the Coward, and they will all give some account of their lives as they see it from eternity, not in Heaven or in Hell, but in a dubious place where the bewilderment of the change has not been lost'. However, as he later recognized, his 'types' remain abstract entities, unable to arouse our interest or empathy because they themselves have no individualized life. Only the Harlot brings her suffering into a recognizable everyday world of 'the traffic's beat', the 'weak lamps [of] the darkening street' where she has to ply her trade. Generally, the attempt to achieve 'pathos of distance in contemplating human life' results in a divorce from human life as we know it.[12]

Edwin was much interested in Eliot's criticism at this early period, and Eliot's essay 'Tradition and the Individual Talent' of 1919, and its insistence that 'the emotion of art is impersonal' and on the need for the separation between 'the man who suffers and the mind which creates', made a strong impression on his thinking about literary creativity.[13] Edwin's early attempts at poetry had drawn on his own dream visions and on the reawakening of childhood memories and his lost island home, but he now needed to find a less subjective way to realize his exploration of what it means to be human. He seems to have had second thoughts about the 'types' in his *Chorus*, for he chose not to include it in the *Collected Poems* of 1960. Yet its theme continued to preoccupy him, and as late as 1955 he would be writing to his friend and poet Kathleen Raine about the temptation to revisit it with a quite different formal approach. Although the poem in its original form appears, technically, to be apprentice work, with its form and choice of language unable to deal with the human dilemmas it poses, it still does raise, even if obscurely, the philosophical questions about human time and experience that were to become the markers of Edwin's mature poetry. In his *Autobiography* he was to describe these as the three mysteries of 'where we came from, where we are going, and,

---

[11] Edwin Muir, letter to Sydney Schiff, 12 July 1926, Schiff Papers, BL, Add MS 52920.
[12] Edwin Muir, letter to Sydney Schiff, 7 May 1924, Schiff Papers, BL, Add MS 52920; *Chorus of the Newly Dead*, *Complete Poems*, p. 42.
[13] T. S. Eliot, 'Tradition and the Individual Talent' (1919), *Selected Essays* 2nd ed. revised and enlarged (London: Faber and Faber, 1934), pp. 22, 18.

since we are not alone, but members of a countless family, how we should live with one another'.[14] Despite its formal inadequacies, however, *The Chorus* must have communicated something of such 'mysteries' to a perceptive contemporary readership, and Edwin followed his letter to Schiff of July 1926 with another mention of the book in his letter of 12 August, saying that a positive review in the *Times Literary Supplement* had not only pleased him, but had resulted in Woolf selling 'over a hundred copies immediately', adding that Woolf 'evidently thinks, what I have never quite believed, though there must be some truth in it, that a favourable review will sell a book'.[15]

Even if Edwin had not quite made the major breakthrough in poetry, which was his aim in the mid-twenties, he had achieved a significant reputation as critic and essayist. In July 1924, T. S. Eliot wrote to Sydney Schiff, returning manuscript verses by Edwin that Schiff had sent him, saying that although he was 'very glad to have seen them', he remained of the opinion that the 'vehicle' of Edward Moore (as Eliot still called him) 'is much more philosophic prose than verse'. He added 'I have been much interested by the two books you lent me [*We Moderns* and *Latitudes*] and I should very much like to meet him when he comes to this country'. At this point Eliot was on the lookout for contributors to the revitalized *Criterion* of which he was editor, and he had also been given a 'tip' about Edwin by Wyndham Lewis, himself part of an Eliot/Schiff literary coterie. Lewis, who did not know Edwin well, called him 'Edwin Moore', saying that he was 'in London for a few days at Schiff's request'. In typical form, he qualified his recommendation somewhat by adding, 'He doesn't seem overburdened with intelligence, but probably is a little more useful than Herbert Read.' Meanwhile, Read himself (doubtless unaware of Lewis's low opinion of his usefulness) was also being asked by Eliot to recommend 'untapped talent' for the *Criterion*. Eliot wrote to him in October 1924 'I have thought of one Orlo Williams and an Edwin Muir. My anxiety about the latter is the fear that his mind has been fed too exclusively on contemporary and on German literature: that his culture, in other words, is too shallow.' And he asks for Read's opinion 'of these people, if you have one'.[16] Anxious to make his name in literary London, Edwin probably did not quite realize in what shark-infested waters he was attempting to swim.

Latitudes, one of the books that interested Eliot, was published in 1924 and derived mostly from Edwin's initial contributions to the *Freeman* in 1921 and 1922, with some essays such as 'A Note on Mr Conrad', 'The Reign of Superstition' or 'Against Optimism and Pessimism' showing his continued indebtedness to an earlier *New Age* style of writing. Edwin's essay and review writing developed

---

[14] *An Autobiography*, p. 56.
[15] Edwin Muir, letter to Sydney Schiff, 12 August 1926, Schiff Papers, BL, Add MS 52920.
[16] T. S. Eliot, letter to Sydney Schiff, 13 July 1924, *Letters of T. S. Eliot*, vol. 2, 1923–25, ed. by Valerie Eliot and Hugh Haughton (London: Faber and Faber, 2009), p. 465; also p. 468 (note 4), p. 515.

rapidly from this point onwards, including his pieces on Hölderlin and Hofmannsthal. An important three-part essay 'The Meaning of Romanticism' grew out of his discussions with von Lücken and his own earlier interest in the English Romantics and Wordsworth. This latter was published in the *Freeman* in December 1923 and January 1924 but was never collected. Back in Britain in the summer of 1924, after the closure of Neill's school on the Sonntagberg, Edwin's mind was already turning towards contemporary writing, and in correspondence with Sydney Schiff he expressed his concerns about the work of Aldous Huxley and other younger writers which seemed to him 'fundamentally an anarchic literature, a literature without orientation'.[17] And after his stimulating conversations with Schiff in London, the idea of an exploration of the zeitgeist, through a series of essays on contemporary writers, began to take hold of his mind as he and Willa were en route to Montrose in Scotland.

In Chapter Three of *We Moderns* Edwin had described people of the modern age as being 'caught in the whirlwind of modern thought which contains as much dust as wind'.[18] In his projected book, which he planned to call 'Transition', he proposed to interrogate the perplexing and contradictory spirit of the age through an investigation of the work of the novelists Virginia Woolf, D. H. Lawrence, James Joyce, and Aldous Huxley, and poets such as T. S. Eliot, Edith Sitwell, and Robert Graves. He also planned to include his friend Sydney Schiff, whose pen name was Stephen Hudson. The introductory chapter to *Transition*, 'The Zeit Geist', argues that the writer of significance is the one who 'wrestles' with his age, as opposed to either attempting to ignore it by retreating into the past, or embracing it unreservedly, thus becoming merely a reflector of predominant fashions. Edwin writes 'For all great writers are of their time, though they sometimes think of themselves as outside and against it; and when they attain expression in art the age is interrogating itself, is being differentiated for the purpose of self-realization.' He continues 'There are two ways in which the writer may avoid being assimilated by the age: one is by struggling with it, the other is by escape.' And for Edwin, 'it is he who wrestles with the age which finally justifies both it and himself.'[19] The critical positions adopted in these short studies are quite revealing of Edwin's own creative position as a poet.

Edwin was not sympathetic to Huxley's writing, and he cites him as 'our best example of the fashionable writer' who has been assimilated by the age, adding caustically that Huxley's 'disillusionment is a thing which, with trifling variations, may be found among half the writers in London and Paris'. James Joyce, on the other hand, is characterized as a wrestler, who expresses the age 'by an uncompromising opposition to it'; and 'when disillusionment is objectified as it is in

---

[17] Edwin Muir, letter to Sydney Schiff, 16 September 1924, Schiff Papers, BL, Add MS 52920.
[18] *We Moderns*, pp. 91–2.
[19] Edwin Muir, *Transition* (London: Hogarth Press, 1926), pp. 5, 7.

Ulysses [...] we are compelled to reckon with it.' D. H. Lawrence he sees as 'the poet of escape' who 'has scoured the globe to find some order of life sufficiently primitive to be the antithesis of contemporary Europe'. Yet in regard to Lawrence, Edwin also acknowledges that in 'presenting in his novels such a radical antithesis to all the age stands for [he] has brought a profound criticism to bear upon it'.[20] Edwin was never entirely at ease with Lawrence's depiction of modernity, as can be seen in his 1923 *Freeman* article 'The Assault on Humanism' in which he attacks Lawrence's philosophical and social ideas, and in *Transition* he finds that the defect of a literature such as that of Lawrence is that it is 'too sweeping [...] It postulates only two things: its vision of truth and beauty, and a world which does not correspond to that vision.' And in his view, in such an escape to the past, there can be no real interrogation of the spirit of the modern age.[21]

Eliot is another writer who does not always respond to the zeitgeist in a way that satisfies Edwin's insistence on the need to wrestle with the age. While appreciative of Eliot the critic, in 1926 Edwin was hesitant in his assessment of Eliot the poet, writing that 'Mr Eliot lacks seriousness.' In contrast, he endorses Eliot's writing on tradition and his idea that writers of the present are not merely 'judged by tradition' but can themselves 'modify' that tradition. He agrees that 'by adding one new work of art to those which constitute tradition we do something that is enough to change, however slightly, its character'; 'thus tradition is a thing which is forever being worked out anew and recreated by the free activity of the artist.' Eliot's poetry, on the other hand, could not at this point satisfy him. 'In the main it is a statement of two opposed experiences: the experience of beauty and ugliness, of art and reality, of literature and life.' He also finds, not without justification, that it communicates a mood in which 'a hatred of squalor disguises a certain pleasure in squalor.' And he links him with Huxley 'Disdain for life, loneliness of soul, the sardonic gesture, the mysterious sorrow—all these are in Mr Eliot's poetry. They are also in Mr Huxley's novels, they have been called the spirit of the age, and it is impossible to take them seriously.'[22] Edwin and Eliot would come to change their views of each other's poetry in later life. Eliot moved from indifference or inattention to Edwin's early apprentice work, but gave strong support to his later collections. Edwin finally recognized Eliot's formal inventiveness, something he did not respond to in the early period, and which was absent in his own early poetry and absent also in his critiques of modern writing.

The writers who are given the strongest support in *Transition* are Virginia Woolf and James Joyce, both of whom are indeed formally innovative writers, but they attract Edwin's particular attention for the way in which they explore and present time in their fiction. Edwin quotes a passage from Woolf's *Mrs Dalloway* in which

[20] 'The Zeitgeist', *Transition*, pp. 12–15.
[21] Ibid., p. 15.
[22] 'T. S. Eliot', *Transition*, pp. 133, 139, 141.

the past is brought into a union with the present through the action of Clarissa Dalloway sewing.

> her needle, drawing the silk smoothly to its gentle pause, collected the green folds together and attached them, very lightly to the belt. So on a summer's day waves collect, over balance, and fall; collect and fall.

Edwin comments—

> The transition here is daring, but wonderfully successful. While Mrs Woolf is describing the falling of the waves, we never forget Clarissa sewing [...] There is something in the ritual of sewing, a memory of another rhythm buried deep within it, which an image such as this, so unexpected, so remote, reveals to us.[23]

As for Joyce, what attracts Edwin's interest in *Ulysses* is not its structuring through the use of classical myth, but the fact that the mythic impulse in the narrative relates to a folk rather than a literary inspiration. He finds that the characters in the brothel scene, for example, are 'figures in a folk-lore which mankind continuously creates, or carries with it', thus bringing the recognition that the spirit of the new age, although breaking new ground, is also part of a timeless human story.[24]

Transition, published in 1926, marks a new maturity in Edwin's criticism, although he was still unconvinced by modernist innovation. It was followed in 1927 by his novel *The Marionette* which had preoccupied him throughout his stay in the south of France. His study *The Structure of the Novel* grew from his experience in fiction reviewing and his own preoccupation with novel writing. It was published in 1928, and his biography *John Knox: Portrait of a Calvinist*, commissioned by Cape, appeared in 1929. His second novel *The Three Brothers* (1931), was set in Knox's Reformation Scotland, most likely derived from research for the biography. Muir's final novel, *Poor Tom*, was set in contemporary Scotland, and appeared in 1932. Neither Scottish novel sold well, although *Poor Tom* has found a new audience in the present century as a significant contribution to the Glasgow novel tradition of harsh realism.[25] Both books are interesting, nevertheless, for their life-writing sources. *Poor Tom* is clearly related to the story of the Muir family's emigration to Glasgow, while several episodes recounted in the autobiographical *The Story and the Fable*, published in 1940, clearly provided material for the earlier fictional narrative of three brothers in sixteenth-century Calvinist Scotland. In 1932 *Six Poems,* in a limited edition of 110 copies, was printed by

---

[23] 'Virginia Woolf', *Transition*, pp. 78–9.
[24] 'James Joyce', *Transition*, pp. 32–3.
[25] *Poor Tom* was republished with three other 'Glasgow' novels in the anthology *Growing Up in the West* (Edinburgh: Canongate Classics, 2003). These were J. F. Hendry, *Fernie Brae*; Gordon M. Williams, *From Scenes Like These*; Tom Gallacher, *Apprentice*.

J. M. Shelmerdine and Flora Grierson at the Samson Press, suggesting that a new phase in Edwin's poetry might be beginning.

With such an output of critical and fictional works (in addition to ongoing reviewing) coming from Edwin from the mid-1920s into the early 1930s, it is not surprising that Willa's own writing ambitions were put on hold as she took the lead in their new occupation as translators, and of course, from 1927 onwards, there were her commitments as a mother. Before her marriage to Edwin and during their stay in London from 1919 until their departure for Europe in the late summer of 1921, Willa's occupation had been as an adult education teacher and lecturer, with no apparent ambition on her part to become a writer. Her first attempts at creative writing of a descriptive nature came with their stay in Prague and their involvement with the Čapek brothers and their theatre circle. She wrote three essays about Prague, 'The Čapek Brothers at Home in Prague' and 'A Woman in Prague', which were never published, although they both have a London Agent's stamp on the front cover; and 'A Western City with An Eastern Accent', which was published in the *Radio Times* of 28 February 1930, linked to a broadcast about the Czech city on the BBC Scottish National Programme. The first two essays, which are undated, were probably written during the Muirs' stay in Prague in the early 1920s, or shortly afterwards, since they both—and 'The Čapek Brothers at Home in Prague' in particular—have an immediacy and a 'surprise' element in their descriptions. The later BBC essay adopts a more conventional and knowledgeable placing of Prague in its historical context and in relation to its contemporary neighbours. All three, however, are marked by an immediacy, a sharpness in observation, and a liveliness in description that would become the hallmark of Willa's mature creative and descriptive writing. (Edwin's early work in this vein was much more stilted.) In her account of their first visit to the Čapek brothers, she takes the reader along the 'old street, quiet and blind-looking' and through the 'big double wooden doors' of No. 11. She describes how Karel takes them into his room, talking about his plays, and drawing their attention to his paintings—'His room is full of pictures, mainly by Vaclav Spala and Jan Zrzavy, two Czech artists belonging to the same group as his brother Josef. There are also sketches by Josef.' And then they meet Josef himself, who 'has the same fresh complexion as Karel, and a pair of very lively brown eyes: his merry look challenges us immediately'. Willa relates how the two brothers 'were students together in Paris and Munich; now they live together in these rooms and Josef's kindly wife, herself a distinguished Czech authoress, looks after both of them'; with Karel pointing out that he himself is 'a confirmed bachelor'.[26] Willa's description of this meeting and her comments on the brothers' collaboration in play-writing bring the encounter alive for the reader. She does not seem, however, to have fully appreciated both the importance of Karel's room full of paintings and his choice of paintings. Vaclav Spala, Jan Zrzavy, and Josef

[26] 'The Brothers Čapek at Home', University of St Andrews, MS 38466, Box 1/1/b.

Čapek himself are now among the principal modernist Czech artists represented by collections of their work in the Czech National Gallery's Museum of Art of the Twentieth and Twenty-First Centuries in Prague, the Veletrnži Palác (Trade Fair Palace). The National Gallery's collection of non-Czech modern art is itself extremely adventurous and extensive, with significant work by Picasso, Braque, Derain, and other important French artists purchased from the exhibitions of French Art which took place in Prague in the early 1920s, and again in 1930. These purchases were an ambitious undertaking for a country that had only recently acquired an independent national identity, and they confirm the Muirs' sense that there was an excitement and vitality in the life of the city. Willa's companion essay 'A Woman in Prague' calls attention to the surprising contrasts found in the city itself where 'electric trams of the best Continental model run rapidly through narrow cobbled streets full of dirt and palaces'; 'women in Turkey red peasant costumes with shawls on their heads sit in the stalls of the National Theatre'; and in a Prague where 'baroque palaces crowd and shoulder each other in every street [...] it is almost impossible to find a lodging free from bugs.' Unlike Edwin, who wrote somewhat romantically of the 'magnificent old women' he saw in the markets and on the boats 'carrying immense burdens with a careless air', Willa notices that 'all the unskilled heavy labour of the town is provided by women.'

> It is not considered a man's job to carry hods of bricks, or to deliver a ton of coal up three flights of stairs. When the coal cart stops in front of a house, the shawled and barefooted women sitting on the back climb down and stand patiently in the gutter while the man in charge shovels the brown coal into the enormous baskets which they carry on their backs.

And 'when a coal-carrier gets too old for her job she becomes a street cleaner in company with superannuated men who are out of work [...] painfully collecting in their aprons the scattered refuse which the dust-carts have left, and sweeping up the leaves and sticks.'[27] Willa's interest in the actuality of the women's lives here, as opposed to Edwin's romanticization of them, anticipates the feminist concerns present in her future writings.

Motivated by her enjoyment of their Prague contact with the Čapeks' theatre circle, Willa had proposed attempting a modernized drama of the biblical Noah's Ark story during their later stay in Dresden. John Holms's correspondence with Hugh Kingsmill from Dresden in July 1922 had talked about an idea Kingsmill seems to have proposed for a Noah's Ark play. 'Your Noah in the Ark idea could be made into a marvellously good intellectual-comic-fantastic play—types well realised (no women of course)'; and he added 'It would also make a marvellously

---

[27] Willa Muir, 'A Woman in Prague', unpublished essay, UStA, MS 38466 Box 1/1/d. Edwin's comment about the 'magnificent old women', *An Autobiography*, pp. 185–6.

good ballet—traditional Noah's Ark toy types simply asks for it—I wonder it hasn't been done.'[28] In the later memoir of this period in her life, Willa would comment that she 'must have picked out of the air' the idea of dramatizing the Noah story in modern terms as a way of 'embodying the making of a new world', but it seems likely that the topic was already mooted during their evening dinner discussions with Holms and Dorothy. On the other hand, unlike Holms's stipulation of 'no women', Willa's plan involved 'important parts for Mrs Noah, Mrs Shem, Mrs Ham, and Mrs Japhet'. She was undecided, however, as to how she would characterize the men: 'Shem, the father of merchant adventurers and bankers, might be a prospective City man [...] while Japhet, the father of land-grabbers and fighters, looked to me like someone in plus fours with a reddish face.' Unfortunately, when she put her idea to Edwin, 'to my dismay he did not like it at all; worse than that, he was shocked by it. The mere suggestion of putting Japhet into plus fours distressed him.' Edwin's view was simply that her idea 'should not be done', and she realized that 'he thought it vulgar.' Discouraged, she took the idea no further, but later noted that 'someone else picked that notion out of the air, or something very like it, and made it into a play; today the transformation of old stories into modern terms has become a commonplace.' In the 1920s, however, Edwin was of the opinion that his later ballad version of the Noah story was 'a more proper way of handling an ancient theme'.[29] His 'Ballad of the Flood', in everyday as opposed to a literary Scots language, was published in MacDiarmid's *Scottish Chapbook* in 1923, and included in his *First Poems* of 1925. Willa had to wait until 1931 before her novel about the difficult relations between women and men in the modern world could be brought to fruition and published.

---

[28] Letter from John Holms to Hugh Kingsmill, 24 July 1922, Holms/Kingsmill correspondence, BL, Add MS 85337.olmsHolm H
[29] *Belonging*, pp. 71–2.

7
Willa and Womanhood 1927–1929

> Since unto us a son is given
> How infinite is grown my worth!
> For the round of my breast is all his heaven
> And the spread of my knee his share of earth.
>
> Willa Muir, 'Nativity', *The Bookman* (1929)

The couple's travels in Italy and Austria kept Willa too busy to fret for long over Edwin's dismissal of her play about Noah's Ark. Her first publication when it eventually came was an extended discursive essay *Women: An Inquiry*, published in 1925 by Hogarth Press in its *Hogarth Essays* series. Edith Sitwell's *Poetry and Criticism* also appeared in 1925, and the series as a whole had been launched the previous year by Virginia Woolf's *Mr Bennett and Mrs Brown*. Willa's first publication was in good feminist company, but it had not been easily achieved, and was not particularly satisfactory when completed. It is not clear exactly when Willa developed the idea of writing about 'a conception of womanhood as something essentially different from manhood', exploring the differences between the creative work of the two sexes. The topic would appear to have been preoccupying her mind on her return from the Sonntagberg to Montrose in the summer of 1924 and throughout the following months. She would say little about *Women: An Inquiry* in *Belonging*, merely noting that while staying with her mother she had been 'thinking out the implications of my inability to detach myself from my emotions, which I suspected might be not only a peculiarity of mine but a characteristic of most women'.[1] Edwin wrote to Sydney Schiff on 1 August shortly after their arrival in Montrose that although they found themselves disappointed at the insularity of Scotland, they would get a good deal of work done while staying with Willa's mother—'Willa will be engaged on her book on women, and I shall have all these things I have mentioned.'[2] So the idea of the book seems to have been firmly on its way by that date.

Willa's correspondence confirms that it was their visit to the Schiffs in London en route to Montrose that inspired her to write her book on women and to dedicate it to Violet. She wrote to both Schiffs in late November 1924 thanking them for

---

[1] *Belonging*, p. 114.
[2] Willa Muir, *Women: An Inquiry* (London: Hogarth Press, 1925), reprinted in *Imagined Selves*, 1996; Edwin Muir, letter to Sydney Schiff, 2 August 1924, Schiff Papers, BL, Add MS 52920.

'heartening letters' and promising to carry out their suggestions for improvement. She addressed Violet in particular.

> I want to ask Violet (may I call you that?) if I may dedicate the essay to you? I had that in mind but I would not ask until I knew if you cared for the work. I should never have written it if it had not been for meeting you (besides condensing the old essay I re-wrote it entirely) and I think I would not have been so encouraged to do so if I had not met in the flesh a woman with a genius for womanhood— I mean you, madam. I found myself, in writing it, insensibly considering 'How would she like that?' and 'would it be true of her?' I don't say that it is entirely a study of Mrs Schiff, but she enters into it largely.[3]

This is a revealing letter in the way it draws attention to Willa's insecurity in relation to her own ideas, and also to her tendency to allow her emotional responses to people and situations to determine how she deals with them. When first sending the essay to the Schiffs for their comments, she had written that 'it is not good enough to make me feel confident: as a matter of fact, I am a little twittery about it. If I had been a man, I could have done it with less effort!'[4] In a follow-up letter she mentions 'the old essay' now condensed and rewritten, and this suggests that a previous draft had been superseded by new insights produced by her meeting with Violet Schiff. The introduction of Violet's ideas, or what Willa understood by them, may help to explain the immaturity and at times the incoherence of the arguments in the published essay. The Schiffs were also involved in the search for a publisher. Willa initially thought of it as an essay for the Hogarth series, but was hesitant about appearing to take advantage of Edwin's relationship with the Woolfs. The Schiffs favoured a small book format, and once again Willa was willing to take their advice. Sydney sent the finished version to Constable, but without success. He may have discussed it with Leonard Woolf, for at the end of a letter to Schiff on14 January 1925, Edwin writes 'I have sent Willa's MSS to Woolf now. I hope it will have some luck.' And after cutting the previously enlarged text to fit the publisher's format, the essay was accepted for the Hogarth Essay series and published in the summer of 1925.

Modern readers who come to Willa's essay on women after reading *Imagined Corners*, or knowing her lively letters to women friends, and her reputation for a quick and caustic tongue in public, must be puzzled by an essay that appears to be so rooted in the deeply conservative ideas about the nature and role of women that were current in pre-twentieth-century social thinking. There is little if any reference here to the campaigns for female suffrage, the arguments in Dora Marsden's *Freewoman* journal, and the greater involvement of women in social, educational,

---

[3] Willa Muir, letter to Violet Schiff, 28 November, Schiff Papers, 1924, BL, Add MS 52920.
[4] Willa Muir, letter to Sydney Schiff, 25 November 1924, Schiff Papers, BL, Add MS 52920.

and artistic life, all of which were redefining women's social roles in these years. Willa's own life as a First Class Honours graduate of the University of St Andrews in 1911, a vice principal and lecturer in a Teacher Training College in London, and then as an adventurous European traveller engaged in the translation of German literature into English, was itself an example of these changed and still changing times.

At the outset of her essay, Willa defines her aim as being 'to find a conception of womanhood as something essentially different from manhood', and within that conception, 'to discover if the division of the human race into men and women involves a division of spiritual as well as of sexual functions, so that the creative work of women is different in kind from the creative work of men'.[5] Willa was not alone in thinking about such differences. Contemporaries such as Rebecca West, Virginia Woolf, and Catherine Carswell were already demonstrating this in their new fiction. In her 1929 essay 'Women and Fiction', Virginia Woolf would argue that the very form of the literary sentence—a sentence created by men—does not suit a woman's purpose in fiction writing 'it is too loose, too heavy, too pompous for a woman's use', so the female author must make a new sentence for herself and her interests.[6] In fact Willa's own investigations would have benefited from a knowledge of Woolf's 1918 review essay 'Women Novelists', which examines sharply, and at times ironically, some of the gender issues raised by R. Brimley Johnson's contemporaneous book *The Women Novelists*. Instead, her influences would appear to have come principally from Violet Schiff, together with a recent book *The Dominant Sex* by Matthilde and Mathias Vaerting, reviewed in the *Spectator* by Julian Huxley in September 1923. More negatively, she may have been influenced by the biological approach of Patrick Geddes and J. Arthur Thomson in their study *Sex*, published in the Home University Library series in 1914—a book that Willa may well have read during her psychology studies and educational work.

Sections I and II of *Women: An Inquiry* discuss perceptions of female and male roles in historical societies of various kinds, an investigation that inevitably leads to the sexual difference of childbearing. 'At the lowest estimate of their powers all women are potential mothers. Men are born of women, and of women only.'[7] This singular focus on childbearing and mothering rather derails the essay's future development. In discussing the differences between the creative work of women and men, it becomes clear that in the author's view the 'creative work' of women is not to be understood in the more usual sense of literary, musical, or artistic performance, but as something that involves the unconscious as opposed to the conscious part of female being, directly related to childbearing, as a creative role not open to men. The mother's role is no less than the creation of a 'human being',

---

[5] *Women: An Inquiry*, in *Imagined Selves*, p. 2.
[6] Virginia Woolf, 'Women and Fiction' in David Bradshaw ed., *Virginia Woolf: Selected Essays* (Oxford: Oxford University Press, 2008), p. 136.
[7] *Women: An Inquiry*, in *Imagined Selves*, p. 4.

for 'the perfection of each individual is women's business.' On the other hand, as with the Indian goddess Kali, Willa suggests that the power of creation can be 'an equal power for destruction', a power she would later find herself exploring in her 1933 novel *Mrs Ritchie*.[8]

In the opening stages of her essay, Willa appears to leave open the 'nurture not nature' arguments presented in *The Dominant Sex* by Mathilde and Mathias Vaerting to which she briefly refers. As the essay proceeds, however, her emphasis on the female creative role of mothering follows the biological arguments of Patrick Geddes and Arthur Thompson, leading her to claim that since all women are potential mothers, they 'must have the necessary reserve of energy for this function whether they intend to become mothers or not'.[9] Men, on the other hand, are not hampered in this way—they 'have more energy to waste on their own individual purposes than women; that is to say, men have more energy at their conscious disposal'. Man is therefore 'the intellectual organiser of life. He arranges life in patterns' and his talents are directed towards the conscious creation of 'systems of philosophy or government'. In contrast, 'woman is the gateway through which the wisdom of the unconscious comes to be translated by man into conscious form.' Her talents are linked therefore to the unconscious work of 'creating individual human beings'.[10] If some women are unfortunate enough to be the 'surplus women' created by the deaths of so many young men in the First World War, and therefore unable to marry and become mothers, then they can still use their biological reserves of energy by carrying out creative succouring roles in the community at large. There is little difference between this 1925 argument, by a supposedly highly educated woman, and that of John Ruskin's *Sesame and Lilies* of 1865 which claimed that man's role is 'active, progressive, defensive. He is eminently the doer, the creator, the discoverer, the defender. His intellect is for speculation and invention.' Woman, in contrast, 'sees the qualities of things, their claims and their places', and for Ruskin her place is 'the place of peace' in the protected home.[11] In her own account, Willa argues that 'the tradition that woman's place is in the home is possibly not entirely determined by the subordinate position of women, but may arise from a sound intuition about the nature of women and their function,' the home being 'a strategic centre for the creation of human beings'; and 'the perfection of each individual is women's business.' Then, in a passage that might well have

---

[8] Ibid., p. 9.

[9] Ibid. It is odd that Willa herself does not specifically allude to the biological writings of Geddes and Thompson, as she does with the Vaertings. But her ideas about the energy given to women for childbearing are so close to those put forward by Geddes and Thompson that it seems unlikely that she had not at some point read their published works. The views of Geddes and Thompson themselves were developed from Herbert Spencer's *Principles of Biology* (1867) and *Principles of Sociology* (1876) which also argued that women had to preserve their 'fund of energy' for reproduction and childbearing.

[10] *Women: An Inquiry*, in *Imagined Selves*, pp. 16, 17.

[11] John Ruskin, *Sesame and Lilies* (1865), reprinted in J. M. Golby, *Culture and Society in Britain 1850–1890* (Oxford: Oxford University Press, 1986), pp. 118–19.

been influenced by her recent translation of Hauptmann's *The Island of the Great Mother* and the female society created there, she adds 'Moreover, a home does not imply a husband: marriage is a desirable but not a necessary condition for woman's creative work.' While this might at first seem dangerously 'modern', anticipating the late-twentieth- and early twenty-first-century world of single parenthood, partnerships as opposed to marriages, and easy divorce, Willa is probably thinking here of the succouring roles in society she referred to previously in her discussion of 'surplus women'. Equally unsatisfactory is her assumption that *all women* (as well as all men) have the same emotional needs and capacities. In her analysis, neither women nor men are treated as individuals with different talents, personalities, and potentialities, nor is the effect of education on women, or the lack of it, taken into account. Some of Willa's broader claims will seem highly contentious to a modern reader, and section IV of the essay, a long passage, is particularly rich. A girl 'values things for their associations, or for the power they give her over other people'; 'nearly every girl wants to be popular, to be an influence for good, to establish a reputation for cheerfulness and kindness'; 'in married life women display the same passionate interest in other people, even though husbands and families absorb a certain amount of it. Neighbours, servants and children are their dearest topics'; 'no woman is bored when she is discussing other people'. And finally, 'when because of some timidity they cannot exercise their creative power on human beings, they readily foster plants or animals instead.'[12]

Towards the end of her essay, Willa comes to consider what are usually thought of as the creative arts, and here she relegates female creativity to performing arts 'like dancing, singing and acting, where the actual personality is the medium of expression'. She considers that women are 'handicapped in those arts, such as literature, painting and the composition of music, where the finished product takes a permanent form detached from the human personality of the artist'. She also denies that 'the domination of men is even partly responsible for the lack of great women artists'. In doing so she ignores the fact that women were, until recent times, denied entry to art schools and life classes and the chance to develop essential skills. She seems equally unaware of the outstanding success at home and in Europe of Scottish women artists of her own time, who studied at Glasgow School of Art under its innovative Director 'Fra Newbery' in the early years of the century. These were women such as Margaret and Frances Macdonald, Jessie M. King, Norah Nelson Gray (famous for her war paintings), and Bessie McNicol. This last-mentioned was a fine artist whose career was brought to an untimely end in 1904 by her death in childbirth, the very act that Willa considers to be the primary role of women.[13] By comparison, the German poet Rainer Maria Rilke saw things very differently in his poem *Requiem: Für eine Freundin* (1908), written for his

---

[12] *Women: An Inquiry*, in *Imagined Selves*, pp. 24, 20, 14, 15.
[13] Ibid., pp. 27-9.

good friend the artist Paula Moderstrom-Becker, who also died in childbirth. To Rilke Paula's death was an 'uneigne Tod', a death that was not her own death, but a falsification of her previous chosen life as an autonomous artist.[14]

Her own anxiety about childbirth and mothering may explain Willa's arguments in the Hogarth essay. A letter to her friend Florence McNeill from Montrose in January 1925, telling of her recent miscarriage, and earlier letters to Florence about her visit to a gynaecologist in London show that mothering had been a strong presence in her mind in the months after her return from Europe. A fortuitous and ironic addition to Willa's preoccupations at this time may have come in the form of the commission from Huebsch in New York for the translation of Gerhart Hauptmann's novel titled *Die Insel der Grossen Mutter, The Island of the Great Mother*. Wholly translated by Willa herself, and published in 1925, this was reviewed in the American *Saturday Review of Literature* on 5 December 1925—around the very time Willa was suffering her miscarriage. Hauptmann's novel tells a fantasy story of the shipwreck of a hundred women, mature and well-educated, on a remote island, who, provisioned by the island's rich store of fruit and livestock, and having organized themselves into a satisfactory life pattern without men, suddenly, one by one, become pregnant, apparently by divine conception. The birth of male children then results in a threat to the continuation of this female-ruled society (although the presence of one male child among the predominantly female survivors of the original shipwreck might have warned the women of potential dangers to come). The *Saturday Review of Literature* praised the book as 'imaginatively translated into English by Mr and Mrs Edwin Muir (who have no finer feather to show in their literary bonnets)'; and as furnishing 'the finest of all modern jokes at the expense of feminism.'[15] Despite her argument for male predominance in affairs of the conscious mind in the Hogarth essay, Willa might well have been indignant to find her role as sole translator of the book so overlooked by both publisher and reviewer.

The Muirs were back in Europe in the spring of 1926, after Willa had recovered from her miscarriage, and they resumed their literary plans at Menton. Here they completed the translation of *Jew Süss*, Edwin finished *The Marionette* and Willa, even as she accepted further translation contracts, started to think again about a novel to be set in her home town of Montrose. Then everything changed. Writing to Sydney Schiff from Villa Soleil in April 1927, Edwin announced—

> I have kept the most important part of my news to the last. Willa is going to have a baby. She has had a very bad time of it for a month or two now, with sickness, but

---

[14] 'Requiem für eine Freundin is collected in Rainer Maria Rilke, *Sämtliche Werke* I (Frankfurt am Main, 1955). Hugh MacDiarmid included a translation of the poem (translator uncertain, perhaps partially himself) in his long poem *To Circumjack Cencrastus* of 1930 in a section on the need for self-realization and independence in art as well as life.

[15] *Saturday Review of Literature*, 5 December 1925.

> she is already a great deal better. We should both have preferred that it should not have come at this present time; but if Willa is to have one it would be better that it should come sooner rather than later; and our prospects for the coming year in the way of money are better than they have ever been before.

And he added—

> I shall be glad when her sickness is entirely over; nature seems to inflict a great deal of stupid suffering on women. However, she like a dear is cheerful, and only complains because she cannot do as much as work as usual.[16]

It was time to return to Britain and the Muirs left France to seek a home in the south of England where they could be close to London and in touch with literary connections. In Dormansland, in the county of Surrey, they found a furnished and inexpensive cottage which seemed to meet their needs. Dormansland was a rural village, established in the nineteenth century, with areas of woodland and parkland related to the local manor house and its estate. The local railway station, also established in the nineteenth century, brought London within easy reach. An additional interest was the cottage's proximity to the nearby Lingfield racecourse, which Edwin would remember with clarity and enthusiasm.

> There was a path through the woods which led down to the course near the starting-point. It was a long, dry hot summer, and we often took the path to the race-course, for horses enchanted us and we could not think of any sound more exciting than the thunder of their hoofs as they swept down on us and flew past, a sound which made the ground hollow, like a great drum. We could watch them by ourselves, away from the bustle and noise of the stand, and without caring whether they lost or won; wishing them all, if that were possible, to pass the winning post together in one glorious line. They seemed to exist in a fabulous world of their own, oblivious of the watchers in the stand or even the jockeys on their backs; as if the race existed only for them.[17]

Much of the summer was occupied by settling into the cottage and working on their translation commitments. Edwin wrote to Sydney Schiff at the beginning of September that 'for the last few months we have been doing nothing but translating Feuchtwanger's other novel [...] the proceeds from it should put us beyond all pecuniary worry, for which I am profoundly thankful.'[18] This was *Die Hässige Herzogin*, *The Ugly Duchess*, which followed the unexpected success of *Jew Süss*.

---

[16] Edwin Muir, letter to Sydney Schiff, 19 April 1927, Schiff Papers, BL, Add MS 52920.
[17] *An Autobiography*, pp. 230–1.
[18] Edwin Muir, letter to Sydney Schiff, 6 September 1927, Schiff Papers, BL, Add MS 52920.

This time they had negotiated royalties on the translation, which accounts for Edwin's optimism about their future financial situation, but unfortunately *The Ugly Duchess* did not find favour with the public and the returns were limited. Their obsession with finishing the Feuchtwanger translation distracted them from Willa's approaching confinement and its necessary arrangements. Neither Willa nor Edwin would appear to have been well informed, or to have been anxious to make themselves well-informed, about the event awaiting them, especially Willa. That summer she wrote to Flos McNeill.

> My dear F. M. Do come down. The train is the East Grinstead line from Victoria (southern) about one hour and then 20 mins walk or so. Send us a card & Edwin will meet you. I can put you up. [...] We came back unexpectedly because (as will be obvious when you see me) I am going to have a baby—end of October, I think. We are still very busy translating another book.[19]

By September, however, Willa was 'learning what it meant to be a heavily pregnant woman'. 'I found that I could not run, nor even walk very fast. I had to progress across fields with a slow, majestic gait, and one day said to Edwin in surprise "Do you know that if a bull came after me I couldn't run away". Now I understand why women need protection.'[20] Willa was equally unsettled at the change pregnancy had brought to her appearance.

> I began to understand something else too, for a sudden glimpse of myself in a long glass gave me a shock. I looked like a bulging fruit, and my head on the top of it seemed small and unimportant. No wonder, I thought, that many men believe women to be mindless. I stared at the figure in the glass and all at once felt a revulsion of sympathy in favour of the poor little head. 'But I am still me!' I said aloud, more than once. 'I am still me!'[21]

Willa's real-life female responses are very different from male-authored portraits of pregnancy, such as D. H. Lawrence's Anna in *The Rainbow* who 'big with child as she was, she danced there in the bedroom by herself, lifting her hands and her body to the Unseen, to the unseen Creator who had chosen her'; or Lewis Grassic Gibbon's Chris Guthrie, 'glad, peeking at herself in the long mirror when she was

---

[19] Willa Muir, letter to F. Marian McNeill, Monday, no further date, perhaps July 1927 since this was a Monday. 'Nov 4' is written in biro in Willa's handwriting, but scored out; also name of cottage changed to 'White Cottage' in biro, but this again must have been a later dating mistake by Willa since the letter is clearly before the birth of Gavin, while Monday 4 November is the date of a letter to Florence McNeill after his birth on 29 October.

[20] *Belonging*, p. 143; and an unpublished draft version, St Andrews University, UStA, 38466, Box 3/11/12.

[21] Ibid.

alone, seeing gradually that smooth rounding of belly and hips below her frock'.[22] Hugh Kingsmill, who visited them in Dormansland, wrote to John Holms that Willa, lying on a couch, was 'monstrous' yet somehow 'magnificent'.[23]

Willa seems to have been strangely indecisive about preparing for the birth itself. In a draft version of *Belonging*, she comments that although her school education had offered botany as a subject for girls, 'the study of flower fertilisation did not tell us much about human conception.' It was therefore 'with great ignorance that I observed my pregnancy'.[24] In view of her earlier correspondence with Flos McNeill and Dr McIlroy, the gynaecologist recommended before her miscarriage in December 1925, Willa might have been expected to make contact again with Dr McIlroy who, if not an obstetrician herself, would have been in a position to recommend someone of good standing and experience in dealing with a first pregnancy by an older mother. Instead, she turned to her old friend A. S. Neill for advice, and his assistant 'Jonesie' recommended an inexpensive nursing home in London. Willa made an appointment with the two doctors who practised there and they advised that as the baby's head was already large it would be dangerous to allow the pregnancy to continue to its full term. Thirty-seven was too old an age to take such a risk with a first baby, they thought, so the birth must be induced a few weeks before its due time. Willa conceded. The result was an extremely long labour—sixty-five hours according to Edwin in a letter to Violet Schiff on 8 November—

> I should have written before, but I have had so much worry about Willa both before and after the event. [...] The baby was born on the Saturday before last, the 29th October: it is a boy. Willa had a very bad and severe time; the labour process lasted about 65 hours: she was twice under chloroform and twice under twilight sleep; and when it was all over, and she absolutely exhausted, she suffered from chloroform poisoning on the top of the rest. But she has now quite definitely taken the turn; she is glad, now that it is over, that it has happened; and she and the baby are both getting on well.

He added 'I never had any idea before that birth was so terrible, or could be so terrible. But it is over and past, and we are both free for the first time for months from anxiety'.[25]

---

[22] D. H. Lawrence, *The Rainbow* (1915: Harmondsworth: Penguin Books, 1961), p. 183; Lewis Grassic Gibbon, *Sunset Song* (1932) in *A Scots Quair* trilogy (Edinburgh: Canongate Classics, 1995), p. 183.
[23] Hugh Kingsmill, letter to John Holms, 11 September 1927, Kingsmill/Holms correspondence, BL, Add MS 83336.
[24] Draft of *Belonging*, UStA, MS 38466, 3/11.
[25] Edwin Muir, letter to Violet Schiff, Dormansland, 8 November 1927, Schiff Papers, BL, Add MS 52920.

Willa and the baby remained in the unsympathetically named Stonefield Nursing Home, Blackheath, until the end of November, while Edwin had to go to Scotland in order to fulfil a lecturing engagement with the English Association. He wrote in his letter to Violet that he wished the lecture had not come at this time, but added 'as I am being paid fairly well, it must be done.' Violet and Sydney were lucky to get a letter from Edwin, for with his worries about Willa and his need to write and make travel plans for his lecture in Scotland, he appears to have been more than usually forgetful about telling friends or, as Willa wrote to Flos McNeill, 'You would look long before seeing any notice inserted by our Edwin in any paper!' She continued 'The bairn was born here last Saturday—a boy; after a hellishly long confinement of more than three days—I can't express it just now; but I am recovering well, and Gavin Muir (provisionally agreed on as name) is sucking lustily.'[26] Despite her recovery, however, Gavin's difficult birth would haunt Willa for some time to come. She had been badly torn during the process, and in the confusion over her chloroform poisoning, the doctors apparently 'forgot' to tell her about this tearing, and even more important, had omitted to stitch her up, thus leaving her with future physical problems. On the other hand, the baby throve. Willa breastfed him and claimed that she 'had milk enough for two babies'. He was a good sleeper, and kept them awake 'only one night during his whole infancy—and that was when a tooth was coming through'. Edwin was proud of him too, although his remark about 'how unlike the human young is to the young of the chimpanzee' did not strike Willa as one she herself would ever have made about their new son. They called him Gavin, a good Scottish name suggested by their admiration for the medieval poet Gavin Douglas, and one that would not challenge the identity of his poet father, as it might have done had they followed the custom by calling him Edwin. One 'Edwin Muir' was quite enough.[27]

In the six months after Gavin's birth, Willa was very much involved with breastfeeding and looking after the addition to their household. She wrote to Lizzie and George in May 1928 that she was 'still feeding him myself, and what with that and work I am just as busy as I can be'—'looking after a baby is nearly a whole time job in itself, I find.' Edwin wrote to Sydney Schiff around the same time that the baby was 'a dear little fellow, and Willa is a mother in a million'.[28] One of the occupations keeping Willa busy during these first six months, and until the summer of 1928, was what she called her 'Marmaduke' journal, a record of her baby's activity and progress from the age of six weeks. She gives no hint as to why she chose this nickname, usually taken to mean 'follower of Saint Maedoc' or 'leader of the seas'.[29] The new parents were also prone to refer to their son as 'it', as in Willa's 'Well, this

---

[26] Willa Muir, letter to F. Marian McNeill, 4 November 1927, NLS, MS 26194.
[27] *Belonging*, p. 144.
[28] Willa Muir, letter of 10 May 1928 to Lizzie and George Thorburn; Edwin Muir, letter to Sydney Schiff, 26 April 1928, Schiff Papers, BL, Add MS 52920.
[29] Internet information about 'Marmaduke' accessed 9 March 2017.

is it. Isn't it nice? A great improvement on its parents, I think! We have called it Gavin', as she sends a photograph of the baby to Lizzie and George.[30] Perhaps too much familiarity with the German language and its neuter gender noun 'das Kind' for 'the child' made the usage seem normal to them.

In addition to its peculiar title, the diary of Gavin's progress is itself a strange document, providing a kind of analytical counterpoint to Willa's *Women: An Inquiry*. While the essay emphasized the emotional responses of women, 'Marmaduke's Journal' proceeds with impersonal rigour. It is not clear how Willa fell into the clutches of Sir Frederic Truby King's childrearing discipline. Generally known as Truby King, this medical doctor and health reformer worked at both Edinburgh and Glasgow Royal Infirmaries before emigrating to New Zealand in the late 1880s to become Medical Superintendent of the Wellington General Hospital and then of the Seacliff Lunatic Asylum in Dunedin, as well as a lecturer in mental diseases at the University of Otago. Later he turned his attention to infant welfare, and, interested in eugenics, he founded the Plunket Society in 1907 in order to apply scientific principles to the nutrition of babies. His regime emphasized regularity in feeding, sleeping, and bowel movements, and rejected cuddling in order to develop character in the infant. Truby King's methods were controversial, and he was challenged by a female doctor as early as 1914, but his publications such as *Feeding and Care of Baby*, published by Macmillan in 1921, and the publicity given to his ideas about routine and strict discipline in the formative years of child development, made his method popular, and his regime was often introduced to new mothers by hospital nurses as they helped them to breastfeed, which he did encourage. Willa spent almost a month in Stonefield Nursing Home, and it is possible that it was there that she was introduced to King's ideas. The method was certainly well established in relation to Gavin's routine when she began her journal when he was six weeks old.

What immediately strikes the reader of Willa's diary is the impersonal, scientific objectivity with which she analyses her baby's behaviour before, after, and during his sucking at her breast. There is no sense of her own involvement as mother in the breastfeeding activity; only a detachment where the provider of the breast milk becomes an observer, holding herself back from participation in a shared physical and emotional experience. Her analysis then turns to his bowel motions—a subject of importance to Truby King who warned that constipation would lead to 'sexual precocity and possibly to masturbation'. She worries when there is an absence of a motion, and it is equally worrying for the reader when, in her entry for 18 December, she is found giving a seven weeks old baby 'catheter earlier, enema salt & water at 6, & a little magnesia'. On 19 December, when the previous day's administrations would appear to have had no positive outcome, she is giving him 'exercise in bath & massage of tummy', followed by '1 tablsp. very weak solution

---

[30] Willa Muir, letter to Lizzie and George Thorburn, 10 May 1928, NLS, Acc. 13226/1.

of magnesia', which is then followed at 2 o'clock by further massage 'with olive oil & enema of soap & water'. This supposedly scientific method shows its weakness when she discovers by chance that the child had actually produced some waste material the previous day, but on her apron instead of in his nappy, and she had not noticed this. The journal continues in this analytical mode. Feeding times and quantities are regulated according to the Truby King book, and as the book dictates that underfeeding is less harmful than overfeeding, when the baby cries, seemingly for more milk, he gets water. He is taken out in his pram in the cold January air, as recommended in the King method, and is allocated 'play-minutes' after his 10 a.m. and 6 p.m. feeds, as well as being taken into the drawing room in the afternoon to lie on the sofa and listen to his parents' voices. Willa is concerned that he does not seem to show interest in his penis, even after it has had an erection; and when he 'shoots out his legs a great deal', she adds in parenthesis '(masturbation?)'. On one occasion, in a rare departure from her objective mode, she speculates about this period of the child's dependency on the mother producing in the human being 'the first idea of God [...] Mother god, a presence rather than a Power'. And she adds a comment in ink 'Men's earliest relations w. women are so undignified that some of them spend the rest of their lives trying to get even.'[31] It is comforting to note, nevertheless, that Edwin was unaffected by Truby King's commands and did the kind of silly things most of us do with babies—the baby 'laughs when Edwin wags his head—or bends his head down & prods him in the tummy with his nose'. On 23 February he has 'a giggling match with Edwin (this happens quite frequently). Made a new high giggling sound, then joined in heartily when E. laughed at it & then did it again, twice, giggling joyfully each time along with Edwin.' And by the end of March the rapport between father and son was such that Gavin 'shouted with joy to E. after he had been away all day'.[32] In the later memoir of her marriage Willa would question whether her earlier adherence to Truby King on the care of infants had been misguided, instead of relying on her own intuitive intelligence to create a more flexible and personalized pattern of care for her child. That she was indeed capable of this is shown by the fine poem written on page 37 at the end of the first section of her diary, and reproduced as the epigraph to this chapter.

The first section of Willa's 'Marmaduke' journal ends in August 1928 with Gavin showing signs of teething. They had managed to have a three-week holiday with friends in Leiston in East Suffolk at Easter and had arranged to stay with Willa's mother in Montrose in the autumn. Edwin had now finished his *Structure of the Novel* book and was working on his life of John Knox for Cape (Knox having replaced Cape's original invitation to write on Luther). He was also now doing some reading for Cape. One of the bonuses of his work on Knox was that it earned him 'escapes' from Dormansland to the British Library in London while Willa was

---

[31] 'Journal of "Marmaduke's" Development (1927–1931)', UStA, MS 38466, 5/1, pp 7–10, 18.
[32] Ibid., p. 25.

confined to the house with the baby. There were three plays and another novel by Feuchtwanger to be translated, but Willa was still hoping to pick up her own long-projected novel again. There were, however, difficulties on the horizon. The owner of their rented cottage in Dormansland decided that she wanted it for herself and so they had to find alternative accommodation. Edwin wrote to Sydney Schiff from Montrose in October that they were about to return to a different house called 'Fairholme'; and in November he wrote to Lizzie and George from their new address, saying that his nieces Irene and Ethel would have to come south to visit them during the next summer when they hoped to have another rented house with their own furniture. He added 'The idea that a spree is a good thing has made me enclose a trifling cheque; I hope you don't mind; and I hope you will have a fling with it, seeing Charlie Chaplin or the theatre. It really does one good.'[33] Edwin's relatives were often hard-pressed for money in the difficult economic times of the late 1920s and especially in the 1930s, so when he and Willa were paid for translation work, he would send a small cheque north. Meanwhile, they settled as best they could into their new house while looking for a place with their own furniture, without having to worry about Gavin knocking things over. Remembering how much they had liked the town of Crowborough and the Ashdown Forest on a previous visit shortly after their marriage in 1919, they decided to look at properties there. They found a semi-detached house on the outskirts of Crowborough with a large garden, well planted with shrubs and flowers stretching down to open fields. As with Dormansland, Crowborough was well connected to London by the railway. They agreed to rent the house at £60 a year and moved there in the spring of 1929.

[33] Edwin Muir, letter to Lizzie and George Thorburn, 12 November 1928, NLS, Acc.13226/1.

8
Crowborough and Literary Life 1929–1931

> I ask but this, to keep a green point growing
> Within myself, whatever winds be blowing,
> To put out blossoms, one or two,
> And when my leaves are thin and few
> To have some fruit worth showing.
>
> Willa Muir, Letter to Mary and Arthur Mason (1929)

One of the last letters written by Willa from Dormansland was to Mary and Arthur Mason, the Americans with whom they had become friendly when living in Menton. They had lost touch over the previous two years as a result of the Muirs' new family preoccupations and the increasing press of their translation work and other writing commitments, while the Masons changed their address. Willa wrote from 'The Nook, Blackness Road, Crowborough, Sussex', with the added note 'After March 26th', and began in a characteristically dramatic fashion.

> What a terrible gap! I mean the gap in my correspondence. I am very sorry about it. And it's even wider than I had thought, for a joyous wire of Xmas wishes which we sent you has just been returned to us (see enclosed) with the information that you could not be found by Cook's. I only hope you get this. Where, in all the immense continent of America, have you got to?[1]

Willa then details the work that had kept them occupied during the previous winter, including 'Sections of Feuchtwanger's enormous new book', which seems as if it may well reach the length of 'half a million words. Who's going to read it? Ask me another. Unfortunately I know who have engaged to translate it.' And then there is 'a German war book by Ludwig Renn which is coming out shortly' and 'a life of Eleonora Duse' which they are still translating, as well as Edwin's biography of Knox. On top of all this there is the new house in Crowborough, rented at £60 a year, which they intend to be their permanent address for the next three years. Willa seems to hope that 'Secker's will pay us to go to Berlin and discover worthwhile novels for them,' out of which commitment they may 'easily sneak a month

---

[1] Willa Muir, letter to Mary and Arthur Mason, March 16 1929, NLS, Acc. 13226.

on the Riviera or elsewhere'. She describes the new house: 'three bedrooms, a nursery, a bathroom, a study, dining room, kitchen, outhouses and a pleasant garden full of flowering bushes and fruit trees'. They have managed to furnish the house 'on the instalment plan' for a sum which she translates to be 'a little more than 500 dollars'. It will be 'a happy and a pretty house to live in' and she hopes to see the Masons in it. They are also to have a telephone, and this will help them keep in contact.[2]

Willa's long-planned novel had finally been sent to Secker, although she received enquiries from Cape and Huebsch in America as well. In addition, she was asked by the P.E.N. Club to partner Hilaire Belloc in a discussion on Bernard Shaw's *Joan* for the *Radio Times*. 'Willa is beginning to emerge from domesticity and come out some more into public life', she writes to the Masons; 'I may be a public figure yet in another's year's time!' The letter ends—'Here are two very bad snapshots of my two boys. The light is better now and I shall photograph Gavin largely one of these days. He is really nicer than these photographs indicate. Going to be very like Edwin, with a touch of me.' As for Edwin and herself, they are 'both looking better than we have done for years. This is partly because we have taken to playing Badminton, without any net or any rules except to hit as hard as you can.' Edwin adds his own greetings, wishing that they could meet again, 'here, in the south of France, or anywhere', adding 'We don't meet real friends like you in a blue moon, and we've never met anybody since we said good-bye to you who has been able to fill the gap.' He also tells them that Willa is 'looking younger & more charming than ever she did.'[3] This is an interesting communication from both of them in the way it signals a continued longing for the European milieu that had suited them so well, the absence of truly like-minded friends among their current English acquaintances, and perhaps also the sense of isolation they had felt in Dormansland with so many literary commitments to fulfil. The letter also reveals, even if humorously, Willa's deep-seated longing to be recognized for her own literary contribution.

Their garden and its Crowborough surroundings were lovely in summertime. Edwin wrote to Sydney Schiff 'We like this part of the country immensely,' and he was enthusiastic about its holiday potential when he wrote to his sister and brother-in-law about the possibility of their daughters coming for a summer holiday. 'There's lots of books here for them to browse among and hills and commons to wander about in, and they'll have nothing to do except enjoy themselves.'[4] The Thorburns were at this time living in Portobello, just outside Edinburgh, and so Edwin suggested that the best way for his nieces to travel to London would be by boat from Leith: 'It's far cheaper and more pleasant,' and he adds, 'I'll certainly come up to London to bring them down here: it would be an awe-inspiring

---

[2] Ibid.
[3] Ibid., postscript by Edwin Muir.
[4] Edwin Muir, letter to Sydney Schiff, 10 December 1929, Schiff Papers, BL, Add MS 52920; letter to Lizzie and George Thorburrn, 23 July 1929, NLS, Acc. 13226.

experience for them to try and find their way from the docks to Victoria among a race talking a foreign tongue, for it takes some time to make out Cockney.'[5] In fact, the girls' summer holiday was a great success, and they would return to Crowborough enthusiastically the following year. Edwin wrote to their parents at Christmas that he and Willa 'still remember the wild doings we had with them,' and asked if they were still 'as great demons at cards'.[6] For the Muirs themselves, on the other hand, the end of summer brought with it some familiar problems and some new ones. Edwin wrote to Mary and Arthur Mason in October 1929, 'Our life here is very quiet, and sometimes rather dull, and we would like to have people dropping in on us.' Their immediate neighbours had proved to be less pleasant than those Willa had mocked in Dormansland for their clichéd responses to bringing up a baby. The Crowborough house was semi-detached, and the residents in the other half were in the habit of playing a gramophone loudly in the garden. When Willa asked if it could be turned down because it disturbed the baby, neighbourliness came to an end. There was also a large garden on the other side of their house, rich with berry-laden pergolas. These berries, however, were found to be hops used for making and selling home-brewed ale, an activity they uncovered only when their cook was found lying drunk in the kitchen. In the winter the house and its environs became as difficult to handle as their previous dank country cottages had been. Edwin wrote 'It's dreary here now, nothing but wet and mud.'[7]

Other problems were more serious. Willa had always been susceptible to throat infections including bronchitis, a situation not helped by her regular cigarette smoking. In the late autumn she developed a quinsy throat that required abscesses to be lanced on three occasions. Then, while she was still in the recovery stage, a telegram arrived from Montrose saying that her mother was dangerously ill and that they should come north immediately. They stayed for three days with Willa's mother, who had terminal cancer and had now also suffered a heart attack, and when they returned south Willa's throat problems recurred. To complicate matters further, Gavin somehow acquired a poisoned finger. At the beginning of December Edwin wrote to the Schiffs—'We're all looking forward now to a long period free of accidents.' But more were to come. By Christmas rain was leaking through the roof and they received word that Willa's mother was dying. Willa felt bound to go north with her child, since her mother had 'set her heart on seeing Gavin this Christmas'. Edwin would stay in Crowborough and attempt to catch up on the writing work that had accumulated. Then Willa's mother's death was followed almost immediately by that of her brother Willie, who had mental health problems and was 'far gone in consumption'. Writing to the Masons, Willa had taken comfort in the thought that 'he will be happier if he dies than he has ever been

---

[5] Edwin's letter to Lizzie and George Thorburn, 23 July 1929, NLS, Acc. 13226.
[6] Edwin Muir, letter to the Thorburns, 23 December 1929, NLS, Acc. 13226.
[7] Edwin Muir, letter to Mary and Arthur Mason, 18 October 1929, NLS, Acc. 13226; letter from Edwin to Lizzie, 23 December 1929, NLS, Acc.13226.

alive,' but she found the death of her mother difficult to deal with, despite the fact that they had never been especially close to each other.[8]

Such disasters came on the heels of an exhaustive period of translation work. Since the publication and success of *Jew Süss* in November 1926, an increasing amount of the Muirs' fragile income had been coming from translation. Feuchtwanger's *The Ugly Duchess* was published in November 1927 and his *Two Anglo-Saxon Plays* in April 1929, followed by Gerhart Hauptmann's *Dramatic Works* Vol. 9 and Ludwig Renn's *War* in June, and Ernst Glaeser's *Class of 1902* in October. Willa's solo translation of Hans Carossa's *A Roumanian Diary* was also published in 1929 under the pseudonym of Agnes Neill Scott, and she was engaged to translate further books by Carossa. In addition to this, Edwin was heavily involved with reviewing commitments until the end of 1928, when he decided to give up reviewing, at least temporarily. Both he and Willa were trying to pursue their own creative writing projects, although Edwin was more successful than Willa who, as the principal and more competent linguist, simply shouldered the burden of the translation work. Nor were all of these commissions satisfying texts to translate, artistically, or intellectually.[9]

A task of a different order, however, was brought to their attention in 1929. When taking a short break in Scotland in the spring to search out sources for his biography of John Knox, Edwin had come upon a book by a German-language author he had not previously encountered, *Das Schloss* by the Prague writer Franz Kafka. The Muirs had heard nothing about Kafka or about his Jewish and German-language background when they were in the new Czechoslovakian Republic in the early 1920s, although *Das Schloss* had been both begun and abandoned unfinished during the period when they were resident in Prague. They realized that they had found something special in the way of modern literature. Edwin wrote to Sydney Schiff from Crowborough on 8 July that he had discovered both Rilke's prose book *Die Aufzeichnungen des Malte Laurids Brigge* and Kafka's *Das Schloss* about the same time, 'and was more moved than by anything I have come across for a long time'. He found Kafka's book 'still more strange in its atmosphere' than the Rilke.

> It is a purely metaphysical and mystical dramatic novel; the ordinary moral judgments do not come in at all; everything happens on a mysterious spiritual plane which was obviously the supreme reality to the author; and yet in a curious way everything is given solidly and concretely. The book was left unfinished when

---

[8] Edwin Muir, letter to Sydney Schiff, 10 December, 1929, Schiff Papers BL, Add MS 52920; Willa Muir, letter to Mary and Arthur Mason, 23 December, 1929, NLS, Ac. 13226.

[9] A fuller account of the Muirs' translation skills and their reputation among other translators will be given in Chapter 12 'Translating for a Living.'

Kafka died a few years ago. [...] it appeals particularly to the part of me which wrote *The Marionette*. It is quite unique, and I think first class of its kind.[10]

Edwin recommended *Das Schloss* to Secker for translation, and once he had completed his biography of John Knox he began to work on the book with Willa. It must have been the principal and most satisfying, as well as their most taxing contract during that first summer and autumn in Crowborough, when Edwin's nieces may have helped to take little Gavin off their hands. Kafka's *The Castle* was published by Secker in March 1930 (a quick turn-around for such a complex book), together with their translation of *Eleonora Duse* by Emil Alphons Rheinhardt. In view of this workload, it is perhaps not surprising that Willa succumbed to a serious throat illness towards the end of the year. Edwin himself was close to nervous collapse when he stayed behind in Crowborough to deal with unfinished work while Willa went to Montrose with Gavin to see her dying mother at Christmas. After the publication of the Kafka and Rheinhardt in the spring of 1930 both were exhausted, and they decided to take themselves off to their much-loved Menton in order to recuperate. They left for France, without Gavin, in the late spring of 1930.

Edwin and Willa could be what one might call a little unreliable with the truth in their memoirs and correspondence. Edwin often misremembers dates and precise details of past situations, and tends to be selective in what he wants or does not want to communicate to friends or the public at large, as in the case of his autobiography. He also kept his correspondents (except, perhaps, his earlier friends John Holms and Hugh Kingsmill) in separate compartments. Willa excused herself for a long gap in writing to the Masons on one occasion, by saying that she had a 'strong disinclination to write letters except out of a fullness of life and energy',[11] a comment supported by the energetic and dramatic nature of her letters to friends such as the Masons and Flos McNeill, even when the information she is communicating is itself concerned with disasters of one kind or another. She appears to wait till she has recovered sufficiently from her troubles to be able to create a dramatic performance out of them or to put a high gloss on their eventual outcomes. This is very much the case with their flight to Menton in the spring of 1930. In *Belonging*, Willa mentions briefly that as a result of the exhaustion caused by overwork and the illness problems of late 1929, they 'engaged a nurse for Gavin and went down to Mentone without him for a recuperative holiday'. In a contemporaneous letter to the Masons of July 1930, however, she writes that 'both Edwin and I were run down so much that we took a month's holiday in Mentone, leaving the baby at a Montessori school near here'. She reports that Gavin is 'a Montessori genius: in other words, he romps through the Montessori apparatus at indecent speed'. And having described his appearance and the physical characteristics he appears

---

[10] Edwin Muir, letter to Sydney Schiff, 8 July 1929, Schiff Papers, BL, Add MS 52920.
[11] Willa Muir to Mary and Arthur Mason, August 1933, no specific day given, NLS, Acc. 13226.

to have inherited from each parent, she continues, 'We love him exceedingly. In fact, when we came back from Mentone, we were as sentimental about seeing him again as any young thing could be about seeing a sweetheart—same queer, tight feeling in the chest!' Neither she nor Edwin appeared to realize how destabilizing it must have been for a child of two and a half years to be suddenly separated from his known environment of home and parents and placed in an unfamiliar educational or nursery establishment. They would also appear to have attempted to place him as a school boarder early the next year when he was just over three years old, but had to bring him home again as a result of his extreme distress. It was clear that he was an emotionally vulnerable child. In his turn, Edwin said nothing at all about leaving Gavin behind when he wrote to his sister at the very late date of 23 July 1930 to ask if his nieces could come to Crowborough again for their holiday in August. In his letter he makes his customary apologies for 'being such a long time in writing', lists all the troubles they had experienced at the turn of the year, and continues

> Finally we both took a complete month's rest—we had to, for we couldn't read a book, far less try to write one. It's the first holiday we have had for three years, and we are both feeling very much the better after it, although Willa is still troubled a little by lumbago; although I think that too is passing over.

He does not say that the 'month's rest' was in France, or that Gavin had to be boarded out in a Montessori School while they were absent.[12]

Another element missing from correspondence and published accounts of this escape to Menton is the fact that mental and physical exhaustion did not prevent them stopping off in Paris to give assistance to John Holms and his new companion, the American heiress and later art collector Peggy Guggenheim. Edwin would appear to have lost touch somewhat with both Holms and Hugh Kingsmill since the return from France in mid-1927 and the birth of Gavin later that year. Holms and his partner Dorothy Jennings had continued to live in St Tropez and the surrounding area, where they met Peggy Guggenheim, who had come to St Tropez with her husband and family. Peggy was unhappy in her marriage, and Holms must have been his usual fascinating self, for he and Peggy eloped together, leaving a distressed Dorothy, a vindictive husband, and unhappy children. In her later autobiography, *Out of This Century: Confessions of an Art Addict*, Peggy Guggenheim describes her various meetings with Edwin Muir, the friendship between him and Holms, and the assistance and advice Edwin gave her after John's untimely death in London in 1934. One of the meetings described by Peggy was in Paris, where she and John were staying in the spring of 1930 and awaiting, with some

---

[12] *Belonging*, p. 151, letter to the Masons, 16 July 1930; Edwin Muir, letter to his sister Lizzie, 23 July 1930, both in NLS, Acc. 13226.

trepidation, the arrival from America of Peggy's mother, who disapproved of her daughter's situation. Apparently the Muirs had been called up from Menton to help with a potentially difficult luncheon meeting, and they seem to have contributed 'a good beginning' to future discussions. They had also, by sheer unlucky chance, chosen a hotel in the Sorbonne area where Dorothy Jennings, Holms's previous long-term partner, had booked a room in the same corridor. In the unpublished draft of *Belonging*, Willa writes that Dorothy was 'hysterical, weeping and shouting by turns, we thought she would never be got out of our room where she was imploring us not to go near "that woman's flat"'. The Muirs had already engaged themselves to lunch at Peggy's comfortable appartement in the Rue Campagne Première, where Peggy's mother was expected imminently, and so they had to 'outwit' Dorothy in order to escape from their own modest hotel. Dorothy was apparently 'always at the door' of the Guggenheim flat, 'screaming and making scenes' so that 'someone had to be kept on guard to prevent her from forcing her way in.' Willa's unpublished account also reports that 'Holms was dressed up to the nines in a new suit, hand-made shoes and gold cuff-links; his beard was pinked to a neat point and he was very elegant.' She continues—

> So was the luncheon. We had scarcely sat down to coffee afterwards when the bell rang and Peggy's mother stood in the doorway; she glared at Edwin and Holms, wondering which of the two was the villain, but with charming tact Holms relieved her uncertainty by merely pressing a wall-button and saying to the parlourmaid: 'Another cup of coffee, please, Mary'.[13]

Willa does not say how Edwin responded to this situation and Edwin himself does not refer to the Parisian aspect of their escape to France in his accompanying note to the Masons of July 1930. He says merely that 'we often thought of you when we were in Menton this last time,' and adds, 'Holms appeared in the scene: he's in with a rich American woman now and living on the fat of the land, but still unhappy, poor chap.' Similarly, in a letter to Sydney Schiff Edwin mentions only that he and Willa had gone down to the south of France 'really because we weren't at all well', and regrets that 'we missed seeing you in Paris' (where the Schiffs would appear to have been staying at that time). He does not mention the encounter in Paris with Holms, Peggy, her disapproving mother, and a distressed and irate Dorothy.[14]

The Thorburn girls' summer holiday in Crowborough in 1930 passed off enjoyably, although it ended with a slight accident when the girls fell off a bike they were riding together down a steep hill. There was compensation, however, in the

---

[13] Peggy Guggenheim, *Out of This Century*, p. 99; Willa Muir, unpublished draft of *Belonging*, Ch. 7, UStA, 38466/3/7.

[14] Edwin Muir, letter to Mary and Arthur Mason, July 1930 (no specific day), NLS, Acc. 13226; letter to Sydney Schiff, 20 June 1930, Schiff Papers, BL, Add MS 52920.

fact that when they arrived home, they discovered that there were two new bikes awaiting them. Willa wrote to their mother in early September.

> I hope you don't mind my giving bikes to the bairns. They won't really hurt themselves. The accident here was caused by the fact that two of them were on the one bike going down a steep hill, and I think it has been well rubbed in to them since that going downhill needs *brakes*. They won't go down a hill in that fashion again.[15]

In later life, both girls always emphasised how generous Willa was in her relationship with them and the whole family. Willa was equally generous in sharing the 'windfall' of money she received after her mother's death, writing that she would be glad if Lizzie 'would accept the enclosed, for you to keep against a rainy day'. In contrast, her behaviour in relation to Gavin was, as always, somewhat puzzling as she tells Lizzie that she and Edwin are 'very relieved because wee Gavin has just been circumcised and has survived the ordeal splendidly. He is a little trump.' It is difficult to understand why the young child should have been put through such an ordeal unless for necessary medical reasons. Perhaps Willa was still under the influence of Truby King's child-rearing methodology. Her further comment to Lizzie is less than tactful when she writes, 'Now that he is turned into a Jew do you think we should call him Moses Muir?'[16]

By the end of 1930 both Muirs had made progress with their novel-writing as well as their continuing flow of translation work. Edwin's novel *The Three Brothers* was completed and due for publication by Heinemann in February 1931. Willa had almost completed her Montrose novel, which would be published the same year as *Imagined Corners*. She had also completed and published her translation of Carossa's *Die Kindheit—Childhood*, to be followed in 1931 by his *Boyhood and Youth*. Edwin seems to claim a translator's role in *Childhood* when he writes to Sydney Schiff that he was thinking of doing an article on Carossa, 'a writer I am very fond of', adding, 'We have just finished translating a book of his called "Childhood" of which you will have a copy when it appears.'[17] All the Carossa books were however translated under a new translation pseudonym of 'Agnes Neill Scott' that is usually considered to be a marker of Willa's identity as sole translator. Edwin's casual use of the Muir translation firm's 'we' on this occasion, when the published book identifies only a single translator, is the kind of slight that Willa would remember in later years, when she felt that her role as principal translator had never been formally acknowledged. On the other hand, Edwin's role was often inaccurately enhanced because he was the one who published the critical articles on several of the authors translated, including Carossa and Kafka.

---

[15] Willa Muir, letter to Lizzie Thorburn, 2 September 1930, NLS, Acc. 13226
[16] Ibid.
[17] Edwin Muir, letter to Sydney Schiff, 29 September 1930, Schiff Papers, BL, Add MS 52920.

Unfortunately, *The Three Brothers* was not the success for which Edwin had hoped. He wrote to the Schiffs thanking them for their 'lovely letters' about the book but saying that it had been 'a pretty complete failure publicly'. Yet at the same time he had 'a feeling—which may be false, however—that only now am I really finding myself as a writer. I hope that is true.' So, optimistically, 'I have started on another one.' On the more positive side, they had received a book for translation that promised the satisfaction they had both found in Kafka's *The Castle*. This was the first part of Hermann Broch's trilogy *Die Schlafwandler*, *The Sleepwalkers*, and it marks the beginning of a strong friendship as well as a translating relationship (especially on Willa's part) with the Austrian author. Edwin told Schiff that this new novel 'seems to me really first rate, and very beautiful, and not unlike Proust in its great truth and psychological subtlety'. And then at last, in June 1931, Willa's *Imagined Corners*, begun so long ago in the south of France, finally achieved publication. Writing to the Masons with a promise to send them a copy, Willa added cautiously, 'I don't know yet what reception it will have.'[18]

In remembering their residence in Menton in 1926 and 1927, Willa contrasted her own approach to creative writing with that of Edwin, saying that while he worked through symbols she relied 'on the empathy of personal feeling and memories'; and she hoped that she might be able to use these emotions 'to present a story in a Montrose setting, imagining what might have happened had I married my Rugby champion and gone to live there.'[19] Willa's 'Montrose' novel is a fine female *Bildungsroman* in which the heroine's growth to maturity and understanding begins after a mistaken marriage in 'Calderwick', a small town on the east coast of Scotland.

Imagined Corners takes its title from John Donne's Holy Sonnet 'At the round earth's imagin'd corners blow / Your trumpets, Angells, and arise, arise / From death, you numberlesse infinities / of soules'. Willa had written to the Masons in October 1929 that she was thinking of calling her novel (which had her 'in its grip like an octopus') 'Houses of Clay', a title that might suggest the collapse of former hopes and relationships, or a recognition that a wrong route has been taken.[20] The eventual title, however, references vigour and new life, both in the energy of word-sound and rhythmic movement in the opening of Donne's actual sonnet and in its philosophical message of new life arising out of death. *Imagined Corners* is therefore a story of journeys of discovery—on the part of the young heroine, Elizabeth, in particular, but also on the part of several of the subsidiary characters whose narratives help create solidity and the sense of a particular community in the plot. Some later critics have compared the novel to the story of Dorothea in George Eliot's *Middlemarch*, or to the narrative in Eliot's *Daniel Deronda*, in

---

[18] Ibid.; Willa Muir, letter to Mary and Arthur Mason, 30 June 1931, NLS, Acc. 13226.
[19] *Belonging*, pp. 125, 126.
[20] For Donne's poem see *The Poems of John Donne*, ed. Herbert Grierson (London: Oxford University Press, 1933), p. 296.

that both these heroines discover, after marriage, how misguided their earlier judgements have been. But neither of these nineteenth-century heroines is given the opportunity for transformation and new growth created by Willa in the open ending she gives to her novel. The last two sections of the book are titled 'The Glass is Shaken' and 'Precipitation', and these chemical metaphors suggest fluidity and change in a way that George Eliot's earlier metaphor of the 'web' in *Middlemarch* cannot manage.

Imagined Corners is a novel written in the context of change, and one that responds to the challenges of change in a female-centred way, even as it uses irony and metaphor to communicate its ideas and viewpoints. The ironic narrative voice in the opening chapter prepares the reader to encounter a Scottish small town on a sunny September day which 'turned its back on the sea'—and by implication on the unknown world beyond it—while looking inward to its own life and its own rigid customs and opinions.

> All this late summer peace and fragrance belonged to the municipality. The burgh of Calderwick owned its golf and its bathing, its sand and its gorse. The larks nested in municipal grass, the crows waddled on municipal turf. But few of the citizens of Calderwick followed their example. The season for summer visitors was over, although summer still lingered, and the burgh of Calderwick was busy about its jute mills, its shipping, schools, shops, offices and dwelling-houses. The larks, the crows and the gulls, after all, were not ratepayers. It is doubtful whether they even knew that they were domiciled in Scotland.[21]

Willa then turns her irony towards her principal character. Elizabeth Shand is a young, inexperienced university graduate, who had surrendered to emotional impulse and married a young man from the leading family in Calderwick, a man with no intellectual interests and a reputation for wild behaviour. In one scene Elizabeth meets with her husband's doubtful spinster aunt, who had cared for him as a child as a result of the death of his mother. (She also represents one of the 'surplus women' in the novel who perform the caring community roles discussed by Willa in *Women: An Inquiry*.) Elizabeth attempts to explain the mutual attraction between Hector and herself in breathlessly erotic and self-extinguishing terms.

> They were both wild and passionate; they wanted the whole of life at one draught; they would sink or swim together. Images flowed through her mind: in the air or under the sea or rooted in the earth she saw herself and Hector, living, growing, swimming, breasting the wind together. She thought of his wide shoulders, his

[21] *Imagined Corners* in *Imagined Selves*, p. 2.

strong neck, his swift and lovely feet ... 'What have brains to do with it?' she asked looking up. 'It's a miracle, Aunt Janet; a miracle that sometimes takes my breath away.'

After one of an increasing number of quarrels with Hector, she begins her road to discovery when she wakes in the night and feels 'that she was lost and no longer knew who she was'.

> She had been dreaming that she was at home, but now the window, faintly perceptible, was in the wrong place, and she knew without seeing it that she would collide with unfamiliar furniture were she to get out of bed. There was a sweat on her brow and her heart was thumping; the world stretched out on all sides into dark impersonal nothingness and she herself was a terrifying anonymity.

Elizabeth 'takes refuge in a device of her childhood', and uses words similar to those her author had used only a few years before, when she caught a sight of her unrecognizable, pregnant self in a long mirror—'I'm me, she thought; me, me; here behind my eyes.'[22]

The ironic narrative voice in *Imagined Corners* is on the whole sympathetic to the young Elizabeth, although less so to her fellow townspeople as it lays bare the self-delusion that marks so many of their lives. What makes the novel such an interesting and fresh account of female self-discovery, however, is its exploration of the heroine's situation through the invention of no less than two, even three 'Elizabeth Shands'. There is the main character, the Elizabeth Shand by marriage, the clever but sexually inexperienced young woman who is beginning to realize that sexual passion is not necessarily the only quality necessary for a fulfilling marriage or for a fulfilling life. Then there is her sister-in-law, known to her family as Lizzie, who as a young girl shocked the community by running off to the Continent with her school's German teacher. She has now returned to Calderwick as the sophisticated Elise, Frau Doktor Mütze, widow of a European scholar, who has come home to Calderwick in search of another Lizzie, her angry young self, in the hope of coming to some understanding of the course her adult life has taken. While all three Elizabeths represent stages in the author's own journey to maturity, this life-writing source developed a life of its own in the making of *Imagined Corners*, serving to widen its range of interrogation and maintaining a creative distance from its autobiographical roots. Implicitly, however, it also provides evidence of its author's continuing sense of alienation in relation to the small Scottish community she herself lived in as a child and young adult, and which in several respects remained with her throughout her life in relation to Scotland as a whole. Willa never seemed to lose that sense of being a 'displaced person' in relation to Scottish life.

[22] Ibid., pp. 50, 64.

Unlike the essay *Women: An Inquiry*, the novel *Imagined Corners* was well received. Willa wrote to Edwin's sister Lizzie that the reviews 'have been good, and some of them very good'. *The Times Literary Supplement* found it 'excellent' in parts although the reviewer was hesitant about the plot's strong focus on the 'two Elizabeth Shands'. The recently established *Modern Scot* was more adventurous in its appreciation, understanding that the book's author was 'concerned with psychological and philosophical problems of moment, and shows her characters in relation not only to the petty standards of the township but to the complex modern consciousness'. While not suggesting that the *Imagined Corners* author 'is a writer on a par with Flaubert', the reviewer nevertheless finds that 'she is definitely the same kind of self-conscious artist, an aristocrat of letters, compared to the democrats who never lift their eyes from the kailyard to contemplate in imagination the "round earth's imagin'd corners"'. Some of Willa's Scottish friends, while praising the novel as a whole, were concerned that it was perhaps not sufficiently Scottish-centred in a positive way. Willa wrote to Flos McNeill in July 1931—

> Your letter took my breath away and I am only beginning to recover it. What a peculiar agitation it rouses in me to find people who have been moved by my novel! Peculiar, for, of course, to move people in some way is obviously the purpose of a novel, so I should be prepared for such an effect; but I am much less serene than you think my book is and commendation from people I know puts me in a painful flutter, just as disparagement from people I know makes me resentful, whereas disparagement from strangers leaves me cold. So I assure you that I was incapable of replying by return!

Willa then comments that she is particularly pleased that the book has moved her friend 'to a positive feeling—that was what it was meant to do; but apparently, some brains are needed for the understanding of my work, since there have been so many utterly stupid comments, stupid both in praise and in blame'. This lack of understanding would appear to have been centred not only on the ultimate positive outcome of the intertwined Elizabeth Shand narratives of female development but, for Scottish readers in particular, on the seeming lack of a positively Scottish dimension in the conclusion of a plot that sees the young Elizabeth leaving Scotland for the south of France in the company of the Europeanised Elise. Willa writes—

> Let me finish off just what I have to say about *Imagined Corners*: you object to my letting Elise leave Scotland. Well, my dear, it was supposed to be 1913, when there was little Nationalism; also, I was thinking more of Elise, when I followed her, than of national sentiment; and Elise would not have stayed in Calderwick, however it might have benefited from her presence—which I don't deny. I was not describing what *ought* to be in Scotland, but what actually would have happened

there in 1913 to the characters in my book; and *I* think I am right in conceiving that Elise & Hector were bound to leave it. Elizabeth was almost equally bound to come back: but all that I left to the imagination of the reader, being more concerned to present an illumination of life in Scotland than a reformation.

Willa would probably have been appreciative of the way in which later twentieth-century and early twenty-first-century readers have recognized the novel's ironic and metaphorical narrative form, together with its philosophical and psychological dimension, both in its main female-development plot and in the accompanying subplot involving a variety of local characters. On the other hand, she may well have felt it necessary to remind later critics who have interpreted the departure of Elise and Elizabeth for the south of France as a lesbian ending, that she was describing what would actually have happened in Scotland in 1913 as opposed, say, to 2013. Committed as she always was to 'belonging with Edwin', Willa may have been unlikely—at least consciously—to offer her character a development that would signal a same-sex conclusion, but the potential does remain. The Schiffs were both appreciative and perceptive readers of the book. Willa wrote to Sydney—

> You are a brick to send me such comforting words about my book. There is much in it that is only suggested and half-stated, because I was afraid of putting more into my characters than probability would bear, and the very suspension of my beliefs in the book seems to have presented some people from seeing that they were there at all. But you have felt that they were there, and I am very pleased.

Then she adds in that surprisingly uncertain way in which she so often speaks of her own creative writing, 'The next one will really be much better. I am learning that one must understand with sympathy the most awful people, if one is to write about them: and I think there will be more real understanding in my next book, and the irony will be less obviously on the surface.' Nevertheless, the irony and the open, often metaphorical, nature of the narrative in *Imagined Corners* do play a major part in giving the book its special quality.[23]

Edwin's nieces again came to Crowborough for their summer holiday in 1931 and this time their mother came with them. Willa wrote to Lizzie that she was looking forward to seeing the two 'kids' again, and it is in this letter that she also communicates that she and Edwin had earlier tried to place Gavin in a school as a boarder (perhaps the Montessori one, or even Neill's Summerhill—she does not give details). What she does say is 'My kid, Gavin, has been at home since

---

[23] Willa Muir, letter to Lizzie Thorburn, 12 July 1931, NLS, Acc. 13226; TLS review (anon.), 2 July 1931, p. 526; *The Modern Scot* 2.2 review (anon.) July 1931, pp. 171–3; Willa Muir, letter to F. Marian McNeill, 21 July 1931, NLS, Acc. 26195; Willa Muir, added piece to Edwin's letter to Sydney and Violet Schiff of 22 March 1932, Schiff Papers, BL, Add MS 52920.

the beginning of February, for he was breaking his little heart at the school, & we brought him home again.' She continues that 'he is a large, strong, affectionate, comical little boy; a mixture of Edwin & of me, to look at, which I think will be a handsome mixture when he grows up. [...] And since he came home for good he has simply blossomed. I have got an excellent nurse who comes every day and takes him out.' Clearly it was an impossible task for Willa to be chief translator, writer of her own creative fiction, carer of a three years old child, and general housekeeper—for although she and Edwin appear to have employed a cleaner and/or cook/housekeeper in their various rented houses, there would still have been a need for someone to oversee the running of the house generally and interact with the employed help. And Edwin himself seemed never to be sufficiently free of writing commitments to help on the domestic front. Gavin's share of his busy parents' time must therefore have been limited. Yet neither parent seemed to be aware of his need for their personal and regular attention. He appears to have been slow in learning to speak, for example, perhaps because his parents did not make enough time to speak regularly with him. When he was 2 years old, Edwin wrote often in letters to family and friends that the child was 'a sweet-tempered little chap, running about at our heels now whenever he can, not yet speaking, however'. Willa wrote to the Masons that he sang to himself 'queer wordless wavering tunes, but he hasn't yet begun to talk intelligibly'.[24] Gavin, however, was speaking by the summer of 1931 when he was on the road to his fourth birthday in October; and he would have plenty of people to speak with when his aunt and cousins arrived. Willa was glad that his relations would also be able to keep Edwin company, if necessary, for she herself was waiting for a specific date to go into hospital for attention to the problems that had followed Gavin's difficult birth. She wrote to Mary Mason, 'I am now held up by a rubber thing, but I have to go into hospital for a fortnight as soon as I can afford it and be put right. After that, a new lease of life for Willa!' Unfortunately, the operation turned out to be more serious than expected and Willa remained in hospital for three weeks and had to stay in bed for another two weeks when she came home. Edwin did not say how he managed to cope with being left in charge of Gavin, and the household generally, when he replied to his niece Ethel's enquires about the outcome of Willa's operation. He told her that Gavin 'often mentions you and Irene'; 'he's mad on signals, telegraph poles and arithmetic in general; and you can hear his voice floating from the nursery at any time, "two eights sixteen" and so on.'[25] Willa's operation put on hold their wish to make a move from Crowborough. Edwin had earlier confided to Sydney Schiff that he would really like to move from the area before another winter set in, since their winters had been fraught with ill-health problems and they felt so

---

[24] Willa Muir, letter to Lizzie Thorburn, 12 July 1931, NLS, Acc. 13226; Willa Muir, letter to Mary and Arthur Mason, 18 October 1929, NLS, Acc. 13226.
[25] Willa Muir, letter to Mary Mason, 30 June 1931, NLS, Acc. 13226; Edwin Muir, letter to his niece Ethel Ross, 6 October 1921, NLS, Acc. 13226.

cut off from their London literary contacts and like-minded friends. For the time being, however, while his relatives were in the process of moving to a new house in Glasgow, and his niece Ethel was preparing for entry to Glasgow University, Edwin, Willa, and Gavin would have to be content with their Crowborough life for a little while longer.

PART III
THE POLITICAL THIRTIES

9
Changing Worlds and a Hampstead Idyll 1930–1933

> For us, living in Hampstead was like living with one's True Love; there was no possibility of ever preferring another part of London.
>
> Willa Muir, *Belonging* (1968)

Housebound in Crowborough, the Muirs were feeling cut off from their London friends, even as they were starting to forge contacts with the literary revival scene in Scotland. While travelling in Europe in the early 1920s, Francis George Scott had persuaded Edwin to send poems and some articles to Christopher Grieve's little magazines to give support to the new Scottish literary movement. At that point Edwin had not appeared to be enthusiastic about the quality of Grieve's publications. Writing from Vienna in December 1923 about Scottish Home Rule politics, he told his sister, 'There's a man C. M. Grieve, a Socialist, running the idea in *The Scottish Nation*—a very bad paper which I sometimes see.' He and Willa went on to meet Grieve and his wife Peggy in Montrose in 1924, after their return from Neill's school on the Sonntagberg, and although they got on together well enough, Edwin was not inclined to become part of Grieve's Scots-language literary revival movement. During his young years in Glasgow he had had no contact with Scottish writers, sending material to Orage's *New Age* and seeking recognition instead in the London literary scene.[1]

On the other hand, after the publication of Hugh MacDiarmid's three volumes of poetry, *Sangschaw*, *Penny Wheep*, and *A Drunk Man Looks at the Thistle* in 1925 and 1926, Edwin appeared to take the Scottish literary revival more seriously as a critic, if not as a contributor. His friend Denis Saurat had written a positive account of the new movement in the article 'Le groupe de "la renaissance écossaise"' in the *Revue Anglo-Americaine* of April 1924, and Edwin produced his own positive review of *Sangschaw*, in the *Saturday Review of Literature* in October 1925. In January 1927 he reviewed *A Drunk Man Looks at the Thistle* in *The Nation and Athenaeum*, in which he commented on the poem's 'characteristic and original' form, and found that the 'synthetic Scots which the author has created himself' is used 'with ease and force'. Edwin was acute in his perception of the 'psychological or philosophical scheme' of this long poem, as he was about MacDiarmid being

---

[1] Edwin Muir, letter to Lizzie and George Thorburn, *Selected Letters*, p. 30; *Belonging*, p. 116.

'as much interested in the possible as the actual'.[2] Later, in a *Criterion* review of 1931, he was one of the few critics to write supportively and perceptively about *To Circumjack Cencrastus*. It would seem, too, that from the late 1920s onwards both Muirs were gradually increasing their contacts with Scotland. Edwin had been north to research his book on John Knox, after all, and since Gavin's birth there had been visits to family and friends in Scotland. In her memoir, *Octobiography*, published in 1976, the Scottish poet Helen Cruickshank recalled Hugh MacDiarmid's founding of the Scottish Centre of International P.E.N. in 1927, and she herself became Honorary Secretary the following year. She wrote that she had set her heart 'on strengthening our Scottish centre by bringing in some of our ex-patriate Scottish writers in London, and we soon added to our list of members the names of Catherine and Donald Carswell, Dr A. J. Cronin, George Malcolm Thomson, Naomi Mitchison, Edwin and Willa Muir, Rachel Annand Taylor and R. B. Cunninghame Graham'.[3] It is not clear exactly when the Muirs joined Scottish P.E.N. (early archives are limited), but their names appear on the List of Members for 1931, with 'The Nook, Blackness Road, Crowborough' given as their address. They are also given as attending members from the London section (with their new Hampstead address of 7 Downshire Hill) in the list of delegates and attendees at the International P.E.N. Congress held in Edinburgh in June 1934.

It may have been through Scottish P.E.N. that Edwin and Willa made contact with James Whyte, a young, wealthy American who had come to live in St Andrews. Even more significant than his association with Scottish P.E.N. was Whyte's founding and editing of a new cultural magazine, *The Modern Scot*, which continued the internationalist and national revival ethos of MacDiarmid's little magazines of the 1920s. Whyte, however, was able to pay contributors and to develop his journal in a more professional and sustained way than MacDiarmid's ill-funded magazines had ever managed. Edwin does not mention the *Modern Scot* in his autobiography, but his correspondence includes a letter to Whyte from Crowborough on 10 September 1931, in which he writes pessimistically about the 'immediate hope of an economically self-supporting Scottish literature', adding, 'and it may be that there isn't ever any ultimate hope of it.' In contrast to Whyte's optimism about *The Modern Scot*, Edwin appears to believe that 'Scotland will probably linger in limbo as long as the British Empire lasts', and that ultimately 'London will become quite literally the capital of the British Isles in a sense that it has never yet quite been; that, in other words, it will become our national capital in just as real a sense as it is the capital of an ordinary English man to-day.' For Edwin, Scotland is 'in a false position' and therefore 'A Scottish writer is in a false position. [...] The very words "a Scottish writer" have a slightly unconvincing ring to me.'[4] Edwin's own thinking

---

[2] Edwin Muir, 'Verse', *Nation and Athenaeum*, XL, 22 January 1927, p. 568.
[3] Helen B. Cruickshank, *Octobiography* (Montrose: Standard Press, 1976), p. 76.
[4] Edwin Muir, letter to James Whyte, 10 September 1931, *Selected Letters*, pp. 70–1.

at this point may have been less dogmatic than such comments might suggest, for he and Willa were going through a particularly difficult stage in their lives, isolated in Crowborough, coping with translation commitments and worries about Willa's health.

Edwin obviously admired what MacDiarmid had achieved in his own poetry, writing that 'Grieve is an exception to all rules'; but at the same time, he was aware that such innovative work had not always received in Scotland the appreciation and support that it deserved. When mixing with the Čapeks and their theatre circle in Prague in the early 1920s, Edwin had admired the vitality of the new republic and the public's positive response to Čapek, hoping that 'Edinburgh might become a similar place and that Scotland might become a nation again.' A few years later, in 1927, writing from Menton to his brother-in-law George about the literary revival, he notes that 'it seems a pity that Scotland should always be kept back by England, and I hope the Scottish Republic comes about.' At the same time, however, 'I feel rather detached, as I've often told Grieve, because after all I'm not Scotch, I'm an Orkney man, a good Scandinavian, and my true country is Norway, or Denmark, or Iceland, or some place like that.' He ends 'But this is nonsense, I'm afraid, though there's some sense in it, as Lizzie will agree.'[5] It seems that neither Edwin nor Willa ever lost a sense of being 'displaced persons' and seem to have felt most relaxed during their European sojourns, where 'not belonging' to the local culture was inevitable. Willa's awareness of not fitting in was mostly felt, perhaps, in terms of her personal relations, while Edwin's insecurity relates more to his identity as a creative writer still to find his mature voice. Despite MacDiarmid's praise for him as a critic 'in the first flight of critics of *welt-literatur*',[6] the power of *A Drunk Man Looks at the Thistle* may have increased his sense of insecurity about his own poetry at the time. Nevertheless, Edwin became a contributor to the first edition of *The Modern Scot* in the spring of 1930 with an essay 'Parallels', which also appeared in the American *New Freeman* in April of the same year. His poem 'The Fall' appeared in the Winter 1930 issue and from then onwards he was a regular contributor in poetry and prose. Willa joined him, and the Muirs introduced Kafka and Broch to Whyte's readers by translated excerpts from their work. The fact that Whyte paid his authors well was an additional factor, and his contributors and reviewers included Rebecca West, Edith Sitwell, William Power, Denis Saurat, Hugh MacDiarmid, and Catherine and Donald Carswell.

It is not surprising, then, to learn from Helen Cruickshank's *Octobiography* that it was James Whyte who provided the finances for Edwin and Willa to be sent as Scottish delegates to the P.E.N. International Congress in Budapest in May 1932,

---

[5] *The Story and the Fable*, p. 228; letter to George Thorburn, 14 May 1927, *Selected Letters*, p. 64.
[6] C. M. Grieve (Hugh MacDiarmid), 'Edwin Muir', *Contemporary Scottish Studies* (London: Leonard Parsons, 1926), p. 108.

although the Muirs themselves appear to have been unaware of Whyte's generosity. Having spent an exhausting year translating, with all the worries of Willa's operation, they were delighted to recharge their batteries with a trip to Europe. Edwin wrote to Lizzie and George shortly before they set off.

> We're managing to keep going in these times, which have hit the publishing (and writing) trade like everything else. The price we've all got to pay for the privilege of supporting Ramsay McDonald and Baldwin and Shawcross—a little too dear at the price, or any price! The Scottish P.E.N. has just given us a free holiday, however, (all expenses paid) by sending us to the international conference in Budapesth. It should be a real spree—the first we've had since we came to this country five years ago.[7]

So, leaving Gavin in the care of the cook and the nanny, they set off excitedly for Europe once again.

Budapest in 1932 presented a very different prospect from the Europe of their travels in the early 1920s. One of the aspects of Broch's *The Sleepwalkers* which had troubled them during their long translation of his trilogy was the disintegration of values played out in the third book, *Hugenau oder die Sachlichkeit*, 'Hugenau or Objectivity', or as the Muirs translated it 'The Realist'. Edwin had written enthusiastically to Sydney Schiff about the first book of the trilogy, *Pasenow oder die Romantik*—translated as 'The Romantic'—when they first encountered Broch's work. By March 1932, after a year's absorption in the translation, Edwin could still write to Schiff that the trilogy 'seems to me the greatest single imaginative prose work of our time'. And he added 'But this is mere beating the air, and you will have to wait until you see the book: it will be out in autumn.'[8] Yet *The Sleepwalkers* was intellectually and emotionally a taxing and unsettling book as its structure and writing style moved from the freshness and hopefulness of 'The Romantic' and the story of the Pasenows (despite their inevitable human difficulties) to the story of Esch and Anarchy, and finally to the story of Hugenau the deserter, with his self-serving realism or objectivity, and the 'predicament of the European spirit' in the wake of World War One. Willa wrote later that she and Edwin 'had refused to be bludgeoned' by the logic of Broch's essay on 'The Disintegration of Values', which he had inserted into the last book of his trilogy, and had 'set up a stout inner resistance to his arguments'. Yet when they travelled to Budapest in May 1932 as the Scottish official delegates to the P.E.N. Congress, they 'were to learn by personal experience that Broch had come

---

[7] Edwin Muir, letter to Lizzie and George Thorburn, 10 May 1932, NLS, Acc. 13,226.
[8] Edwin Muir, letter to Sydney Schiff, 22 March 1932, Schiff Papers, BL, Add MS 52,920.

nearer the truth than we thought and that Europe was indeed getting ready to break up'.[9]

As delegates to the Congress, Edwin and Willa had to prepare an official report to the Scottish P.E.N. Committee. In a private letter to Honorary Secretary Helen Cruickshank, however, Willa gave a rather franker account of the problems that had confronted them in Budapest. One important commission was to ensure that they were presented at the Congress as official independent *Scottish* delegates, not as regional members of English P.E.N. In her later memoir Willa would recall 'I do not know the Hungarian language, but I have never forgotten the sentence drilled into me: Nem Angol vodyok, Skōt vodyok'. *Belonging* duly reports that when the delegations were presented to Admiral Horthy, 'the Scottish delegation of two was presented separately, quite independently of the much larger English delegation'. Her letter to Cruickshank, however, recounts their dismay when they were actually listed as 'angol' and were in fact treated as members of the English delegation. They had to protest to the Congress Central Bureau before they were allowed free accommodation in their hotel as independent official delegates. Willa continues her complaint to Cruickshank, saying that they had to 'assert ourselves continuously as being at least on the same independent footing as the delegates from Esthonia (!)' The high (or low) point of their demotion came during the official reception by President Horthy. The delegates were arranged in a semi-circle, with the delegation heads in front and members behind, but unlike her account of the reception in *Belonging*, there was no separate place provided for Scotland, whose members were expected to be grouped with the English party. After further protests, their names as individual delegates were hurriedly added in pencil to the typed list, and Edwin, as the Head of the Scottish group was finally presented separately to Admiral Horthy. Willa writes that 'all this made Edwin so nervous that he forgot to present me, I might say; and I had the dubious distinction of being the only person in the room who did not grab Horthy's hand'.[10] The difficulties of precedence have their amusing side, but more disturbing was Willa's account (now detailed in *Belonging*) of the Hungarian government's control over decisions made with regard to prize-winning publications, of the seemingly cowed nature of the mass of the people, and of the political violence that erupted during the conference itself. Willa wrote in her letter to Cruickshank—

> Shortly before we came, a tailor (I think a tailor) suspected of giving out Socialist pamphlets, was bound hand and foot, hung upside down in his house on a bar between two chairs, and bastinadoed on the soles till he was unconscious: when he came to he was beaten again and, finally, he jumped out of his window, bound

---

[9] Hermann Broch, *The Sleepwalkers*, trans. Edwin and Willa Muir (Berkeley, California: Northpoint Press, 1985), p. 640; *Belonging*, p. 152.

[10] Willa Muir, letter to Helen Cruickshank 26 May [1932], *Selected Letters*, pp. 74–5.

as he was, and broke both his ankles. His wife, who was pregnant, was forced to witness his bastinadoing, and when she heard her husband land with a thud in the courtyard below she thought he was killed, and she died herself of shock.

She continues—

In short, the general atmosphere is filled with hatred, revenge, and cruelty. Perhaps this should not have depressed us, but it did; and I spent Thursday afternoon of Congress week in roaring and greeting in my bedroom over the state of Central Europe.[11]

Discussions away from the Congress venue, with delegates such as Ernst Toller, whom they already knew and liked, confirmed such repression in Hungary, and their fears that the P.E.N. International Congress in Budapest was being used to give respectability to a harsh regime. Both Muirs were glad to cross the frontier at the end of the event, with Willa saying 'This was the first time in our lives we experienced political fear, which is more faceless and more like a chill, penetrating fog than any other fear in the world.' Once over the border into Austria, they made their way to a Vienna familiar from their earlier travels, and met with the author of *Die Schlafwandler* in the flat where he lived with his mother. Perhaps feeling like a sleepwalker herself, Willa commented that 'from his tall height Broch looked down on us compassionately as on a pair of children who had just been learning the facts of European Life.'[12]

When they returned to Crowborough further troubles—even if less serious—lay in wait. While they were in Budapest, the cook and the nanny had been quarrelling over which of them was the principal employee left in charge of the household, and the friction between them resulted in Gavin developing episodes of nervous wheezing. In addition, the increasingly difficult economic environment made a move to London necessary in order to maintain literary contacts and to source writing commissions. They had already decided to try to avoid spending another damp winter in their Crowborough house, and so the summer was spent househunting and exploring Sussex in the second-hand car they bought in 1930 with their 'windfall' from Willa's mother's estate. Both had learned to drive, although Edwin seems to have done most of it during their country excursions at a modest speed of twenty-five miles an hour, while Willa sat with Gavin on her lap. With the help of new P.E.N. friends such as Catherine and Donald Carswell, and the money left by Willa's mother, they finally found a house at 7 Devonshire Hill in Hampstead at a rent of £120 a year—double the cost of the Crowborough house. Sending a copy of *Poor Tom* to Lizzie and George on 29 September, Edwin wrote

---

[11] Ibid., p .73.
[12] *Belonging*, p. 157.

that they were '"flitting" in a week's time', adding 'We'll be glad to get back into human society again, after almost six years of living among English grass and clay. The street we're in—and we were lucky to get in it—is just beside Keats' Walk, very quiet and old fashioned and near the Heath.'[13] Hampstead was indeed one of the most pleasant residential parts of London and was a popular living area with exiled Scots. Just around the corner, in Keats' Grove, was the home of Catherine Carswell, whose sexually frank *Life of Robert Burns* had caused a furore throughout the Scottish Burns Clubs when it was published in 1930. Her husband Donald was also a writer who had written a biographical study of Walter Scott and his circle in Edinburgh. And in Holly Terrace, close to Highgate Village and Hampstead Heath lived George Malcolm Thomson who, with Roderick Watson Kerr, had founded the Porpoise Press in Scotland in 1922 (the same year as the first issue of Grieve's *Chapbook*). The Porpoise Press played a strong part in the encouragement of the interwar Scottish literary revival by publishing new poetry and fiction until it was taken over by Faber in the 1930s. Now its co-founder George Malcolm Thomson worked in London for the Beaverbrook Press but still kept his eye on Scottish affairs. Like Catherine Carswell, although for different reasons, his books on the condition of Scotland such as *Caledonia: or The Future of the Scots* (1927) and *Scotland: That Distressed Area* (which Edwin would review in *The Criterion* in 1936) caused a sensation in his native country.

Expatriate Scots and young, cosmopolitan, political poets would make up a significant number of the Muirs' new friends and acquaintances in Hampstead, together with the return of many old friends with whom they had lost touch while living in the English countryside. First of all, however, they had to tackle a familiar problem. Willa wrote to Lizzie and her family on 31 October apologising for not having answered an earlier letter of enquiry.

> My dearest Lizzie—George—Irene—Ethel—
>
> Talk about the pangs of conscience! Ever since Ethel's letter came enquiring about books (which, I am sorry to say, we haven't got) I ought to have had pangs: but when your lavatory is condemned and dismantled, and bricks fall down the kitchen chimney, and a large portion of plaster narrowly misses Edwin as it falls from the ceiling in the dining-room, and rain soaks in at every corner of the roof, a mere failure to write letters becomes as nothing. We have been living in a nightmare, not a house, and I have not been able to think two connected thoughts.

Perhaps surveyors' reports were not so rigorous in the 1930s, or the Muirs in their innocence had not thought to commission one before renting the property, but clearly their new residence was not without its drawbacks. On the other hand,

---

[13] Edwin Muir, letter of 29 September 1932, *Selected Letters*, p. 78.

Willa had fallen in love with Hampstead and Downshire Hill, and by the end of the letter she was writing more optimistically to her relations.

> This house is going to be charming when it is watertight and the lavatory is working. Really, *much* better than Crowborough, so don't regret The Nook. You can have a prime holiday here: the Heath is just like open country and the air is good and there is so much to see.

Then she adds—

> Gavin is taking to it enormously; he thanks you for his coloured pencils, and has been making grand messes all over the pictures. He is such a big boy now, and has got rid of all his troubles about the school, and is so nice and sweet and mischievous that we are amazed at the speed with which he is developing. You would find him much improved: the nervous complexes are gone and he is tremendously happy.[14]

Gavin was even happier when the family took on the care of a golden cocker spaniel called Matthew, bred by their friends Flora Grierson and Joan Shelmerdine, who had published Edwin's small collection *Six Poems* at their hand-printing Samson Press in Surrey in April 1932. The dog had been bought by a young woman who was out at work all day and Matthew was left howling beside the dustbins in a little backyard while his owner was absent. Since she was now being threatened with eviction, Flora and Joan had come on her behalf to beg the Muirs to take him in. Willa remembered the day Matthew arrived to become part of their family.

> The yelping and the laughter brought Edwin down from his study, and this is the picture that stays in my mind: Edwin in an open-necked shirt and grey flannels coming across our back lawn looking gay and beaming a welcome, Joan and Matthew inextricably mixed up with the lead and a deckchair, Flora helpless with mirth and the sun shining brightly over all.[15]

Willa's initial responses to people and places tended to be definitive, and so it was with Hampstead and their house in Downshire Hill. In remembering her life with Edwin, she would write—

> For us, living in Hampstead was like living with one's True Love; there was no possibility of ever preferring another part of London. In the mode proper to True Love I embraced it all, including the shops and the woman who sold flowers halfway up the Hill. The tradesmen and the flower-seller were like friends

---

[14] Willa Muir, letter to Lizzie Thorburn, 31 October 1932, NLS, Acc. 13226.
[15] *Belonging*, p. 161.

rather than acquaintances. I did not stop to wonder if these feelings of mine were one-sided but perhaps my simple friendship gave pleasure too.[16]

Edwin shared her feelings—

Hampstead itself, its old streets and old houses, the Heath five minutes' walk away, the little shops like shops in a village, the sense of seclusion and leisure on the verge of a great city, the need to walk only a few steps if one wanted to see a friend: all these were parts of the happiness.[17]

By the spring of 1933, however, Edwin was preoccupied with what he described, in a letter to his brother-in-law George, as the 'dreadful world that we're living in just now: like the Dark Ages, when one civilisation was breaking up and another forming with painful fragmentary slowness'. Coming to live in London seems to have quickened his sense of civilization being between worlds, a process 'both of death and birth'. He wrote that 'London gives me very strong feelings of it, and lots of friends of mine feel that something like this is happening.' Yet it was not all bleak, for he and his friends also felt that something positive would eventually come out of it. 'We're in the trough between something that has been great and something that will be great: an extraordinary, even if painful, time to be living on earth.' He confessed to George, nevertheless, that his family had been in something of a 'trough' after coming to London. The cost of fixing their charming but dilapidated house in Hampstead must have used up most of what was left of the money from Willa's mother. More seriously, perhaps, shortly after they had taken over the house, Edwin lost his reader's job with Secker, 'on which we were depending for a livelihood. (They couldn't afford to keep me in any longer).' He tells George that 'at Christmas we were down to £1-10, with no job in prospect, the rent due, myself down with the flu!'[18] Secker had been the British publisher of the Muirs' German translations starting with Gerhart Hauptmann in 1925, and they had done well with Feuchtwanger's *Jew Süss* in 1926. Willa's solo translations of Hans Carossa were also published by Secker, who had relied to a significant extent on the Muirs bringing interesting writers (notably Franz Kafka) to the firm's attention. Losing contact with their principal publisher in the difficult financial times of the early 1930s must have taken some of the glow off Hampstead.

Fortunately, their poverty was short-lived. In the first week of the new year Edwin reported that he had 'got a job from Gollancz and also a huge book to translate; and the same week *The Listener*, quite out of the blue, offered me the job of reviewing novels for them. So that out of hopelessness we were raised in a few days to comparative comfort'. Telling George that he had hardly ever felt more

---

[16] Ibid., p. 162.
[17] *An Autobiography*, p. 239.
[18] Edwin Muir, letter to George Thorburn, 11 March, 1933, *Selected Letters*, pp. 79–80.

thankful in his life, he adds, characteristically: 'I'm sending £4 for you and Lizzie as a thanks offering, and hoping that it will be of some little use. We're all right for several months to come at least, and can quite well afford it.' His brother-in-law must have been having his own employment difficulties at the time, for Edwin goes on to ask him about the Means Test which had been introduced before out of work benefits could be given. 'If you have saved anything, does it mean that they will penalise you for it?' And he adds 'I would get round it some way if I were you. It must be dreary beyond words, this writing for work, a perpetual empty Sunday.' He asks George if he had ever thought of writing down his own experiences and thoughts, 'telling what your life had been'; and says he himself would be willing to give him 'a hand with it' if he would like to have a try. He also conveys their impressions of London more generally: 'We like being in London after the deadness of the country: the people we meet are more human than I had expected.' And he tells George, who had been a regular reader of *The New Age*, that he has seen its editor, who has now returned to London, a few times. Edwin thinks that Orage is 'a somewhat sorry figure now, without knowing it; still leading an advanced army that has long since fallen into the rear'; and he adds 'I don't think he feels quite at home. But he's a nice man.'[19]

A welcome aspect of Hampstead life was the connections they made with younger poets. Edwin wrote that his own 'apprehension about the state of the world, which had darkened the poetry I had written in Crowborough became far less troublesome now that I was in London, where everyone I met had been talking about it for a long time, until it had become an ordinary theme for conversation'. Hampstead was especially 'haunted by young poets despairing over the poor and the world' but to Edwin it seemed that their 'despairing together' brought a 'comforting communion'. The poetry of Auden, Spender and Day Lewis was a regular topic of conversation, and among the group with whom Edwin became friendly were Spender himself, Dylan Thomas, George Barker, a very young David Gascoyne, 'still in his teens', and Geoffrey Grigson, editor of the journal *New Verse*. For Edwin, 'a new generation had appeared from a country which I had never guessed at [...] now they appeared to belong in a specific way to the present, as if it were theirs exclusively, or as if they had been forged by it alone.'[20] The Muirs' Hampstead home became a regular venue for many of these writers, especially George Barker who 'dropped in at all hours'. Barker had met the Muirs as a result of Edwin reviewing a novel he had written with the hope of earning enough money to enable him to 'move into a larger attic'. If the novel did not earn him any money, at least it introduced him to Edwin, who invited him to Downshire Hill. Barker later wrote about the friendship that developed.

[19] Edwin Muir, letter to George Thorburn, 11 March 1933, NLS, Acc. 13226.
[20] *An Autobiography*, pp. 232–3.

I think often with gratitude of evenings spent in his company, because here I learned that words were not only delightful things in themselves but also—this mysterious fact still fascinates me—they stand for far more than most people either think or are. Muir was like a silent clock that showed not the time but the condition, not the hour but the alternative.

Willa also left a strong impression as Barker recalled—

that occasion when the overpowering caryatid of Willa Muir took up Homer and began to recite that opening passage in the Greek, so that the whole of the tasteful room in Hampstead gradually filled with the loud-mouthed rolling parallels of the poem and the sea—until I was witnessing the living demonstration of Eliot's assertion that a poem can communicate before it is understood.[21]

The move to Hampstead brought the Muirs to feel that they were once again in touch with the pulse of the times. Their loss of contact with Europe, which had so inspired them during the 1920s, was regrettable, but they could keep in touch with the Continent through their translations of European writers, their correspondence with Hermann Broch, and the company of their European friends in London such as Denis Saurat and Janko Lavrin, the latter of whom would found the *European Quarterly* with Edwin in 1934. There were new Scottish friends, too, such as George Malcolm Thomson and the Carswells who lived a few minutes away, and Janet Adam Smith, Assistant Editor of *The Listener*, who had unknowingly helped them escape financial disaster by offering Edwin regular reviewing when they first came to Hampstead. Willa wrote of meeting MacDiarmid when he was staying with the Carswells, and Lewis Grassic Gibbon when on a visit to London from his home in Welwyn Garden City. Old friends such as Hugh Kingsmill and John Holms renewed contact. John was now living with Peggy Guggenheim in Woburn Square and Edwin was surprised at his enthusiasm for the new political poetry. Kingsmill, who lived in Hastings, visited whenever he came to London. And despite the problems with their new home, which Edwin described as 'an old dilapidated Strawberry Hill Gothic house, which vibrated gently whenever the underground train passed beneath it', he confessed that he and Willa 'were in love with its sweet, battered Mozartian grace, and for that were prepared to forgive it anything'.[22]

During 1933, their first full year in Hampstead, Edwin's principal literary work was his monthly reviewing contract with *The Listener*, together with occasional

---

[21] George Barker, 'Coming to London', *London Magazine* vol. 3, no. 1, January 1956, pp. 49–54 (p. 51).
[22] *An Autobiography*, p. 237.

reviews for *The Spectator* and the Scottish *Modern Scot*. The translations of Franz Kafka's *The Great Wall of China, and Other Pieces*, and *Little Friend* by Ernst Lothar, were published by Secker in May and June 1933, and *Three Cities* by Shalom Asch, which was the first translation of the new contract with Gollancz, appeared in October that year. Edwin had been disappointed but not surprised by the lack of interest in his novel *Poor Tom*, which had been published by Dent in September 1932 when they were moving from Crowborough to Hampstead. He had written almost apologetically about it to Sydney Schiff in May of the previous year, thanking him for what he had said about it, but adding that he did not expect the book to sell well. *Poor Tom* was to be Edwin's final attempt at fiction writing. Unlike the Knoxian *Three Brothers*, it had a modern Glasgow setting, but like his previous book it drew on personal experience and was closely related to the story of his own family's disastrous time in the city. The book's occasional German-language epigraphs such as Nietzsche's 'Warum? Wofür? Wodurch? Wohin? Wo? Wie?' ('Why? For what? How? Where? Where? As?') might suggest that its already bleak philosophical discourse had been further darkened by their translation of Broch's *The Sleepwalkers*, which was published around the same time as *Poor Tom*. James Whyte's *Modern Scot* was one magazine that did appreciate the novel. As with Rebecca West's positive review of *The Three Brothers* in the Spring 1931 issue of the magazine, the anonymous reviewer in Autumn 1932 (perhaps James Whyte, himself) found *Poor Tom* 'the most interesting work in prose written by a Scotsman since—the war, if you like—or even the year in which *The House with the Green Shutters* was published.' The reviewer also wrote that the author 'imposes an artist's order on his material, recalling Percy Lubbock's words in *The Craft of Fiction*', and singles out for special attention the fine episode of the socialist procession in chapter ten of the novel.[23] Edwin would surely have been encouraged by this review if the complexities of their move from Crowborough to Hampstead had allowed him an opportunity to read it. And had he been able to see into the future, he would have taken heart to know that several decades later it would be in print again as an important contribution to the tradition of the Glasgow novel.

Willa's second novel, *Mrs Ritchie*, published by Secker in July 1933, was a very different book from *Imagined Corners*. She had been surprisingly insecure about *Imagined Corners*, despite several positive reviews and her own initial excitement. She took various quibbles about its lack of Scottishness too seriously, along with comments about the nature of its ending, or its too great focus on the two Elizabeths. Writing to Sydney Schiff, to thank him for being 'a brick to send me such comforting words about my book', she promised that her next book would 'really

---

[23] Anonymous review of *Poor Tom*, *The Modern Scot*, 3.3 Autumn 1932, p. 250.

be much better.'[24] Yet in contrast to the liveliness of *Imagined Corners*, with its interlinked story of two young women, *Mrs Ritchie* suffers from a lack of narrative irony and flexible narration, and in many ways it seems more like a companion book to the harsh Calvinist spirit of Edwin's John Knox. Willa wrote to her sister-in-law shortly before publication that the new novel had 'some hopes of success. It's a lot better—ever so much better—than the first one I did. Nobody knows what a shock Scotland is going to get.' And in a later post-publication letter to the Masons she writes that she is going to send them a book, 'this time a really good book, called *Mrs Ritchie*, which came out in July, and was recommended by the Book Society'. She tells them that it 'has gone into a second printing, and has sold over 2000 and has been praised largely', and in customary dramatic fashion she adds, 'On the strength of my book I was even invited to write an article for the Evening News! So I may blossom into remunerative journalism yet.'[25] In the end, however, *Mrs Ritchie* did not do as well as Willa hoped, and it received mixed reviews. The *Times Literary Supplement* found too strong a narrative control, with a narrative voice like that of a lecturer, lacking in satiric humour or irony. *The Modern Scot*, on the other hand, found that 'the puritanical Mrs Ritchie, of Calderwick, is "large as life"'; and the book 'one of the grimmest challenges offered to puritanical Scotland since *The House with Green Shutters*'. It also found it 'a beautifully wrought piece of imaginative prose', with a 'unity that *Imagined Corners* lacked'. Friends such as Flos McNeill and Helen Cruickshank protested that it gave too harsh a depiction of small-town Scotland, especially of Montrose, and Cruickshank who, like Willa, came from Montrose thought that it was 'too full of phallic symbols for my liking'. She later realized that her criticism of the book 'had incurred Willa's displeasure' and they lost contact in later years.[26]

Willa herself would say little about *Mrs Ritchie* in *Belonging*; merely that she 'lost control of it in the second half, although the first half is quite good'. This is probably an accurate summing-up of the work, although present-day feminist critics admire it for its study of what can happen to a young woman of academic promise when her ambitions are cruelly thwarted by societal mores. Willa's own life during the writing of the book was itself an example of the difficulties facing an ambitious woman attempting to be mother, principal translator, organizer of household help, and—if there was any time left over—creative writer. She would later reflect on her literary life, comparing it to that of her poet and critic husband.

---

[24] Willa Muir, note to Sydney Schiff added to Edwin's letter of 22 March 1932, Schiff Papers, BL, Add MS 52920.
[25] Willa Muir, letter to Lizzie Thorburn, 26 May 1933, NLS, Acc. 13226; letter to Mary and Arthur Mason, August 1933 (no specific day), NLS, Acc. 13226.
[26] Anonymous review, *The Modern Scot*, Vol. 4:2. Summer 1933, p. 158; Helen Cruickshank, *Octobiography*, p. 150.

> In his study at the top of the house which contained only a table, a chair, an ink-pot and a fine view over roofs and tree-tops, Edwin now and then produced a poem. The bareness of his study was how he liked it [...] My study on the ground floor was neither so spare nor so secluded. Here I was intruded upon at all hours by household staff, the weekly washerwoman, any casual caller ready for a gossip, and Gavin whenever he came home from school. [...] I envied Edwin's power of sitting down immediately after breakfast to concentrate in solitude on what he wanted to do.[27]

Edwin was asked to visit Europe again when Scottish P.E.N. sent him to the Congress in Dubrovnik in May 1933. Remembering Gavin's distress at the squabbling between cook and nanny when they attended the Congress in Budapest, Willa decided to stay at home with their son. Besides, there was a great deal of translation work to be done. Edwin duly set off, and was spared the identification difficulties—Scottish, not English—that he had faced in Budapest, nor was the political atmosphere quite so threatening. Yet the Dubrovnik conference had its own difficulties because the German delegation would not accept the passing of a resolution condemning intellectual persecution, including the burning of books by the Nazis in Germany. Having failed to protest about this at home, the members of German P.E.N. had virtually become a Nazi-supporting organization, and even attempted to prevent Ernst Toller, who was Jewish, from speaking at the conference. Membership of International P.E.N. was subsequently withdrawn from this group, and it was decided that in future German P.E.N. would be represented by authors in exile such as Toller and Thomas Mann, together with Lion Feuchtwanger, whose work, of course, the Muirs had translated. Yet Edwin missed all this controversy. Perhaps he had been sightseeing, reporting that he was deeply moved by the beauty of the city and its surroundings, especially during a cruise between Dubrovnik and Trieste. He seems to have thoroughly enjoyed himself, breakfasting in his hotel with H. G. Wells, who had in fact led the campaign against the book-burning. On his return to Hampstead, Edwin wrote to his niece Ethel, who was about to graduate from university.

> Here is the form back with my signature. I'll probably be seeing you all soon, when I come up for my week-end. [...] You didn't say anything about yourself and your triumphs in the university. I'll hear about that later. I've been moving in very 'high' company lately, breakfasting with H. G. Wells, and flirting with the editors of 'Vogue'.

He added that he had 'managed to cram in a day in Venice on my return journey, and sit for a few hours in the square of St Mark's, watching the church and the

---

[27] *Belonging*, pp. 162–3.

pigeons flying about and getting them to feed out of my hand.'[28] Edwin's apparently untroubled and enjoyable European sojourn would, however, be followed by a serious family upset shortly after his return, an event that disrupted their Hampstead happiness and led them to leave their much-loved home.

One of Willa's most difficult tasks as organizer of the household was the finding and keeping of cooks and housemaids. This is a topic she would say little about in her later memoir, although it forms a significant part of her unpublished Hampstead novel *Mrs Muttoe and the Top Storey*. Edwin recalled the problems, writing that 'we endured our maids too for the sake of the house'. There was—

> the quiet (Welsh) one who left to get married, taking a selection of our sheets and pillow-slips with her; the (Scottish and Northern English) ones who introduced suspicious characters into the house under our noses, and left secretly one night after having drunk all our wine and whisky; the sad little Cockney (from Camden town) whom my wife engaged out of pity, but who felt lost away from her pub and her friends.[29]

Absent from this list is another Irish maid whose obsession—like Willa's Mrs Ritchie—with human sinfulness and retribution, resulted in a serious accident to Gavin. Willa had engaged a new cook who was an Irish Catholic. Housekeeping staff were difficult to find, and the cook had made it clear that she would only come if her niece could also be employed. Willa 'loved at sight' the aunt called Mary and agreed. But she would later remember that the niece Julia, 'a tall gaunt girl who looked rather like de Valera in petticoats and had hard suspicious eyes behind her spectacles, gave me a sinking feeling which I ignored, for I was busy with a press of work'. Willa delegated Julia to take Gavin and the dog to the Heath in the afternoons, but became aware that something was troubling her son, and that this had something to do with the pond on the Heath. After questioning Gavin, when she herself took him for his walk, she discovered that Julia had told him that bad boys were drowned there. Willa did not take the matter further, apart from telling the maid not to frighten her son with such stories. But a few days later she was disturbed at her translation work by a boy coming to the door to say that Gavin had been knocked down by an oil tanker when running home across the steep road that led from the Heath to their house. His right leg was broken in two places and he was severely concussed. It turned out that he had been running home to get away from Julia, who was frightening him with more stories of sin and Hell. When questioned, the over-religious housemaid, whose brother was a priest, was unrepentant, saying that Willa's house was a 'godless house' and that Gavin was being brought up to be 'a little heathen'. Willa was sorry to lose the

---

[28] Ibid., pp. 169–70; Edwin Muir, letter to Ethel Ross, 11 June 1933, NLS, Acc. 13226.
[29] *An Autobiography*, pp. 237–8.

aunt, who was a good cook, but since Julia had to go, the aunt would not stay without her.[30]

Willa blamed herself strongly and repeatedly for this disaster, until Edwin became distressed. Recounting the incident in *Belonging*, Willa remembered him saying, 'If thu keeps on saying that thu'll make me believe it.' Edwin's love and respect was always a priority with Willa, so she stopped talking about it and 'began preparing an inward sump of self-accusation and grief'.[31] Whether Edwin was ever told the whole 'sin and hellfire' story is not clear from his own memoirs, and it may be that his version is simply what they chose to tell their friends.

> The oil-tank was coming down the hill, and Gavin, being a daring little boy, thought he could beat it. He might have succeeded, but at the last minute he hesitated. The lorry driver braked desperately, but could not quite avoid him. The nurse stood chained to the dog.

Willa wrote to the Thorburns a few weeks after the event, sending them a copy of the forbidding *Mrs Ritchie* and promising a 'black & white frock' for Ethel's graduation. Then she added 'Gavin was run over by a lorry and got his leg broken and we have been very harassed.' Her account of the event to the Masons in August was, as always, cheerfully dramatic.

> Gavin is large and a highly individual kid: his individuality went so far that on July 1st, he tried to beat a petrol lorry across the road and had his right leg broken: he was lucky not to be killed. [...] he is now running about, but he'll not run in front of an automobile again, thank goodness! A drastic way of acquiring traffic sense, isn't it?[32]

The Muirs spent most of August in Orkney to allow both Gavin and his parents to recuperate. Edwin wrote that from the windows of the farmhouse where they lodged—

> We looked down on the isle of Damsay, with its one farm and the ruins of a chapel said to have been built by Adamnan, the disciple and biographer of St Columba. A path across a field led down to the beach, and we spent most of our time there. I had not been back to Orkney for many years; few of the people I had known were there still; but the beauty of the light showered from the wide sky and reflected

---

[30] *Belonging*, pp. 170–2.
[31] Ibid., p. 172.
[32] *An Autobiography*, p. 241; Willa Muir, letter to Lizzie and George Thorburn, 17 July 1933, NLS, Acc. 13226; letter to the Masons, August 1933, NLS Acc. 13226.

from the spreading waters, and diffused, a double radiance, over the bright fields, was the same beauty I had known as a child.[33]

This visit reawakened Edwin's feelings for Orkney. The family would return the next summer when Edwin undertook a trip throughout Scotland to research a 'Scottish Journey' book for a travel series for Heinemann and Gollancz. Gavin, however, continued to show anxiety amid the increasing London traffic, even at the end of their own quiet road, and they came to the reluctant conclusion that they should leave Hampstead to find a house in a more peaceful location in Scotland.

---

[33] *An Autobiography*, pp. 241–2. Edwin was, however, mistaken in the passage that follows this entry, when he closed the chapter by saying 'after a month we moved south to St Andrews'. The move to St Andrews did not take place until August 1935, after a second summer holiday in Orkney and two years of literary activity, involving both the journey and the writing of *Scottish Journey*.

10
Scottish Journeys 1933–1935

> It represented the only desirable form of life that I found in all my journey through Scotland.
>
> Edwin Muir, *Scottish Journey* (1935)

Gavin's accident prompted their reluctant decision to leave London, but this did not happen immediately. On their return from Orkney in the late summer of 1933 the family had a stroke of domestic luck in finding two very suitable employees. Hilde Weissenseel, an anti-Nazi German, became their cook and housekeeper, and a student from Finland, Eja Bergmann, in England to learn the language, became the housemaid. The young women worked well together, although the German-speaking Hilde spoke little English, and Eja spoke English but very little German. Willa remembered how the girls bought small English-German dictionaries from Woolworth's and tied these to their belts, 'exchanging words with much laughter as they went about the house'. Hilde and Eja brought order and stability as well as laughter to the household, and they joined the Muirs on holiday in Orkney, with a still fragile Gavin, in the following year. Meanwhile there was much literary work to be done, and in late November 1933 Edwin wrote to Hermann Broch to tell him that Gavin had been ill and that 'Willa was really very run down, and at last reached the stage when she was allowed neither to speak nor to read. If she did not take an immediate rest she was told that she would have to rest later for six months.' He continued 'It was partly the worry about our little boy, and partly over-work. She is now much better, but not yet back to what she should be. I hope she will be by the end of the year.'[1]

Edwin had heavy reviewing commitments. He was writing regularly for *The Listener* and *The Spectator*, as well as contributing to James Whyte's *Modern Scot* and London magazines such as *The Bookman*, *The New English Weekly*, and *The Criterion*. He was one of the best-known and respected critics in the London scene, reviewing both English-language and European new writing. Between late 1933 and the spring of 1934, for example, his reviews included work by William Faulkner, Oswald Spengler's *Jahre der Entscheidung* (*Years of Decision*), Eliot's *The Use of Poetry* and *After Strange Gods*, *Tales of D. H. Lawrence*, and Sholokhov's *And*

---

[1] *Belonging*, p. 172; Edwin Muir, letter to Hermann Broch, 20 November 1933, *Selected Letters*, pp. 81–2.

Quiet Flows the Don. In cooperation with Stephen Spender, he was also negotiating with Heinemann for a proposed edition of Hölderlin's poetry. May 1934 saw the launch of the *European Quarterly*, which he founded and co-edited with Janko Lavrin, the first issue of which contained his own article 'Bolshevism and Calvinism'. In the same month Edwin's survey of the literary revival in Scotland appeared in *The Spectator*, which had announced its intention, in October 1933, to follow Scottish affairs because 'developments are in progress in Scotland that are far too little understood or discussed outside Scotland.' In particular, their editorial policy had declared that 'the cultivation of Gaelic and the conscious development of a modern Scottish literature are movements demanding not only observation but discussion.'[2] Thus Edwin became the principal contributor to the *Spectator*'s coverage of Scottish affairs, increasing his own involvement with affairs in the north. Although his creative writing, and especially his poetry, was progressing at a slower rate than his critical writing, *Variations on a Time Theme* was published by Dent in April 1934, the first substantial poetry collection since *First Poems* appeared from the Hogarth Press in 1925, followed by the less successful *Chorus of the Newly Dead* in 1926. Influenced, perhaps, by Eliot's poetry, the *Variations* collection showed Edwin finding new ways of formal expression and moving away from the thematic search for the 'lost lands' of his childhood that had dominated his early verses. Yet the opening section of the first 'Variation', with its questioning imagery, 'How did we come here to this broken wood [...] Where did the road branch? [...] Or did we choose?' could be seen to continue his long preoccupation with the nature of the human story, and even to anticipate the empty Highland glens and the slums of Glasgow that lay in wait for him on his travels later that year for the *Scottish Journey* book. Geoffrey Grigson's *New Verse*—which had initially supported Edwin as poet—published a negative review of *Variations* by Louis MacNeice, but on the whole the new collection was well received. Edwin wrote to George Barker in May 1934, 'Thank you so much for your letter. I am so glad—and relieved!—that you like my poems; for many people's opinion I should not have cared at all; but there it is, you seem to me to have quite a different *kind* of honesty from other people.' And he added 'The book has been getting me quite a lot of bouquets, public and private, far more than I've ever got in my life before, and I must say I like it.'[3]

A less happy event in early 1934 was the death of John Holms who died from heart failure in January under anaesthetic for what appeared to have been a minor operation for an injury to his wrist, carried out by doctors in his Woburn Square home. Edwin dedicated *Variations* to the memory of Holms who had been such a significant and supportive critic of his early attempts to write poetry. Edwin's

---

[2] Editorial, *Spectator*, October 1933, p. 434.
[3] *Complete Poems*, p. 51; letter to George Barker, 10 May 1934, Harry Ransom Center, University of Texas at Austin, George Barker collection, MS-00216.

contact with him had diminished as the Muirs developed their family and writing life in the south of England, but they met again in Hampstead when Holms and Peggy Guggenheim came to England in 1933 to rent a house in Woburn Square in addition to Hayford Hall, their country house in the Dartmoor area. Neither Willa nor Edwin would say much about this renewal in their later memoirs, but it is clear from Edwin's correspondence of the time, and especially from Peggy Guggenheim's memoir *Out of this Century: Confessions of an Art Addict*, that there was significant contact between Holms, Peggy, and Edwin, during this early 1930s period. In her memoir, Peggy writes about the support she received from Hugh Kingsmill and Edwin, who both attended the cremation service, and how Edwin had insisted that she have a lawyer present at the inquest into Holms's death 'in case any trouble arose', presumably about the manner of the death in an operation carried out in his home as opposed to a hospital. She also writes that after Holms's death, 'Edwin Muir and Hugh Kingsmill came often to my house. They felt that by sitting there they could in some way be closer to John. We were all most unhappy.'[4] Peggy Guggenheim is not always the most reliable of narrators, but the account of Edwin's friendship with Holms, which she asked Edwin to write after his death, was reproduced in her later memoir, and Edwin included a revised version of it in the enlarged version of his own autobiography in 1954. The first version of his autobiography, *The Story and the Fable* of 1940, had already told of his meeting with Holms, brought to his door in Glasgow by Hugh Kingsmill one Sunday Morning in 1919. Edwin never forgot Holms's support, and in July 1934, he mentioned it again in a letter to George Barker. Barker had published his first novel, *Alanna Autumnal*, the previous year, but was going through difficulties with his own work. Edwin had a suggestion.

> Two old friends of mine, Emily Coleman and Peggy Guggenheim (both American) have just read your 'Alanna' and are so in love with it that they've asked me to send them your address. They were both very close friends of the oldest and closest friend I have ever had, who died in January of this year; his name was John Holms and he was certainly a man of genius, though various things kept him from realising his gifts. I think it would be well worth your while to know Emily and Peggy; first because I'm sure you would like them and that they would like you, and secondly because I think they might be of some use to you, Peggy especially, who is one of the nicest women I know.

He adds that Emily Coleman 'has a very fine and true appreciation of poetry and a quite unusual passion for it, and has written some poems which I like very much.'[5]

---

[4] *Out of this Century*, pp. 127–8.
[5] Ibid., pp. 100–102; *The Story and the Fable*, pp. 199–201, 210–17; *An Autobiography*, pp. 167–9, 177–81; letter to George Barker, July 1934, HRC, MS-00216.

It is clear from this that Edwin had kept in contact with Holms and his new ménage in London, and with Peggy after Holms's death.

Before the family's July holiday in Orkney there were two significant Scottish-based events that occupied him in particular. The Scottish Centre of International P.E.N. had been chosen to host the International P.E.N. Congress of 1934 in June in Edinburgh. This was a splendid affair, described enthusiastically by journalist and P.E.N. activist William Power in his autobiography.

> From every country in Europe, except Russia and Turkey, but including Catalonia, where the Congress of 1935 was to be held; from the United States, Canada, Latin America, Iceland, South Africa, Australia, New Zealand, China, came bands of influential authors. There was a garden party at Holyrood, where the delegates were received by the Secretary of State for Scotland, the late Sir Godfrey Collins. Edinburgh Castle was floodlit. There were receptions by the municipalities, the universities, the R.S.A. [Royal Scottish Academy], and other bodies. There were tours to the Borders, the Highlands, and the Land of Burns [...] These things helped to convince our guests that Scotland was not an English county.[6]

The Scottish P.E.N. Secretary Helen Cruickshank also describes the Holyrood garden party in her *Octobiography*, the first time, apparently, that any group apart from the General Assembly of the Church of Scotland had been allowed to hold a garden party there. Sir Godfrey Collins, who presided, was unwell at the time—'a sick man'—and had indicated that he could not receive more than twenty guests for tea within the palace itself. Cruickshank tells how she had 'the invidious task of selecting, as unobtrusively as possible, that number from the hundreds strolling about the gardens or eating strawberry ices in the tea marquees'. She took care to invite Ernst Toller, the German-Jewish playwright, whom she describes as having 'suffered insults from the Italian Fascist poet Marinetti at a business session earlier in the day'. Cruickshank had met Toller previously, when P.E.N. helped to organize a lecture tour for him, and she remembers how, on a journey with him to Glasgow, he had told her about 'sinister signs already evident of Nazi persecution of the Jews', and how one of his own friends became so overwhelmed with apprehension concerning what might lie in store for the Jews in Europe that he 'suicided'. Cruickshank comments that that was the first time she had ever heard Toller use an English word incorrectly and that the conversation with Toller, and his distress, remained in her mind to resurface after the Second World War, when she heard that Toller had hanged himself in a New York hotel bedroom after the successful launch of one of his plays on Broadway.[7]

---

[6] William Power, *Should Auld Acquaintance: An Autobiography* (London: George Harrap, 1937), pp. 175, 177.

[7] *Octobiography*, pp. 93–4.

Both Muirs attended the Edinburgh conference, with Edwin taking part in some of the smaller discussion sessions. Then they set off for their second summer holiday in Orkney. Edwin had been invited by Heinemann and Gollancz to write a 'Scottish Journey' book in a series of three travel books commissioned by the publishers in 1933. *English Journey* by J. B. Priestley and *European Journey* by Sir Philip Gibbs appeared first, with Edwin's *Scottish Journey* to be published in 1935. This commission would finance their household's travel and their long summer holiday in the north. Having given away their own elderly car when they moved to Hampstead from Crowborough, Edwin was presented with another old car belonging to his Orkney painter friend Stanley Cursiter, then Keeper of the National Galleries of Scotland in Edinburgh. It was in this car that he proposed to make his circuitous journey to the Orkney Isles, where he would join Willa, Gavin, Hilde, Eja, and the dog, who would sail from Leith, and arrive before him.

Edwin's Scottish journey started from the country's capital city, the manners of whose inhabitants he would discuss good-naturedly, but also ironically, in the opening chapter. He set off on a bright Sunday in July in Cursiter's 1921 Standard car, with his friend's guarantee that 'if it could be made to start it would keep going.' Edwin found that it 'skittered along the roads quite briskly, except for a trick of dancing like a high-spirited colt' when he took it to a speed of over thirty-five miles an hour.[8] From Edinburgh he travelled south to the Borders, stopping for 'excellent stew and milk pudding' in a Galashiels decorated for its annual festival and busy with holidaymakers, before continuing to Melrose, Dryburgh, and then to Jedburgh where he planned to spend the night. These journeys were full of reminders of a past Scotland and its pre-Reformation ballad traditions, and it seemed to him that, 'as soon as one is within sound of the Tweed one can feel the presence of history, in the landscape and in the faces and manners of the people.' Yet that sense of history did not appear to have exerted a constricting force on the life of the border towns, because they continued to have an active life of their own. His travels in the Borders included a visit to Scott's Abbotsford, 'a fantastic house in a fantastic place'. Edwin, an experienced European traveller, was intrigued.

> Abbotsford is a very strange house. It is a place certainly well-suited to be displayed, to astonish, to stagger, and to sadden; but that it should ever have been lived in is the most astonishing, staggering, saddening thing of all. One feels, while wandering through it, that one is on the track of a secret more intimate than either Scott's biography or his written works can tell; and that if one stayed here long enough one would at last understand the mania which drove him to create this pompous, crude, fantastic, unmanageable, heartless, insatiable, comfortless brute of a house, and sacrifice to it in turn his genius, his peace of mind, his health and his life.

[8] Edwin Muir, *Scottish Journey* (1935: Edinburgh: Mainstream Publishing, 1979), p. 40.

Two items especially remained in his mind—the walls of the drawing room, covered with emerald-green Chinese wallpaper, which 'show scenes of Chinese life interwoven with floral scrolls; and near the door Mr George Bernard Shaw, in a Chinese robe, can be seen talking a century before his time'. Edwin found this illusion 'an astonishingly faithful likeness; easily, indeed, the best I have ever come across'. Equally impressive in a less ironic way was Raeburn's original painting of Scott, a portrait of 'a very remarkable man' but one 'expressing simultaneously consciousness of power and of defeat. The face might be that of a lifelong outcast or a lifelong prisoner who has never resigned himself to his lot'.[9]

From the Borders Edwin turned north to Glasgow, via Ayrshire with its reminders of Burns and the Burns Cult—a cult that in his view 'is not a literary cult, but a social one [...] based on a firm foundation of sanctified illusion and romantic wish fulfilment'.

> This legendary figure is a Scotsman who took upon him all the sins of the people, not to redeem them, but to commit them as ideally as they should be committed, that is, freely and guiltlessly, in an imaginary world beyond good and evil, a Paradisal Kailyard with a harmless domesticated serpent. [...] The Burns of popular legend is an imaginative incarnation of a people's desires, unfulfilled in life. It has no fundamental resemblance to Burns himself.[10]

Then, from his encounters with what he considered to be the romantic falsehoods of Abbotsford and the Burns Cult, he travelled to Glasgow and the all too evident reality of post-industrial decline. The next stage in his travels took him north, through the empty glens of the Highlands to reach the Pentland Firth and finally the ferry to Orkney, the place that would mean most to him at the end of his tour.

As one might expect from Edwin's writing in general, *Scottish Journey* is not a travel book in the usual sense of the term. His journey is an interior journey, where the traveller does not merely report on the surface terrain of the territory and peoples he encounters, but uses the voyage to explore his own and their essential being, and that of the times in which they live. In his book, descriptions of landscape and incident become a metaphor for a deeper psychological and philosophical search, what his fellow Scottish writer MacDiarmid would call, in his 1939 book *The Islands of Scotland*, the attempt 'to express through the physical form the spiritual meaning of Scotland today'.[11] It is also a political and sociological book, especially in the sections that deal with the conditions of the slum dwellers in 1930s Glasgow, and the empty landscapes of the Highlands, which had never recovered from the depopulation of the Clearances in the later eighteenth and nineteenth centuries.

---

[9] Ibid., pp. 41, 45, 57, 58, 59.
[10] Ibid., p. 90.
[11] Hugh MacDiarmid, *The Islands of Scotland* (London: Batsford, 1939), p. xix.

George Malcolm Thomson, Edwin's Hampstead neighbour, and Andrew Dewar Gibb, Professor of Scots Law at Glasgow University, had already written accounts of what they saw as an economically and socially deprived Scotland in books such as *Caledonia or The Future of the Scots* (1927) and *Scotland in Eclipse* (1930). But in addition to dealing with economic decline as a result of businesses moving their headquarters southwards to London, and the resultant emigration of the most able and adventurous in the population in the search for opportunities abroad, Thomson and Gibb had laid much of the blame for what they believed to be Scotland's current sickly situation at the door of Irish immigration and the Catholic inhabitants of the slums found in the city of Glasgow. Dewar Gibb quoted 'an eminent geographer' who had written 'A large foreign population, chiefly Irish, is taking possession, ousting Scotsmen and doing by peaceful penetration what no previous invaders were ever able to do by force'. And for Gibb himself, these immigrants

> are responsible for most of the crime committed in Scotland, which otherwise would be the most law-abiding country in the world. Wheresoever knives and razors are used, wheresoever sneak thefts and mean pilfering are easy and safe, wheresoever dirty acts of sexual baseness are committed, there you will find the Irishman in Scotland with all but a monopoly of the business.

For Thomson, 'Half Scotland is slum-poisoned. The taint of the slum is in the nation's blood; its taint in their minds has given birth to a new race of barbarians.' And for him also, Irish immigrants with their large families and their religion's ban on birth control are much to blame for this situation—'a family of eight people sleep in one bed in a room into which the daylight never penetrates.'[12]

Edwin's *Scottish Journey* would have none of such arrant racism. He was equally concerned about the slums of Glasgow, but unlike Thomson and Gibb he had first-hand experience of them when, left as a teenager to make his own way in the city, he had to pass through such slum areas daily, on his way to poorly-paid work, and was himself often unemployed. Now, observing the still present slums and the results of the economic crises of the 1930s, he focused on the lack of financial help for the unemployed, and their inability to buy the kind of food that would help their children grow healthily. He writes that 'the situation of an unemployed man and of everybody dependent upon him is one of complete helplessness'; and what he calls the 'cast-iron hieroglyphics' of unemployment 'are a sort of black charm keeping them in a state of semi-animation and making them a race of "the dead on leave", "die Toten auf Urlaub", to use Rosa Luxembourg's phrase'. On the

---

[12] Andrew Dewar Gibb, *Scotland in Eclipse* (London: Humphrey Toulmin, 1930); George Malcolm Thomson, *Caledonia or The Future of the Scots* (London: Kegan Paul, Trench, Trubner & Co., [1927], quoted in Margery Palmer McCulloch, ed., *Modernism and Nationalism: Source Documents for the Scottish Renaissance* (Glasgow: Association for Scottish Literary Studies, 2004), pp. 235, 228.

other hand, he believes that Scottish slums are distinguished from English slums in their 'open publication of their degradation, which springs partly from their hopelessness and partly from a feeling that it is wrong that misery and vice such as theirs should be ignored'. Edwin's view is that 'to publish one's degradation is a moral protest', and that this most probably rises 'from a last-ditch sentiment of justice'.[13] He believes that the imperative is to find a way to create social justice, and this leads him, at the end of his journey, to support a socialist as opposed to a nationalist solution to Scotland's problems. For Edwin, neither the Glasgow slums nor the empty Highland glens could be changed merely by the Scots taking charge of their own affairs. He was not necessarily against the Scots regaining a separate national identity and political self-determination, but in the present social and economic condition of Scotland he believes that aim to be divisive.

> Looking, then, at Scotland as impartially as I could, in the little room of the hotel on that last evening of my run, I seemed to see that it was ripe for two things: to become a nation, and to become a Socialist community; but I could not see it becoming the one without becoming the other. [...] The Socialist movement in Scotland is still strong, in spite of the countless discouragements it has suffered; it is strong because it has behind it the drive of economic and historical reality. The National Party has nothing behind it but a desire and nothing before it but an ideal; and it is numerically so weak as to be negligible. These are the facts that no amount of publicity and no degree of romanticising of realities can alter.[14]

Scottish Journey comes to an end with the boat journey across the Pentland Firth and the arrival in an Orkney, which for Edwin was 'the only desirable form of life that I found in all my journeying through Scotland', although he also realized that Orkney's was an 'erratic fruition'[15] and not one that could be repeated in the conditions of early twentieth-century Scotland. Willa and Gavin were waiting for him as the boat docked and—once Edwin had been reminded by the boat staff to take his brake off—the elderly borrowed car took them to the house they had rented for the next three months.

Remembering that summer in Orkney in later writings, both Muirs would tell how they did much less work than they had intended to do, and had a much fuller social life than they had expected to have. The writer Eric Linklater had his home on Orkney, with many of his relations also living close by. They met up with former schoolmates of Edwin who regularly returned to Orkney with their families in the summer. Cursiter's car—still running—took them on expeditions to various parts of the island, as well as to lunch parties or dinner parties, and they welcomed friends to their rented summer house. Freed from city traffic, their dog had

---

[13] *Scottish Journey*, pp. 137–8, 122.
[14] Ibid., p. 234.
[15] Ibid., p. 241.

a new life chasing hares on the hillsides, while Gavin gradually regained his lost confidence. The two young household helpers, Hilde and Eja, tramped over the hillsides or swam in the sea, and Willa gradually became aware that Edwin seemed to be thinking quite seriously about the possibility of Orkney as a replacement for their Hampstead home. James Whyte had earlier tried to persuade them to move to St Andrews where he was building two modern houses in North Street, close by the Abbey and its grounds. He would keep one of them for Edwin and Willa, he suggested. Willa was attracted to the idea, since she had happy memories of her time at university there, and she thought that St Andrews would be a good place for Gavin to grow up. Unfortunately, their delay in coming to a decision led Whyte to let his newly built house to a French lecturer at the University, but he was still willing to look out for a suitable furnished property for them to rent if they decided to move north. Rather than consider St Andrews, however, Edwin seemed to Willa to be looking for a home in Orkney. There appeared to be a number of redundant manses on offer for rental; why not go and have a look at some of them? Willa would remember how the more manses they looked at—'all in country parishes full of light and fresh air'—the more uneasy she began to feel about committing herself permanently to Orkney. Orkney was Edwin's place—he was familiar with its weather, its darkness in the winter as well as its long summer days and light quality. As in Dormansland, so long ago, she worried about having to deal with an unfamiliar coal-fed range, and having to carry coal to light fires in cold upstairs bedrooms. She worried about being able to cope with the darkness of the Orkney winter. The problem of making a decision was unexpectedly taken from her however, when, playing a game of football with Gavin and Edwin, she experienced a recurrence of the prolapse problems that had resulted from her difficult childbirth with Gavin. The island doctor could give only limited treatment, so they had to make arrangements to return to the mainland. The idea of making Orkney a permanent home was tacitly abandoned, and Edwin duly asked James Whyte to look for something suitable in St Andrews. Willa rationalized the decision by telling herself that Edwin would be 'less cut off from the contemporary world in St Andrews'. After all, he himself had said that Orkney was an 'erratic fruition', and that it 'lay outside the main stream of future social development'. St Andrews would be a more suitable home for the family.[16]

This was an uncertain time in their family life, and neither Edwin nor Willa would be generous with information or entirely accurate in dating their later accounts of the period. *The Story and the Fable*, from 1940, ends with a short discussion of their time in Prague and Dresden between 1921 and 1922. The *Autobiography* of 1954 deals economically with some of the following years. It covers the period of Gavin's accident in 1933, their summer holiday in Orkney, and their move to St Andrews in less than two pages, suggesting that the St Andrews move

---

[16] *Belonging*, pp. 181, 183.

came immediately after their first (rather than their second) summer in Orkney. Willa, unusually, misdates the Edinburgh P.E.N. International Congress as taking place in Edinburgh in 1933 as opposed to 1934, and—perhaps relying on Edwin's 1954 volume for her own later account in *Belonging*—she appears to suggest that the family's move to St Andrews took place immediately after her prolapse problems in Orkney in the summer after that conference. In fact, it was not until late August 1935 that they were able to move from Hampstead to St Andrews. The intervening twelve months were, as had become normal, filled with literary commitments. Edwin had to write the account of his journey throughout Scotland and he was still busy with regular reviewing and other magazine contributions, which now included writing for the *Scotsman*. In December 1935 his small book *Social Credit and the Labour Party: An Appeal* had developed out of his belief that socialism was the only way to deal with the desperate conditions he had witnessed in the empty Scottish glens and the city slums.

Yet another publishing venture had arisen shortly after their Orkney summer in 1934, when both Edwin and Willa agreed to contribute to a series of books on Scotland to be edited by Lewis Grassic Gibbon (James Leslie Mitchell), author of the recently acclaimed novel *Sunset Song*, and the poet and journalist Hugh MacDiarmid. Provisionally titled 'Meanings in Scotland', the series had been concocted and the idea sold to Routledge in the autumn of 1934, when Grieve was in London for several months and in regular contact with Gibbon who lived in Welwyn Garden City. Discussion of possible contributors and topics travelled back and forward between putative editors and the publisher, and in October a letter from Edwin to Gibbon confirmed that he and Willa were prepared to give up an idea they themselves had been considering for a series of books on aspects of Scotland, and instead join in with the 'Meanings in Scotland' project. It was agreed that Edwin would write on 'Scott and Scotland' and Willa on 'Mrs Grundy in Scotland'. Edwin's letter makes it clear that he finds the amount of the advance to be immediately paid by Routledge—consisting of only half of the entire fee—not particularly satisfactory, since he had generally been given the whole fee 'for books which require a certain preparation, as the Scott will do'. Willa's letter to Gibbon was characteristically unconventional. She wrote 'My dear Leslie, Edwin and I have decided after all to put our eggs into your basket—this might be given a Freudian interpretation!—and I have agreed to come in on the series on the same terms as Edwin, for the sake of domestic harmony.'[17] The new project was, however, another burden to add to the existing commitments of translation, largely carried out by Willa, and the writing of books, reviews and essays by Edwin. What turned out to be a discordant relationship between Gibbon and the publisher,

---

[17] Edwin Muir, letter to Lewis Grassic Gibbon, 19 October, 1934; Willa Muir, letter to Lewis Grassic Gibbon, 19 October, 1934, Routledge archive LGG Voice of Scotland Series RKP8/1, University of Reading.

as well as difficulties in matching writers and topics, could not have made the project any easier for the already harassed Muirs. As the more experienced and best-known of the two editors of the new series, MacDiarmid was anxious that he should have an equal say in the choice of contributors and topics, as well as the reading of submitted manuscripts, but Gibbon appeared to think that, as the originator of the idea, he should be the first among equals. Mr Paterson of Routledge wrote to MacDiarmid on 9th October.

> The question arises as to whether you or Grassic Gibbons [sic] would be the best person to undertake the correspondence with the proposed authors. There are a lot of problems related to these negotiations, for as you can well appreciate, unless we can assume an enormous spectacular sale (and I am not quite so optimistic as all that) the advances would have to be modest. [...] I genuinely feel that as your position in Scottish letters is of so infinitely more defined a quality than Gibbons', you would be much the better editor. Or as an alternative, you might feel that joint editorship was preferable.

And he added—

> I have an uneasy feeling that Grassic Gibbons will consider these advances all too modest. There is no doubt that he has got ambitious ideas on the subject of advances. While I quite sympathise with this outlook, there is at the same time still the economic situation to be considered. There is of course the chance that the books will be really big sellers, but that remains to be seen and I do not want to gamble with the firm's money too much without some more concrete certainty.[18]

In point of fact, senior partner or not, MacDiarmid had rather more experience of poor sales than Gibbon, whose earlier books as James Leslie Mitchell, as well as *Sunset Song* from 1932, had found favour with American readers. The question was eventually settled in favour of joint editorship, but by late December 1934 relationships between Gibbon and the publisher had become increasingly difficult, with Mr Warburg of Routledge consulting the firm's lawyers as to whether they would be justified in sacking Gibbon. MacDiarmid, who had received a copy of the letter from Gibbon which had precipitated the consultation with the lawyers, wrote to the firm's Mr Paterson from Whalsay (where he was now principally based) that he was 'utterly astounded and disgusted at Gibbon's letter, copy of which you sent me (and which, of course, I regard as absolutely confidential)'. And he continued—

> Many of us who have been interested in his work have feared that his potentialities would be drastically restricted by this incredible coarse strain under his veneer,

---

[18] Letter from Mr Paterson of Routledge to C. M. Grieve, 9 October, 1934, Routledge archive RKP 8/9 MS 1489, University of Reading.

and, indeed, his money-grabbing propensities were discerned and discussed by us when the present arrangements were first mooted. They are bad enough in themselves but when they are conjoined to such impudent expressions towards Mr Warburg the matter is, of course, insufferable.[19]

In the end, Routledge decided to persevere with Gibbon, while assuring MacDiarmid that he would read the manuscripts for the series as they came in. And by the beginning of 1935, Gibbon himself seemed to be adopting a more cooperative tone. Then, suddenly, came the tragic news that he had died from peritonitis on 7 February three days after an operation for gastric ulcers. It seems that the peritonitis that killed him had already set in, but it had not been detected by his doctor. His wife Rebecca, known as Ray or Rhea, wrote to Valda and Chris Grieve that he was in severe discomfort before the end of the year, but the doctor continued to prescribe a mixture of powders that eased the pain temporarily but did not treat the cause. This undetected illness may have been responsible for the aggressive correspondence that so upset the Routledge directors, although Gibbon did have a reputation for liking to get his own way. His death came as a considerable shock to the literary community in Scotland and to his friends in London. Edwin and Willa had visited him only the weekend before his death and Edwin was one of the writers who successfully supported an application to the Royal Literary Fund on behalf his widow, to whom they made an award of £300.

The 'Meanings in Scotland' series—which was soon to change its name to 'Voice of Scotland'—seemed to cast a shadow beyond the death of Gibbon. Now, the sole editor, MacDiarmid, was himself hospitalized in August 1935 and out of touch with publishing affairs for six weeks. '[N]o ordinary illness,' he wrote to Routledge's Paterson, 'but a touch and go one—a horrible immanence of death from which I was only rescued by a miracle of specialist treatment.'[20] Willa Muir was also unwell, with Edwin writing to Stephen Spender in May 1935 that he had had 'to take Willa down to the country for a holiday; she has not been very well for some time; she is much better now, but still in the country, but I've returned.'[21] And July found Edwin writing to his sister Lizzie in Glasgow, after the sudden death of his brother-in-law George. 'I can't say how sorry and shocked I am by the sad news. There is nothing I can say to comfort you at present, and Ethel and Irene too. But, if you need any help of any kind, Willa and I will be more than glad to do anything we can.' He added, 'I wish we had been in Scotland already; we will be up there in a fortnight, by the middle of August; we're making preparations now.' He gives Lizzie their new address of 'Castlelea, The Scores, St Andrews', and says that they will be staying in Scotland for a few years. 'So that if there is any difficulty you can always come

---

[19] Letter from C. M. Grieve to Paterson 10 January 1935, RKP 8/9 MS 1489, University of Reading.
[20] Letter from C. M. Grieve to Paterson, 13 October 1935, RKP 8/9 MS 1489, University of Reading.
[21] Edwin Muir, letter to Stephen Spender, May 1935, NLS, Acc. 13226/1.

there.' And he asks her to 'get Ethel or Irene to write to me and tell me if I can do anything now [...] We are so distressed about it.'[22]

With such troubles on top of their writing commitments, it is not surprising that both Edwin and Willa had difficulty in keeping to the agreed schedule for their contributions to the Routledge series. Regular letters arrived from the publisher asking for blurbs to be used for publicity purposes, and asking Edwin for a decision as to whether he intended to write on Scott, as previously arranged, or on Burns, the topic that Gibbon had chosen, but which now needed a new author. Edwin asked Routledge if he could borrow the manuscript of William Power's book in the series, *Literature in Scotland*, to see what he had said about Burns and Scott and so help him decide which writer he himself should write upon; and as late as July 1935 the publisher was writing to Edwin to 'please let me have back now Power's book on Scottish literature, quite apart from whether you have made up your mind yet for Burns or Scott. We must have Power's book back to go to the printers.' Previously, at the end of June, Routledge's Mr Paterson had written to Mr Warburg agreeing with his view that 'Edwin Muir is likely to write a more profitable book on Burns than on Scott' and that he believed that Muir 'is considerably more knowledgeable on Burns which will mean an earlier delivery of the manuscript'. In the end, however, Edwin decided to stay with Scott, and in mid-August 1935, shortly before the family finally moved to St Andrews, Routledge was sending a request for publicity material 'which almost takes the shape of an S.O.S' because of the short time available before the publication of the first books in the series. This exasperated correspondence from the publisher continued into the autumn with a warning at one point that, 'unless we can be sure that one or other of the books will be delivered to us within the next two months, we shall have seriously to consider cancelling the contracts.'[23] Promises of delivery continued throughout November and December and into 1936, when Willa eventually sent off the manuscript of *Mrs Grundy in Scotland* on 7 February. It is not clear exactly when Edwin delivered the manuscript of *Scott and Scotland* (promised for November 1935), but it was still missing in January 1936. The book itself was eventually published in September 1936, but its troubled gestation only heralded the controversy it aroused when it finally appeared.

---

[22] Edwin Muir, letter to Lizzie Thorburn, 29 July 1935, NLS, Acc. 13226/1.
[23] Correspondence between Routledge and Edwin and Willa Muir, 30 Sept 1935, RKP 13/13, University of Reading.

11
Scotland and Europe 1935–1939

> The world seems to be showing its shape more and more clearly every year, almost every month, and warning us more and more that it will have to be changed.
>
> Edwin Muir, letter to Sydney Schiff (1938)

The decision to move to St Andrews appeared to be a good one when the family arrived there in late August 1935. Their new home, 'Castlelea', was a semi-detached stone-built villa situated at the end of a long residential road called 'The Scores', close by the ruins of St Andrews Castle with all its historical associations, and also close to the university and the Abbey. The front rooms of the house looked outwards across the wide stretch of the sea and a footpath led to the East Sands. All the necessary facilities of a town such as shops and schools were also within walking distance. When Edwin wrote to Stephen Spender in October 1935, confirming the final outcome of their problematic negotiations with Heinemann over the proposed Hölderlin poetry translations project, he ended his letter by saying, 'I like being here very much, and I find that I am beginning to write poetry again. If you wish to see us, and at any time you wish to see us, please come and do so.'[1] For the moment, however, as the increasingly urgent correspondence from Routledge makes clear, their top priority was to deal with their accumulating literary contracts. They did of course meet with James Whyte. He showed them over his bookshop and one of the newly built houses he had hoped they would occupy and they dined with him at his own house in nearby South Street—a building he had completely modernized. Willa felt that she was being 'ushered into a whole new world, since in James's house the furniture, the pictures, the lighting, as well as the music, were all fashionably *avant-garde*'.[2] The bookshop was equally *avant-garde*, with shelves of recently reviewed books and contemporary magazines, including some of the most modern journals from France and the United States, all displayed on the counter.

Edwin's *Scottish Journey* was published shortly after their arrival, followed by his *Social Credit and the Labour Party* in December. By the end of 1935 a large group of his reviews were published in the *Listener, Scotsman, New English Weekly,*

---

[1] Edwin Muir, letter to Stephen Spender, 16 October 1935, Stephen Spender Correspondence, HRC, Box 5.1, HR 88.
[2] *Belonging*, p. 184.

and the *London Mercury*. Similar commitments lay in wait for the early months of the new year, together with his much overdue manuscript for *Scott and Scotland*. Willa in her turn was trying to meet new deadlines for her equally overdue manuscript of *Mrs Grundy in Scotland*, with repeated promises of completion dates regularly unfulfilled. Eventually, in the autumn of 1935, their long-suffering publisher threatened to cancel both contracts, which prompted Edwin to promise that Willa's book would be delivered within two months and his own within three. Routledge had their doubts, but Willa eventually delivered *Mrs Grundy* on 7 February 1936, with a surprisingly jaunty letter, given her history of broken promises.

> Here is Mrs Grundy in Scotland. I can send you a list of chapter titles in a day or two. I can also provide, if you like, a marvellous picture, which is hanging in a hotel in Wester Ross, depicting the Broad and the Narrow Way, and the evils of dancing, gambling, Sunday trains etc. It would make a double illustration, or end covers, or a jacket. It is an incredibly funny and solemn picture. The copy I have procured can be posted to you, if you like.[3]

The book, without the picture (copyright for which was owned by the North of Scotland Biblical and Tract Society), was published on 4 May, and had a mixed reception. Under the title 'Counterblasts to Knox', George Scott Moncrieff in *The New Statesman* enjoyed the presentation of Mrs Grundy as 'a medley of unpleasant and social phenomena', along with Compton Mackenzie's *Catholicism in Scotland* also from the *Voice of Scotland* series, saying how much he enjoyed both writers' attacks on the Presbyterianism of Knox and its effect on Scottish mores over the centuries. Catherine Carswell, a discriminating reviewer, did not appear quite so impressed when she reviewed these books in *The Spectator*. She found Mackenzie 'magnificently biased' in favour of Catholicism, adding that 'in the long and eloquent account of Protestant wrongdoing, only one paragraph is allotted for the failure in Scotland of the main body of the Catholic clergy. Yet what could Protestantism have done but for that failure?' In her review of Willa's book, her choice of verb in the sentence, 'Mrs Muir rumbles on' suggests that she was not overly impressed either, given her criticism of Willa's use of 'slang expressions which carry neither rapier point nor bludgeon weight'.[4] While some present-day critics have attempted to see *Mrs Grundy* as another example of Willa's feminist writings, the study, like *Women: An Inquiry*, suggests that her talents do not lie in the area of analytical essay writing. The book is too short to develop a full account of the actual historical situation in Scotland, which might

---

[3] Willa Muir, letter to Routledge, 7 February 1936, Routledge archive RKP 13/13, University of Reading.
[4] Catherine Carswell, 'The Grundy Women', *Spectator*, 22 May 1936, p. 946; George Scott Moncrieff, 'Counterblasts to Knox', *New Statesman*, 27 June 1936, p. 1040.

have underpinned Willa's satire, and it is too long in its repetitive and tiresome descriptions of how this English theatrical character had somehow smuggled herself into Scotland to change the nature of the country and its female inhabitants. It is difficult to envisage the readership she had in mind for the book. Willa states in the dedication that it 'was planned for the delectation of LEWIS GRASSIC GIBBON', with whom she (as well as Francis George Scott) shared a kind of wild, undisciplined sense of humour; and it may be that 'Mrs MacGrundy' was written with that coterie in mind. Willa's acknowledgements also express her 'debt to Mrs Mary Litchfield'—another unconventional friend—'who provided much of my information', a comment that may to some extent explain the lack of informed, discursive argument in the book, as well as the second-hand nature of her accounts of the Mrs Grundy phenomenon.[5] It seems likely that Willa's book, planned as a satirical squib, was just too hurriedly produced under a heavy workload, and recurring poor health.

The reception of Edwin's *Scott and Scotland* proved rather more controversial when it eventually achieved publication in September 1936, for its thesis struck at the heart of the interwar literary revival initiated by the writings of MacDiarmid in the early 1920s, a movement that was experiencing its own difficulties by the mid-1930s. As is clear from Edwin's correspondence and his prose writings generally, including the recently published *Scottish Journey*, he was socialist in his politics, but not attracted to communism like MacDiarmid and many of the younger poets he met in Hampstead. For Edwin, as he had argued in 'Bolshevism and Calvinism' in the *European Quarterly*, Russian communism was too close to the restrictive ideology of Scottish Calvinism. His own vision of an ideal society was the kind of socially cooperative one he had experienced in his early years in Orkney. He was not against a self-determining Scotland, but he was against a narrowly nationalistic one. For Edwin it was socialism that had 'the drive of economic and historical reality'[6] behind it and his case had much to support it at this time. The two nationalist parties in Scotland—the National Party of Scotland formed in 1928 and the more right-wing Scottish Party, brought into being around 1930 by George Malcolm Thomson and Andrew Dewar Gibb—decided to come together to form the Scottish National Party in 1934, the year of Edwin's Scottish journey. But the new party was not free from internal divisions, as became clear in the late 1930s and early 1940s, when war with Germany became a reality and some activists such as the poet Douglas Young from the Aberdeen branch, campaigned against Scotsmen being called up to fight what they saw as England's war. In 1936, however, it was Edwin's views on the future of Scottish literature that were to prove so controversial that his breach with MacDiarmid was never to be healed.

[5] Willa Muir, 'Dedication' and 'Acknowledgement' in *Mrs Grundy in Scotland* (1936), reprinted in *Imagined Selves*.
[6] *Scottish Journey*, p. 234.

What caused MacDiarmid such pain was a statement, in the short 'Introductory' section to the book, that seemed to dismiss all that he himself had fought for in the literary revival movement.

> The practical present-day problem may be put somewhat as follows: that a Scottish writer who wishes to achieve some approximation to completeness has no choice except to absorb the English tradition, and that if he thoroughly does so his work belongs not merely to Scottish literature but to English literature as well. On the other hand, if he wishes to add to an indigenous Scottish literature, and roots himself deliberately in Scotland, he will find there, no matter how long he may search, neither an organic community to round off his conceptions, nor a major literary tradition to support him, nor even a faith among the people themselves that a Scottish literature is possible or desirable, nor any opportunity, finally of making a livelihood by his work.

This challenging proposition—which may well have persuaded some nationalist readers to explore the book no further—was compounded by a comment in the following 'Language' chapter that Scottish poetry at that time had 'shrunk to the level of anonymous folk-song'. There are 'half-truths' here, poorly developed, and Edwin's argument continued—

> Hugh MacDiarmid has recently tried to revive it by impregnating it with all the contemporary influences of Europe one after another, and thus galvanize it into life by a series of violent shocks. In carrying out this experiment he has written some remarkable poetry; but he has left Scottish verse very much where it was before.[7]

Actually, Edwin's writing on the Scots language and MacDiarmid's achievement had been expounded more satisfactorily in the American *Saturday Review of Literature* in 1925 and in his review of *A Drunk Man Looks at the Thistle* in *The Nation* of January 1927. In the former he pointed to the 'essential difference between literary language and spoken language' and how in Scottish poetry since the time of Burns this difference had weakened, resulting in the Scots language used by a dialect poet being the same as the daily language used by his village neighbours. In making this distinction, Edwin in this early article was clear that Burns' own poetry still sustained this linguistic difference, and that the Scots language of Burns 'was really artificial, a composite language, like Mr M'Diarmid's'. Nevertheless, over time and as English became more widely used in Scotland, 'there has been no Scottish literary instrument for over a century, no larger speech transcending the bounds of everyday speech, and capable of dealing with every variety of

---

[7] Edwin Muir, *Scott and Scotland* (1936: Edinburgh: Polygon, 1982), pp. 4, 9.

experience.' Edwin is dealing specifically with the use of *language* in Scottish *poetry* here, and in his subsequent review of *A Drunk Man* in *The Nation* he had further discussed how MacDiarmid's language and the overall design of his new long poem 'might be called indifferently psychological or philosophical: it is the picture of a mind; it is an image of the world as symbolized in the thistle. The world changes its shape, is lost, appears again as Mr M'Diarmid follows the transitions, daring and yet natural, in the mind of the monologist.' He considers that the variety and value of the poem is created by its 'translations from Russian, German and French, parodies of contemporary poetry, love songs, sacred and profane, pictures of Scottish life, satire on the Kailyard School, and a long address to Dostoyevsky'. So, in Edwin's view, *A Drunk Man* was not only a linguistically adventurous poem, but also one that brought together the national and the wider international human world, along with deeper investigations into the nature of human life itself. As the Drunk Man himself says, 'He canna Scotland see wha yet / Canna see the Infinite, / And Scotland in true scale to it.'[8] Edwin understood what MacDiarmid had achieved in his own poetry, but he was also aware, as he wrote in *Scott and Scotland* that 'a really original Scots poet like Hugh MacDiarmid has never received in Scotland any criticism of his more ambitious poems which can be of the slightest use to him.' And even more provocative, the final part of the introductory section suggests that the poet who consciously decides to root himself in Scotland will find no opportunity there 'of making a livelihood by his work'—a conclusion only too painfully relevant, perhaps, to MacDiarmid's actual situation at that time.[9]

In her own later comments on the *Scott and Scotland* controversy, Willa blamed 'the uncharacteristic acerbity of Edwin's remarks about Scotland' on 'the effect living in St Andrews had had on him, and I knew that I was responsible for his being in St Andrews'.[10] She was certainly behind the move to St Andrews, but the pessimism of *Scott and Scotland* had deeper roots. Edwin had never felt entirely at home in relation to mainland Scottish culture, preferring to call himself an 'Orkneyman' with Scandinavian influences. More than that, his sense of himself as a person and a writer had been formed by his early exposure to German literature and his European travels, as MacDiarmid acknowledged when he judged him 'in the first flight of contemporary critics of *welt-literatur*'.[11] Edwin was quick to recognize that MacDiarmid's new poetry reached beyond its Scottish context to belong to a wider modern movement in literature and ideas, but he did not believe that the Scots language was the way forward for himself or indeed for

---

[8] Edwin Muir, 'Scottish Renaissance', *Saturday Review of Literature* (NY), II, 17 October 1925, p. 259; 'Verse' [including *A Drunk Man Looks at the Thistle*], *Nation* XL, January 1922, p. 568; quotation from *A Drunk Man*: Hugh MacDiarmid, *Complete Poems 1920-1976*, vol. 1 (London: Martin Brian & O'Keeffe, 1976), p. 162.
[9] *Scott and Scotland*, p. 4.
[10] *Belonging*, p. 195.
[11] 'Edwin Muir', *Contemporary Scottish Studies*, p. 108.

Scottish literature in general. Less impressed than Willa by the modernity of James Whyte's bookshop, he commented on the incongruity between the culture on its shelves and the Scotland he witnessed in *Scottish Journey*. He noted, too, that the bookshop was not patronized by the public or by St Andrews students as he had expected it would be. Indeed, the girls of St Leonard's School, situated in a sizeable historical building with extensive grounds almost immediately opposite the Abbey bookshop, were forbidden to enter it on account of the nature of its books and magazines and the large fresco 'caricature of John Knox astride a beer-cask' which faced the entrance door.[12] Mrs Grundy would have felt at home. In fact, *The Modern Scot* was experiencing difficulties by the spring of 1936, and Whyte had entered into a coalition with another magazine, *The Scottish Standard*, to form a new monthly titled *Outlook*. Whyte would be literary editor and the overall editor would be David MacEwen, a close friend of the novelist Neil M. Gunn, who had been instrumental in forming the Scottish National Party in 1934, and whose own English-language fiction was making a substantial contribution to the literary revival. As it happens, it was the new *Outlook* that featured a pre-publication excerpt from *Scott and Scotland* in its third issue of June 1936, serving to increase the debate about Edwin's book. Neil Gunn made clear his respect for Edwin as a literary critic, but he took him to task in *The Scots Magazine* for October that year, for what he considered to be the simplistic political analysis in *Scott and Scotland*. For Gunn, the faults Edwin perceived in Walter Scott derived from Scott's need to work in a country that had lost its sense of nationhood and was no longer self-determining, and his view was that Scott himself was only too aware of that loss, having in the end called the historical material he dealt with 'stuffing my head with the most nonsensical trash.'[13]

Yet Edwin was not entirely wrong about the conservative nature of contemporary Scottish society and the lack of publishing outlets for innovative writing. James Whyte's cultural aims, and even his style of living, did not fit easily into St Andrews' social mores, and Willa herself began to realize that her own sense of belonging to the town of her student days was no longer applicable to the St Andrews of her adulthood. Indeed, she experienced this soon after their arrival, when she enrolled Gavin in the junior school of Madras College where she had done her training as a teacher of Classics many years previously, and which she remembered as an excellent school. She was sure that her son, who was now approaching his eighth birthday, would do well in its junior department. But she noticed that Gavin became more and more nervous about going to school, and began 'to jerk and twitch' as he had done in London after he was run down by the lorry. On enquiry, the child told her that his teacher was strapping him almost

---

[12] *Belonging*, p. 184.
[13] Neil M. Gunn, review of Muir's *Scott and Scotland*, *Scots Magazine* 26, October 1936, pp. 72–8, reprinted in Alistair McCleery, ed., *Landscape and Light: Essays of Neil M. Gunn* (Aberdeen: Aberdeen University Press, 1987), pp. 122–6, (p. 123).

every day. Willa had already informed the headmaster about Gavin's earlier accident and his nervousness as a result, so she was surprised and disturbed at this information. Leaving the child at home, she went to the school and interviewed his teacher at break time, expecting to be able to resolve the situation. To her surprise, she was told that Gavin had been disobedient in not folding his arms when told to do so, and had even stuck his elbow into the little girl sitting next to him. Boys had to be hardened if they were to grow into men, and so Gavin had to be strapped in order to learn not to be disobedient. Furious, Willa intimated that she would not leave her child to be hardened by such 'drill-sergeant methods', and that Gavin would not be returning to her class.[14] This outcome only brought further problems. Where could Gavin now go for his schooling? If strapping small children was the norm in Madras College, it was unlikely to be absent in the local primary school. That left the prospect of a new fee-paying preparatory school, called New Park, a school on the English model for young boys that was being increasingly patronized by the professional classes in St Andrews. The Muir family could not afford a private school, but felt they had no alternative but to send Gavin to New Park, where neither the cane nor the strap was in use.

As the Muirs began to have a little more time to explore activities in the town, they found that other aspects of St Andrews were not quite as expected—or at least not as Willa had expected. She found herself rebuffed when she went to visit a former friend from student days who was now teaching in the Latin Department at the University—a post Willa herself had held for a year at the outbreak of war in 1914. The friend was not anxious to renew the acquaintanceship. In fact, the Muirs found that the university community at large, especially the English Department, where they had expected to meet like-minded people, was intent on keeping its distance from 'a man who wrote for the papers'. The academics took their cue from the professor of the time, who did not believe that any contemporary work could be considered as 'literature'.[15] Edwin and Willa did eventually make friends with two Europeans, a classical scholar and a mathematician, who took refuge in the town from Hitler's Germany. They also met up with the newly appointed Head of the Psychology Department, a Dr Oeser from South Africa, who had obtained his doctorate from Imperial College, London, and his wife Drury, also a Doctor of Psychology, who had studied at Cambridge. Willa tells how on one occasion they were told by their classical scholar friend that a distinguished classicist, Werner Jaeger, was due to give a lecture in St Andrews about his pilgrimage from Germany to the United States, but that no arrangements had been made for any hospitality after the lecture, apart from the booking of a hotel room. To Willa, this seemed a poor welcome from her own university to a foreign guest, and so after consulting their housekeeper Hilde, who had come with them

---

[14] *Belonging*, p. 188.
[15] Ibid, pp. 189–90.

to St Andrews, Willa invited the speaker to eat with her and Edwin after the lecture, when they had 'a delightfully uninhibited European evening with plenty of wine'.[16] They repeated the invitation some time later when the Prager Quartet from Czechoslovakia performed at the university, and again they had an enjoyable European evening. London friends such as Hugh Kingsmill and Hesketh Pearson stopped by on their way to expeditions further north, and the writer and editor Janet Adam Smith, who had given Edwin his first reviewing contract with *The Listener* and was herself now married and living in Newcastle, also visited. In summer they met up with F. G. Scott, whose family came regularly to St Andrews on holiday, as in St Tropez so many years before, and Willa and 'F. G.' were particularly lively and noisy when brought together. Valda Grieve, the young Cornishwoman who was MacDiarmid's second wife, was taken aback when she first encountered them when visiting St Andrews—Willa 'sprawling on the beach in one of those modern bathing costumes—four sizes too small' and 'holding forth unnecessarily on her favourite topic—phallic symbolism'.[17]

Gradually, then, Edwin and Willa began to make new acquaintances among a group of more adventurous residents in conservative St Andrews who were interested in topics such as psychology, sociology, and politics, although they knew less of the modern literature that so engaged the Muirs. A Discussion Club was formed on the suggestion of Oscar Oeser, consisting of a small group of thirteen members including Oscar and his wife Drury and Edwin and Willa, and this group met alternately in the house of the Muirs or the Oesers. The Thirteen Club, as they named it, continued until just before the outbreak of the Second World War and had a varied number of skills among its members, including workers from the local paper mill as well as young teachers from St Leonards School for Girls. Willa was probably more fulfilled than Edwin in belonging to this club, which she regarded as an experiment in adult education where they all learned from each other. They dined regularly with Oscar and Drury Oeser on Saturday evenings, either in their own house or at the Oesers' flat in Howard Place, where they listened to recordings of Mozart, including Edwin's favourite opera *Don Giovanni*—music that must have reminded them of Salzburg and Vienna. There was no one in St Andrews, however, apart from James Whyte and his partner John Tonge, who could relate to Edwin's literary interests, or indeed understand the importance of the writings of Broch and Kafka that he and Willa had translated and with whose work they were still involved. The Muirs were still in touch with Broch, but few in St Andrews had ever heard of him or Kafka. Edwin would later write that he was 'more unhappy in St Andrews than I had been since the time of my obscure fears and the course of psychoanalysis that dispelled them'.[18] Whyte would not for long continue as

---

[16] Ibid, p. 190.
[17] Alan Bold, *MacDiarmid: Christopher Murray Grieve: A Critical Biography* (London: John Murray, 1988), p. 333.
[18] *An Autobiography*, p. 244.

a resident of St Andrews after *The Modern Scot* was recast as *Outlook*. His early enthusiasm for Scottish national identity and Scotland's literature had not turned out as he had envisaged and his bookshop seemed to be out of bounds for both university and school students. He was saddened by MacDiarmid's harassment of Edwin after the publication of *Scott and Scotland*. He had little patience with the round robin letter against the Muirs that MacDiarmid was circulating, including the charge that Edwin and himself had been responsible for the publishers Lawrence and Wishart rejecting MacDiarmid's 'Red Scotland' book after Routledge had decided not to include it in the *Voice of Scotland* series. Whyte wrote to MacDiarmid from the Isle of Barra on 10 September 1936, 'I had not answered your letter of August 11th because I thought that my own position in your controversy with Edwin Muir had been made sufficiently clear, but your second letter makes it necessary to reply to your allegations point by point.' He states his surprise 'that in the not-so-distant past you should have written so enthusiastically on Muir's literary achievement in *Contemporary Literary Studies* and still more recently. You can scarcely blame me for "falling under his influence" in view of what you wrote and that it was in your own house that I first met him.' Whyte then takes up the more serious allegation about the publication of MacDiarmid's 'Red Scotland' book. 'As far as the publication of 'Red Scotland' is concerned I have an absolutely clear conscience, being informed by Messrs Lawrence and Wishart that they had already decided not to publish the book before my writing to them. In view of the hysterical tone of your circular letter and the many mis-statements which it contained, Muir and I considered ourselves perfectly justified in writing to see a copy of "Red Scotland".' Whyte ends by advising MacDiarmid that if he thinks that Muir's arguments in *Scott and Scotland* are 'so pathetic it is up to you to argue with him in intellectual terms and not in those of a spoilt schoolgirl. If you wish to substantiate your claim to be Scotland's greatest man of letters that is the only course which lies open to you.' And in a postscript, he warns his correspondent that 'I am keeping a copy of this letter should the occasion arise when it must be published in full.'[19]

In addition to the *Scott and Scotland* dispute, MacDiarmid had blamed Whyte for the fact that he himself had not been included in the 1936 issue of the *Left Review*, which featured contributions by Scottish socialist writers such as the Muirs, Catherine Carswell, James Barke, and Neil Gunn, in addition to Whyte himself. Whyte had spent a large part of the summer of 1936 away from St Andrews staying with his family in Braemar as well as travelling to the Western Isles, and F. G. Scott, always a great communicator of gossip, wrote to MacDiarmid on 1 September, immediately after arriving home from his own summer holiday in St Andrews, to the effect that Whyte's relationship with John Tonge appeared to be

---

[19] James Whyte, letter to Hugh MacDiarmid, 10 September 1936, *Dear Grieve: Letters to Hugh MacDiarmid (C. M. Grieve)* ed. John Manson (Glasgow: Kennedy & Boyd, 2011), pp. 172–3.

ending and that Whyte was going off with his family to America around the 20th of the month. On 2 October he wrote again—

> I haven't heard a word of any kind from St Andrews since we left. Willa Muir wrote to Lovey about something or other and invited her through for a farewell party they were giving Jimmy before he went off to America. I think things had been messed up a bit at the time—Tonge's brother in RAF was killed about the middle of Sept. and Whyte was leaving on the 23rd.

He added, 'At any rate he didn't write to me about our proposed golf game at Gleneagles so he went away without any blessings from Glasgow'. Whyte may at that point have been only too glad to get away from the problems of literary Scotland and well able to depart without Scott's blessings. Whyte's final letter to MacDiarmid on the topic of the *Scott and Scotland* excerpt in *Outlook* and the 'Red Scotland' accusations, was headed 'French Line, S.S. Normandie, 27 September 1936'.[20] *Outlook* did not survive beyond 1937, bringing Whyte's brave attempt to create a culturally modernist Scotland to an end. He remained in the United States, opened an art gallery with his brother in Washington, and later married.

Whyte's decision to return to his birthplace may have been conditioned not only by his disillusionment with the cultural and political situation in Scotland but also by the deteriorating political situation in Europe with the outbreak of the Spanish Civil War in 1936 and political events in Hitler's Germany. Edwin wrote to Stephen Spender in late 1936 that he wondered if there was 'any hope of beating off the Fascists in Spain, with Italy and Germany and Portugal for them and apparently nobody against them but the Spanish people'. Spender had asked Edwin to send a poem for *The Left Review*, but Edwin was finding difficulty in writing 'anything that I feel would be suitable'. He told Spender that he had written 'one poem inspired by the situation in Spain and generally, but I feel for the present that I had better keep it to myself, it is so hopeless'. He had previously written that while he was consciously 'a Socialist, and would like to write poetry that would in some way express that fact, when I actually start to write, something else comes up which seems to have nothing to do with Socialism, or is connected with it in some way too obscure for me to detect'. He could not write in the directly political way of the younger poets like Spender. Yet he was conscious that there was a need for such involvement, and wished to be part of it.[21] In a less obvious and perhaps, even to themselves, less conscious way at the time, he and Willa were indeed contributing to the condemnation of fascism by their translation of Kafka's *The Trial*, which was to be published in the spring of 1937. Kafka's great novel was begun in 1914 shortly before the outbreak of the First World War, but it can be seen to foreshadow the

---

[20] Letter to Hugh MacDiarmid from F. G. Scott, *Dear Grieve*, p. 176; Whyte's final letter, p. 175.
[21] Edwin Muir, letter to Stephen Spender, [July–November, 1936], and letter of 19 November 1936, *Selected Letters*, pp. 92, 93.

inhuman developments that would engulf the whole of Europe twenty-five years later. In October 1937, Edwin was writing to Spender again, expressing his 'delight' that 'you like my poems so much: thankful, for I never expect them to be liked, and your way of looking at life, I feel, is so different from mine, though I think they must be similar somewhere'.[22] Spender had reviewed Edwin's new collection *Journeys and Places*, published by Dent in September 1937, and had written appreciatively about it, although making the point that at times he felt the argument of a poem was existing outside the poem itself. As a whole, however, the collection seemed to be moving in a new direction, with Edwin's use of Greek myth in poems such as 'Troy' and 'A Trojan Slave' anticipating his mature use of Greek myth as metaphor in later collections such as *The Labyrinth* and *One Foot in Eden*. It was an increasingly worrying time politically, however, and *Journeys and Places* did not receive the attention Edwin might have wished from the London literary world.

Unhappy in St Andrews and increasingly concerned about political developments in Europe, Edwin and Willa, in their different ways, turned to writing for succour. Edwin began to keep a diary, jotting down thoughts, observations, and memories that would eventually lead him to write his own life story, from his childhood in Orkney to his new beginnings as an author. Willa looked back to her happy years in Hampstead and began to create a third novel. Both activities, however, were coloured by the insecurities of the present, which in Edwin's case surfaced in his dream life. One diary entry describes a dream about T. S. Eliot 'who was taking Willa and myself to his country house: very kind and even mildly jolly, as he has become in the last few years, pleasant and yet with a touch of willed bonhomie which give the pleasantness a slight appearance of falseness, though it is perfectly real'. He remembers, however, that in his dream he himself was 'uneasy'. The road to Eliot's house 'led through a wood; it was quite dark, yet we walked among the trees without stumbling or knocking into anything'. They passed a house with a family sitting in a drawing room which was 'nevertheless in the open air: two walls were ordinary walls with pictures hanging on them, while where the other two walls should have been there was nothing but the wood, with the trees set in good order'. Then, when they eventually reached Eliot's house with its 'old English sitting room with a fire burning on a wide open hearth' and walls looking 'somewhat dilapidated with patches of damp', Eliot 'began to change his clothes, beginning with his trousers'. At that point the dreamer Edwin 'suddenly realised I should have taken my evening suit, and E's behaviour is an indirect rebuke to my remissness'. He awoke 'feeling my shortcomings, how little I had made of my life, and the guilt that comes from the feeling that I am not what I should have been, and have not realised the powers within me that I should have realised'. He wondered, 'Do all people or most people who have reached my age have that feeling?' In relation to his time in St Andrews, his diary also notes how he has

---

[22] Edwin Muir, letter to Stephen Spender, 6 October, 1937, *Selected Letters*, pp. 97–8.

'often been conscious of an ache, walking down these streets here, looking at these people, and the cause of that ache is the *knowledge* that I do not fit these people, and that they do not fit me'. Yet he senses, too, that 'this is a general disharmony not one personal to myself. For these people do not fit each other, and for all of them society is like a furnished house which they have rented for their life here and in which they will never feel at home.'[23]

Willa's new novel, to be called 'Mrs Muttoe and the Top Storey', moved slowly, interrupted by periods of illness and translation work. Like Edwin's diary, it turned out to have a latent life of its own, for its life-writing source seems to have transformed itself into an account of its principal character's underlying fears and everyday harassments quite different to the Hampstead idyll portrayed in its author's autobiography and her letters to friends. In addition to recurring difficulties with domestic help, resulting in an accident to her son, Alison Muttoe, the novel's protagonist, and a barely disguised stand-in for Willa, becomes increasingly obsessed with the negative aspects of a capitalist society in which she, along with her servants, is struggling to survive. Her nightmares of finding herself lost in huge constructions, sometimes new buildings under construction, and others disintegrating, give surreal life to the mental and emotional pressures of an everyday life that is becoming unviable, although not yet acknowledged as such. It is Alison Muttoe, too, who is the chief translator of the work of 'Garta' (a clever reuse by Willa of Max Brod's name for Kafka in his own fiction featuring the Czech author), and this translation work too features in her nightmares. For Alison Muttoe—

> It was true that Garta's work seemed to come straight out of the region which evoked dreams and nightmares. He showed an uncanny skill in describing the twists and turns of frustrated feelings; merely to read him was like having an anxiety dream by proxy. And every incident in his stories, almost every phrase, carried so many implications that the translation had to be done slowly, with extreme care. Yes, Garta is making me fearful, decided Alison Muttoe, opening her jotter.[24]

Despite its many interesting features, the *Mrs Muttoe* book never found a publisher, perhaps because of its author's recurring periods of illness in these difficult years, or because of wartime conditions; but also, perhaps, because the manuscript needed more severe editing on Willa's part, to give her personal sources an independent fictional life of their own.

1938 was a particularly difficult year for the Muirs. In June they decided to move from the 'Castlelea' home to a less expensive house in Queen's Gardens where they

---

[23] Edwin Muir, Diary 1937–39, 23 April [1938], NLS, MS 19668.
[24] Willa Muir, 'Mrs Muttoe and the Top Storey', unpublished typescript, Willa Muir archive, UStA, 38466, 1.2, pp. 252–3.

were at last able to have their own furniture installed. Gavin's schooling was costing them more than they could afford and translation contracts were beginning to dry up. Kafka's *The Trial* had been published by Gollancz in the previous year and would be followed in the autumn of 1938 by his *America*, this time published by Routledge. Two other translated books were published in February and April of 1938, but there would be no translation work for the Muirs in 1939 or 1940. Edwin was still reviewing, with the *Listener* and *Scotsman* as his regular outlets. He also went to Edinburgh for BBC broadcasts, and gave an occasional evening lecture, but on the whole their finances were stretched to their limit, and sometimes beyond that limit. Edwin had been trying to help his younger London-based friend, the poet George Barker, to find work by contacting some of his own BBC connections, and had invited him to come to St Andrews to stay for a time with him and Willa. Barker appears not to have had the money for such an expedition, and Edwin wrote that he would 'gladly send you the money if I could, but the moving of our furniture up here, where we hoped to live cheaper, has bogged us in debt, and when we shall be out of it, except by good fortune, I don't know'. Nevertheless, he added 'Do come, if you can come at any time.'[25] Hermann Broch was another friend about whom they worried. They had repeatedly tried to persuade him to leave Austria and to come and stay with them in St Andrews. But he was reluctant to leave his country which would also mean leaving his mother and son behind, although he did send some manuscripts to the Muirs for safekeeping. After Hitler's annexation of Austria in March 1938, however, it was clear that he had to make plans to leave. Broch had been arrested and put in prison immediately after the *Anschluss* because of his anti-fascist writings, but was fortunate to be released after a month. Now his problem was to get a British Home Office visa to allow him to enter the country and come to St Andrews. This was not an easy achievement, for since a man in Broch's situation would not be allowed to return to the annexed Austria, he must have someone willing to support him financially in Britain before a visa could be granted. Edwin and Willa were willing to do this temporarily, but their own financial circumstances were such that this could not be a lasting solution. As so often in the past, Edwin turned to his old friend Sydney Schiff, with whom he had lost contact during the later 1930s. As it happens, Schiff had already heard of Broch's plight from Broch's friend and assistant Anja Herzog, and he expressed his willingness to help. Edwin wrote thanking Schiff for his offer, and told of his own enquiries, through a civil service friend in London, as to what could be done to forward the visa application. He also contacted Herbert Read and Aldous Huxley, both of whom admired Broch's work, to see if they, too, could aid the visa application. Huxley, unfortunately, had by this time gone to South America, but Read was willing to do what he could. By the end of May it appeared that Broch's visa application would be granted, and Edwin and Willa

---

[25] Edwin Muir, letter to George Barker, 15 October 1938, HRC, MS-00216.

waited anxiously for news of his safe departure from Austria. Edwin's diary for 15 August 1938 announces Broch's arrival at their home.

> Hermann B. has come, strange and fine creature. Talked about many things, the three of us. The pettiness of the Nazis. Benches on the streets in Vienna: 'Here no Jews may sit'. Parks: 'Jews enter here at their peril', with a death's head as a device. Mean and ignominious exercise of power.

Then he adds, somewhat incongruously 'W. is interested in what H. said about the ugliness of people in the West of Scotland—Glasgow mainly. I'm sure this has something to do with Calvinism.'[26] In *Belonging*, Willa would remember Broch's stay with them and how 'the spare bedroom at the top of the house—all we could offer Hermann—was spare enough in comfort, like our other bedrooms, and had only a small gas fire to warm it.' She tried to persuade Broch to come downstairs to the warmer drawing room, but he insisted in staying in the cold bedroom, 'answering letters from desperate people in Vienna who thought he might help them to get out too', and leaving his 'solitary confinement only for meals, for going walks in the afternoon, and in the evenings'. Willa continues, 'He was glad to have escaped from Austria, glad to be with us, but he was profoundly unhappy.'[27] Broch stayed in St Andrews for a little over a month, but left for the United States just before the Munich Agreement of 29 September, and the postponement of war with Germany. Edwin explained Broch's departure in a letter he wrote to George Barker on 15 October, because 'he could stand it no longer; he saw the War and an interment [*sic*] camp straight before him, and he went off to the United States.' He continued 'But he said that even that terror of waiting was nothing compared with the terror in Vienna for the month or two before he got out of it.' Edwin, like many people at the time of Munich, seemed at first to think that war would not now happen, continuing 'Well, it's past, and I think for a long time; I expect we'll have ten or twenty years of reaction now, with all the big powers, Germany, Italy, France and England, united in an unholy accord. I may be wrong.'[28] He was wrong, of course, and Chamberlain's Munich Agreement could not stop the inevitable conflict. Then on Christmas Day came news of the death of their Czech friend Karel Čapek. He had been a strong supporter of the new Czech Republic and its president in its optimistic years, and a fierce critic of fascism in his later writing. Friends had urged him to leave Czechoslovakia after Munich, but he had delayed until it was too late, unwilling to leave his country. He died of pneumonia on Christmas Day, although many friends and supporters, including Edwin, believed he had died also of a broken heart after the betrayal of Munich.

[26] Edwin Muir, Diary 15 August 1938, NLS, MS 19668.
[27] *Belonging*, p. 199.
[28] Edwin Muir, letter to George Barker, 15 October 1938, HRC, MS-00216.

The post-Munich period brought different problems to the Muir family. The German Hilde, who had been the mainstay of their household since Hampstead decided that she wanted to return to Germany. She was no fascist supporter, but like many others she believed that the Munich Agreement had turned the tide against war and now it was time for her to return home to find a husband. This was a shock to Willa, who lacked house-management skills at any time, but was regularly unwell in these later years. Initially, and after some difficulty, Willa found a refugee from Berlin to replace Hilde, but this young woman was well educated with a doctorate and she appeared to resent the fact that she had to do housework while Willa translated books from German, a task she might have deemed her own. Whatever the reason, she and Willa did not fit together, and she was replaced by a local household help whose cooking skills left something to be desired. And then in January 1939, Willa fainted. Her heart was missing beats and her whole system appeared to have become overstrained by the gynaecological problems of Gavin's birth, which had never really been properly attended to. In response to an earlier letter about Broch, Edwin wrote to Sydney Schiff on 16 January—

> Forgive me for not replying sooner. But Willa has been unwell; she has been ordered by the doctor to lie on her back and rest; her heart is weakened and missing its beat; and after her rest she must have a minor internal operation. I have been unwell too, and have had to have out all my remaining teeth but two; after this I shall be all right again. In the middle of all this, Gavin has had chickenpox but that is a minor matter, and he is almost well again. But it has been a troubled time, and as far as Willa is concerned, still is.

News about Broch in the USA was better. Schiff's letter included a letter from Broch with reassuring information about his situation. The Schiffs and the Muirs had been concerned about his lack of communication, apart from a few postcards which said he was 'working wildly'. But at least they had an address for him now and could contact him again.[29]

Spring in 1939 seemed slow in coming, despite Willa's gradual improvement in the Cottage Hospital. While she was away from home, Edwin found company by occasional visits to the Oesers and other St Andrews acquaintances, talking politics, sometimes disagreeing openly, sometimes silently. He was fond of Drury Oeser, 'one of the nicest women and the most lovable I know.' One evening he went to the Oesers' house specially to see a new philosophy lecturer she wanted him to meet. But the lecturer became involved in 'abstruse philosophical questions' with another philosopher in the room, and when he eventually turned to Edwin he said, 'I believe you do some translating or something. I'm sure I've seen your name on some book or other.' Then the general conversation turned to politics, where the

---

[29] Edwin Muir, letter to Sydney Schiff, 16 January 1939, Schiff Papers, BL, Add MS 52920.

tone seemed to Edwin equally belittling. He wrote in his diary that he got up and walked around the room looking at books, left early, and as he walked home found himself saying over and over again to himself 'A dreadful, awful time! A terrible, terrible time!'[30] But a more truly terrible time arrived in mid-March, when the Germans invaded Czechoslovakia.

> Yesterday Hitler marched into Prague, and he is installed now in the Hradčany. The Prague Policemen keeping order with tears running down their cheeks. I have read the newspapers until I am tired out. I do not know what to think of Chamberlain's speech. Willa said, 'Britain's only policy is to keep the Stock Exchange going'. [...] Women weeping in Prague. Many suicides, mostly among the Jews, who are being driven out from there too.[31]

Edwin had previously written to Sydney Schiff in his January letter—

> I am as sick, I think, as you can be, over the dreadful things that are being done to the Jews, and the darkness that has fallen over them. I am ashamed, as every citizen of this country should be, of the part England has played. And share, with everyone else, part of the responsibility for it; for we have all been too easy-going and thoughtless and hopeful.[32]

Now there was no more reason to be hopeful, as many had been after Chamberlain's visit to Munich and the on-paper abandonment of Czechoslovakia, and when Hitler broke the Treaty by invading Poland, war became certain. Its declaration by the British government on 3 September 1939 brought the uneasy 'peace' to an end, and with it, on a much less momentous but personally significant scale, the end of the Muirs' financial support as translators of German-language literature.

---

[30] Edwin Muir, Diary, 4 March 1939, NLS, MS 19668.
[31] *The Story and the Fable*, p. 257; earlier version in Diary for 16 and 17 March 1939, NLS, MS 19668.
[32] Edwin Muir, letter to Sydney Schiff, 16 January 1939, Schiff Papers, BL, Add MS 52920.

Figure 0.1 Willa Muir in 1944. Portrait by Nigel McIsaac
Source: National Galleries of Scotland. © The McIsaac Family

Figure 0.2 Edwin Muir in 1955
Source: From Willa Muir, *Belonging. A Memoir* (London: The Hogarth Press, 1968)

12
Translating for a Living

> And the fact remains, I am a better translator than he is. The whole current of patriarchal society is set against this fact, however, and sweeps it into oblivion, simply because I did not insist on shouting aloud: 'Most of this translation, especially Kafka, has been done by ME. Edwin only helped'.
>
> Willa Muir, Unpublished Journal (1953)

Before following the Muir family into a new world of Europe at war, this chapter will consider their work as translators of German-language literature, an opportunity that was brought to an end in 1939. Their occupation as translators had begun by chance in 1924, when the American *Freeman* magazine ceased publication and its publisher Huebsch asked if they would be willing to translate three verse plays by Gerhart Hauptmann at a fee of 100 dollars a play. They jumped at the chance and Willa realized that Huebsch's request would allow her to contribute to their earnings without depending on Edwin. Her years of travel in Germany and Austria, together with her time as a teacher in Neill's Hellerau school, gave her confidence and, as Edwin told his Glasgow relatives, she spoke 'almost like a native'.[1] She looked forward to this new occupation with a great deal of pleasure. The three plays duly arrived from Huebsch while they were still living with Neill on the Sonntagsberg and they made a start on the work, with Willa taking the lead in ensuring accuracy in their initial translations, followed by revision when they left Austria and were living for a time with Willa's mother in Montrose. Edwin did not have a high opinion of Hauptmann, despite his winning the Nobel Prize for Literature in 1912, writing to Sydney Schiff from the Sonntagberg that he and Willa were 'tired out' translating and typing up the three plays, saying, 'I really think it has not been the labour which has exhausted us so much as the stupidity of the original. We did not choose Hauptmann for translation (we would never have thought of doing so); it was the publisher's suggestion.'[2] What Edwin does not acknowledge to Schiff, who was at that time still a very new acquaintance, is the fact that these translations had saved them from financial disaster. Willa would appear to have been the sole translator of Hauptmann's fantasy novel *The Island of the Great*

---

[1] Edwin Muir, letter to Lizzie and George Thorburn, *Selected Letters*, p. 26.
[2] Edwin Muir, letter to Sydney Schiff, *Selected Letters*, p. 39.

Mother, which was done when she was preoccupied with *Women: An Inquiry*. The translation, was, however, published under both their names.

It was another writer for whom they did not greatly care, the Munich-born Lion Feuchtwanger, who brought the Muirs to early prominence through their wildly successful rendering of *Jüd Süss*. Again, Willa appears to have been the principal and at times the sole translator of this novel, which they had read for Secker and recommended for publication while they were in Montrose. Willa wrote later that while Edwin was finishing his *Transition* essays, she was 'getting on as fast as I could with this translation, which was wanted by the month of May'. In the spring of 1926, they took the book with them to St Tropez 'to polish off *Jew Süss*'. Willa called this 'polishing off' an 'apt phrase, for I cannot say that we translated *Jew Süss*; what we produced was a polished rendering of it'. And she adds 'In Montrose I had already begun to tailor the style to what I felt would better suit an English public, and in St Tropez we went on doing that, cutting out adjectives and shortening sentences.'[3]

The outcome was a popular success, but without negotiating a royalty on the book's sales they had to settle for only £250 as the translation fee. The Feuchtwanger translation had a backstory they may not have known about. Before asking the Muirs for their view of the book in December 1925, Secker had in February approached D. H. Lawrence for a verdict on its suitability for translation, and Lawrence had replied negatively '*Jud* [sic] *Süss* is a vulgar affair'. After the Muirs' successful translation was published, Lawrence wrote to S. S. Koteliansky, who had asked his advice about a publication project of his own, 'I am a useless person to consult commercially. You know Secker asked me if Jud Süss was worth publishing in translation and I said no! Luckily he did it and saved his life and almost made his fortune. So there am I, as a business adviser!' He held to his original opinion, however. Writing to Secker from Florence, with thanks for sending *Women in Love* and *Sea and Sardinia*, he added 'What a Godsend that *Jud Süss*! Even here people think it is *so* good. Only old Vernon Lee has no use for it—bottle-washings.[4] Edwin and Willa, did negotiate royalties for *The Ugly Duchess*, the next Feuchtwanger novel Secker commissioned, and in Willa's words produced a "faithful" and "good" translation—"authentic Feuchtwanger". But it was not a success with the English-speaking public, and they made little money from it.'[5]

This changed in 1929 when they encountered the German-speaking Czech writer Franz Kafka, whose reputation as one of the most significant modernist writers was significantly enhanced by the Muirs' first English-language translations of his work. Kafka's novel *Das Schloss* had been begun and left unfinished in Prague when Edwin and Willa lived there in the early 1920s, but they heard

---

[3] *Belonging*, pp. 125–6.
[4] *The Letters of D. H. Lawrence*, ed. James Boulton (Cambridge: Cambridge University Press, 1979–2000), vol. 5, letter 3613; vol. 6, letters 4003, 4163.
[5] *Belonging*, p. 134.

nothing about it during their time with the Čapeks and their Czech theatre circle in the city. First published in Munich in 1926, two years after its author's death, *Das Schloss* was edited by his friend Max Brod, and somehow came to Edwin's attention when he was in Scotland in early 1929, researching material for his book on John Knox. Edwin wrote to Sydney Schiff that this new discovery was a 'purely metaphysical and mystical dramatic novel' where 'everything happens on a mysterious spiritual plane which was obviously the supreme reality to the author; and yet in a curious way everything is given solidly and concretely.'[6] The Muir translation of *The Castle*, was duly published by Secker in March 1930, which means that they must have worked extremely hard on it during the summer of 1929 into early 1930, a period when they also had to deal with the death of Willa's mother and Willa's own bouts of illness.

In *Belonging* Willa described the process by which she and Edwin together translated Kafka. She noted a 'difference of emphasis between our separate appreciations of *The Castle*', with Edwin 'more excited by the "whence" and I by the "how"'. She explains this difference by adding 'That is to say, Edwin tried to divine and follow up the metaphysics of Kafka's vision of the universe, while I stayed lost in admiration of the sureness with which he embodied in concrete situations the emotional predicaments he wanted to convey.' As to how they worked together, 'It was simple enough.'—

> We divided the book in two, Edwin translated one half and I the other, then we went over each other's translation as with a fine-tooth comb. By the time we had finished the going-over and put the two halves together the translation was like a seamless garment, for we both loved the sinuous flexibility of Kafka's style—very unlike classical German—and dealt with it in the same way.[7]

This is most probably the method they employed for all their major Kafka translations, such as *The Great Wall of China and Other Pieces*, published in 1933, *The Trial* in 1937, and *America* in 1938. (Their translation of *The Penal Settlement, Tales and Short Pieces* appeared much later in 1948.) Willa was clearly the trained grammatical expert in this process, for although Edwin would appear to have had a wide reading vocabulary as a result of his involvement with German poetry, he had never been trained in the intricacies of grammar like his wife, and was not able, as she was, to come to terms with the complex grammatical structures of the German language. On the other hand, his experience as poet and his interest in imagistic and metaphorical communication, not to mention a penchant for the metaphysics of human existence, made him an essential partner in the Kafka translations, as his own critical essays on Kafka demonstrate.

---

[6] Edwin Muir, letter to Sydney Schiff, *Selected Letters*, p. 67.
[7] *Belonging*, p. 150.

Although the Muir translations did so much to bring Kafka to the attention of an English-speaking readership in Britain and the United States, their versions—most of them still in print today—have fallen out of favour with more recent specialists. Criticism has been directed towards what has been perceived as an over-religious interpretation of *The Castle* in particular, together with a general overreliance on the background material and interpretations as published by Max Brod, Kafka's friend and editor. In fact, Brod had disregarded Kafka's instructions to destroy the work still unpublished at the time of his death in 1924, but few readers—whether general or specialist—would blame him for saving some of the twentieth century's most significant fiction. Even so, Brod's personal interpretations of Kafka's work, together with his editing practices, are no longer found acceptable, and new German-language editions of Kafka, edited by the scholar Malcolm Pasley, are now available for reading in the original language and for translation into other languages.

One of the most severe late twentieth-century criticisms of Edwin and Willa's English-language translations, and their Brod-influenced approach, appeared in an article published in the journal *New Literary History* in 1996. This article, '"Digging the Pit of Babel": Retranslating Franz Kafka's *Castle*', was written by the Kafka scholar and translator Mark Harman, whose own English-language version of *The Castle* would be published by Schocken Books in 1998. This was the first title in a project to retranslate the entire body of Kafka's work by a series of respected individual translators, based on the newly edited German editions by Malcolm Pasley. Although Harman appears to begin his 1996 critique with sympathy, writing, 'I am loath to criticize the Muirs, whose smooth translation I read with relief, alongside the more puzzling original, while still an undergraduate in Dublin', his remark that he is glad not 'to cast the first stone' points more accurately to what is to come. One of Harman's most severe criticisms of the Muirs was their use of what he called Brod's 'deeply-flawed editions'[8]—a point that is rather difficult to sustain, given that there were no other editions to choose from when they began with *The Castle* in 1929. More relevant, perhaps, is Harman's criticism of their interest in fluency—what Willa herself called Kafka's 'sinuous flexibility'[9] which led them to fill out Kafka's abrupt transitions, and make the translation appear natural in the English target language. This 'invisibility' of the translator—in the sense of making it seem as if a text was actually written in its target language was a common practice at the time—and largely responsible for the success of their *Jew Süss*. But translation practices and theories have changed over the years, leaving the naturalizing approach of earlier translators open to criticism. More serious, however, is Harman's claim that the Muirs' version of *The Castle*, especially as shown in Edwin's introductory note, had been adversely affected, not only by their

---

[8] Mark Harman, 'Digging the Pit of Babel', *New Literary History*, 27 February, 1996, p. 294.
[9] *Belonging*, p. 150.

acceptance of Brod's religious interpretation of the novel, but also by Edwin's own Calvinist religious background. Quoting from George Steiner, Harman called this Edwin's 'Kierkegardian Calvinism'.[10] Yet if Edwin and Willa are to be accused of not fully understanding Kafka's religious and linguistic context, as Harman and the critics he cited argue, it can be equally strongly argued that Harman himself did not fully understand the philosophical and literary background of Kafka's Scottish translators, especially Edwin's life-long battle *against* Calvinist ideology.

In his letter to Sydney Schiff, Edwin felt *Das Schloss* to be 'a purely metaphysical and mystical dramatic novel', so it is not surprising, perhaps, that he did not question Brod's interpretation of the book as a symbolic religious journey or quest. Harman criticizes Edwin's introduction for comparing K's journey to Bunyan's *Pilgrim's Progress*. Yet Edwin significantly qualifies that reference by noting that 'the "progress" of the pilgrim here [i.e., in *The Castle*] will remain in question all the time, and will be itself the chief, the essential problem.'[11] And he adds that while Christian in Bunyan's *Pilgrim's Progress* 'knows from the beginning what the necessary means are [...] K., the hero of *The Castle*, has to discover every one of them for himself, and has no final assurance that even then he has discovered the right ones'. Edwin was always hostile to the certainties of Calvinism. In his 1934 essay 'Bolshevism and Calvinism', published in the *European Quarterly,* which he edited with Janko Lavrin, he compared Scottish Calvinism to Russian Bolshevism, and rejected both ideologies. And towards the end of his life, in his poem 'The Incarnate One', he would praise the Italian Giotto's 'Word made flesh' in his paintings compared to 'King Calvin with his iron pen, / And God three angry letters in a book'.[12]

There is more substance to Harman's criticism that it is Kafka's ironic scepticism as well as his black humour that are missing from the Muirs' translations. This is particularly relevant to their 1938 translation of Kafka's first novel *Der Verschollene*, left unfinished in 1912 and again published by Brod along with Kafka's other unpublished fiction in the 1920s. Brod gave the title *Amerika* to this publication, and on one level it is a kind of travel book about a young man's departure from Europe to try his luck in the New World—a common magazine theme of the time. So, on the surface it looks like a much lighter, less personally and psychologically tortured journey of exploration than is to be found in *The Trial* and *The Castle*. Yet Kafka's own title for the unfinished book hints at a darker side. *Der Verschollene* means 'The Missing One', or as Ritchie Robertson's Oxford World's Classics edition of 2012 translates it, *The Man Who Disappeared*. Despite the riot of superficially comic incidents and unforeseen happenings in the narrative, the modern title points more truly, if subtly, to the ways in which human cruelty towards the

---

[10] Harman, 'Digging the Pit of Babel', p. 296.
[11] Edwin Muir, 'Introduction', *The Castle*, translated from the German by Edwin and Willa Muir (London: Martin Secker, 1930), p. vii.
[12] Edwin Muir, 'The Incarnate One, *Complete Poems*, p. 213.

unsuspecting newcomer, and the nightmarish outcomes to his initially innocent activities, are always present in the text. In the absence of an ending to the book (it was left incomplete) such possibilities continue to haunt the reader. Yet in his 1938 introduction, Edwin writes '*America* is one of the happiest of Kafka's stories. In his other two long stories, the fantasy is never far from nightmare; but here, except in the description of the country house and of Delmarche's quarters with Brunelda, it is pure enjoyment, free improvisation without any or without much serious afterthought.'[13]

The later 1930s were difficult years for both Edwin and Willa, unhappy in St Andrews, contending with fears of approaching war, illness, and a shortage of money. So perhaps the apparently surface jocularity of the events in *America* came as a relief to them. Yet links to Kafka's later, darker books are there also, especially in its relationship to *The Trial*. Karl Rossman, *America's* inexperienced teenage protagonist, has been despatched to America by his irate parents as a result of his being seduced by a servant girl who has given birth to his child. Yet he does not seem to realize what has happened to him, and a pattern of innocence exploited or misunderstood and unintended mishaps, is repeated throughout Karl's American travels. His visit to the country house belonging to a business contact of his uncle, and his later involvement with the characters Delmarche and Brunelda—episodes specially mentioned by Edwin—are indeed obviously nightmarish. But even when Karl's adventures are recounted in seemingly trivial, at times even comical ways, the theme, as in *The Trial*, is of innocence somehow made inexplicably guilty. The quotation from Kurt Tucholsky, printed on the back cover of the 1993 Fischer Taschenbuch edition of *Der Verschollene*, catches the double-edged philosophical depth of the tale.

> Am schönsten an diesem grossen Werk ist die tiefe Melancholie, die es durchzieht:
> Hier ist der ganz seltene Fall, das seiner das Leben nicht versteht und recht hat.
> (Finest of all in this great work is the deep melancholy which runs through it: here is the quite rare situation in which someone does not understand life and is in the right?)[14]

Not quite, perhaps, 'the happiest of Kafka's stories', as Edwin put it.

Shortly before Edwin discovered *Das Schloss*, Willa was translating another German-language writer whose work brought her satisfaction, enjoyment, and much-needed income. This was Hans Carossa, a medical doctor and poet whose memoir of his childhood and early life was a form of life-writing that drew on

---

[13] Edwin Muir, Introduction, *America*, translated from the German by Edwin and Willa Muir (London: Routledge, 1938), p. viii.

[14] Kurt Tucholsky, *Der Verschollene* (Frankfurt am Main: Fischer Taschenbuch Verlag, 1993), back cover quotation. The present writer is grateful to Professor Ritchie Robertson for his suggestion of 'in the right' as a translation of the complex 'und recht hat' in the quotation.

aspects of fiction and poetry. Her translation of Carossa's *A Roumanian Diary* was published in 1929 to be followed by *A Childhood* (1930), *Boyhood and Youth* (1931), and *Doctor Gion* (1933). Willa adopted the pseudonym of Agnes Neill Scott (the middle name and surname perhaps borrowed from her friends A. S. Neill and F. G. Scott). She is generally understood to have been the sole translator of these works, and Willa also used the name 'Agnes Neill Scott' alongside her printed Crowborough address, on notepaper she used for correspondence with her American friends Mary and Arthur Mason in October 1929. The explanation she gives for this pseudonym, however, in her letter of 18 October, is ambiguous, appearing to suggest that the Carossa translation was either a joint venture under disguise, or that she was hesitant about admitting to be the sole translator behind her new nom de plume. Willa writes to her American friends—

> I see you have retreated into the country again—like us: it's the best place for working in. This place, in fact, is too damned good for working in; we have translated so many books this summer that we are ashamed of them, and have taken the pseudonym of Agnes Neill Scott for one. Now we are both busy now [sic] by our novels, which will be finished before Xmas. Hallelujah! After that, we hope and pray—the Deluge.[15]

The summer and autumn of 1929 were certainly busy, for their joint work on *The Castle* was published in March 1930, and Ludwig Renn's *War*, published in June 1929, would most probably have been completed before they began the Kafka. It is likely that Ernst Glaeser's *Class of 1902*, published in October, would have had some revision to be done in the early summer, while Carossa's *A Roumanian Diary*, appeared in October 1929, quickly followed by *A Childhood* in 1930. Also published in 1930, under the joint names of Edwin and Willa Muir, was *The Life of Eleonora Duse*, which appeared in March, the same month as *The Castle*, and was most probably translated at least in part in 1929, along with Lion Feuchtwanger's *Success*, published in November 1930. With such a workload, it is not surprising that Willa fell ill in the late autumn of 1929, and that when she went north with Gavin to visit her dying mother at the turn of the year, Edwin had to stay in Crowborough, to recover from a nervous illness of his own and catch up with undone work. When *The Castle* and *Eleonora Duse* were delivered to Secker for publication in March of the new year, they were more than ready to escape to Menton for recuperation, leaving Gavin behind.

It is surprising that apart from that brief comment in Willa's letter to the Masons, she never mentions 'Agnes Neill Scott' in *Belonging*, or in her journals and correspondence. There is no record of how she felt about the translation of Carossa's writings as sole translator as opposed to the works they jointly translated.

---

[15] Willa Muir, letter to Mary and Arthur Mason, 18 October, 1929, NLS, Acc. 13226.

Edwin wrote to Sydney Schiff in September 1930 that he had 'in prospect an essay on Hans Carossa, a writer I am very fond of'; adding '*We* [my emphasis] have just finished translating a book of his called "A Childhood" of which you will have a copy when it appears. It is exquisite, and I think you will like it.' Nevertheless, *A Childhood* is usually considered to have been translated by Willa alone. Edwin's 'A Note on Hans Carossa' was published under his own name, like his other essays on their translated authors, in the New York *Bookman* in December 1930.[16] Despite Willa's comment to the Masons, there was little to be ashamed of in the heavy workload of 1929, but perhaps she chose a pseudonym to conceal her anxiety about how *A Roumanian Diary* would be received. If so, she need not have worried, for when the book appeared, Arnold Bennett wrote in the *Evening Standard* that '*A Roumanian Diary* is translated by Agnes Neill Scott. I know of no better translation from the German than hers.'[17] The reviewer in the *London Mercury* found that Carossa's book 'takes rank with the best of the war books', adding that 'the translation is amazingly good', while the *New Statesman* noted that 'the beauty of his style is apparent even in translation.'

The next Carossa translation, *A Childhood*, was not quite so successful in capturing the beauty of its author's style. It is a book where the author's skills as a poet, as well as a doctor and life-writer, are much in evidence throughout its narrative. This appears in descriptions of the young child's responses to a world he does not yet understand, in evocations of the natural world as it appears to him, and in the fairy-tale nature of his childhood explorations. But the often matter-of-fact style of the Agnes Neill Scott translation does not capture the poetry of the Carossa narrative. Surprisingly, the translation also opens inaccurately by leaving out the evocative part of Carossa's initial description, thus changing the place of the speaker's birth from Tölz in Upper Bavaria to the nearby Königsberg, where his doctor father had his practice. Carossa's original account of his own origins begins—

> An einem Wintersonntag des Jahres 1878 wurde ich zu Tölz in Oberbayern geboren. An diesen schönen vielbesuchten Badeort, bei dem die grüne Isar aus den Alpen hervorschäumt, sind mir leider nicht viele Erinnerungen geblieben; mein bewusstes Leben begann erst in dem nahen Königsdorf, wo sich mein Vater bald nach meiner Geburt als Arzt niederliess.[18]

In these opening lines the reader's imagination is immediately captured by the 'winter-Sunday' of the day of his birth, and the emphasis on the 'lovely, much

---

[16] Edwin Muir, letter to Sydney Schiff, 29 September 1930, Schiff Papers, BL, Add MS 52920.

[17] Arnold Bennett, also reproduced on a publicity leaflet, cited in Margery Palmer McCulloch, 'Edwin and Willa Muir: Scottish, European and Gender Journeys, 1918–69', in *Edinburgh History of Scottish Literature, Vol. 3, Modern Transformations*, ed. by Thomas Owen Clancy, Susan Manning, and Murray Pittock (Edinburgh: Edinburgh University Press, 2007), p. 87.

[18] Hans Carossa, *Eine Kindheit*, Insel Taschenbugh 291 (Leipzig: Insel Verlag, 1922), p. 9.

visited Spa town', lying alongside the 'green river Isar frothing down from the Alps'. But the speaker goes on to tell us that, unfortunately he has no memories of that birthplace, and that his known or conscious life ('mein bewusstes Leben') first began in the nearby Königsdorf, where his father set up practice soon after the boy's birth. Inexplicably, this captivating opening is much reduced in the Agnes Neill Scott translation, which reads as simple information-giving, except for the fact that it is wrong.

> On a Sunday in the winter of 1878 I was born at Königsdorf, in Upper Bavaria, where my father had settled down as a doctor some little time before.[19]

Such a mistake is surprising in a reasonably simple piece of German prose, and a matter-of-fact approach to what should have had something of the 'magical' about it. This is, alas, a feature of the translation more generally. A little further on from the opening description of his birthplace, Carossa's child remembers the house he lived in during his early years, and particularly a large transparent blue glass bead that someone had hung at the top of his window. He could make it swing to and fro just as he pleased, and in his description of the memory Carossa creates a synaesthetic phrase in which the contrasting short and long vowels and the rhythmic movement between the first and second part of the phrase create the movement of the bead as the boy pushes it gently, 'schnell und kurz, langsam und weit'. This loses its magic when rendered as 'quickly in short jerks, or slowly and largely'. There is a similar loss, this time in relation to the child's anticipation of the magical busyness of the natural world, in rendering the upward movement of 'Im Spätsommer wimmelte das Moor zwischen Königsdorf und Beuerberg von Kreuzottern' as the rather flat statement, 'In late summer the moor between Königsdorf and Beuerberg was alive with adders'. It is true that the German language has a certain advantage when the author starts his sentence with a phrase—'Im Sommer', 'In summer'. German grammar insists that the verb must come next and so there is a sense of anticipation created as to what exactly 'teemed' ('wimmelte'), only to be revealed at the very end of the passage. The rhythmic pattern of the sentence moves upwards and onwards to its end in the creation of that anticipation. But the English translation reads prosaically, without the magic of 'Spätsommer', 'wimmelte', 'zwischen'. There are a number of such unimaginative passages, and more surprisingly the first chapter omits an interesting section concerning the little boy's spending a large part of one day cooped up as a visitor in the local schoolroom. He has been inclined to wander and his mother has asked the schoolteacher to teach him a lesson. This is a fairly complex but amusing episode, and the boy is all too happy to run home to his mother at the end of his 'imprisonment'. It is difficult to understand why it was omitted from Willa's translation. Nevertheless, like a *A Roumanian Diary*, *A Childhood* was welcomed by its reviewers. Roger B.

---

[19] Hans Carossa, *A Childhood*, translated by Agnes Neill Scott (London: Martin Secker, 1930), p. 11.

Lloyd in *The Fortnightly Review* called Carossa's book 'a masterpiece in miniature' and added 'The author owes much to the translation of Miss Agnes Neill Scott.' L. A. G. Strong in *The Spectator* was equivocal about the original Carossa, 'feeling that too much adult knowledge has been brought to the survey of childhood', but concluded 'The translation, by Agnes Neill Scott, is excellent.'[20]

Willa's role as lead translator is clearly seen in Hermann Broch's trilogy *Die Schlafwandler, The Sleepwalkers*, published in 1932 (Figure 12.1). This loosely linked set of three novels was Broch's first foray into prose fiction. He started work on it in 1928, and sought to cover the years from 1888 to 1918, through the experiences of a Prussian aristocrat, Joachim von Pasenow in the first book, followed by a middle-class bookkeeper and embezzler August Esch in the second, and Willhelm Hugenau in the third, a ruthless pragmatist and a deserter from the army. In the grim final volume, all three characters find themselves in a small town on the Mosel river, rife with disaffected soldiers, hunger and social unrest in the chaotic closing years of the war, a foreboding, according to Broch, of the rise of fascism in future years. The trilogy, with its evolving narrative styles, was a critical success, often likened to the work of Thomas Mann or Kafka. It was much admired by Stephen Spender and Aldous Huxley when it first appeared, and praised by Milan Kundera in his study *The Art of the Novel* (1986).

Figure 12.1 Hermann Broch
https://medium.com/@mjcantinho/hermann-broch-da-poesia-como-absoluto-edd06ac320e

---

[20] Carossa examples, pp. 9, 11, 11–12; Agnes Neill Scott, pp. 11–12, 15.

This commitment was a new departure for the Muirs in that they were now dealing with the work, indeed the 'work in progress', of a living author, and Willa exchanged many letters with Broch during the process. In April 1931 Edwin had written to Sydney Schiff about Schiff's own translation of Proust (he had translated *Time Regained* when Scott Moncrieff died), saying that he could well understand him finding the task a fine experience since in his own experience 'translation does take one closer to a writer, closer probably than anything else.' He adds 'and when the writer is a great one, like Proust, one is bound to gain an intimate insight into the workings of the human mind at its best which is really valuable, and is worth all the immense difficulty that has to be encountered.' Then he tells Schiff that he and Willa 'are translating a novel at present by a new German writer, Hermann Broch, which seems to me really first rate, and very beautiful, and not unlike Proust in its great truth and psychological subtlety'. This was the first book in the *Sleepwalkers* trilogy, and they were still working on its final stages when Edwin wrote to Schiff almost a year later in March 1932, confessing that he had not had time to read much contemporary literature as a result of both himself and Willa being 'absorbed' in the Broch, which he called 'the greatest single imaginative prose work of our time'. He adds 'It is astonishing in its newness, its vast scope, its perfection of detail, its style, and its balance and clearness of structure.' And he tells Schiff that 'it will be out in the autumn.'[21] The trilogy had evolved greatly since Edwin's first mention of it to Schiff, and he would probably not have used the Proust comparison in relation to its later stages as he had done for the first book *Die Romantik*, 'Romanticism', translated by the Muirs as *The Romantic*. In Book One of the trilogy there is indeed a late romanticism that hovers over its account of the gradual disintegration of traditional customs and values in the life-time of the von Pasenow family. But this is replaced by the chaotic, opportunistic, and yet unproductive social interaction of the second book, titled *The Anarchist*, and in the final book, *The Realist*, by the almost total disintegration of human values in the wake of the First World War. Translating *The Sleepwalkers* had been a taxing and sober journey for both Muirs, and although they themselves could not fully accept the seemingly despairing message of Broch's final book, with its inclusion of an essay titled 'The Disintegration of Values', they were in no doubt about its importance.

The respect and friendship they felt for Broch comes over in their correspondence, which was mostly conducted by Willa. She wrote to Broch from Crowborough on 14 May 1931 when they had finished translating the first book about the Pasenows and were now working on the second, whose main character is Esch, a clerk suddenly dismissed from his office job as a result of a violent argument with his boss. Neither Willa nor Edwin could understand a word used on the first page of the Esch story, where the dismissed man is continually turning

---

[21] Edwin Muir, letter to Sydney Schiff, 11 April 1931, *Selected Letters*, p. 69; also letter of 22 March 1932, Schiff Papers, BL, Add MS 52920.

over in his mind the unsatisfactory way he has handled the dispute with the boss. The unfamiliar word was 'Gözzitat', used again on a later page, and Willa opens her letter by asking for Broch's help in deciphering its meaning. This would seem to be a very early letter in their correspondence, probably the first one.

Dear Herr Broch,

My husband and I are translating into English your trilogy 'The Sleepwalkers' (which we admire more and more as we do it) and I write to ask you if you would be so good as to tell us exactly what is the Gözzitat referred to on page 1, and again on p.104 of Esch. It is probably clear to all Germans what you intend—is it a particular saying from the Götz von Berlichingen?—but we simply do not know.

She continues, '*Pasenow* we have already finished. I hope you can read English with pleasure (I am sure you know English) and that you will find pleasure in our translation. It is at once a challenge and an inspiration to have such a masterly work to translate.' And she signs herself simply 'Yours sincerely, Willa Muir'. Broch replied one week later, first of all addressing Willa with an elaborate form of the customary German designation of 'Dear Madam', 'Hochverehrte gnädige Frau', before moving quickly to an explanation that he is writing in German because she and Edwin are translating *Die Schlafwandler* (and so, presumably, will be able to understand a letter in German), going on to apologize for the letter being typewritten ('dass ich mit der Maschine tue'). But the use of both the German language and the typewriting machine will, he believes, speed up both the process of getting the letter written on his part, and its (machine-made) readability when they receive it. On the other hand, Broch clearly finds himself in some difficulty in this initial exchange as to how to answer Willa's query about 'Götzzitat'—an expression translated in modern-day German/English dictionaries as 'the V-sign', but with a rather more demotic translation available for the full passage as it appears in Goethe's play. Broch tells Willa she is correct in believing that all Germans would understand this expression, and that it does indeed have something to do with Goethe's *Götz von Berlichingen*, but that his typewriter is too prudish—'zu prüde'—to put the meaning down on paper. He refers Willa instead to the passage from Goethe's work, Act III, at the end of the third-last scene. This describes how the beleaguered von Berlichingen angrily dismisses a messenger from the Kaiser's army by saying 'Mit wem redet Ihr! Bin ich ein Räuber! Sag deinem Hauptmann: 'Vor Ihro Kaiserliche Majestät hab ich, wie immer, schuldigen Respekt. Er, aber, sag's ihm, er kann mich im Arsche lecken!' ('With whom do you think you're speaking? Am I a robber! Tell your Captain that for his Majesty the Kaiser I have, as always, the respect due to him. As for himself, tell him he can lick my arse!'). The Muirs do not say whether or not they explored the directions to Goethe's text given by Broch, but in their translation of the problematic passage they followed Broch's prudish typewriter by translating the phrase as 'guttersnipe abuse'.[22]

Willa was the principal correspondent with Broch during the months of work on his trilogy, except for the brief period when she was in hospital in the autumn of 1931, when Edwin dealt with the correspondence. Her letters show her deep engagement with the *Schlafwandler* text and its underlying meanings, while Broch's responses make clear his own trust in her as translator. On 21 May 1931, in reply to Willa's letter about the Gözzitat problem, he says how happy he is that his book is with her 'dass das Buch zu Ihnen gelangt ist'; and he then adds the recommendation he had received from his publisher, Rhein-Verlag—'zu Ihnen, "der besten Übersetzerin aus dem Deutschen", wie mir der Rhein-Verlag soeben schrieb'. This recommendation, 'the best translator from German', uses the feminine ending to the word 'translator'—'Übersetzerin', and this, together with its related grammatical features, assumes a female translator. In her responses to Broch, Willa is always clear that the translation is a joint venture between herself and Edwin, apologizing at one point for their having finished the second book about Esch so quickly and before Broch was ready to send the next part. 'If we seem to have translated the books at shameless speed, it is only because we are *both* doing it, and doing with zeal.' Despite Edwin's significant input, as with his interpretation of Kafka's vision, and his sensitivity to linguistic expression (confirmed by his essays on Kafka and Broch), the correspondence with Broch suggests that Willa was the principal contributor as far as the initial and accurate translation from the German is concerned.[23]

A striking topic in this correspondence is the relationship between Broch's trilogy and James Joyce's *Ulysses*. Although the actual letter appears to be missing in which Willa compared Broch's trilogy to Joyce's innovative work, while stating her preference for the Broch, Broch's response of 21 June 1931 expresses his happiness at what she has written about the Esch part of his trilogy, but rejects any comparison to Joyce as being 'allzu schmeichelhaft; das muss ich ablehnen'—it is 'too complimentary' and so he must reject it. He goes on to tell her that if he had known Joyce's *Ulysses* before he had written *Die Schlafwandler*, then the latter would have remained unwritten. He had found in Joyce's novel a complete realization or production of a kind that is not usually given expression in novel form. He had himself tried to write 'unter der Haut', 'under the skin', in his books, but found that in *Ulysses* Joyce had completely fulfilled this aim. His view was, therefore, that if literature was to succeed in giving expression to modern life, then it would more

---

[22] Willa Muir, letter to Hermann Broch, 14 May 1931; Hermann Broch, letter to Willa Muir, 21 May 1931, in Hermann Broch, *Die Unbekannte Grösse und Frühe Schriften. Mit den Briefen an Willa Muir* (Zurich: Rhein-Verlag, 1950–1961), pp. 50–1.

[23] Willa Muir, letter to Hermann Broch, 7 July 1931, NLS, Acc. 13634/41; Hermann Broch to Willa Muir, 21 May 1931, *Die Unbekannte Grösse und Frühe Schriften*, p. 50.

and more have to come under the influence of Joyce's way of writing. He tells Willa that the final book of the three, which deals with Huguenau, the realist, will possibly employ a new form of expression in contrast to the earlier books, and he is in some suspense as to what she will have to say about it.[24]

Willa was not easily deflected from her preference for Broch over Joyce, commenting in her next letter that she felt Broch had a peculiar genius for 'rendering what, I think, has not yet been made conscious in literature, what you so well describe as the sleepwalking of the human race' and she echoed Broch's comments on Joyce by saying that if she had read *Die Schlafwandler* before writing her own book (*Imagined Corners*), then that book would have been 'written differently'. She tells him that she too was trying to get 'under the skin, to use the knowledge of psychology without any of its jargon, without betraying, indeed, my knowledge of psychology and you have done it better than I did'. But she adds, 'my novel is a good one, so the compliment means something.'[25] This letter had been written to Broch partly to acknowledge the receipt of the first part of the third book of the trilogy concerning Huguenau. Edwin and she had already read it with interest and she confirmed that they found that the Huguenau section had indeed brought 'a new element' to Broch's technique, in the way it briefly introduced so many new characters, one after the other, without development or establishment in the narrative—at least in the sections of the book they had as yet received. They were to find that this Huguenau section, or *The Realist* as it was called in the final publication, was the most difficult and pessimistic volume of the trilogy. Its disconnected form and its vision of disintegrating values marks a theme played out, not only in the fragmented action, but also in an intellectual essay inserted into the sleepwalking narrative in sections, together with passages of rhymed verse, which Willa succeeded in translating into a reasonably comparable verse form. It was, however, only when they experienced what Willa called the 'political fear' of the International P.E.N. conference in Budapest in the summer of 1932 that they realized, in Willa's words, that 'Broch had come nearer to the truth than we thought and that Europe was indeed getting ready to break up.'[26]

Broch was happy with the Muirs' translation of *De Schlafwandler*, with the patience they showed for his corrections and late changes in pagination, and his decision about the need for a specific and more intellectual title for the 'Disintegration of Values' essay chapters. He asks after Willa regularly and with concern in his correspondence with Edwin during her absence in hospital—his first comment in letters most often being 'wie geht es der gnädigen Frau?' (how is the dear lady doing?); and in his letter of 17 November he expressed his happiness at her recovery and also his 'egoistischen Freude', his egotistical joy that she is back on the job

---

[24] Hermann Broch, letter to Willa Muir, 21 June 1931, *Die Briefe, Gesammelte Werke 8* (Zurich; Rhein-Verlag 1950–1961), pp. 316–17.
[25] Willa Muir, letter to Hermann Broch, 7 July 1931, NLS, Acc. 13634/41.
[26] *Belonging*, p. 152.

in relation to Huguenau—'dass Sie wieder beim Huguenau sind'. Broch was equally pleased with Edwin's essay 'Herman Broch' which appeared in *The Modern Scot* in August 1932, followed by publication in the New York *Bookman* in November. As in his compliments about the translation, he was especially happy because he believed that they understood the underlying ideas in his book, and understood what he was exploring in his trilogy in relation to human life. Their friendship deepened after their meeting in Vienna at the end of the Budapest P.E.N. Congress in June 1932, although Edwin wrote to Broch on his return home about how he was 'sorry all the time I was in Vienna for my faltering German—we both used to speak it far better, indeed fairly well, years ago when we stayed in Austria and Germany'. He felt it was 'most unfortunate that it should fail us just when we particularly wanted to summon it'.[27] Edwin is probably speaking about himself here, for Willa's occasional use of the German language in her letters to Broch suggests that—at least in writing—she was still able to communicate fluently. On the other hand, Edwin tells Broch how much he had enjoyed and appreciated rereading the 'Pasenow' and 'Esch' books in preparation for his essay for *The Modern Scot* and *The Bookman*, saying that this had 'brought all my first surprise back, all the first joy of discovery of something undreamed of'. He tells him that he cannot think that *The Sleepwalkers* will ever be forgotten (as Broch seems to have feared when they met in Vienna) 'at any rate it will not be forgotten by me, for I really think it has given me the deepest experience I have ever had from an imaginative work, since the time, in my 'teens, when I discovered poetry.' He concludes, 'You have done something decisive for my generation—lost though it may be.'[28]

Edwin and Willa continued to correspond with Broch after their meeting in Vienna and after the publication of *The Sleepwalkers*. They published the translation of a smaller work *The Unknown Quantity* in 1935, Willa translated a novella, 'A Passing Cloud' for *The Modern Scot*, and they succeeded in placing another with *The Criterion*. Much of their later correspondence deals with the worsening situation in Europe, when they tried to persuade Broch to leave Austria and come to them in St Andrews. Although they did not realize it at the time, Broch's anticipation of future horrors in the final book of *The Sleepwalkers* also signalled their own approaching demise as translators. The most significant works they were to translate after the Broch volumes were the titles by Kafka, by which time Broch had come to St Andrews and, like the protagonist of Kafka's *Der Verschollene*, left for a new life in America. By 1938 their translation work in German was coming to an end. Their strong friendship with Broch was also waning, partly as a result of his new residence in the United States, but also because of misunderstandings that arose in relation to the translation of his later, and now better-known novel, *Der Tod des Vergil*, *The Death of Virgil*, written during his exile in the United States.

---

[27] Edwin Muir, letter to Hermann Broch, 2 June 1932, *Selected Letters*, p. 76.
[28] Ibid.

Broch seems to have believed that the Muirs had agreed to translate this work also, but Willa did not feel comfortable with it, and by the late 1930s and early 1940s she was too unwell to undertake such a major task, even if there had still been a market for German literature in wartime. Her illness, their financial troubles, and Edwin's own difficulties with employment and his health, brought about a lapse in their correspondence, which Broch interpreted as an unwillingness to respond to his attempts to maintain contact with them. This was a sad end to such a positive partnership. *The Death of Virgil* was eventually translated by Jean Starr Untermeyer and published by Routledge in 1946.

PART IV
A SINGLE, DISUNITED WORLD

13
The Second World War in St Andrews 1939–1942

> St Andrews will be plastered. It's only three miles from Leuchars aerodrome; of course it will be plastered with bombs. Simply plastered.
>
> Willa Muir, Belonging

Many people in Britain did not expect a second world war to break out as soon as September 1939. Leader-writers and newspaper correspondence pages praised Chamberlain for the seeming success of the Munich negotiations, as in the St Andrews *Citizen*'s proclamation in its issue of 8 October 1938 'The European Crisis: Mr Chamberlain's Great Achievement: Signs of a New Dawn'. Edwin's ironic comment in his letter to George Barker shortly after Munich spoke for those who were dismayed at the sacrifice of Czechoslovakia while still hoping that the unsatisfactory agreement had halted the immediate possibility of war. 'Well, it's past, and I think for a long time; I expect we'll have ten or twenty years of reaction now, with all the big powers, Germany, Italy, France and England, united in an unholy accord.' Yet Edwin and Willa could not support Chamberlain's comment about 'a quarrel in a far-away country between people of whom we know nothing'.[1] Czechoslovakia and Prague meant a lot to the Muirs, and they were co-signatories in 1938 of an open letter, drafted by their fellow writer Eric Linklater, which criticized Chamberlain's actions in Munich and pointed out that his government had been returned to power 'in response to a pledge given by its prospective members to defend the principles and observe the Covenant of the League of Nations'. In the view of the signatories, 'the crisis produced by Herr Hitler's threat to Czechoslovakia was made possible by the weakening of international law for which this Government is largely responsible by reason of its failure to fulfil its original mandate.' And the letter continued—

> The crisis produced an emotion in Britain which was in many places frankly discreditable, but not incomprehensible. Fear is the obvious reason for the widespread gratification with which the Munich Pact was received. The people of

---

[1] Edwin Muir, letter to George Barker, 15 October 1938, HRC, George Barker Collection RECIP, 30/31. Chamberlain comment quoted in James Joll, *Europe Since 1870*, p. 370.

this country found themselves in a position wherein the issues were, for many, not clearly defined; and being confronted with a danger whose origin was obscured by time, were momentarily grateful to anyone who could extricate them from it.[2]

The question of Munich was laid aside temporarily in the Muir household by family problems in early January 1939. Willa was hospitalized with a weakened heart, followed by home rest before returning to hospital for a minor operation. Gavin caught chickenpox and Edwin needed to have most of his teeth taken out. A welcome break in the bleakness of those months was provided by occasional visits from friends, including Mary Litchfield who was then renting a cottage in nearby Cupar belonging to MacDiarmid's former wife Peggy Grieve. One Saturday afternoon, Mary brought with her a young novelist, Fred Urquhart, whose first book *Time Will Knit* had been well reviewed by Edwin in June of the previous year. Urquhart was immensely excited at the prospect of meeting Edwin, writing 'I was twenty-six and ecstatic with delight'. His own skills as novelist are clear in this memoir from 1987, as he catches the setting and atmosphere of the Muirs' new home, now in a terrace house in Queen's Gardens in the centre of town. He is sharp in his characterization of the occupants and their visitors and the interaction between them. He particularly remembers the upstairs sitting room, where guests were entertained, in which there were 'small mirrors, like car mirrors, that were fixed to the insides of the windows, slanting downwards so you could see who was passing along the street or knocking at the front door'. He wrote that he had 'always felt that it was Willa who rigged up these mirrors; she was much more inquisitive than Edwin'.[3] Edwin was in his study when the visitors from Cupar arrived in that spring of 1939, writing his fiction review for the next week's *Listener*, and so they were entertained by Willa until teatime when Edwin finally appeared. Although Urquhart describes himself as 'a bright, friendly young man' in these early days, and one who usually 'got on better with women than with men', like many other acquaintances of the Muirs he remembers that he always found Willa 'intimidating'. Even at the time of this first visit, when she was unwell and waiting to go into hospital, she 'exuded a kind of aggressive energy that nearly always upset me'. Perhaps Urquhart was uncertain of his own sexual identity at the time, for he adds, 'I think the truth is that Willa, despite her display of intellectual tolerance, her left-wing views and her bohemian behaviour, didn't really like young men she suspected of being homosexual'. Whatever the reason, he would never feel at ease with her, and his comments chime with those of other acquaintances, especially when they met Willa in company with F. G. Scott who also enjoyed being dramatic and dominating in public. For Urquhart, the still developing young

---

[2] Typed draft of Open Letter [1938] with signatories Eric Linklater, Edwin Muir, Willa Muir, NLS, Eric Linklater Acc. 10282.
[3] Fred Urquhart, 'Edwin and Willa: A Memoir', *Chapman* 49 (Special Centenary Issue on Edwin Muir), vol. ix, no. 6, Summer 1987, pp. 11–14 (p. 11).

novelist, 'She tried jocosely to be one of the boys, and she would often leer and give me metaphorical digs in the ribs. After all, I had written a novel that some people thought Rabelaisian, and she was not going to let me forget it.' Edwin, on the other hand, was a very different character—he was 'a gentle, quiet, kind man, very sensitive to other people's feelings'. Urquhart made many other visits, until in September 1939 he became Mary Litchfield's lodger and made weekly trips to the Muirs with her, where he talked with Edwin about books and writing, before returning to the cottage in Cupar with two or three of Edwin's review books, duly recommended for reading. He still felt 'indebted to him for an introduction to Raymond Chandler'.[4]

Despite Edwin's concern about the increasingly unstable situation in Europe after Hitler entered Prague in March 1939, and family worries about Willa's health, he did find some refuge in writing. In addition to his regular reviewing, he published in April his critical study *The Present Age* in a series on English Literature edited by Bonamy Dobrée, and he was making progress with the autobiography he had tentatively started two years before. When summer came, Willa's health seemed to have improved after rest and her operation at the Cottage Hospital. Then on the first day of September, Hitler's troops attacked Poland and the British Government declared war on Germany two days later. By the end of the month the German invasion of Poland had been successfully completed, and there was panic in cities and towns all over Britain. Hitler's bombers were expected to bring devastation to British urban areas, and hasty plans were made for the evacuation of children to safer homes in the countryside. The east coast seaside and university town of St Andrews was no exception to these fears. To Willa's surprise, 'the intellectuals in the town were loudest in their prophecies of doom—even the Oesers '"St Andrews will be plastered", they both said, "It's only three miles from Leuchars aerodrome; of course it will be plastered with bombs. Simply plastered."'[5] On the other hand, the emergency brought a new sense of comradeship among the various social classes of the town. Edwin joined the Home Guard, which consisted of men from all sections of society—professors, divines, teachers, and shop assistants— and they were drilled in the evenings in the grounds of the university by a sergeant major from the First World War. Willa remembered Edwin practising this new and unfamiliar drill 'shyly, almost furtively, in a corner of his study, using an old golf club instead of a rifle'. Edwin took his turn guarding the telephone exchange in the evening, 'armed with a silver-mounted shotgun which had been presented by a local landowner, but with no ammunition'.

> To pace alone around the telephone exchange from two to four in the morning emptied the mind of the cares of the day and removed the war itself to an inconceivable distance. In the room where we slept between our turns of

[4] Ibid.
[5] *Belonging*, p. 203.

duty, there was peace and a complete sense of identity among us, except for occasional flurries of gossip in which the secret cupboards of the town were opened with almost affectionate candour. My return in the morning through the empty streets prolonged the tranquil pleasure of these night vigils, until, with breakfast and the newspaper, the war and my personal worries rushed back again.[6]

These worries related principally to the question of earning a living. Edwin wrote to Stephen Spender in October, 'We have enough work at the moment to keep us going for a few months, but how long that will last I don't know, if this war goes on for long.'

On the positive side, a shortage of commissions enabled Edwin to carry on with his autobiography. He wrote to his friend, Alec Aitken, at the beginning of January, 'Forgive me for not replying sooner, but I've been working day and night to finish my autobiography before the end of the year; I simply could not bear to have it dragging on into 1940. I managed it, and the book left for the publishers in 1939.' He seemed satisfied with what he had done, now that it was finished, although he lamented to Aitken that the writing of his life had made him aware that he had no philosophy of life.

> I find with some dismay, after going over my life, that I have no philosophy—here am I, a middle-aged man and a professional writer, and I have no philosophy. I had a philosophy when I was 27, but it was not my philosophy. I have no philosophy now—that is no rational scheme for accounting for all the time I have lived in the world, or comprehensively for life itself.

He continues—

> I suppose what I mean when I say I have no philosophy is that I have no explanation, none whatever, of Time except as an unofficial part of Eternity—no historical explanation of human life, for the problem of evil seems insoluble to me; I can only accept it as a mystery, and what a mystery is I do not know. All these thoughts have been roused (and clarified a little in my mind) by writing my life: there is very little in the book itself about them.[7]

One striking passage in the book, which would be published by Harrap in May 1940 as *The Story and the Fable*, comes in its first chapter 'Wyre', where he tells of his Orkney childhood and also of the dreams that he experienced when he left the Orkneys. He writes, 'Our minds are possessed by three mysteries: where we came from, where we are going, and since we are not alone, but members of a

---

[6] *Belonging*, p. 203; *An Autobiography*, p. 248.
[7] Edwin Muir, letter to Stephen Spender, 27 October 1939, HRC, Stephen Spender Collection Box 5.1; letter to Alec Aitken, 4 January 1940, *Selected Letters*, pp. 111–12.

countless family, how we should live with one another.'[8] Although Edwin claimed to have no 'philosophy', readers of his earlier poetry can see that there is indeed an exploration of human life and its possible meanings going on in those poems, if only at a formative stage.—'What shape had I before the Fall? / What hills and rivers did I seek? / What were my thoughts then?'[9] The recapturing of his years in Orkney and Glasgow in *The Story and the Fable*, together with revisiting that early life in fictional form through *The Three Brothers* and, especially, *Poor Tom*, would appear to have freed Edwin's imagination and allowed him to move on from the past. His mature writing skills could now explore his three mysteries, most especially how we should live with one another in an increasingly disunited twentieth-century world. This new direction is evident in his poetry from the early 1940s onwards.

At Christmas 1939 the Muirs gave a party for friends including Mary Litchfield and her young novelist lodger and 'two young pretty teachers' from St Leonard's Girls School, perhaps the same ones who took part in the Oesers' discussion club. Fred Urquhart stayed overnight with the Muirs, while Mary Litchfield was given a bed by the two teachers. There were students at the party too, and late in the evening Willa, the young women, the visiting novelist, the students, and other guests all went for a walk around the castle where Willa and the students (in an activity reminiscent of D. H. Lawrence and Frieda's behaviour in the First World War) began to sing the Christmas carol 'Stille Nacht' and some other German songs. Fred Urquhart thought nothing about this activity at the time—he himself could not 'sing in tune' and did not understand German, but he remembered how Mary Litchfield and some of the older guests scolded them when they returned, saying it was a foolish activity, given the war and the anti-German feeling in the town.[10] With Christmas over and Edwin's autobiography despatched to the publishers, it was time to focus once more on how to improve the family income. Willa was well qualified to teach with her St Andrews degree and teaching experience, but to take advantage of her qualifications at a reasonable level it would be necessary for her to leave St Andrews during the week, returning home only at weekends. This did not seem a satisfactory solution to the problem, not least because of her fragile health. Edwin had a wide knowledge of literature and was now a respected critic and writer, but he had no formal post-school educational qualifications. His name was brought forward at a meeting of Senate in St Andrews University as a possible temporary lecturer, to help fill the loss of teaching staff conscripted in the war. But the English Literature Professor of the time would on no account allow Edwin to be considered, dismissing him as 'a crofter's son who had never been to university', adding that his St Andrews–educated wife was 'nothing but a pain

---

[8] *The Story and the Fable*, p. 64.
[9] 'The Fall' from *Journeys and Places* (1937), in *Complete Poems*, p. 75.
[10] Fred Urquhart, 'Edwin and Willa', *Chapman* 49.

in the neck'.[11] Edwin wrote to Alec Aitken, himself a Professor of Mathematics at Edinburgh University, that his 'lack of an academic degree is a most astonishing obstacle: in Scotland nothing but a certificate of some kind seems to be recognised as really meritorious—a curious preference of faith to works, for surely by this time I've done some work that should count'.[12] Testimonials from leading writers and academics of the time such as T. S. Eliot, John Buchan, Walter de la Mare, Bonamy Dobrée, and Denis Saurat seemed to have little influence. Edwin wrote to Stephen Spender, to say that Gavin's headmaster had advised him to apply for a post as English master at some public school. Edwin thought that he might enjoy teaching, but he had no public school connections and wondered if Spender or any of his friends might be able to give him advice about how to set about making applications. In the meantime, Willa decided to take up the offer of a teaching post at New Park School where Gavin was a pupil, replacing the male Classics teacher who had been called up for war service. The post was badly paid, at three pounds a week with lunches included, and she found herself doing more teaching than she was contracted to do, but the money helped and allowed her to stay at home with Edwin and Gavin. In the autumn Edwin found employment with the Dundee Food Office, stamping ration books and doing other routine clerical tasks, also for three pounds a week (but no lunches), which was less than he had been earning as a clerk in 1919. So, Willa cycled to New Park every morning, returning about six o'clock in the evening after supervising the boys' preparatory work, and Edwin took the train from Leuchars to Dundee and the Food Office. In the evenings he taught adult education classes in English Literature in St Andrews and took his turn in the town's Home Guard.

The relatively quiet months after the outbreak of war, sometimes called the 'phony war', were an uncertain time for everybody. In Scotland, the Scottish National Party was conducting an internal debate as to whether it was still feasible to put up candidates in parliamentary by-elections in wartime or whether this would weaken the government in its conduct of the war. Back in 1938, MacDiarmid's *Voice of Scotland* magazine had published the nationalist Wendy Wood's article 'We will fight no more in England's wars', but MacDiarmid changed his mind after Munich and the betrayal of Czechoslovakia, writing an angry anti-Chamberlain, anti-Hitler poem which he dedicated to Karel Čapek, who had died shortly after the Munich Agreement. Nevertheless, there was a strong anti-conscription group within the Scottish National Party, led by Douglas Young, a Classics scholar who was secretary of the Aberdeen section of the party and employed as assistant to the Professor of Greek at Aberdeen University. He, too, was a visitor to the Muirs' home in St Andrews. Young had been cavalier in his

---

[11] Kirsty Allen, interview with Ronald Cant, 3 June 1995, quoted in *The Life and Work of Willa Muir, 1890–1955,* PhD research repository, University of St Andrews, 1997. https://research-repository.st-andrews.ac.uk/handle/10023/9073.

[12] Edwin Muir, letter to Alec Aitken, 12 June 1941, *Selected Letters,* p. 130.

attitude to the possibility of war, departing on a visit to Greece in August 1939, 'thinking on the whole there would be no war, and even if there were still I would have had a little try while the going was good'.[13] When war did indeed break out in September, Young was one of the strongest anti-conscription protesters, arguing not on the basis of pacifism, as did his fellow Scottish poet Norman MacCaig, but by making the contentious case that the ('broken') Treaty of Union of 1707 between Scotland and England did not give the present-day Westminster government the right to conscript Scotsmen for war. He would serve two periods of imprisonment as a result of the court cases he lost in opposing conscription, but his campaigns exacerbated the political tensions of the time in Scotland, especially after Hitler's forces occupied Denmark and Norway in the spring of 1940. After the occupation of the Netherlands and Belgium in May, and the fall of France in June followed by the evacuation of British troops from Dunkirk, no one was sure what might happen next and many families feared for their children. Edwin wrote to Stephen Spender shortly after Dunkirk, 'We've been terribly troubled about Gavin, whether to send him to America or keep him here, pulled to and fro in the most agonising way by two impossible choices. He gets asthma and begins to gasp and choke as soon as the thought of crossing the Atlantic is suggested to him: we have no choice at present but to keep him.' Then he added more positively 'His music is going on in the most astonishing way.'

Gavin did indeed seem to show signs of having outstanding musical ability. He performed well at the piano and composed his own melodies, as well as improvising on classical pieces. Yet at the same time he had a nervous disposition and his psychological equilibrium was easily disturbed. Remaining close to his parents was clearly important for his well-being. Edwin and Willa would appear to have discussed Gavin with Alec Aitken, who although a specialist in mathematics was also very interested in music, an affinity he shared with Gavin. Edwin wrote to Aitken in July 1938.

> We are often bothered pretty deeply about Gavin, as Willa says. The slightest psychical stimulus produces almost immediately such a strong physical response, driving the blood from his face, often actually hollowing his cheeks. Excitement can turn him green. I don't know what is to be done with a sensibility like that. On the one hand it is a strength, and goes with his enjoyment of music; on the other, it is sometimes almost paralysing to him. We have never encouraged him consciously in following out the intellectual and musical drive within him; for I can only think of it as a drive. Actually we have discouraged him sometimes, put on the brake, not directly but by drawing his attention to other things.

[13] Douglas Young, letter to Rupert Allan, 20 January 1940, NLS, Acc. 6419, Box 4.

In the same letter, Edwin mentions his own childhood to Aitken and his severe breakdown as a teenager after the deaths of his parents and two brothers in Glasgow, and he wonders if Gavin could be 'feeling the reflection of a breakdown of my own'. He adds 'I'm very attached to Gavin and very moved by him in all sorts of ways, powerfully and happily', and acquaintances have confirmed that Gavin was equally attached to Edwin. Clearly this was a child whose emotional well-being would not be furthered by sending him across the Atlantic to America, however worrying the home situation might be.[14]

Tensions of a different kind arose in the summer of 1940, when police raids were carried out in several houses throughout Scotland, including Mary Litchfield's rented cottage in Cupar. British Security Services had kept a number of Scots (as well as other UK nationals) under surveillance during the 1930s. MacDiarmid was a principal target because of his nationalism as well as his communism, and his correspondence was regularly opened and examined. The Muirs were also under suspicion for a time because of their left-wing politics and their association in Hampstead with writers who were either members of the Communist Party or known sympathizers. No one who had read Edwin's 'Bolshevism and Calvinism' essay of 1934, and his *Scottish Journey* book of the next year, could have accused him of an attraction to communism, which he had called 'a coffin of human freedom' in a letter to Spender in 1937.[15] But, like Spender, their friend Mary Litchfield was a member of the Communist Party who had been politically active in London, and was still involved when living in Scotland, especially in relation to the party's ongoing difficulties with MacDiarmid's nationalism. In Cupar, she had many visitors who seemed 'foreign' to her small-town neighbours. These guests included BBC producer and actor Moultrie Kelsall, James Barke the left-wing novelist, poet Tom Scott, and others involved with the theatre and artistic activities. She also allowed the local Labour Party to use her sitting room for its monthly meetings. So it was, that in the dark days after Dunkirk, Mary Litchfield's home was raided by the police, apparently as a result of an anonymous letter accusing her of being 'the head of a nest of Fifth Columnists'. Fred Urquhart, her lodger, remembered the occasion.

> About nine o'clock in the morning I was in the kitchen making tea when I heard the front door burst open, the tramp of many feet, and a man's voice reading something like a proclamation. I headed for the door but was stopped by two policemen who had come in the back door and up the cellar stairs. I asked what was wrong, but was told nothing. Instead I was propelled by them into Mary's

---

[14] Edwin Muir, letter to Stephen Spender, 20 July 1940, *Selected Letters*, p. 123; letter to Alec Aitken, July 1938, *Selected Letters*, p. 102.
[15] Edwin Muir, letter to Stephen Spender, 6 October 1937, *Selected Letters*, p. 98.

room next to the front door. She was sitting up in bed while the head policeman read an announcement about a search of the premises. Each of us was then given a body search. Mary wore only a nightgown, so it didn't take long for the policewoman to find she was not concealing any weapons. I wore only a pair of pyjama trousers, a thin silk dressing-gown, a pair of socks and slippers. I even had to take off my socks when they searched me. And every time I went to the lavatory in the next few hours I was taken there by a policeman who stood inside the door and kept an eye on me.[16]

It would appear that Mary was a hoarder of correspondence. Urquhart wrote that stored in the house were 'hundreds, if not thousands of letters and other documents dating back to the 1920s'; and in the attic were 'two or three hundred volumes of *The History of Soviet Russia*' which Mary seemed to be storing for a communist friend. It took the police the best part of the day to search through all this material, until the late afternoon when they announced they were leaving with the books from the attic and several bundles of papers—a departure watched with much interest by neighbours. Whether the books and documents were ever returned, and much of the correspondence would have been of historical interest rather than politically subversive, is not known. Just before the police left, Douglas Young arrived on a visit that apparently helped save the cottage's inhabitants from 'fits of delayed hysterics', but must have added to their neighbours' curiosity about such happenings. With Young's 'black beard, his tall thin figure—he was several inches over six feet—and his black hat and bright green tweed suit', it was not surprising that the good folk of Cupar took time off to 'gape' at them when Urquhart walked him down to the bus station.[17] On his return, Urquhart found Mary on the telephone telling Edwin in St Andrews all about the day's activities, and the next morning Edwin himself arrived to see what he could do to comfort them. He managed to persuade them that the best way forward was to try to forget what had happened and go on with their lives as before.

It was shortly after this incident that Edwin found employment in the Dundee Food Office. A friend reported seeing him standing in the corridor of the Leuchars/Dundee train absorbed, and appearing to make notes—perhaps for the striking poem that became 'The Wayside Station', published in the *Listener* in March 1942 and included in *The Narrow Place* the next year. 'Here at the wayside station, as many a morning, / I watch the smoke torn from the fumy engine / Crawling across the field in serpent sorrow'.[18] Generally, however, there was little time or little inspiration for poetry writing at the Food Office, and things became more difficult when Edwin tripped and fell one evening in the Dundee

---

[16] Fred Urquhart, 'Edwin and Willa', *Chapman* 49, pp. 12-13.
[17] Ibid., p. 13.
[18] *Complete Poems*, p. 96.

blackout, hitting his head against an iron post. The wartime blackouts had many such casualties and indeed Catherine Carswell's writer husband, Donald, was knocked down and killed by a taxi in the London blackout. Willa reported that Edwin arrived home looking ill and persuaded him to lie in bed for a couple of days. He would not stay off his work or his Home Guard duties for longer, but collapsed with chest pains when moving sandbags one evening. Edwin was diagnosed as having overstrained his heart and was ordered to stay in bed for at least six weeks or he might not last the year. A piece of good luck in the midst of this trouble came as a result of the house next door being used as a boarding house, and so the woman who ran it brought Edwin a hot lunch each day, which kept him going until Willa and Gavin arrived home after school. But it must have been a long and lonely six weeks. Willa remembered the difficulties she had keeping her cycle from skidding on the frozen roads, and at the end of the winter term she found she could not afford to pay Gavin's already outstanding school fees. She continued to let them slide, perhaps simply not knowing what to do about the problem, but at the start of the new term in 1941 she was informed by New Park School that they would use her weekly wage to pay off her debt. This meant that there would be no money to run the household, and she would be teaching all day only for the reward of a lunch-time meal. In addition, she was obliged to teach more subjects for the same pay, and found herself taking Latin, English, History, Greek, and Scripture. Willa enjoyed teaching, although having Gavin in her Greek class was awkward, since he tended to expect special treatment. Later comments, from those who had been in her classes during this period, suggest that she was a stimulating and meticulous teacher whose love of Greek enabled her to take her class beyond the syllabus. She herself 'liked the little boys I taught: it had already struck me on Sports Day how much nicer they were than most of their parents.' On the other hand, her opinions were not always welcome, and one former pupil recalled that 'around the classroom table she was instructing us in socialism and complaining about New Park School. She spoke about politics, equities and justice—and she laid it on thick [...] She was certainly guilty of indoctrination.'[19]

When spring came, Edwin was once more able to go about his business, although he stopped going to the Dundee Food Office and no longer moved sandbags for the Home Guard. He continued his regular book reviewing for the *Listener* as well as contributing to other journals and writing occasional broadcasting scripts for the Scottish Home Service, with programmes for St Andrews Day and on the life of Mary Queen of Scots. Although wartime conditions did not encourage sales, he had received admiring letters from literary colleagues and positive reviews for his autobiography. Around this time, his correspondence with Leonard

---

[19] *Belonging*, p. 206; Kirsty Allen, doctoral thesis, University of St Andrews.

Woolf suggests that he was seriously considering writing a book about Virginia Woolf, whose writing he much admired, and who, fearing the onset of another period of insanity (perhaps brought on by the terrifying London bombings of 1940) had drowned herself in the river Ouse in March 1941. Unfortunately, nothing was to come of this project, and events in the next few months were to change the future direction of Edwin's and the family's life.

During Edwin's enforced bed rest in the early months of the year, Willa had been struggling to cope with her own declining health, as well as looking after him and Gavin and meeting the demands of her school-teaching post. By the time Edwin could get out of bed, she herself was 'worn with anxiety and persistent belly-pains, later discovered to be the result of bowel ulcers'. Somewhat oddly, she tried to remedy this by eating charcoal biscuits 'till I must have been sooted inside like an old chimney'.[20] Despite feeling so unwell, she continued to work, until one day her friend and doctor Dorothy Douglas met her by chance in the street, and was so shocked at her appearance that she insisted on a medical examination. After a stay in the local hospital, Willa's health seemed to improve a little, although when Edwin wrote to John Lehmann in August, apologizing for not having sent a promised article, he had to explain that Willa was back in bed with a series of complications. And writing to the BBC about a script that was not up to his best, he described further worries about Willa's recovery after she suffered a relapse. Her health continued to deteriorate, and in January 1942 she was taken into hospital where she underwent a serious operation. Willa remembered none of this until one day she became conscious of Edwin sitting beside her bed, in a strange awakening.

> Before opening my eyes I had been lost in a bleak region where there was no living thing, not even a microscopic insect or a minute speck of lichen, nothing but ice, deep clefts and high ridges of bluish ice, with jagged peaks of ice rising beyond them which I knew I had to climb. This frozen landscape was still around me, yet I knew that the man beside my bed was Edwin. He saw me open my eyes and laid his hand on mine. I turned the hand over and looked at it; the fingers were slim, tapered and heavily stained with tobacco. It was only a hand, not very clean, an irrelevant hand, yet I told myself: But this is Peerie B's hand! And I was sorry that I had no feelings about it. Tears began to trickle from my eyes because I was sorry for being so unfeeling, and the faster they flowed the sorrier I felt, until all at once I was flooded inside with warm love; the icy peaks faded; I held on to Edwin's hand and knew that things were coming right for me again. From that moment I began to recover.[21]

---

[20] *Belonging*, p. 207.
[21] Ibid., p. 208.

Edwin's own memories of Willa's illness make clear just how serious her situation was.

> She did not get any better, and was driven off to a nursing home to undergo a difficult operation. She awoke from it in such weakness that the doctors feared for her life; for some days she had to be kept alive with sips of champagne. One day when I went to see her I realized that my being there no longer had any meaning for her; she had gone too far away and she did not have the strength to reach out her hand to me. That was our worst day. Then very slowly she began to recover.

It was a long time before Willa recovered, 'and when she came home at last she had shrunk as if by some chemical process, and life, of which she had been so full, had sunk to its inmost source. Years passed before she returned to the semblance of what she had once been.'[22] She was barely 52 years old.

A happier outcome in the autumn of 1941 came with a letter from H. Harvey Wood, an Edinburgh University academic who had moved to a wartime post as the Scottish Representative of the British Council, based in Edinburgh. He invited Edwin to give a talk on contemporary English literature to a group of Polish officers stationed in the city. There were many European servicemen and European refugees in Edinburgh at this time, and the Poles were by far the largest group, with a Polish House established to cater for their needs with funding assistance from the British Council. Harvey Wood had never met Edwin, although they had friends in common with Orkney connections, including the writer Eric Linklater and the painter Stanley Cursiter, who was now Keeper of the National Galleries in Edinburgh. Wood had read *Latitudes* and *Transition*, which had given him an impression of the author as a man of 'immense authority and assurance'. To write, as Edwin had done in *Transition*, 'As a poet, Mr Eliot lacks seriousness', could only have been done by 'a rash or a supremely confident critic', and Harvey Wood confessed that he himself 'shrank from coming under the appraising eye of this Arbiter, to whom my puny achievements in art and scholarship must inevitably seem contemptible'.[23] When one of his Orkney friends told him that Edwin was 'not lording it in Bloomsbury but working for a pittance in a Government office in Dundee', he took courage and contacted him. They met in Edinburgh to discuss a lecture series, and he found that his preconceptions did not match the person in front of him—'his manner was modest and hesitant, yet eager and friendly; his voice had that Orcadian lilt that I knew in Stanley Cursiter; his eyes were candid and gentle; and his laugh was the kindest and yet the most infectious laugh I had ever heard.' Edwin's lectures to the Poles were a great success, and 'as each series came to an end, a succession of Polish officers came to me to plead for more of "Pan Professor

---

[22] *An Autobiography*, p. 249.
[23] H. Harvey Wood, typescript for BBC talk on Edwin Muir, 31 August 1969, pp. 2–3. Theatre Archive, University of Glasgow.

Muir'".[24] When a Free French House and a Czech House were added to the existing Polish House (with an American Centre created when the Americans entered the war), an organizer and deviser of programmes for these Allied Houses became necessary. Harvey Wood persuaded his British Council colleagues in London that Edwin would be the man for the job, and he was duly appointed to a temporary post with the British Council. He began his new duties at the beginning of March 1942, initially working in Edinburgh during the week and returning to St Andrews at weekends, until Willa's health had improved sufficiently for her and Gavin to join him in the flat he found for the family at 8 Blantyre Terrace. One final difficulty to be overcome, however, was their son's unwillingness to leave St Andrews for Edinburgh.

Gavin had been moved from the private New Park School to Madras College junior school at the beginning of the new school year in September 1941, when Willa could no longer pay his school fees. Although a number of his fellow New Park pupils were transferring to Madras with him, it was not an easy move for a sensitive and nervous child who needed stability, and Gavin found the transition difficult. Gradually, however, he established a role for himself, playing the piano at school concerts and expanding his musical knowledge when the school's music department gave him his first formal tuition in harmony and counterpoint. At the end of his first year at Madras, he won the Prize for Sight Reading at the piano. At the same time, his mathematical abilities were being extended and he won the school's Mental Arithmetic Prize. By the end of his transfer year he had become part of his new school environment, and the idea of another uprooting to go with his parents to Edinburgh was not one he welcomed. St Andrews, he now felt, was his home. Willa tried to find what she called a 'bunk-lady', someone with whom he could lodge and have his meals, if he stayed behind and continued to attend school in St Andrews. She could find no one who would take him, however, and even advertising in the local papers brought no results. So, much against his own wishes, Gavin had to move with Willa to join Edwin in Edinburgh in the summer of 1942.

[24] Ibid., p. 4.

14
Edinburgh and a New Poetry 1942–1945

> His work [...] has caught a flame—from the fire that is burning the world.
>
> Neil M. Gunn, 1942

Edinburgh was difficult for Edwin, especially the first day in his new office. He would later write of how Harvey Wood arranged for a number of the people he would be dealing with to come and meet him when he arrived. In St Andrews, visits from friends and acquaintances had been limited, but now he met more people in a day than he had 'in a twelvemonth' back in Fife. He remembered that when he returned to his lodgings in the evening, he 'went up to my room and did not stir from it again for fear of meeting someone else'. He soon settled in, however, and found his new work interesting and, importantly, he 'felt at last that I was doing something useful, like everybody else'. He wrote to his American friends Mary and Arthur Mason in early April.

> My work is arranging for lectures and concerts to the foreign population here, Poles, Czechs and others, and bringing them in intelligent relations with our own people. Itis work worth doing, and should have a permanent effect surviving the war—at least I hope so. It means for me quite a different kind of life from the one I have been used to; I meet lots of different people every day, and move about, and take chairs at meetings, and so on; it is probably very good for me as well as being good in itself.[1]

The Scottish Allied or International Houses—collectively they went under either name as well as their own specific national name—were established in Edinburgh in the wake of the fall of France in 1940. The Scottish Polish House was the first to be set up as a result of the large number of Polish servicemen stranded in Edinburgh as well as non-combatant Polish refugees. Situated at 7 Greenhill Gardens, it was opened on 1 June 1941, and offered entertainments and hospitality generally to the exiles in Edinburgh, such as the series of lectures which Edwin had been invited to give in the autumn of 1941. Later, on 17 July 1942, the Polish General Kukiel opened another Polish refuge in the city, the Polish Soldiers' Home (Dom

---

[1] *An Autobiography*, p. 249; Edwin Muir, letter to Mary and Arthur Mason, 9 April 1942, NLS, Acc. 13226.

Zolnierza) at 9 Moray Place in Edinburgh. The aim of this second home was to provide a house with sleeping accommodation for sixty servicemen, 'which the Polish soldiers would feel was their home in Scotland'. It was reported at the opening that 'already, since the home was informally opened on June 29, 748 men had been given beds, and 3194 meals had been served'. The motto of the home was 'Czem chata bogota, tem rada', freely translated as 'Everyone shares alike; what is mine is yours'.[2] In the home itself, the dormitories were allocated to the various branches of the Polish forces—with the name of the specific branch marked on each door—and the walls of the dormitories themselves were decorated with photographs and designs relevant to their specific units. There were also many people in Edinburgh with French connections—either refugees or those with marriage relationships—and by late 1941 there was talk of a Free French Centre. This came to fruition when the Free French House was opened by General de Gaulle on 23 June 1942, not long after Edwin had taken on his new British Council role. He was listed among the 140 invited guests at the opening and the lunch that followed, which he attended in place of Harvey Wood, who was unwell. Later he accompanied Miss Parkinson and Sir Eugene Ramsden from the British Council in London on a visit to the Scottish Polish and Scottish Czech Houses. Sir Eugene had been one of the speakers at the opening and had 'charmed the large French portion of the audience by finishing his speech in their native language'. He later sent a note to Edwin thanking him for the arrangements he had made, while Miss Parkinson noted in a memo that 'despite Hitler', she thought the day had been 'a very great success'.[3] Edwin had come a long way from his isolation in St Andrews.

The French House was the third Allied House to be opened in Edinburgh, following the Scottish Czechoslovak House at 34 Lauder Road, opened by President Beneš on 23 October 1941. The Czech House was Edwin's favourite among the Allied Houses, partly because of his relationship with Prague in the early 1920s, but also because of the strong friendship he developed with its young Warden, Lumir Soukup. When war broke out, Lumir had been working in Edinburgh for a doctorate in theology on the topic of 'T. G. Masaryk: Analysis of his religious, philosophical and political ideas'. He volunteered for military service but was rejected for health reasons, which gave him the year needed to complete his thesis and graduate. On graduation, he worked for various organizations such as the Ministry of Information, the BBC, and the Scottish Army High Command, but he wanted to be involved in the war effort in a more direct way. A Czech friend, Olga Revilliod, the sister of Jan Masaryk, son of the first president of the newly independent Czechoslovakia after the first war, had come to Edinburgh with her sons, and through her, Lumir heard of a large empty house in Lauder Road, which the Church of Scotland once used as accommodation for missionaries home on

---

[2] *The Scotsman*, 27 July 1942, p. 3.
[3] British Council Archives, BW 2 / 273 'Free French Centre', National Archives, Kew.

leave. He thought that this might serve as a meeting place and accommodation for fellow Czechs in Edinburgh. So, on the basis of £100 in his bank account, and the hope that other helpers might come along before this was exhausted, Soukup rented the house for £10 a month. With voluntary help, he turned it into a cultural centre and a place of relaxation and entertainment, where Czech soldiers and airmen could stay when on leave. Lumir had not known about the British Council's financial involvement with the Allied Houses project when he started up the Czech House, but two retired academics—Professor Herbert Grierson and Principal David Cairns—whom he consulted about funding and who came to the activities at the newly opened Czech House, suggested that he should contact Harvey Wood. And so, Lumir's voluntarily funded Czech House with its 'first class piano' in an upstairs drawing room, and 'five bedrooms and two dormitories, all with beds', came under the auspices of the British Council and benefited from its greatly superior funding. Lumir commented that this help had come 'long before my initial funds and hope were exhausted', while the British Council representatives 'did not believe that till then I had run the House on a monthly budget which would not have covered a single day of their expenses'.[4]

The Czech House was a popular venue for both Edwin and Willa when they settled in Edinburgh, and Lumir and his future Scottish wife Catriona left interesting memories of the Muirs at this period in their lives. Catriona recalled the first time she met them together.

> After one of the lectures at Czech House, while we were talking and laughing in the hall, I suddenly noticed two people standing apart, watching us. One of them, Edwin, I knew. He had his hand on the elbow of an older looking, white-haired woman, who was leaning on a stick, and he looked happy, proprietorial. She, I thought, seemed slightly on her guard, but also alert and amused. I went up to them. 'Don't tell me, Edwin', she said, 'this must be Catriona. Now let me see whether I can find Lumir'.

Like many who met the Muirs for the first time, Catriona was 'impressed by Edwin's apparent gentleness and vulnerability and by Willa's strength, in spite of her physical infirmity'.[5] Later, however, she realized that it was Edwin who was the stronger character, the resilient one. In a broadcast talk in 1969, Harvey Wood remembered that Edwin 'called forth the most affectionate and protective instincts of all my staff, and yet in many ways he was the most remote, the most self-sufficient of them all'. He imagined him sitting 'in his room in Melville Street, running his nicotine-stained fingers through his hair, and spinning the web in which he entrapped almost every notable creative artist in Britain at that time'. He

---

[4] Lumir Soukup in 'Lumir and Catriona Soukup: Edwin and Willa Muir: A Memoir', NLS, Acc. 12007, p. 9.
[5] Catriona Soukup in 'Edwin and Willa Muir: A Memoir', NLS Acc. 12007, p. 39.

added 'How Edwin did his work I never found out. I never heard him dictating a letter, nor did I ever find him writing or typing one by himself, and he always seemed to handle the telephone charily and mistrustfully.' And not only did Edwin 'manage his own business with enviable ease', but he had another seemingly more mundane but extremely important skill which led to him being 'a final court of appeal when, as so often, the monthly office accounts refused to balance. He would point to a column or a total, and say, "I think *that's* wrong", and careful rechecking would prove that it was.'[6] This was a skill from his early Glasgow clerking days, and it must have helped to keep his own family's head above water, too.

Among the many writers, artists, musicians, and critics who were persuaded to come and talk or perform in Edinburgh were T. S. Eliot and Stephen Spender, two poets at opposite poles both in their manner of appearance and their lecturing. Lumir Soukup had never met Eliot, and when he saw Edwin entering the lecture room with 'a gentleman in a black jacket, silver tie, striped trousers, bowler hat, carrying a rolled-up umbrella', he commented ironically to Willa, 'Is the accountant in Edwin blossoming out into the City? Just look at the stock-broker he's with.' Unsurprisingly, he was hurriedly 'hushed' by Willa, who whispered to him that it was T. S. Eliot. Lumir was even less impressed by Eliot's manner of lecturing, finding that he read his paper, titled 'The Music of Poetry', 'in a monotonous, emotionless voice, as if it were a balance sheet or financial report to a shareholders' meeting, never lifting his eyes from his notes'.[7] Spender's appearance and performance was very different. His jacket and trousers were 'baggy, of no special cut', his hair was 'unruly' and seemed as if it had not been cut or 'groomed' for months, and his body was 'in constant movement, involved in the debate, arms and hands emphasising his words'. Spender's lecture was not written down but extempore; 'he was thinking aloud, and one could feel it.' He was a very popular speaker, 'People always asked Spender to come back, and he did, willingly.'[8] Despite his more distant manner, Eliot was also invited to return, which he did equally willingly.

As Catriona Soukup's account suggests, and as Edwin's own memories confirm, Willa was particularly vulnerable when she and Gavin joined Edwin in Edinburgh in the summer of 1942. She was still weak after her hospitalization, and lacked confidence when she went out in the evenings to events at the International Houses. Among the many difficulties to be faced was the evening blackout in wartime Edinburgh. The Muirs' friend the poet Helen Cruickshank remembered making her way home to the suburb of Corstorphine from her daytime civil service commitments in the city centre.

---

[6] H. Harvey Wood, Typescript of BBC broadcast talk on Edwin Muir, Theatre Archive, University of Glasgow.
[7] Lumir Soukup, 'Edwin and Willa Muir: A Memoir', NLS, Acc. 12007, p. 74.
[8] Ibid., p. 77.

Coming home in the dark was something of a nightmare but I always found the hazards of city streets worse than in the country. Walking up the unlit Corstorphine Hill road to my own home was quite easy. After all, I had been used all my childhood to unlit country roads where, as one's eyes got adjusted, even the darkest night would reveal the friendly glimmer of countless stars. In the city streets, the hazards of uneven or invisible kerbs, unlit lamp-posts, litter bins and collisions with human bodies were many; and leaving the pavement for a street island to await one's tram was a particular risk, for a tram in those days showed up only as a dim blue moving light, with an almost invisible destination board. The city's proximity to the Forth Bridge and Rosyth dockyard, always an objective of enemy bombers, made total black-out imperative and our Air Raid Wardens did a marvellous job in attaining it, chivvying offenders into complete obedience.[9]

It took Willa some time before she felt sufficiently confident to take a tramcar to the Czech House and Catriona and Lumir were ready to help. She would telephone beforehand and be met, sometimes at the tram stop, to be escorted upstairs to the room where the lecture was to take place. A comfortable chair was always reserved for her in a corner so that she could have room to stretch out her legs. Things were easier in the daytime, and she soon became accustomed to standing in queues at the butcher's, grocer's, and fish-shop, becoming well enough known to get 'occasional extras from under the counter'. Helen Cruickshank's kind butcher once gave Helen a sheep's head for an 'extra', which ended up hanging on her clothes line where 'the crows and gulls speedily spread the news and picked the skull clean'. More welcome were the wild strawberries, raspberries, and gooseberries that invaded Cruickshank's untended garden and helped to make up for the wartime absence of fresh fruit.[10]

Housekeeping was never one of Willa's skills, and being solely responsible for shopping and general housekeeping in a wartime city was particularly taxing for her. Events took a more positive turn in February 1943, when Morley and Flora Jamieson, a young couple who had begun their married life in the Edinburgh house of the historian Dr Mary Ramsay, moved into the Muirs' home in Blantyre Terrace, and Flora agreed to help Willa with running the household. Morley was an aspiring writer who had met Edwin at a lecture in Edinburgh, and both Jamiesons got on well with Edwin and Willa, with Flora taking 'all of Willa's old-fashioned "rationalism" in good part'. Flora and Gavin went to the cinema together, especially enjoying 'some George Formby farce'.[11] Gavin had eventually settled at George Watson's school, despite his previous wish to remain in St Andrews. Initially, however, his parents were contacted by Watson's headmaster, who advised them that

---

[9] Helen Cruickshank, *Octobiography*, p. 116.
[10] *Belonging*, p. 210; *Octobiography*, pp. 117, 114.
[11] Morley Jamieson, 'Recollections of Edwin and Willa Muir', University of Edinburgh Centre for Research Collections, Gen. 2180 / 4, pp. 1, 14.

Gavin was not turning up at school. Apparently, he would leave home and board a number 23 tram, only to stay on it 'in a continuous tour to and from Granton Harbour'.[12] Absorbed in working out the permutations and variations of his new transport system, Gavin seems to have forgotten that the tram was supposed to take him to school. Jamieson, whose memoir tells this story, does not say how this particular mathematical problem was eventually solved. He does, however, paint a lively portrait of the Muirs' social life at 8 Blantyre Terrace, which he called 'a cultural Piccadilly Circus'.

Edwin and Willa had been isolated from congenial company during their early years in Dormansland and Crowborough, and again to a significant extent in St Andrews. Now, in Edinburgh, as previously in Hampstead, their home became a regular meeting place for friends and visitors who came to lecture or perform at the various Allied Houses. Jamieson remembers the many Orcadians he met there, including Stanley Cursiter, Robert Kemp, and Eric Linklater, although he adds that only Edwin had kept his Orcadian accent. There were retired university professors such as Herbert Grierson and Alexander Gray, the painter Nigel McIsaac, and film-maker T. R. Ritchie. The Highland novelist Neil Gunn was a regular visitor to Edinburgh at this time and he, too, was often to be found at Blantyre Terrace. Although both wrote in English, Edwin and Gunn had seemed to be at opposite poles of the Scottish literary revival movement in the mid-1930s, but Gunn did not agree with MacDiarmid's angry personal pursuit of Edwin in articles and books in the wake of *Scott and Scotland*. Nor did he approve of the caricature of Edwin and Willa by Barbara Niven that had been published in MacDiarmid's *Voice of Scotland* magazine in 1938. Asked many years later about this sketch of Willa as an aggressive Amazon and Edwin as a 'little doe licking her fingers', Gunn explained 'No, that's not fair at all. She may have been a bit positive. She was intellectually self-reliant', adding 'Although she treated Edwin like a mother at times, she was a fair, good person, and he in his delicate, quiet way was actually wiry and tough, too'. In addition, and despite their earlier *Scott and Scotland* disagreement, Edwin and Gunn shared many qualities in their philosophical and literary thinking, with Gunn quick to appreciate the new direction in Edwin's poetry, which would appear with his *Narrow Place* collection of 1943. Edwin was equally appreciative in his *Scots Magazine* review of Gunn's novel *The Serpent*—'a mature book'—in June of the same year. Other Scottish writers who were to be found regularly at Blantyre Terrace were Sorley MacLean, who had been invalided out of the army and lived just round the corner from the Muirs, and, as in St Andrews, Douglas Young, who had seen MacLean's important Gaelic-language poetry collection *Dàin do Eimhir* (*Poems to Eimhir*), with illustrations by the young artist William Crosbie, through its publication process in 1943, while MacLean himself was recovering in hospital from the injuries he had received in

[12] Ibid., p. 13.

the battle of El Alamein in 1942. In addition to his visits to the Muirs, Young's time in Edinburgh also included two spells in Saughton Prison in consequence of his refusal, as a Scotsman, to be called up for army service by the Westminster Government. A surprising absentee among these visitors to the Muirs' home (apart from MacDiarmid, who had been conscripted for industrial war work on the Clyde) was the poet Sydney Goodsir Smith, who lived nearby, whose poems such as 'On Readan the Polish Buik o the Nazi Terror' ('Poland, the warld is greetan as they read'), 'Ballad o the Defence o Warsaw, 1939', and 'Epitaph for a Pilot' might seem to have made him a likely supporter of Edwin and his work for the Allied Houses, especially the Polish House. Rejected for war service as a result of poor health, Goodsir Smith was one of the younger poets in the second wave of the interwar Scottish poetry revival and, like Edwin himself, he published in new magazines such as *Poetry Scotland*, whose editor Maurice Lindsay, like many of the contributors, sent their material directly from the war front. Goodsir Smith followed MacDiarmid in writing in a revitalized Scots language, and he followed him again in his rejection of Edwin and the views he had expressed in *Scott and Scotland*. Morley Jamieson tells of an unpleasant encounter at a party held in the Czech House at Lauder Road where 'the wine was flowing rather freely' and Smith 'proceeded to get more and more buoyant and even outrageous'. When Willa—who herself had a reputation for being 'outrageous' in company—at one point made some general remark, 'Sydney threw back his head and laughed so loudly that the whole room went quiet. Then, still sniggering, he gave Willa a friendly push and said loudly, "How can you—a staid old-fashioned body like you—know anything about it?"', increasing the offence by adding, 'an old grey-haired wummin like you'. In earlier times Willa would have given the speaker a suitably acerbic reply, but still fragile, she was only too aware of how she might appear to those who did not know her. She told Jamieson afterwards that 'Sydney would never appear at any such party again', but his barb clearly distressed her and did not help to heal the divisions between MacDiarmid's supporters and the Muirs.[13]

Much more congenial were the European writers who came to the Allied Houses and Blantyre Terrace, who included Louis Aragon, Paul Eluard, and Max-Pol Fouchet. Willa did not care much for Aragon, finding him 'too arrogant for our liking'. In the post–First World War period Aragon had been involved with the Dadaist movement and became a founder member of Surrealism. Having won the *Croix de guerre* and the military medal for bravery in the Second World War, he was a member of the National Front Resistance movement after the fall of France, involved with setting up the National Front of Writers in the Southern Free Zone of the country. Perhaps his communism was a problem for Willa, or perhaps he had a reserved artistic nature which contrasted with her own ebullience. Paul Eluard, in contrast, she found 'a delight'. His poem 'Liberté, j'écris ton nom', written in 1942,

[13] Ibid., pp. 11–12.

had quickly become an emblem for the French Resistance movement. It had been first published in an underground book of poetry *Poésie et verité 1942* and was reprinted in June of that year in the magazine *Fontaine*, retitled *Une seule pensée*, and so reached the southern Free Zone with which Aragon was also involved. Poet and critic Max-Pol Fouchet was a joint founder of *Fontaine*, and claimed responsibility for persuading Eluard to reprint his poem in it. Willa described Fouchet, who, unlike the other two, did not lecture at the Allied Houses, as 'our most amusing visitor' and one who 'had escaped from Algeria with only one ragged shirt to his back and no money at all'. Fouchet had spent his youth in Algeria, to which his family had emigrated, and his magazine *Fontaine* brought together Resistance writers in Algeria before becoming the platform for a wider French intellectual Resistance movement. When he came to Edinburgh, the British Council provided money to buy him some clothes, but according to Willa he became so fascinated with Princes Street's tartan souvenir shops that he spent most of it on 'tartan ties and waistcoats', a 'Scottish bonnet', and 'flamboyant oddments' from the souvenir shops. She added 'War or no war, he was like a schoolboy on holiday'. It is not clear whether their Edinburgh hosts entirely realized the exceptional quality of these visiting French poets, together with their outstanding contribution to the Resistance movement in their own country; or indeed whether they realized the place of communism in the thinking of many French intellectuals and artists of this time. According to Willa, neither she nor Edwin 'could ever understand how such a gentle, sensitive poet [such as Paul Eluard] could be a Communist'.[14]

Another visitor to the Muirs' wartime home was Dora Dymant, the young woman whom Franz Kafka had met at a holiday camp on the Baltic in the summer of 1923, and who lived with him in Berlin during the last year of his life. Dora came from a Polish Jewish family, and in the 1930s she joined the Communist Party in Germany and married the editor of the Communist Party newspaper, *Die Rote Fahne, The Red Flag*, by whom she had a daughter. She and her daughter left Germany in 1936 to join her husband, who was already in Russia, but when he was arrested during Stalin's purges, she crossed Europe to reach England just before war broke out. Sent to an internment camp on the Isle of Man during the early years of the war, they were transferred to the north of England at some point, for when she came to stay with the Muirs in Edinburgh she was on leave, without her daughter, from a camp near Berwick on the Scottish–English border. Unfortunately, and surprisingly, neither Willa nor Edwin mentions this Kafka-related meeting in their later memoirs, although Morley Jamieson remembers Dora's small stature, loose-fitting clothes, and her 'good face' which 'smiled a lot, with her head slightly inclined like a bird'. He writes 'We liked her and she was friendly though our lack of German and her poor English

[14] *Belonging*, p. 211.

made it difficult to get far in friendship.' Edwin had to stand as guarantor for her visit, which was limited to three weeks, and the authorities, would 'on no account' extend her leave. Jamieson does not mention Edwin and Willa conversing with Dora in German, although Willa at least would still have been able to do so. He does say that he thought they would have liked to keep her with them for longer.[15]

A significant happening in February 1943, in addition to the coming of the young Jamiesons to lodge with the Muirs, was the publication of Edwin's poetry collection *The Narrow Place*. Richard Church had been the editor at Dent who oversaw the publication of *Variations on a Time Theme* and *Journeys and Places* of 1934 and 1937 respectively, and when Dent decided not to continue with new poetry, Church succeeded in placing Edwin's latest collection with Faber and Faber. Edwin wrote to him on 2 February 1942, confirming that 'Eliot has taken my poems, thanks to you' and added 'And now I feel, for some reason, that I'm going to write better poetry; I've written so little.'[16] *The Narrow Place* certainly seemed to herald a new beginning when it was published exactly one year later. Reviewing the collection in May 1943 in the *Scots Magazine*, Neil Gunn wrote that this new work 'has caught a flame—from the fire that is burning the world'. He had found that Edwin's previous poetry had 'at its best [...] always been spare and austere', noting that 'occasionally one had the strange feeling that Muir could not get life's sure outline until years of death had fixed it permanently'. But now in this new collection he 'frequently deals with life in its living moment in the world of to-day'.[17] All the poems in *The Narrow Place* were written in St Andrews before the move to Edinburgh in 1942, and many of them would appear to have been inspired by the situation of the time, with images that point to the destruction and futility of war and its cycles of recurrence in human history. 'The Wayside Station' opens and proceeds by means of a despondent but enigmatic mood and strongly everyday visual imagery, 'Flat in the east, held down by stolid clouds, / The struggling day is born', before coming to a close with the image of 'the lonely stream'—not referred to previously in the poem but now seeming to have an essential place in its underlying argument—which 'leaps the gap of light, / Its voice grown loud, and starts its winding journey / Through the day and time and war and history'. There are no commas in this final line to separate out its items, and its heavy uninterrupted stress pattern seems to make it longer than it actually is 'day and time and war and history' seem to have become both inseparable and everlasting.[18] In the poem which follows 'The Wayside Station', 'The River', the stream moves on through history to show repeated patterns of destruction caused by war 'a blackened field, a burning

---

[15] Morley Jamieson, 'Recollections', University of Edinburgh Centre for Research Collections, Gen. 2180 / 4, pp. 28–9.
[16] Edwin Muir, letter to Richard Church, 2 February 1942, *Selected Letters*, p. 133.
[17] Neil M. Gunn, *Scots Magazine*, 2 May 1943, p. 163.
[18] *Complete Poems*, p. 96.

wood, / A bridge that stops half-way, a hill split open / With scraps of houses clinging to its sides', and their contents—'planks and tiles and chips of glass and china' scattered 'among the grass and wild-flowers'.[19] 'The Refugees', first published in a slightly longer form in the *New Alliance* of 1939, raises the question of responsibility that would recur in Edwin's later Prague poetry and was already part of his philosophical thinking in the late 1930s. In this respect, Edwin must have been influenced, too, by his discussions with Hermann Broch in St Andrews, and the discourse of Broch's *Sleepwalkers* trilogy, especially in its final book. Many people in the 1930s had been either ignorant of, or had paid little attention to the plight of peoples still displaced in the aftermath of the First World War; and they appeared to be unaware of the treatment of Jews in Europe that led to the Holocaust. So 'The Refugees' bears witness to those of us who 'lived in comfort in our haunted rooms', who have looked on without involvement or full understanding, as 'We saw the homeless waiting in the street / Year after year, / The always homeless, / Nationless and nameless'.[20] Such unpersonalized images transfer readily to crises of displacement and neglect throughout human history, and reinforce Muir's vision of war and the condition of war as a repeated cycle in human life, raising difficult questions about responsibility. In contrast, 'The Return of Odysseus', first published in the *New York Times* of August 1942 as 'The Return', takes its theme from the faithfulness of Penelope as she waits for the return or even for news of her husband Odysseus, whose journeying has taken him far from home and family. This use of Greek myth as metaphor, which had begun tentatively in Edwin's earlier poetry, would become a major source of imagery in his late work. Two specifically personal, although still imagistically expressed, poems in the collection are its opening poem 'To J. F. H. (1897–1934)', written for Edwin's friend John Holms who had died so suddenly in 1934, and 'The Confirmation', a love poem to Willa, written during Edwin's enforced bed rest in the spring of 1941. Edwin recalled that the poem to Holms came when he was walking in St Andrews after a period of illness, and a soldier on a motorcycle flashed past, strongly reminding him of his dead friend. For a moment 'the worlds of life and death seemed to fuse for an instant.' The opening lines of the poem catch the speed of the motorcyclist, the lively, searching mind of his dead friend and the suddenness of his death.

> Shot from the sling into the perilous road,
> The hundred mile long hurtling bowling alley,
> To-day I saw you pass full tilt for the jack.
> Or it seemed a race beyond time's gate you rode,
> Trussed to the motor cycle, shoulder and head
> Fastened to flying fate.

---

[19] Ibid., p. 97.
[20] Ibid., p. 98.

Then the speaker remembers that his friend is 'seven years dead', but he is there 'so clearly' that he cannot himself be sure 'in the hot still afternoon / What world I walked in, since it held us two, / A dead and a living man'.[21] The poem is a moving tribute to Holms as well as a meditation on the mystery of life and death. Willa was much moved by 'The Confirmation', the poem written for her when she was feeling unwell and low in her own estimation. It proceeds through a series of metaphors through which the speaker tries to catch the qualities of the loved one and what she means to him 'a fountain in a waste, / A well of water in a country dry', ending with the simple appreciation 'Not beautiful or rare in every part, / But like yourself, as they were meant to be'. Willa would write in *Belonging* that the last line '"But like yourself, as they were meant to be", sent me privately into a passion of tears, because I knew too well that I was only a botched version of what I was meant to be.'[22]

The poems in Edwin's next collection, *The Voyage*, published in 1946, were all written during his residence in Edinburgh. A few, like 'The Return of the Greeks', 'The Rider Victory', and 'Reading in Wartime' continue the war theme prominent in the earlier collection, but the majority move towards a more positive outlook on human affairs, something that is present even in the collection's war poems. In the opening poem, 'The Return of the Greeks', Edwin turns to Homer and his story of the siege of Troy, but here we have the Greek soldiers returning to their homes, 'sleepwandering from the war'. While that borrowing from Broch's *Die Schlafwandler* has echoes of Broch's Europeans moving blindly towards the disaster of two world wars, in Edwin's poem it is used primarily to show the personal psychological as well as the physical destabilizing effect of war. 'All the world was strange / After ten years of Troy' to the veterans whose ships came 'blundering' over the bar and into the harbour. Their homes were especially strange to them—'a childish scene / Embosomed in the past', with their 'grey-haired wives / And their sons grown shy and tall'. Yet the poem ends with the possibility of renewal, as it returns to the idea of the faithful Penelope from 'The Return of Odysseus' in *The Narrow Place*. In this later poem she watches from her tower and sees 'within an hour / Each man to his wife go, Hesitant, sure and slow', while she remains 'alone in her tower' still waiting for the return of Odysseus.[23] Another poem, 'The Rider Victory', points to the futility of war in its image of the sculptured 'Victory' reigning his horse 'Midway across the empty bridge', where 'In front the waiting kingdom lies'. Yet, although 'The bridge and all the roads are free', the sculptural metaphor suggests the hollowness of the supposed victory—'But halted in implacable air / Rider and horse with stony eyes / Uprear their motionless statuary'.[24] Other poems in *The Voyage* display the new, free, personal approach that Neil Gunn singled out

---

[21] Ibid., p. 95; Edwin Muir, letter to Raymond Tschumi, 10 June 1949, *Selected Letters*, pp. 152–3.
[22] *Complete Poems*, p. 118; *Belonging*, pp. 210–11.
[23] *Complete Poems*, pp. 125, 126.
[24] Ibid., p. 139.

in his review of *The Narrow Place*. 'Song: (Why should your face so please me)' is another love song to his wife; 'On Seeing Two Lovers in the Street' was thought by Morley Jamieson to have been written after Edwin met him and Flora walking hand in hand in Edinburgh, although Lumir Soukup also thought it related to himself and his future wife Catriona. 'For Ann Scott-Moncrieff' speaks of the qualities of a friend who had died too young, while in 'A Birthday', the poet looks back on his own life and expresses his present sense of gratitude for his continuing capacity to fully appreciate the living world: 'I never felt so much / Since I have felt at all / The tingling smell and touch / of dogrose and sweet briar, / Nettles against the wall.'[25] 'The Myth' also looks back to his past life: 'My childhood all a myth / Enacted in a distant isle'; and the content of this poem links with the essay 'Yesterday's Mirror', which he published in 1940 shortly after the publication of *The Story and the Fable*. At the beginning of that essay Edwin wrote, 'At last the proofs arrived; I made the last correction; there was no further turning back. And suddenly I felt that now that my autobiography was finished, I could really write my autobiography. I had cleared up a few things in my mind.'[26] This was an insightful comment on his part. Writing an autobiography, and allowing himself to revisit the lost childhood he had searched for in his very earliest attempts at poetry, would appear to have finally freed him from the trauma of the family's move to Glasgow so many years before. From now onwards he would be free to deal with both the present and the future in his poetry, with the mature writing skills developed from a long apprenticeship in poetry and prose.

By the time *The Voyage* was published in April 1946, Edwin's thoughts were elsewhere. Recalling Dora Dymant's visit to the Muirs, Morley Jamieson believed that her presence had added 'a certain colour, not only to their past, but to their post-war intentions what they were going to do and where they were going to live'. It seemed to him that they both thought of Prague—Kafka's city—'as a kind of dream or mythical city and even the herring bone thoroughfare of the Lawnmarket and High Street reminded them nostalgically of other days there'.[27] As the war seemed to be moving towards its end, some planning for the future became a necessity, so Edwin asked the British Council whether there was any work he could do for them after the war, especially in relation to Czechoslovakia. They replied that although he was now too old for them to put him on a pensionable list, if he would accept that condition, then the post of Director of the British Institute in Prague was vacant and they would be willing to appoint him to it. At the end of August 1945, therefore, he left Edinburgh and its Allied Houses for Prague, while Willa remained to settle their affairs and help Gavin prepare for his return to St Andrews, this time as a student at her old university.

[25] Ibid., p. 152.
[26] Ibid., p. 141; 'Yesterday's Mirror', *Scots Magazine* xxxiii, September 1940, p. 404.
[27] Morley Jamieson, 'Recollections', University of Edinburgh Centre for Research Collections, Gen. 2180 / 4, p. 29.

15
The Cold War and Prague 1945–1948

> When the times darken
> Will there be singing even then?
> There will be singing even then,
> Of how the times darken
>
> Bertolt Brecht, translated by Edwin Morgan

After six years of Nazi occupation, the Prague to which Edwin returned in 1945 was a very different place from the optimistic city of the early 1920s. As he left for his new post at the end of August, he was asked to take a private car out to Prague belonging to the British Council representative in the city. The Librarian, Cyril Saunders, was to drive the official Council car, and they were to be joined by a young man appointed to a post in the Information Service of the Embassy, who was also going by car. All three decided to travel together. Edwin wrote later that as they drove through Belgium and Germany—

> there seemed to be nothing unmarked by the war—the towns in ruins, the roads and fields deserted (Figure 15.1). It was like a country where the population had become homeless, and when we met occasional family groups on the road they seemed to be on a pilgrimage from nowhere to nowhere (Figure 15.2). In the towns and far out in the countryside we met them pushing their belongings on hand-carts, with a look of dull surprise on their faces. Few trains were running; the great machine was broken; and the men, but for the women and children following them, might have been survivors of one of the medieval crusades wandering back across Europe to seek their homes. Now by all appearances there were no homes for them to seek.

When they reached Cologne, it seemed for a moment as if its previous life might still be there. They drove along the fine straight avenue which led into the city from the north and they could see the outline of houses as they approached. As they entered, however, they found this to be an illusion: 'The spacious houses were roofless, the windows empty gaps.' And presently, 'the sour stench of the corpses buried under the ruins rose about us.' What was even more surreal about the seemingly 'dead' city they had entered, was that 'people were out as usual for their Sunday evening walk in their Sunday best, the children decked in chance remnants of finery.' It was 'a lovely late summer evening', and to Edwin's imagination, 'the peaceful

THE COLD WAR AND PRAGUE 1945–1948 219

Figure 15.1 Refugees. 'On a pilgrimage from nowhere to nowhere'
Source: dpa picture alliance / Alamy Stock Photo

Figure 15.2 'The towns in ruins.' Prague after the American bombing
Source: https://albumwar2.com/prague-after-the-american-mass-bombardment/

crowds in that vast graveyard were like the forerunners of a multitude risen in a private resurrection day to an unimaginable new life.'[1]

The journey to Czechoslovakia took longer than they expected. A few miles past the town of Godesberg, the car Edwin was driving began to rattle alarmingly before stopping entirely. It was decided that the young Embassy man should drive back to Godesberg, which had been the first district in Germany to be transferred peacefully to Allied control, and get help from the British Army now stationed there. Meanwhile, Edwin and Saunders would wait in the broken-down vehicle. As they waited, they watched a bearded man with a collie dog sitting on the hillside across from them, as if he were on the look-out for someone or something. They later learned that the pair might have been on the alert for displaced persons living in the woods, who were responsible for raiding farms and even for murder. Edwin got out of the car to speak to a woman walking along the road with a little girl by the hand. They were coming back from a prayer meeting, to a farm close by, and the girl had been sent to stay there from Munich where her parents had been killed in an air raid. Edwin remembered that when he told the woman that he had just come from England, she looked at him in wonder, as if England was a fabulous place beyond anything she could imagine. Eventually, late at night and in pouring rain, an army lorry arrived to tow the disabled car back to Godesberg, where the drivers found a meal waiting for them, with 'lots of wine'. The commanding officer was astonished when he heard that their ultimate destination was Prague, and he advised them strongly against this. The liberation of Czechoslovakia had been allocated to the Soviets at the end of the war, and the commanding officer appeared to distrust their motives. 'You'll never get through', he told the travellers, and every so often during their stay in Godesberg he would repeat 'When I visit the salt mines in Russia in twenty years' time, I'll look down and say, "What, is that you there still, Muir and Saunders? Well, you should have taken my advice."' He looked after them well, however, during an extended stay of several days in Godesberg, accommodating them in one of the luxury summer villas that bordered the river of this former spa town. They were free to walk about, but the townspeople seemed subdued and unwilling to make contact with strangers. Eventually they were informed that the car would take several weeks to repair since spare parts would have to be brought out from England, and so they proceeded to Prague in the two remaining cars. En route they ate in the mess room of the American Army in Frankfurt, and slept in a hotel 'which had been split in two, so that the passage outside our bedrooms had only one wall and hung precariously over nothing'. At Nuremberg they 'clambered over the ruins of the old town', and Edwin remembered the few days he had spent there with Willa when they were living in Hellerau. At that time the town had 'enchanted' them. Now there was nothing left but 'jagged blocks of masonry'. As he navigated the ruins, Edwin tried to revisit

---

[1] *An Autobiography*, p. 252.

the house of Albrecht Dürer, painter and printmaker of the late fifteenth-, early sixteenth-century German Renaissance, but discovered only fragments of the city wall.[2]

It was an unfamiliar Prague that awaited them, when their documents were eventually accepted by the Soviet border guards, and they drove to the city itself. During his first few weeks in Kafka's city, Edwin's thoughts seemed to echo Kafka's sense of its dual nature, as he recalled the old Jewish ghetto that had once been part of it—'With our eyes open we walk through a dream: ourselves only a ghost of a vanished age.' Edwin felt strangely dislocated. 'I felt I was in a strange place, and was teased by the fancy of another city, the same and yet not the same, whose streets I or someone very like me had walked many years before.'[3] One of his first actions, when he arrived in post-war Prague, was to visit Mělnik, about one hour north of the city by car, where the elderly parents of Lumir Soukup lived. Lumir was now working with the Czechoslovak Embassy in London, but would return to a post in Prague the following year, and Edwin wished to reassure his parents that he was well. His mother wrote later to Lumir about Edwin's visit, saying that 'a very distinguished gentleman' with a 'beautiful head' had arrived in his car and told them all about him and Catriona. Lumir's father would appear to have been particularly reassured by Edwin's information, since he was concerned that Catriona might find it strange to come to a city that had changed so much since pre-war days, and whose future was still uncertain. In a postscript, Mrs Soukup noticed Edwin's raincoat and wondered 'how was it possible that such an important person could wear such a dirty garment?' Lumir and Catriona were much amused by this comment, for they both 'remembered that coat of Edwin's which had acquired such a rich patina after withstanding light years of Scottish, English and now European weather.'[4] Apparently Lumir's mother believed that unless outer garments were cleaned once a month, they were unfit for use. How she managed to hold on to this belief during the privations of Nazi occupation is not clear, but Lumir was grateful that Edwin had taken the trouble to visit his parents so soon after his difficult journey across Europe.

Although Prague itself had not been destroyed like so many of the places Edwin had passed through on his journey, everyday living was still difficult. The people in the streets looked undernourished and apprehensive. Edwin noticed a man 'jerking his head over his shoulder, as if the memory of being watched and followed still lingered in his nerves'. From past acquaintance, he remembered the Czechs as 'a noisy, somewhat unruly people', but now he found that they hardly spoke to each other. And in a reminder of the Godesberg major's half-joking comments about the Russian salt mines, he took note of the Soviet soldiers in the

---

[2] Ibid. p. 253, p. 254. (The house was unroofed and broken, but not entirely destroyed.)
[3] Franz Kafka, quoted by Gustav Janouch, *Conversations with Kafka* (New York: New Directions Paperbook, 2012), p. 80; *An Autobiography*, p. 255.
[4] Lumir and Catriona Soukup memoir of Edwin and Willa Muir, NLS, Acc. 12007, p. 87.

streets, 'short powerful hairy men, who seemed to be lost in the alien city and only half-aware of the power they possessed and the fear they inspired'.[5] The shop windows showed the same dried food packets that they had seen throughout their overland car journey, and there was no meat to be found in their hotel or in the restaurants, but it was arranged that the institute staff should have their meals sent from a restaurant on the Mala Strana, on the small town side of the river, which served as the British Embassy Mess. It was not easy to get the working life of the institute up and running. Edwin had come with instructions to make contact with people in the city, and to organize the institute as a place where they could learn about the British way of life and literature. When he arrived, however, only a skeleton British Council staff was in existence, and its members were housed temporarily in a small flat off a side street, one room of which was reserved for the Council representative, with another tiny closet put aside for his secretary. The rest of the staff had to try to do their work at a large shared table in the only other room in the flat. As more staff arrived from Britain, the work table became more and more crowded, there was no place to keep papers, and the papers had to be cleared away every day when lunch was brought by car from the Embassy mess.

Unsurprisingly, Edwin felt tense and ill at ease in this situation, and with no private room in which to receive people, there was little possibility of serious planning, especially without a secretary or typist. He communicated his frustration in letters to Willa, asking when she would be able to fly out to join him. Finding a seat on a plane to Prague, however, appeared to be no easier than finding a working place at the institute or a nourishing meal in a Prague restaurant. In her turn Willa was discovering that every furniture repository in Edinburgh seemed to be 'crammed to bursting point'. Eventually their friend Joseph Chiari, who was at that point the French vice consul in Edinburgh, offered her the use of an empty room in his house for her furniture, and she was 'able to save as many pieces as could be packed into it'. She then packed a suitcase for herself, saw Gavin off to St Andrews, and travelled down to a boarding house in her much-loved Hampstead, where she would more easily be able to lobby the British Council about a flight to Prague. Eventually it was Lumir Soukup who came to her rescue. He discovered that there was a weekly flight to Prague to carry diplomatic mail, and that that particular flight was leaving the next day, with a place on it. The only problem was that it was a converted Junker bomber, captured in Prague during the final days of the war. Lumir warned Willa that there were no seats, only deck chairs. In addition, the bomb door in the floor did not shut properly, so a continual stream of freezing air would enter the passenger cabin, which was also storing crates containing the belongings of people returning to Prague after wartime exile in Britain. Willa would not be discouraged, and armed with rugs to keep herself warm on the

---

[5] *An Autobiography*, p. 255.

journey, she embarked on her first ever air flight on what, fortunately, turned out to be a different aircraft on the day.

> I climbed happily into the converted Dakota, which carried eight passengers, sat down by a window and forgot to feel scared. We left the ground smoothly and it seemed the most natural thing in the world to be airborne; we flew low enough to have the irregular small fields of Kent, the white-streaked channel, the larger, more geometrical enclosures of northern France spread out beneath us like a map easy to read, except that at first I could not tell whether round objects in the noonday sun were humps or hollows, corn-stacks or shell craters. By the time we came to the Rhine, where broken bridges were sticking up out of the water like blackened teeth, the sky to the right of us had thickened into deep cloud and we coasted along beside these white cliffs of vapour like a pleasure-craft sailing down a river, while Europe flowed past underneath, a unity, as I felt it should be, interrupted by no artificially drawn frontiers.

She added that it was 'a fascinating journey', and that like all good journeys it 'ended appropriately in a lovers' meeting. Edwin was at the airport.'[6] On Edwin's part, it was probably not only the 'lovers' meeting' that he welcomed, but also the arrival of a partner whose linguistic ability had in the past enabled her to learn enough Czech to translate a play by Karel Čapek and who would now be able to take over the Czech language communication that was so often a necessity. This was a language, he had decided, that was not for him, despite his new appointment in Prague.

October in Prague saw the celebration of the founding of the new Czechoslovakian Republic in 1918, with Thomas Masaryk as the first head of the provisional government, and then as president of the republic. This was followed in November by the withdrawal of the remaining Soviet troops from the city. Portraits of Stalin had disappeared from the shop windows during the anniversary celebrations, and now the crowds threw bottles of wine and flowers after the departing troops, with Willa taking part as well. The Muirs were housed in the Šroubeck Hotel on Vaclavské Namesti, Wenceslas Square, which Edwin remembered as uncomfortable, cold, noisy, and expensive. At Christmas, however, there was a Christmas tree on the square opposite the hotel, and they listened to the first sounds of singing in the streets, finding it a strangely forlorn and yet reassuring sound. In the spring the institute was housed in the Kaunic Palace, a small, attractive building in a narrow street that lay behind and parallel to Wenceslas Square—home nowadays to an Alfons Mucha museum. And around this time the Muirs were allocated a ground floor flat in a pleasant open part of the city close by the wooded Stromovka Park, formerly called 'The Royal Hunting Forest'. Prague people called this area 'Little

---

[6] *Belonging*, p. 212, p. 213.

Russia', since the Russian Embassy was situated at the far end of the street. The top flat of their building was occupied by the family of Edwin's second-in-command at the institute, who was a musician as well as a good English teacher. He had already made contact with the best string quartets in Prague, so they had companionable neighbours. In addition, this new home meant that they could have their own furniture around them once more, and Willa succeeded in engaging a cook who had previously been cook to the Slovakian ambassador in Berlin, from the period of Slovakia's so-called independence during the Nazi occupation of Czechoslovakia. Willa found Ella's cooking to be properly 'ambassadorial', and they began to give dinner parties again. She was later to find that her good cook's distinguished past brought some rather less tolerable attributes.

The late spring saw Lumir and Catriona Soukup in Prague. They arrived in May 1946, by which time Edwin was established in the Kaunic Palace, with a desk of his own and suitable rooms for the Institute's teaching and secretarial staff. Writers from Britain would arrive to give formal lectures and meet with Czech writers in the city, and the institute's film shows were particularly popular with the public. Lumir and Catriona were temporarily homeless, and Edwin and Willa offered to put them up in their own flat. Because of the official governmental positions of both men, this could only be a short-term arrangement, but they enjoyed their reunion until the Soukups were allocated their own accommodation. Unfortunately, this was at the opposite end of Prague, far from the Muirs in 'Little Russia', and so future meetings were mostly at functions and receptions or at the theatre, although they did manage some informal get-togethers in one or other family home. Edwin and Willa received tickets to all the activities organized by the institute, and because the Czech Ministry had a box in the principal theatres in Prague, the friends were able to offer hospitality to each other. Lumir remembered that Edwin and Willa 'learned to love Smetana, Dvořak, Janáček, especially under Václav Talich's baton', although he himself could not reciprocate their enthusiasm for the Sadler Wells Ballet, brought over from Britain. Of all the arts, ballet was 'right at the bottom of the list' for Lumir, an opinion that 'shocked' Willa when they met at the interval of the performance. She told Lumir that she was the one who had introduced Edwin to the ballet in the early days of their relationship, and that after seeing Diaghileff in London, he had said that he wanted to be a ballet dancer himself. Lumir's response to Edwin was that he was very glad that he had not followed this inclination, and that he much preferred Edwin's 'choreography of words to that of legs and pirouettes'.[7]

Soukup's memories of this time are significant in relation to Edwin's relationship with Charles University, where, as a part of his institute duties, he was appointed a Visiting Professor of English Literature. Edwin had discovered how much he enjoyed teaching when he worked with the British Council's Allied Houses in

---

[7] Soukup Memoir, NLS, Acc. 12007, pp. 89–90.

Edinburgh during the war, and the success he achieved with foreign servicemen and other refugees in the city would appear to have been repeated with his Prague students. Apparently, it had not been the policy of pre-war students to attend lectures regularly. There was the practice, instead, of 'buying scripts'. Since most lecturers did not change their material from year to year, enterprising students copied the lectures in shorthand, transcribed them, and sold them on to the next generation, who did the same in their turn. Edwin's method of lecturing put a spoke in the wheel of this practice. Lumir reports how, to the astonishment of the waiting students, he 'would arrive in the lecture room, and without even one page of notes, start to give his exposé, evaluating the authors and communicating his love of literature'. And what was strikingly absent was 'that oratorical delivery which, although foreign to English lecturers, is yet common, and even expected, on the Continent.'[8] When Edwin wanted to illustrate a point, he would quote lines of poetry and even prose, relying only on his memory, and in his own soft but clear voice. The result was a hugely increased attendance at lectures, and with no 'scripts' to be passed on, a good relationship grew up between Edwin and his students, with many of them accompanying him on the long walk back from the university to the institute close by Wenceslas Square, continuing to discuss as they walked. H. Harvey Wood, who had appointed Edwin to the Allied Houses post in Edinburgh, came to visit Prague as part of his British Council duties and remembered how 'it was heartwarming to cross the quadrangle [of Charles University] in his company and note the affection and regard with which he was greeted by his students'. Harvey Wood also reported how the students of St Andrews University, hearing of the 'book famine' in Prague, 'started up a "Books for Edwin" drive, and cases of books, oddly assorted but all useful, were sent off to Prague'. This was a welcome, if surprising, change of heart from a university that once had no time for 'a man who wrote for the papers'.[9]

As in St Andrews, however, Edwin's popularity with the students and his manner of lecturing were not always appreciated by his fellow academics in Prague. Some asked if all professors in British universities lectured in the same way, others complained that their students arrived late to their classes as a result of their discussions with Edwin, and some even believed that the dignity of the professorship was being devalued by such familiarity. Lumir recalls the comments of one member of staff who complained that Edwin's relationship with his students was as if 'a congregation were to start interrogating the priest at the end of his sermon while he was still in the pulpit. We cannot allow "orationes ex cathedra" to be questioned', was his view.[10] On the contrary, Edwin believed that his job was to stimulate his students' interest in a subject and to encourage them to

---

[8] Ibid, pp. 91–92.
[9] H. Harvey Wood, typescript for BBC talk on Edwin Muir, 31 August 1969, pp. 2–3. University of Glasgow Library, Archives & Special Collections, Sp Coll STA Kc7/6.
[10] Soukup Memoir, NLS, Acc. 12007, pp. 92–93.

think for themselves. Even so, similar issues were brewing with some of the British Council officials. The institute that was developing under Edwin's leadership, with the support of his second-in-command Bill Allen, and even the local employees who made the institute tearoom so popular, was offering truly open and interactive links between the local population and the British Council presence in the city. Unfortunately, however, there were some who believed that as the wider political situation in Czechoslovakia became more difficult, too much equality and too much contact between local consumer and foreign provider was not appropriate for British staff on a foreign posting.

Edwin and Willa, busy with helping the city and its people, and busy with their own adjustment to the new Prague, saw things very differently. As they got to know more of the local people in the city, and these people began to feel more at ease with them, they heard personal stories of the hardships of the Nazi occupation, and began to understand the trauma that many inhabitants were still suffering, from experiences that they themselves were only now beginning to be able to talk about. Edwin recalled a man of high character, the curator of an historical museum, who had remained in his post during the occupation because he considered himself the guardian of irreplaceable national treasures. Yet he was blamed by some Czechs, and praised by others, for this was the kind of difficult choice that many had had to make, and one that was difficult to judge fairly. Edwin and Willa attended meetings of the International P.E.N. Club in the city, at one of which the current General Secretary, the English author Herman Ould, visiting at the time, expressed his hope that the Czechs would now be reconciled with their former enemies. But some of the people at the P.E.N. meeting had suffered so badly at the hands of the occupiers, that any such reconciliation was too painful and still far off. One woman rushed out of the meeting room and returned with a shirt box containing a neatly folded bloodstained shirt, with little pieces of torn skin on it. This had been sent to her by the Gestapo who had tortured and finally strangled her husband, who had been the head of an underground group that sent information to Britain. It was not always easy for visitors to understand the pain of those who had lived under occupation.

Willa described a shopping experience when she joined a queue at a market stall where the first cherries of the year were on sale. Willa's Czech was reasonably good by this time, but she had a problem with the word for cherries, which began with the letters 'tž'—a difficult sound for non-Czechs to pronounce. The fruit-seller refused to give her the cherries until she could pronounce the word for them properly, telling her 'This is *our* country, and these are *our* cherries, and I won't hand out any of them to someone who can't even say their names.' Willa was not to be defeated, however, and told him defiantly, 'I have come a long way from Scotland to be of use to you Czechs and you shouldn't speak to me like that.' She reported that this aroused 'a ripple of excitement in the queue, and several women cried "She isn't a German, give her the cherries"', while a man nearby added '"If she was a German she wouldn't be able to speak two words of Czech.'" Willa went off with her cherries, in the end, but the market stall assistant was 'still hostile'.[11] She wrote later that this was an experience of *political* hostility, and that she had not understood how the Nazi occupation had struck at the heart of Czech identity.

As they settled into their new life in Czechoslovakia and understood more fully the difficulties and tensions around them, Edwin and Willa had personal issues of their own at the back, and sometimes at the front of their minds. Their son Gavin had embarked on his own adventure of university study in St Andrews, and this was the first time he had been left to look after his affairs entirely by himself. Gavin had always appeared to need the security of his parents' presence in his life, and although he was excited at the prospect of returning to St Andrews, his letters show a continuing need for that presence. In an undated letter, probably of early spring 1946, since he mentions that it is now 'several months since we last met', he ends with a strongly felt hope that he may meet up with his parents again sometime soon. He wrote, 'Is there any chance about my coming to Prague in the summer? And is there any chance of your coming to this country for a few days?' He adds, 'Although I am extremely happy here, and have completely recovered all the ground I ever lost anywhere, I would still like to see you again sometimes, and it is now several months since we last met.' A second undated letter was apparently written in June, since he mentions arriving in Prague 'on July 15th' and looking forward to seeing them 'in a month's time'. In this letter he comments that his parents 'are now staying in a palace', but seems to be preparing the way for disappointing news, writing that he thinks he is 'through my exams, but in all subjects, particularly physics, the standard was raised considerably without warning, and this will catch a considerable number of people who expected to get through'. He tells them not to be disappointed if he fails 'because that will be the reason'. His music studies, on the other hand, seem to be going well, with success in competitions in Edinburgh, and he hopes to be 'studying it quite hard' when he gets to Prague in July.[12]

Edwin and Willa say little about Gavin's difficulties in their own memoirs of this period, or indeed of any period in their lives, apart from his childhood accident with the road tanker in Hampstead. Their anxiety comes across, however, in Willa's *Belonging*, and in an incident—at times terrifying and at others hilarious—recounted by Edwin in correspondence with his Edinburgh friend Joseph Chiari. The Muirs had been at a summer school in the Slovakian High Tatras, and had to rush to Prague's Wilson rail station. During this journey, the institute car had three punctures between the Tatras and Bratislava, and another three between Bratislava and Prague, so that they found themselves in a lonely forest area without

---

[11] For Herman Ould visit and Occupation information, *An Autobiography*, pp. 260–61; for Cherries incident at the market, see Willa Muir, draft of *Belonging*, UStA, MS. 38466, 9/4/3 (Prague, 1945–48), p. 8.

[12] Gavin Muir, NLS, Acc. 13226, 3/2.

a spare wheel in the early hours of a Saturday morning, with Gavin due to arrive by train in Prague at 8 o'clock. Worse was to come when they were given a lift by a passing driver, who then took them on a mad drive throughout the countryside, making no apparent attempt to get to Prague, but regularly asking Willa, who was seated beside him, 'Are you afraid yet, gracious lady?' Edwin in the meantime was seated in the back of the car with a pot of honey spilled all over his trousers. The 'madman'—for it seemed that he could be nothing else but mad—eventually appeared to tire of his adventure and finally dropped them off in the town of Tabor, still some distance from Prague. As usual with a disastrous happening, Willa would make a humorous drama out of the details when she wrote about it in her future memoir. She was particularly entertained by Edwin's confession that, during the terrifying journey, he had been sitting in the back with the spilled honey pot in his hand, trying to decide whether he should hit the mad driver on the head with it and bring the journey to an unpredictable end. Edwin speaks more seriously when he tells of Willa's distress and loud weeping, when she discovered that no train could take them to meet Gavin in Prague by eight o'clock. Her cries brought help in the form of a hotel night watchman, however, and this good Samaritan took them into his hotel to allow Edwin to change his honey-steeped trousers, and found a taxi to take them to Prague in time to meet Gavin. Edwin's letter to Joseph Chiari of 18 August 1946 retails their amazing night-time adventure in the Bohemian countryside, and thanks him once more for all his help and kindness to his son. (Gavin had indeed failed his end of session exams, and when Edwin went to Scotland to see him, he stayed with the Chiaris for two weeks, perhaps arranging for Gavin to stay with them for a time as well.) After all the excitement of Gavin's arrival in Prague, Edwin and Willa decided that he should not return to St Andrews to resit his examinations in September, but would remain with them in the city until the beginning of October and the start of the new term. '[H]e needs our care for some time', Edwin wrote to Chiari.[13]

When Gavin returned to Scotland in the autumn of 1946, Willa embarked on a more personal venture. In November she began to keep a regular diary of her own feelings about herself and about events in Prague. The first entry involves measurements which seem to relate to kitchen curtains—'Kitchen: (70 broad—4 ½ metres) 5 metres needed for window, if 70 broad (doubled)'. This is one of the few domestic tasks entered in the diary, for it is followed more typically by short enigmatic poems and prose comments which are surprisingly insecure in their implications, especially from a woman whose correspondence with friends and relatives is so characteristically dramatic and confident, no matter the circumstances. An early entry on 13 November is a poem titled 'Wartime Old Style', which tells a story of 'Our tigers [who] were happy at home; / they kept the babies warm;

---

[13] For Tatras adventure and Gavin, see *Belonging*, pp. 221–23; Edwin Muir, letters to Joseph Chiari, 27 July and 18 August, 1946, *Selected Letters*, pp. 141–42 and pp. 143–45.

/ under the tent of the great counterpane / none of us came to harm'. Then things changed high up on the 'windowless wall, / so high, so high we missed it, / was a wide round hole / And our tigers could not resist it'. The tigers escape, dogs bark and snap outside, there is shouting and screaming, the babies begin to cry, and outside, 'there are guns, there are traps, there are nets', and the speaker calls for the tigers to return, 'O come back, our darlings, our tigers, our pets'. This is a strange piece of writing, hardly a poem, although in poetic form, yet it is compelling, and seems to point to some unspoken trouble, even panic, in the writer's experience. She writes that 'a rush of words to the imagination is like a rash on the skin, and is just as distracting. A painter at least puts his pigments on canvas, but a writer's own skin itches with unwritten and irrelevant words.' Perhaps she is realizing that even after her health has improved, her life as a writer seems to have run dry, at least for the present. It would be another year before the translation work to which she made such a significant contribution would revive, with a contract for Kafka's *In the Penal Settlement* to be published by Secker in 1948.

The post-war residence in Prague must have been the first time in Willa's married life that Edwin had undertaken a public occupation quite separate from their previous shared lifestyle as translators and writers, where their work was carried out principally in the family home. Edwin had held an official post in Edinburgh with the Allied Houses, but because of the wartime circumstances this had an informal aspect to it, and although Willa shared his activities, her main priority had been to regain her health and strength. In Prague, however, she had to learn that Edwin had a public persona beyond the home and his marriage; and since his position was a governmental one, linked to the British Embassy with a visiting professorship at a foreign university, it was one that necessarily left her on the outside. Like the Embassy wives, her new role seemed to be to accompany her husband to official functions. Her awareness of this colours her journal writing in early 1947. There is a comment on her husband—'Edwin—a document indecipherable even for home reading', and a poem titled 'Metamorphosis', dated 21 February 1947.

> My only love, daily I see you change,
> donning hard rows of buttons, buckled, braced,
> brushed smooth and shaven till you are bare-faced,
> and then disguised with large and horn-rimmed glasses [...]
> lined with edged note-books for your students' classes ...

The speaker of the poem asks 'Should I not find this frightening and strange?' This piece is followed by an entry of 9 March, with a disturbing account of what seems to have been a dream where the dreamer is confronted by 'a large pie with a raised puff crust; and inside it lay a dead baby on its back, with wide open *brown* eyes glazed and blank'. At the end of March there is a short poem where the speaker 'seek[s] a love / I cannot find. / The people tread / before, behind'. But there is no happy conclusion 'Among their feet / I seek in vain: / I shall not see / my love again'. Then, in April, in a poem specifically titled 'Address to Edwin', the despondent speaker lists the negatives of her present-day personal appearance, despite her own belief that she 'was not born to be a comic figure, / but life has changed me into one at last'. The poem ends with a hope that when she is dead and 'among the elementals', Edwin himself 'will forget the accidentals / remembering rather what I meant to be'.[14] Willa would continue to be haunted by such personal insecurity, writing in June 1947 how it was 'queer that it should be important to wash one's hair and powder face & dress neatly, that one's own appearance should be a reality'. And she adds—

> For it is. If I neglect my appearance I look ugly, and Edwin sees that I am ugly, and insensibly is affected by the fact. Even queerer that, left to myself, I am ugly; queer, because I don't *feel* ugly. I feel that I am an attractive interesting well meaning me, and so I don't feel ugly. Yet I look ugly without some care. I think probably I always did.[15]

In contrast to such poignant and deeply insecure fragments, Willa's diary entry in mid-May 1947 is a celebratory one that tells of Edwin's award of an honorary doctorate from Charles University on the occasion of his sixtieth birthday. She writes 'May 16. Yesterday, Edwin's sixtieth birthday, he was made a Ph.D. honoris causa by Prague University, Alma Mater Carolina.' Then, more informally, she records the anxiety as to whether they would get Edwin's dark suit back from the cleaners, where it had been sent five weeks previously. His jacket and trousers eventually arrived with one day to spare, and since it was a 'hot, breathless day', the missing waistcoat was not needed. She adds proudly, 'Edwin looked highly respectable. So did I, in my new doctor's-wife's outfit.' She goes on to give a detailed account of the splendidly choreographed occasion.

> The performance began at eleven o'clock plus the 'academic quarter of an hour' which is traditional here. The University banner came in to the music of trumpets & drums, 'Carolus, MCCCXXXXVIII', a lion rampant in blue and silver, with two girl students beribboned & badged, & two men students, beribboned & gauntleted, carrying naked swords; another student carried the banner. Then the professors in their black gowns, doctors' gowns, and gold chains, then the Promotor, Vočadlo, the Spectabilis, the Dean, Kràl, and the ex-Rector & the present Rector Magnificus, Bělohradek and Bydžovsky, in red with squirrel fur edgings. Among all these, Edwin, in his plain dark suit, the University Bedellus, and— oh, I forgot, six beautiful maces, each carried by a gorgeous bedellus. The ritual

---

[14] Willa Muir, Prague Journal, November 1946-47, March/April 1947, UStA, MS 38466/5/2.
[15] Ibid., June 1947.

proceeded, every move heralded and finished by a flourish of trumpets. The Promotor, the Dean, the Rector in inverse and reverse order, with a XIV century piece of music in between, & near the beginning Smetana's Song of Freedom. Then Vočadlo gave an oration about Edwin; then the Rector assented, & Edwin answered the very impressive Latin oath, Hussite in origin, with its emphasis on the seeking after truth, 'non ad vanam captandam gloriam'. While he answered, Handel's Largo played softly. Then he was chained & given the diploma in a leather case, and then he made his speech, beginning with a Czech sentence & finishing with a Latin one, thanking everybody first, and then talking about poetry & its real function in life, to express the indefinable, those universal feelings that unite men and that science or mere factual knowledge cannot express.[16]

Willa's account ends with the processions out, the ceremonial lunch, and Edwin's comment, 'I have never had such a birthday before: I don't suppose I shall ever have such a birthday again.'[17] This ceremony (followed shortly afterwards by the award of an LLD from the University of Edinburgh) was an important moment in Edwin's life, a recognition of what he had achieved in his lifetime as poet, critic, and teacher, despite his difficult beginnings and his lack of a university education. It was a moment to share with his Prague friends and to celebrate their hopes for a promising future. It was also to be the high point of Edwin and Willa's long-standing attachment to the city and its culture, for there were political movements afoot that would eventually result in a second loss of freedom for Czechoslovakia.

Edwin's new doctoral status did not solve Willa's sense of being adrift from her own ambitions, but she attempted to find a place for herself in her new life by becoming involved with the more general running of institute activities such as the tearoom, which served the institute staff as well as local visitors who came to classes or the library. She was always ready to listen to the problems brought to her by other institute wives, or junior employees and Czech visitors, and to advise where she could. She would write later, when reporting a disagreement with the new Council representative, Reginald Close, that she 'felt personally responsible for Edwin's staff, for keeping them happy', and was even a 'safety valve'.[18] This had its own problems, however. Reginald Close's comment, that that she was not aware of her own influence, as 'junior members of the staff chattered about "Willa said this, or that"', may not have been as unjustified as she clearly thought it was at the time.[19] She was on more secure ground as hostess to the Writers' Circle, which met weekly in the Muirs' flat, keeping them au fait with goings-on in Prague generally; or entertaining the many local friends and visiting speakers who came for dinner or an evening's talk. Perhaps most of all, in an intellectual context, Willa enjoyed

---

[16] Ibid., May 16 1947.
[17] Ibid.
[18] Willa Muir, Prague Journal October 1947-January 1948, UStA, MS 38466/5/3.
[19] Ibid.

the summer schools held beyond Prague, such as the one they attended in 1946 that ended with their mad car journey, and the one held in Mariánské Lažné, or Marienbad' in the late summer of 1947.

There were many such events. In June 1947, the Czech International P.E.N. organization invited both Edwin and Willa to accompany the Czech delegates to the Congress in Zurich held between the 2nd and 6th of the month. British Council Reports for 1947 also note Edwin's tour as director to Austria, where he apparently lectured in Vienna, Innsbrück, and Graz. Neither Willa nor Edwin mentions this tour in their memoirs, and it may be that Edwin was accompanied by institute staff only. After their P.E.N. visit to Zurich, Willa's diary mentions Edwin speaking about going to Greece to lecture, saying that if this proposal became an actuality, then she would 'certainly' accompany him. She writes, 'Tears welled up at once in my silly eyes. How deep I must have buried my desire for Greece!' Then she adds, 'It was thundering weather, electric, and perhaps that was why I got so worked up.' Such comments once again show how vulnerable and excluded she was feeling at this time. The British Council have no records of a lecture tour in Greece, but Willa's diary for October 1947 contains a poem titled 'To Edwin absent' that could refer to an Austrian lecture tour, listed by the Council, that may have replaced it. Whatever the background to Edwin's absence, Willa writes—

> A roof I have in Prague, four walls, a floor,
> a bed, a desk, an easy-chair much more
> than simple need demands, more than my due;
> yet I am homeless, homeless lacking you.

The poem continues.

> The trees are friendly still, though bare and blown,
> Neighbours are kind, I breathe a friendly air;
> And yet I fit no pattern, left alone;
> My home is in your bosom, only there.[20]

Willa's second Prague journal, running from October 1947 to January 1948, continues to demonstrate the earlier document's sense of personal insecurity, but now she finds those feelings reflected in the wider Prague community. She begins by remembering her own early days in Montrose and their effect on her—'All emigrants are Displaced Persons. My parents were D.P.'s in Angus. So I grew up not fitting into Angus tradition and therefore critical, resentful, unsure.'[21] She finds Scotland itself to be 'deformed by commercialism and Calvinism helps to keep the deformation rigid'. She then turns to the Czechs, and the rigidity and unfairness of their society, and how if a householder does not pay health insurance

---

[20] Willa Muir, Prague Journal, 23 October 1947, UStA, MS 384665/2.
[21] Willa Muir, Prague Journal, October 1947-January 1948, UStA, MS 38466/3.

for a maid when it is due, then an execution officer will come to value anything among the person's household goods that matches the outstanding health insurance debt, followed by a notice that that piece of furniture will be sold at auction. This seems to have happened to the Muirs while they were absent in Switzerland for the P.E.N. Congress. Ella, their Slovakian cook and housekeeper, had put the insurance letter in the kitchen drawer and not told them about it. They paid up when they returned home and eventually found the letter, but still received notice that their hired piano would be auctioned. A visit to the insurance office by Ella with the receipt appeared to settle the matter, until yet another official arrived to demand the supposedly outstanding costs. Willa wrote in her diary, 'I am ridiculously upset by this kind of thing: it makes me tremble. There is something frightening about a foreign state office which is not trustworthy in its accounts: I could be easily intimidated by some Czech-speaking official I could not understand.' After these trials Willa dreamed about being turned away from a British hotel at night-time because 'you are not the kind of people we usually accommodate.'[22] There were frustrations at the institute, too. A newly appointed Council representative tried to acquire the flat above the Muirs in 'Little Russia' for his own deputy, now that Bill Allen, who had done so well as Edwin's deputy, had been transferred for supposedly temporary, but likely to be permanent duties in Bratislava. The fact that Bill had a wife and children still living in the flat, and accommodation for a family in Bratislava was almost impossible to find, did not deter the new representative in his aims. Willa became much too involved in this internal conflict, with her sympathies totally on the side of the soon-to-be-evicted Allen family. The dispute did not help Edwin's attempt to keep on reasonable terms with a Council representative who was only interested in hierarchy and tidy organization.

Tensions in the life of the British Council and institute were echoed by the political life of Prague as 1947 drew to its end. Willa's journal signals a growing political uncertainty, with anxieties about the secret police and a friend's warning to be careful about what one writes in letters apart from the Council's bag letters. As she and Edwin sit in the Stromovka Park on a December afternoon watching the children play, she speculates, rather astutely, that 'the Russians are playing politics much as they play chess: a move here, a move there, all over the world.' Earlier, in October, she had written 'I am in a queerly apprehensive state, and a gun went off just now (4 p.m.) and made me jump. Probably only nerves.' But in November a Czech friend who worked for the government as a liaison officer had been arrested, 'charged with espionage on behalf of a foreign power', and there were reports of others 'belonging to some Anglophile "British Society"' having been arrested also.[23]

[22] Ibid.
[23] Ibid.

Such fears were temporarily laid aside by what Willa in her diary called the 'Red-letter day' of 13 December, first with the arrival of Gavin for the Christmas holidays and then with the news that a Czech friend, who had been arrested in November, was now freed and at home once more. Yet personal worries remained. Although Gavin looked to Willa to be 'well' and 'cheerful', if thin, he seemed to have developed a problem with his hearing. Willa writes that Gavin's deafness 'varies' and now seems less 'dense' than it had been previously, so that an operation might not be necessary. Yet she was clearly worried, with nightmarish dreams about him, and diary reports about an attack of 'asthmatic bronchitis', which he suffered after performing a Chopin Polonaise, at a Christmas party given by the Council representative. Gavin's health seems to have been closely linked to his emotional state, and Willa remembered his distress when she and Edwin expressed their disapproval of communism, to which Gavin was attracted, or his asthmatic attacks when they left him to go to the P.E.N. Congress in Budapest, or when they discussed sending him to the United States in 1940. Gavin had been on his own in St Andrews since the autumn of 1945, and comments by fellow students of that time suggest that he was often to be found walking alone on the beach, or arriving at morning classes a little late and disorganized in appearance. He continued to need resits for some of his annual examinations. Willa writes in her diary in early January that she had 'soothed, encouraged, cosseted him' and that 'he is now all right: sense of division, I think, smoothed out', but this was clearly a young man who needed a more constant family situation in order to feel himself secure.[24]

A hopeful change on the domestic front arrived in late 1947, when Willa eventually found the courage to sack her rather difficult ex-ambassadorial housemaid and cook. Willa wrote that 'Ella never wants to establish a truth or even a fact, but merely to cause an instant emotional effect.' She was replaced by Poláková who said she was a 'born Hungarian' but was reluctant to give much more information about herself. The departing Ella said dismissively that Poláková was 'from the Lager' in Tabor, but she turned out to be an 'unassuming' and efficient housekeeper. Willa tells how Poláková's arrival uncovered many interesting aspects of Ella's reign 'so many kilos of butter vanished! Tradespeople giving Poláková sidelong glances as if expecting something (probably butter)'. Willa adds that Poláková is going to change most of the shops used previously and start afresh, for there is a suspicion that Ella got two prices in her shopping expeditions, one for herself and one for Willa's shopping book, and 'made a good bit on the side for herself'. She would also appear to have used up all the family's ration coupons, so that Poláková was immediately limited in her shopping. When Ella departed, Willa was 'surprised at the lift in my spirits. I felt gay, for the first time in many weeks, & all difficulties seemed miraculously lightened. Happiness & courage welled up!'[25]

[24] Ibid.
[25] Ibid.

The lightening of Willa's spirits would be only temporary, however, as tensions in Prague and the wider Czech community came to a head early in 1948. Willa's journal of January 1948 to May 1948, titled 'The Putsch, and after', begins, as in previous journals, with a mixture of personal information, anxiety dreams, a poem, institute problems, and also successes such as the much-appreciated visit of the writer Elizabeth Bowen to speak at one of the institute's literary evenings. And here, too, is to be found one of those passing comments that support Willa's case to be recognized as the main actor in the Muirs' translation partnership, especially in their Kafka translations. She had written on 13 December in her previous journal, when delayed by some family sickness, 'I must finish this translation.' Now, after writing of her enjoyment in meeting Elizabeth Bowen, she chides herself 'This is Thursday—tonight I am tired & have been reading Stella Benson's life (Ellen Roberts) instead of translating!' As the final Kafka translation under the Muirs' joint names, *The Penal Settlement, Tales and Short Pieces*, was published by Martin Secker and the American publisher Schocken in 1948, it is most probable that it was this work to which she was referring in her journal, and she would appear to have been solely responsible for it. The general strain she was living under at this time is given expression in a dream about her unhappy childhood in Montrose and the family difficulties she experienced there. 'I realised how much I feared and loathed that house [...] too many dead people have been carried out of it'; and also, in a humorously ironic poem 'Fever Train', she compares the train struggling through the snow to her own sense of exhaustion, 'You need cough syrup / to stop your choking / I need fuel / Yes, I need stoking.'[26]

The outstanding section of this final Prague journal is the account given by Willa of the coming to power of the communists—what she calls the communist 'Putsch'—which took place in February 1948. President Beneš, in exile during the occupation, had returned to Czechoslovakia after the withdrawal of Soviet troops in late 1945, and free elections were held in May 1946 with the Communist Party achieving 38 per cent of the vote. As a result, a coalition was formed. The Communist Party provided the prime minister and the post of Minister of the Interior, but the majority of the other representatives in the coalition were non-communist. As time went on, however, the Communist Party and its allies from the Socialist Party became dominant, filling important positions in the police force and other organizations with their own supporters, a situation that resulted in the resignation of non-communist members of the government. The telegraphic drama of Willa's journal entries powerfully communicate the tensions of the time. The page begins with the heading 'Attempted Putsch (premature?)' followed by the comment 'written Tuesday 14 Feb'. There then follows a taut list of the happenings that eventually led to the communist takeover, with brief personal comments by Willa as in the opening items of 19 and 20 February: '19th Thurs.—"Winter

---

[26] Willa Muir, Prague Journal January 1948-May 1948, 'The Putsch and After', UStA, MS 38466 5/4.

Programme—Bronchitis"'; and '20th Friday—Bed—"12 Ministers Resigned" Brit. Wireless'; and 'They shouldn't have resigned. One shouldn't give up an inch.'[27] Event follows event after the resignations, and the sense of an unstoppable movement is conveyed by Willa's stark entries. On Sunday 22 February a token strike is called, and on the 23 February, police raid the premises of the National Socialists and announce a plot against the state.

> police everywhere with rifles—ministries, banks etc. No one to leave country without Wosek's permission. 24th Tuesday: Police raided Social Democrats. [...] Some liveliness in Václavské Namesti at night, after 6 o'clock. Demonstrations and slogans.

On Wednesday, Polaková comes back from buying milk with the news that 'high officials' in various ministries, including the Ministry of Justice, have been arrested. There are now no newspapers apart from the Communist papers, and one Social Democrat paper, and she reports 'more indignation about the stopped newspapers than about anything else so far!' Willa goes on to comment 'This is therefore the day on which people will waken up to realise that the Putsch is here.'[28]

There follows a period when the diary recounts attempts to recover the political situation. An action group puts up notices; there is an appeal for a reconstruction of the government, bringing about a 'National Front of Unity'; a newly formed National Defence committee also puts up notices, intimating that this is a 'political' crisis and that the army 'stands at the disposal of the President'.[29] Students continue to demonstrate. But the outcome seems inevitable, as Polaková reports that senior ministers are being dismissed from their posts and forcibly removed from their offices, including the Minister of Justice. Then comes the announcement that the ageing and unwell President Beneš has accepted the new government. A student is killed and several wounded in an attempt to meet with the president. Non-communists are removed from offices, schools, and university posts; foreigners begin to make arrangements to leave if they can. Finally, the journal gives the news that on Wednesday 10 March, the former Foreign Minister Jan Masaryk would appear to have committed suicide by falling from the window of his former ministry. Masaryk, who was the son of the first president of the new Republic of Czechoslovakia, had visited President Beneš on 'Masaryk Day', the day which celebrated the life of his father. Now, on the day that the Czech Parliament was due to meet under its new communist government, he was dead. Willa reports comments on the BBC which suggested that 'he gave his life for his country.' And she asks 'What will happen?'[30]

[27] Ibid., February 1947.
[28] Ibid.
[29] Ibid.
[30] Ibid.

Initially, both Edwin and Willa hoped that things might settle down politically, and that the institute's work in Prague would be able to continue. Lumir Soukup, who was working in the Foreign Office, was not so sanguine. He wrote in his own memoir of that time that the Putsch 'had been planned as a single-parent family event, and that the spoils and inheritance were to be shared "per stirpes" only'. He added that when Jan Masaryk returned from his visit to the castle, after the ailing President Beneš had made the 'difficult and painful decision to accept the inevitability, as he saw it, of the new Government', he was told by the communist leader Gottwald that the Polit bureau 'had searched for months to find a method of taking power, but that it had never occurred to them that it would in fact be so easy; they simply could not believe their opponents would be so stupid as to hand it to them as a gift'.[31] Soukup's post in the Foreign Office had involved acting as Masaryk's secretary, and now he was dealing with his estate after his death. When he visited Masaryk's sister Alice, she was clear in her belief that her brother had committed suicide, both from the testimony of friends who had heard him express such an intention, but also because she herself had seen his body and read the autopsy report. The only significant marks on his body were those resulting from the impact of landing, on his feet, on the paved courtyard. She commented that only a fully conscious person could stand on a window-ledge, just broad enough to give him a foothold, and then jump down to land on the courtyard, striking it first of all with his feet. 'I am glad he died standing up, like a Sokol', she said.[32] Lumir was aware that a considerable amount of Masaryk's important private papers had to be sorted quickly before they were confiscated by the regime now in power. He managed to rescue a great many of the most significant ones, sorting the less important into bundles that were left in his office, soon to disappear into government 'archives', as he had predicted they would. He was also aware that he was himself under surveillance, with one watcher for the daytime and another following him at night. The day watcher followed him from the time he left his home in the morning till he reached his Ministry, staying behind the partition for messengers and chauffeurs at the entrance of the building until Lumir left again in the evening. He then telephoned his colleague, waiting at the underground station at Wenceslas Square, where Lumir changed trains, and he took over from there. Lumir tells how an accommodation was eventually reached by which watcher and watched ate separately in a designated little restaurant, and if Lumir went out for any reason, he would tell his watcher when he would return. After a few 'tests', the watcher accepted the arrangement, which eased his night-time duties and helped Lumir's own evening manoeuvres.

Being watched in this way meant that Lumir could no longer meet freely with Edwin and Willa, and it was dangerous to communicate with them by telephone.

[31] Lumir Soukup memoir, NLS, Acc. 12007, p. 97.
[32] Ibid., p. 101.

Edwin found it difficult to believe that free association in Prague could change almost overnight in this way, and was troubled by the fact that when he tried to telephone Lumir, the phone was put down immediately on hearing his voice. A method of contact was eventually arranged, but meetings had to be clandestine. One solution took advantage of the fact that the Muirs' flat was in Little Russia, with the Russian Embassy at the end of their street. Lumir's watcher would follow him partly up the road but would hold back before he came to the Embassy gates themselves. This allowed Lumir to redirect his path just before the Embassy gates to make a quick detour to Edwin and Willa's flat. Another method of meeting involved the various Prague walks that he and Edwin had regularly done together in the days before the Putsch, such as the one they called the Mala Strana walk. They would set out separately to meet at a prearranged point where they could no longer be 'watched'. Eventually, however, it became all too clear that it was no longer possible to continue the work they had both hoped to do in post-war Prague. Application forms for Communist Party membership began to appear on office desks and in domestic letter boxes, leaving the recipients with a dilemma similar to that experienced previously by so many during the Nazi Occupation. Lumir was scornful of what he called a 'sneer' of a comment by the *Manchester Guardian*, about 'the leech of collaboration', remembering his father's view during the occupation that 'a person who has never been in a similar situation has no right to sit in judgment, adding "Who was I, then or now, to say that to protect one's family and friends was wrong."'[33] Edwin found it difficult to deal with the news that one of his own female staff was acting as an informer about institute affairs, trying again and again to find an excuse for her behaviour. He would write later of this difficult time.

> I had been in Prague for two and a half years, had made friends there, had seen the city forgetting the fears bred by the Occupation, and growing prosperous. The people in the trams talked to one another freely, as in the days before the Occupation, without needing to be reminded of old Masaryk's saying that he would know Czechoslovakia was a democracy when anyone could stand up and say in public, 'God damn the government'. In Prague houses no one started with apprehension when the door-bell or the telephone rang. Now all was changed. The old stale fears were back. No one opened his mouth in the trams. No-one said 'God damn the government', knowing that he would be arrested if he did. No one dared to tell what he really thought, except in his own house or to a friend he could trust. No one telephoned if he could help it, though in a very short time people knew by the slight diminution in the volume of the sound when the line was being tapped. And men at last became suspicious even of their friends.[34]

[33] Ibid., p. 98.
[34] *An Autobiography*, p. 267.

Lumir himself was increasingly in danger because of his non-communist political beliefs as well as his previous closeness to Jan Masaryk. His wife Catriona had already left for Edinburgh and now he turned to planning his own escape from the city. This meant leaving furniture and many treasured belongings and books behind, but once he had confirmation that Edwin's application for a transfer from Prague had been successful, he began to move a few of his most important books to Edwin and Willa, during his clandestine evening visits. He hoped they might take them to London with their own belongings, and Willa suggested he should do the same with some of his clothes too, so he would duly arrive to visit them, dressed in two suits. Lumir chose the date of 6 July for his intended departure. This was the anniversary of the burning at the stake of the great fifteenth-century religious reformer Jan Hus, and Prague would be busy with the patriotic gymnastic Sokol Festival that was being held in the city. The possibility of public demonstrations was high, and police were being drawn from frontier and other areas to cover the capital city, so it seemed a favourable time for his departure. Lumir would write later that he 'crossed the two streams that after a few yards joined to become the Vltava, with Smetana's symphonic poem singing in my head'.[35] Having made the crossing, he would eventually reach safety in the American zone in Germany and finally in London.

Edwin, meanwhile, having been granted his transfer request, completed with a heavy heart his summer term course at Charles University on the Literature of the Victorian Age, along with seminars on John Donne and Contemporary Poets. His imminent departure left a gap that British Council reports for the period acknowledged was impossible to refill. He wrote about this summer term in his autobiography—'all was changed; my class, once eager to discuss everything, was silent.' Yet, despite the two communist watchers in attendance, who took down everything he said, Edwin recognized that he was in a privileged position. Other lecturers in the employment of the state had to conform to the wishes of the new government or risk dismissal, or worse. Professor Vočadlo, who had given the supporting speech at Edwin's honorary doctoral ceremony, was one who continued to lecture in his own way, and paid the price for this. Edwin took advantage of his freedom to lecture on John Stuart Mill and his ideas on liberty, an event that caused some agitation on the part of his communist watchers and appeared to bring his students temporarily to life again, as if 'fearfully enjoying a forbidden pleasure'.[36] But his class soon dwindled in numbers. Willa organized an end-of-term party in their flat for the students who remained, and the final meeting of the Writers' Circle was held there as well. The Muirs' belongings were packed up, checked by the authorities, and on the last day of July they found

---

[35] *Má Vlast*, 'My Homeland', by the Czech composer Smetana consists of six symphonic poems, one of which is titled 'Vltava', the name of the river crossed by Lumir in his escape from his homeland.
[36] *An Autobiography*, p. 272.

themselves on a train to the border. The train stopped at the hot, dusty border station for about two hours, with people in various carriages being ejected, their luggage thrown out of windows. Then at last it moved on and they were running through the American zone of Germany, leaving behind the Prague whose 'sizzling' atmosphere had so inspired their own lives when they first encountered it in the early 1920s, but which now appeared so negatively and seemingly irreparably changed.

During their secret Prague walks together after the Putsch, Lumir Soukup remembers how Edwin told him that he had been writing a good amount of new poetry despite the distress of the situation. He read some of these poems to Lumir as they walked, or during Lumir's evening visits to their flat. These poems would be published by Faber and Faber in 1949 as *The Labyrinth*. As with his earlier wartime collection *The Narrow Place*, which Neil Gunn had characterized as catching a 'flame from the fire that is burning the world', the poems in *The Labyrinth* derive their significant power from their creator's responses to the situation he witnessed in post-war Prague. In an essay published in 1987, the Irish poet Seamus Heaney would hail Edwin as the translator of Kafka and as a witness to the communist takeover in post-war Czechoslovakia, commenting that *The Labyrinth* and the subsequent collection *One Foot in Eden*, are 'not like anything that was going on just then on the home poetic front'. Heaney argued in particular that 'The Interrogation' poem from *The Labyrinth* 'anticipates by a couple of decades the note which would be heard when A. Alvarez began to edit his influential Penguin *Modern European Poets* series in the late 1960s'.[37] 'The Interrogation' begins 'We could have crossed the road, but hesitated / And then came the patrol'. Neither speaker nor setting is identified, the action begins *in media res*, but the potential danger of the situation and its tense atmosphere are powerfully and economically communicated by the poem's short lines and the irregular chiming of end-rhymes as in 'intent / indifferent' in lines three and four, and 'hesitated' in line one with a gap of several lines before it chimes with 'waited' in line five; by the tension and expectation created by the silent beat after 'patrol' at the end of line two. This tense, but unspecific opening, is then contrasted with the rapid questioning of the patrol leader which immediately follows, before the pace slows again as the poem brings in the everyday life going on around the captives—'the careless lovers in pairs go by'—before moving to an ending in which 'Endurance [is] almost done', a sense reinforced by the slow, heavily stressed movement of the final line: 'And still the interrogation is going on'.

The long poem 'The Good Town' was one of the first poems Edwin read to Lumir on their secret walks—'Look at it well. This was a good town once'. Lumir was much taken with it, but felt that Edwin should have made clear its identity as Prague, destroyed by the communist Putsch, or indeed by the Nazis. For Edwin,

---

[37] Seamus Heaney, 'The Impact of Translation'. *Yale Review*, Autumn 1987, pp. 8–9.

however, the impersonal approach was important. He said the poem had been in his head before the events of February 1948, and it seems clear that its non-specific setting was linked in his thinking to his sense of the pointless cycles of warfare throughout human history, something that was already present in poems from *The Narrow Place*, such as 'The Wayside Station' and 'The River', or 'The Rider Victory'. The title poem 'The Labyrinth' derives from Edwin's interest in Greek mythology and his increasing and subtle use of it in his late poetry. As early as in his *We Moderns* of 1918, he had argued that the Greeks 'did not aim at the reproduction but the interpretation of life [...] a symbolizing of the deepest questions and enigmas of life'.[38] His 'Labyrinth' poem therefore does not attempt to use the myth of Theseus and the minotaur explicitly, but brings it to mind through occasional words and phrases—'Since I emerged that day from the labyrinth'; 'the bull [...] dead on the straw'—creating a psychological drama of confusion and dislocation. The poem also has clear resonances with K's constantly frustrated attempts to reach the Castle in Kafka's novel, with its imagery of 'deceiving streets / That meet and part and meet, and rooms that open into each other / And never a final room'. Speaking some years later about this poem, which he had started to write while staying at the Writers' House in Dobris in Czechoslovakia, he said—

> Thinking there of the old story of the labyrinth of Cnossos and the journey of Theseus through it and out of it, I felt that this was an image of human life with its errors and ignorance and endless intricacy. In the poem I made the labyrinth stand for all this [...]
>
> The poem begins with a very long sentence, deliberately labyrinthine, to give the mood.[39]

This mood is captured again in the shorter poem 'The Helmet' which uses a similarly symbolic and imagistic approach to capture the loss of human identity and human feeling as a result of war. Its taut regularly rhyming four-line verses reinforce the sense of isolation and entrapment: 'The helmet on his head / Has melted flesh and bone / And forged a mask instead / That always is alone'. The first line of the final verse: 'But he can never come home' seems to echo the comment of Broch's one-armed amputee soldier in the final book of his *Sleepwalkers* trilogy, who tells the hospital sister that he thinks that 'none of us will ever really get home again.'[40] Like the story of the 'Good Town', and Edwin's prose account of the displaced human beings he saw wandering the roads during the journey to his new posting in Prague, this 'impersonal' approach, working through image and metaphor, allowed him to write a poetry that is relevant to the human story for all

---

[38] *We Moderns*, pp. 15, 16.
[39] Edwin Muir, BBC broadcast, 3 September 1952 (BBC archive).
[40] Hermann Broch, *Die Schlafwandler / The Sleepwalkers*, p. 545.

times and not just our own. As with Brecht's own 'singing' in the face of the rise of Hitler in Germany, Edwin's *Labyrinth* poems confirm the continuing importance of the response of the artist—whether literary, visual, or musical—in the face of darkening times.[41]

---

[41] The poems referred to in this final section are from *Complete Poems*: 'The Interrogation, p. 172, 'The Good Town', pp. 173–76, 'The Labyrinth', pp. 157–59, 'The Helmet', pp. 168–69.

16
Roman Interlude 1948–1950

> I'm much struck with Rome [...] Edinburgh I love, but in Edinburgh you never come upon anything that brings the thought of Incarnation to your mind, and here you do so often, and quite unexpectedly.
>
> Edwin Muir, letter to Joseph Chiari (1949)

After crossing the channel, Edwin and Willa went first of all to Cambridge where a friend had booked them into a boarding house called 'The Hermitage', said to have had associations with the Darwin family. It did not prove much of a refuge, however, since Edwin immediately had a nervous breakdown, which he later described as falling 'plumb into a dead pocket of life which I had never guessed at before'. He found himself waking each morning 'feeling that I had lost or mislaid something which I was accustomed to but could not name [...] I wandered about the colleges, seeing but not feeling their beauty'. Willa remembered her own attack of indifference when she was so seriously ill in St Andrews, and felt certain that Edwin had similarly 'lost touch with the feelings that give immediate meaning to life'. All that he had tried so hard to accomplish in Prague seemed to have been destroyed or blighted and Edwin felt that he had lost 'the little spring of hope, or interest, with which the day once began'. Willa records a visit from E. M. Forster, whom they had never previously met. The novelist must have heard that they were in Cambridge but he could get no response from Edwin, and after a little while he went quietly away. Edwin seemed distant whenever Willa suggested how they might spend their days, and she found this 'formal politeness' to be 'heart-rending'. Gradually he began to show more interest, however, helped by their finding a little local pub in the evenings where Gavin, who was with them at this time, charmed the regulars and made their visits especially welcome by playing jazz and Chopin on the pub piano. As Edwin recovered, they went to stay with friends in London, then to a boarding house in Hampstead, where Edwin found that 'our old happy memories of the place gathered around us.'[1] In the meantime, the British Council was trying to find an appropriate transfer situation for him. Portugal at one point seemed a possibility, but fell through, and then in December he was offered an appointment in Rome as Director of the British Council Institute in the city. He accepted, and Willa and he set out for a new Roman adventure at the beginning of January 1949.

---

[1] *An Autobiography*, p. 274; *Belonging*, pp. 244–6.

In their future memoirs, both Muirs would write in detail and with appreciation of the happiness their stay in Rome brought them. With an updated autobiography in mind, Edwin's account of their difficulties in Prague had to bear in mind Lumir Soukup's worries that a publication date in 1954 was too close to the events of 1948 for the safety of some of the participants. His experience of Rome, however, brought a happier problem. He confessed that his affections were still so 'deeply attached to the Italy I discovered then—for the few months I had spent in it twenty-three years before had told me little or nothing—that if I were to write at length about it now, gratitude would make me say too much, or dread of appearing extravagant tempt me to say too little'. And he adds, in a way that reads sadly in relation to his happy memories of 1920s Prague, that 'perhaps the fact that Rome made my wife well again and let me forget Prague was enough to account for part of the gratitude.'[2] One immediately welcome element in his new situation was the warm friendliness that already existed in the Rome Institute. This seemed to have been created to a large extent by the director who Edwin was replacing. Roger Hinks was an art historian who had spent a year at the British School in Rome in the 1920s. As a linguist, he was interested in Europe and its languages and literature, and was at the opposite end of the spectrum from the aloof, hierarchical, organization-obsessed Council representatives Edwin had encountered in Prague. Hinks had joined the British Council after the war, had been appointed Director of the British Institute in Rome from 1945 to 1949, and was now moving to a post as British Council Representative in the Netherlands. The institute staff were very sorry to see him leave and Edwin records how the Secretary at the Institute, Laura Minervini, took him aside to tell him how happily everyone had worked together in the institute under Hinks, and how she hoped this would continue under him. She offered to give him an idea of the Italian character, explaining how Italians would do anything for their friends, but could not be 'driven'. Edwin said she need not fear being driven, and the atmosphere she described was exactly the kind he hoped would continue. And it did continue, with Edwin calling the institute 'a sort of talkative Eden', adding 'In it and from it I made most of my friends.' He was aware that in Rome, 'the poor, certainly, were dreadfully poor, and the rich senselessly rich.' But writing of the character of the Romans he encountered during his work at the institute, he compared them to the farmers he remembered in Orkney 'I had known fresh and natural speech among Orkney farmers living close to the cattle and the soil, but not until now among men and women moulded by city life, and sometimes of subtle mind.' He continued—

The people we knew had the air of stepping out completely into life, and their speech, even at its idlest, had something of the accent of Dante, who spoke more directly from the heart than any other poet but one. I was reminded of the paint-

[2] *An Autobiography*, pp. 274–5.

ings of Piero della Francesca and Michelangelo, not so much by the faces of our friends, as by their expression and carriage, which seemed an image of full humanity. The humanity was perfectly natural, but I knew that naturalness does not come easily to the awkward human race, and that this was an achievement of life.[3]

Willa was equally captivated by Rome, but her primary preoccupation—apart from regaining her health—was finding a suitable flat to live in. The hotel the Council had initially booked for them was too noisy, being situated near the Porta Pinciana, the Pincian Gate, in an area close to the Villa Borghese. Nor did the area of Parioli, one of Rome's fashionable quarters, attract them when they went flat hunting there. Willa remembered 'one Parioli living-room with tomato-red Pompeian walls diversified by alcoves in which white porcelain nymphs simpered', with magenta plush chairs arranged round a large table 'where a huge spiky glass fish leered at us, a most sadistic-looking fish'. They suggested to the housing agent that perhaps Old Rome would suit them better than fashionable Parioli, and after rejecting sombre rooms in old palaces, they by chance found a small penthouse at the top of an apartment block beside the Tiber on Lungo Tevere Marzio. Willa was certain that this was the flat for them. 'Once we stood on its wide terraces we knew that this flat was ours. The east terrace looked towards the Quirinal, over some of the oldest roofs in Rome; the west terrace faced the Tiber and the Palace of Justice.' Although the indoor living space of the flat was small, they decided that it was big enough for them, 'since we meant to live as much as possible in the open air on the roof'.[4] It is worth noting that the location of this flat beside the Tiber was very similar to their accommodation in Prague overlooking the Vltava, and to their Neustadt Dresden accommodation, in a square looking down to the banks of the Elbe. Another welcome reminder of the past was Hilde, their housekeeper who had returned to Germany after Munich to look for a husband. Willa does not say how she managed to keep in touch with Hilde during the war and early post-war years, but Hilda had found an Italian husband, as opposed to a German one, and was now living with him and their small son in a village at the top of Lake Como. Willa sent her a telegram, and in a short time she came to Rome with her son and took up her former role as Willa's housekeeper, while her husband found a hotel job in Rome, living initially with relatives. Life in Rome began to promise all they could have hoped for. Willa wrote to Violet Schiff, with whom she had regained contact, that the 'wonder of penicillin' had restored her mobility, 'I can now walk and sit- and- stand all in one piece—even run if need be.' Edwin too had recovered 'from the minor nervous breakdown which Prague induced in him'. They felt that a new life was beginning for them, and Willa added 'Also,—and this is not

[3] Ibid., pp. 276, 275.
[4] *Belonging*, p. 252.

unimportant,—we feel that a new life is beginning to emerge for Europe, however slowly. I am actually beginning to hope!'[5]

Edwin was kept very busy—enjoyably so—with his work in the Rome Institute. Membership of the institute among the Roman public was low compared to the numbers of language students, and Edwin and his second-in-command Joe O'Brien aimed to do something about this. Edwin suggested that they open a tearoom and, as in Prague, this proved a very popular innovation, singled out for comment in the Council reports sent to London. Willa reported that the fame of the tearoom had spread to the extent that it became a popular meeting place for Romans who arranged with each other to meet 'at the British', without feeling the need to say 'at the British Institute Tearoom'. Magazine evenings at the institute were also a popular innovation, and membership increased again, with a general in the Italian Army even presenting the institute with a box of its own at the theatre. Members of staff were equally well connected with various layers of Roman society. Laura, the secretary so concerned about the office's happy atmosphere, had an assistant with a brother in the Pope's Noble Guard, so that Edwin and Willa could expect to be allocated seats at any ceremonial taking place in St Peter's. Joe O'Brien had a close friend who was a Monsignore, and he introduced Edwin to the Scots College where Edwin gave a talk on literature to the students. There were also official visits to towns such as Florence, Venice, and Siena on which Willa was able to accompany Edwin. When Edwin undertook a more extensive lecture tour of Sicily, taking in places such as Palermo, Messina, Catani, and Syracuse—an activity in which Council wives were normally not permitted to accompany their husbands—Willa had succeeded in becoming sufficiently fluent in Italian to be able to join the tour as a lecturer in her own right. Unlike his lack of success with the Czech language, Edwin made some progress with Italian, writing to Pat Swale, a former Prague colleague and friend about his impressions of Rome, 'I like the people, and (you will never believe it) I'm learning the language: perhaps because I like it.' He told Pat that Rome was a good place 'for coming across English people one wishes to see for they all come there sooner or later: we've seen in the last few weeks Auden, Graham Greene, Rex Warner and V. S. Pritchett'. Most of these visitors would end up at some point on the Muirs' large roof terrace, and Edwin added, not quite in the manner expected of a good host 'That's one of the advantages of it—people who come in flying visits, or pass through, and one can see for once, and then not see again.'[6] Douglas Young visited them in Rome as did George Scott-Moncrieff, nephew of the translator of Proust and editor of *The New Alliance*, to which Edwin was a contributor. And in the hot summer of 1949, they escaped the Roman heat by spending time in Cremia on Lake Como where

---

[5] Willa Muir, letter to Violet Schiff, 21 April 1949, Schiff Papers, BL, Add MS 52920.
[6] Edwin Muir, letters to Pat Swale, 10 June 1949 and 18 December 1949, Orkney Library (Kirkwall) Archives D1/245/9 and D1/245/12.

housekeeper Hilde still had a small family house, and where she succeeded in renting a larger house from one of her acquaintances for the use of the Muirs and their visiting friends. This small village, Willa reported, made its living largely by smuggling goods from Switzerland, with young men inheriting their fathers' shares in the smuggling gangs as if they were part of a family business.

Writing to his Edinburgh friend Joseph Chiari, Edwin was very taken with his new life.

> I'm much struck with Rome, and all its wealth of associations; you feel the gods (including the last and greatest of them) have all been here, and are still present in a sense in the places where they once were. It has brought very palpably to my mind the theme of Incarnation and I feel that probably I shall write a few poems about that high and difficult theme sometime; I hope so. Edinburgh I love, but in Edinburgh you never come upon anything that brings the thought of Incarnation to your mind, and here you do so often, and quite unexpectedly.

He added, 'I'm rather afraid of writing on such a theme and though it occupies my mind whenever my mind is free from daily affairs, I feel nothing is ready yet to be written down.'[7] In her own memoir of their time in Rome, Willa was somewhat troubled about Edwin's involvement with the theme of incarnation. She wrote that ever since the beginning of their marriage she had been aware of Edwin's preoccupation with the biblical story of the fall and the idea of original sin, and she wondered if his experience of the Putsch and its aftermath in Prague had reanimated such ideas in his mind, leading to his relapse when they left Czechoslovakia. Now it seemed that he had been released from ideas of original sin, by discovering in Rome what she described as the 'warm, new love for Jesus'.[8] During their stay in Menton in the later 1920s, when both of them were occupied with writing novels, Willa had thought about what she perceived to be the very different approach to creative writing on her part as compared with Edwin's. She noticed that Edwin's approach to his theme was more detached, and that he 'transmuted it into symbols' while she herself relied 'on the empathy of personal feelings and memories'.[9] Her tendency to personalize their creative relationship is clear from her memoir and the testimony of friends, for if Edwin seemed especially quiet or preoccupied when they were in company, she would announce 'Look, a poem is coming', as if Edwin was some kind of exhibit she was responsible for, and the sense of 'belonging' to each other, which was so important to her, also extended to his creative life as a poet. Willa did not claim to possess the high creative ability she saw in Edwin. She had strong talents of her own, of course, but this capability was a of different kind from what is required to write or interpret poetry, especially a

---

[7] Edwin Muir, letter to Joseph Chiari, 20 December 1949, *Selected Letters*, pp. 154–5.
[8] *Belonging*, p. 250.
[9] Ibid., p. 126.

poetry that uses metaphor and symbol as opposed to straightforward description or argument. Willa hardly, if ever, mentions in her memoirs the innovative work of writers such as Eliot, Joyce, Lawrence, and Woolf, which Edwin critiqued in his 1926 *Transition*, and Edwin's discussions of poetry and poetic ideas seem to have been conducted to a large extent in his correspondence with friends and fellow poets.

It is unfortunate, therefore, that the difference between their ways of seeing the world led Willa almost always to interpret Edwin's poetry biographically, relating the poem to his personal life—often his past life—and what brought that particular poem into being. Willa was not alone in this. The success of Edwin's autobiographical *The Story and the Fable* of 1940 led many other commentators to link his early poetry exclusively to his Orkney childhood and his difficult teenage years in Glasgow, and to consider him as a primarily religious poet because he used the biblical story of the fall as a kind of objective correlative for his ideas about human life. A strictly biographical interpretation of his later, more sophisticated poetry is even more misleading. For Peter Butter, for example, 'The Labyrinth' from the 1949 collection of that name, deals with 'Muir's state of alienation in his Glasgow years, his escape from it and his later efforts to reconcile two apparently contradictory conceptions of human life'. Butter quotes a passage about the maze image in the poem which 'swept me smoothly to its enemy, / The lovely world', and claims that this description 'corresponds in Muir's life to the time of his marriage and the recovery of a sense of vivid contact with nature on the Continent afterwards'. This is a simplification of both Edwin's philosophical thought and the formal maturity of his late poetry, and stands at a far remove from Seamus Heaney's broader assessment, referred to earlier, that a poem such as 'The Interrogation' from *The Labyrinth* collection 'anticipated by a couple of decades the note that would be heard when A. Alvarez began to edit his influential Penguin Modern European Poets series in the late 1960s'. For Heaney, Muir's late poetry was 'European' in its wider philosophical thought and in the imagistic communication of that thought.[10] As Heaney went on to say in another essay on Muir, 'in the Forties and especially in this 1949 volume, [*The Labyrinth*] we can watch the gratifying spectacle of a solitary poetic endeavour attaining representative status; or to put it another way, by then Muir's subject was everybody's subject.'[11]

The dangers of biographical interpretation also apply to Edwin's engagement with what he understood as incarnation, and the poems later published in the 1956 collection *One Foot in Eden*. These are not simplistically Christian poems despite their frequent biblical references. Like many people of his age in Scotland, Edwin had come under the influence of revivalist preachers who called their

---

[10] Peter Butter, *Edwin Muir: Man and Poet*, p. 216; Seamus Heaney, *Yale Review*, Autumn 1987, pp. 8–9.
[11] Seamus Heaney, 'Edwin Muir', in *Finders Keepers*, p. 254.

congregations to come forward and give witness that they were 'saved'. In his Glasgow years he rejected this kind of religious ideology and gave his commitment instead to socialist organizations such as the Clarion Scouts and the Guilds movements that worked to improve the everyday earthly lives of ordinary working people. Edwin's later writings, such as his 1929 biography of John Knox and his 1934 *European Quarterly* article 'Bolshevism and Calvinism', denounced the creeds of Calvinism and communism as equally inhuman. Yet at the same time he did have a belief in what he called 'immortality', perhaps something similar to D. H. Lawrence's reference to 'the beyond'. He was aware of what he called the 'mystery' of human existence, recalling his 'three mysteries' in *The Story and the Fable* especially the third mystery, how we should live with one another'.[12] This is a consistent theme in his poetry. It is especially strong, if often metaphorically expressed, in his wartime and post-war collections of the 1940s and 1950s, but the preoccupation is present in all his work, going back to his early and continuing interest in the poetry of Hölderlin. It seemed to Edwin that Hölderlin's philosophical ideas expressed a continuity between human past and present experience, while the 'gods' in the scenarios of his poetry come down to earth and interact with human life, as opposed to being something apart.

At a particularly difficult time in St Andrews, when Willa was ill in the Cottage Hospital, when the threat of war with Germany was increasing, and the news about the treatment of Jews in Europe was becoming more and more distressing, Edwin had found himself one night, when preparing for bed, suddenly reciting the Lord's Prayer, something he had not done for years. He wrote in his diary of that time—

> Last night going to bed alone (Willa being in Cottage Hospital) I suddenly found myself (as I was taking off my waistcoat) reciting the Lord's Prayer in a loud emphatic voice—a thing I have not done since my teens—with urgency too, and deeply disturbed emotion. As I recited it I grew more composed; my soul, as if it had been empty and needed replenishment, seemed to fill; and every word had a strange fullness of meaning, which astonished and delighted me, and gave me not so much hope as strength. It was late; I had sat up reading; I was sleepy; but as I stood in the middle of the floor half undressed reciting the prayer over and over, the meanings it contained, none of them extraordinary, indeed ordinary as they could be, overcame me with joyful surprise, and made me seem to realise that this petition was always universal, always adequate, and to life as it is, not to a life such as we long for or dream of: and for that reason it seems to sanctify common existence.[13]

---

[12] *The Story and the Fable*, p. 64; *An Autobiography*, p. 56.
[13] Edwin Muir, Diary, 1 March 1939, NLS, MS 19668.

What had struck him so forcibly was that this old prayer was dealing with 'human life, seen realistically, not mystically. It is about the world and society, not about the everlasting destiny of the soul.' He realized also that the 'we' and 'us' in the prayer made it a 'collective' prayer—'for all societies, for all mankind as a great society', and a prayer, which, in its collective nature, could be seen as 'revolutionary'. This recognition reawakened his interest in the biblical stories of Jesus's teachings, which seemed to him to be especially applicable to how we live our earthly lives. Jesus himself, like Hölderlin's gods, lived his life on earth alongside others, as opposed to being separated from them. A few years after his St Andrews 'Lord's Prayer' experience, Edwin wrote to Stephen Spender from wartime Edinburgh in March 1944—

> The problems are terrifying, as you say. The religions exist, I suppose, to provide an explanation of them. I can't accept any religious explanation that I know of, any more than you. I would rather have the problems themselves, for from an awareness of them and their vastness I get some sort of living experience, some sense even of communion, of being in the whole in some way, whereas from the explanations I should only get comfort and reassurance and a sense of safety which I know is not genuine.

He goes on, 'I don't know why, this being so, my religious experience is not without hope: I do not think it is because of my belief in immortality; I still hold it, but for some reason it doesn't mean so much to me as it used to do; whether this is a bad sign or a good I really don't know.' He agreed with Spender that 'love is the supreme quality and more closely connected with immortality than any other, immortality either as you or I conceive it. And in a way I feel it is more important than immortality'.[14]

Coming to Rome, with all its reminders of past and present now living together, and especially the religious heritage of its churches and paintings, had reawakened Edwin's earlier interest in the *New Testament* and the story of Jesus and incarnation. This, in a somewhat similar way to the stories of Hölderlin's gods, seemed to point to the possibility of living a 'good' life in this world. His poem 'The Annunciation' came from this awakened sense, and was prompted by a small plaque on the wall of a house in a quiet side street not far from the busy Spanish Steps and Keats's House. Edwin remembered—

> stopping for a long time one day to look at a little plaque on the wall of a house in the via degli Artisti, representing the Annunciation. An angel and a young girl, their bodies inclined towards each other, their knees bent as if they were overcome by love, tutto tremante, gazed upon each other like Dante's pair; and that

---

[14] Edwin Muir, letter to Stephen Spender, 21 March 1944, *Selected Letters*, p. 137.

representation of a human love so intense that it could not reach farther seemed the perfect earthly symbol of the love that passes understanding.

Edwin realized that such a representation would have 'shocked the congregations of the north',[15] but it seemed to him that its open declaration of the presence and power of love, present among us in the physical world, was what distinguished Christianity from the older pagan gods associated with the city. 'The angel and the girl are met. / Earth was the only meeting place.'[16] Edwin did not write many poems during his stay in Rome, being kept extremely busy with the institute affairs and his lecture tours, but the experience of Rome clearly inspired the poems of *One Foot in Eden*, including those that used Greek myth. It is important to realize, however, that these more overtly 'religious' poems belong to an ongoing philosophical and material exploration of 'how we live with one another', and that this can be found in all his poetry and prose works, early and late. In his essay 'Tradition and the Individual Talent', T. S. Eliot insists on the 'transforming catalyst' and on the separation between 'the man who suffers and the mind which creates', and this applies as much to Edwin as a poet as it does to Eliot himself.

Edwin and Willa had hoped that they would spend around three years in Rome which would have taken them up to Edwin's sixty-fifth birthday in May 1952, and to British Council retirement age. However, in January 1950 the staff was informed by Ronald Bottrall, the British Council representative in Italy, that for financial reasons the Rome Institute, together with the institute in Palermo, would be closed at the end of June that year. Willa told of their surprise and disappointment in a letter to Violet Schiff which had begun as a Christmas greeting at the end of December, but as a result of illness on both her and Edwin's part, had been set aside and continued only at the end of January. After opening with an apology and an explanation for the Christmas card which 'is now more than belated', she continued—

> Part of our trouble was the sudden news, which came as a shock, that the British Council is going to close the Rome Institute this summer, as a dollar economy. (Edwin has brought it into a flourishing condition, and felt like the father of a lusty infant which was being ear-marked for Herod.) We shall therefore be leaving Italy in June or July, as far we can tell. It looks as if we shall be going to Scotland in some capacity or another; but we do not yet know anything for certain.[17]

She continues by telling Violet that they had gone to Capri early in January to recuperate from their various troubles and had 'a very peaceful, sunny holiday there'. They were 'beginning to feel less numbed and apprehensive; indeed, we

---

[15] *An Autobiography*, p. 278.
[16] 'The Annunciation', *Complete Poems*, p. 206.
[17] Willa Muir, letter to Violet Schiff, 13 December 1949–23 January 1950, p. 2.

achieve a cheerful faith that there will still be work which we can do'. Edwin was further heartened to win the Foyle Prize for poetry for *The Labyrinth* collection, and Willa adds 'never was prize so timely. He has a lot of poetry in him still, and please God he will get it written.' One member of the family who was pleased by their return to Scotland was Gavin, who was coming to the end of an honours degree in Astronomy and Mathematics at St Andrews University. Willa tells Violet that 'he hates to have us always so far away', and she hopes to see her when they pass through London, probably in June.[18]

In some ways it is surprising that Edwin, or at least Willa, had not heard any rumours about the British Council's cost-cutting in Italy. Willa had been impressed by Ronald Bottrall, whom she described as 'a poet and likely to behave humanly rather than as a bureaucrat'. He had entertained them when he 'held up to our ridicule, with loud guffaws, London's warning to him before our arrival that Edwin was a trouble-maker and Willa a dangerous woman', and 'we thought we knew where that assessment of the Muirs had come from, even if Ronald might have embroidered it a little.'[19] Ronald, from Cornwall, and a poet himself, seemed to be a very different representative from the two bureaucrats they had met in Prague, but British Council reports and unpublished archival material on post-war activities in Italy clearly show that Bottrall was himself involved with the closure of the Rome Institute.

In the post-war years of the British Council, there were problems of communication and friction between locally based teaching and organizational staff, the representative for the wider area, and London itself. Bottrall, as representative, was particularly irritated at being unable to make his own decisions as to what should happen to the various Italian Institutes, while London considered Italy, as well as Greece, to be an immediate priority and wanted to be strongly involved in any decision-making. Reports from the British Institute of Rome, before Edwin was appointed as Director, show concern with poor enrolment of non-language student members, problems with accommodation as a result of a split campus between language teaching and cultural activities, and on one occasion what seems a dismissive attitude towards the Romans themselves, who are said to have 'hardly suffered from the war', but are 'prone to grumble at real or fancied inconveniences which are ignored by those who have more serious difficulties to contend with'. Many of these Roman 'backsliders' who do not renew their enrolment subscriptions, are seen to have 'joined the Institute mainly for snobbish reasons, while it was the fashion to do so'.[20] Even the popular Roger Hinks had not been able to increase

---

[18] Ibid.
[19] *Belonging*, p. 251.
[20] British Council Archives, National Archives, Kew, BW 40/30 'British Institutes in Italy', Appendix D, Extract from British Institutes of Rome Report for February, 1947. For a published account of the difficulties of the Rome Institute, see Simon Pocock, *the British Council in Italy: An Early History (1938–58)* (British Council, 1965), especially sections '1948–49: storm clouds over Rome' and

non-student membership sufficiently to satisfy the representative, whose letters and reports to London regularly emphasized the costs and other disadvantages of the Roman split-site accommodation, and especially 'the gilded splendours of the Palazzo del Drago', as an unsuitable venue for more intimate meetings. By the summer of 1948, the question of accommodation was still unresolved, and in the face of Treasury cuts to the Council budget, Representative Bottrall was writing to the appropriate overseas director that he had 'followed the line [...] that first priority must be given to geographical coverage', and that 'the logical conclusion of this would be to make the first cut the abolition of the Rome Institute, which would provide a net saving of £10880.' Later, in October, when the institute was about to move into new premises in the Palazzo Doria Pamphlij, which would serve both teaching and cultural needs, Bottral reported that with the chance of an adequate number of students for the future, he did not think it would be wise to close it before July 1950. It is clear, however, that the decision to close Rome had already been taken, and that this must have been known when the officials in London decided to offer Edwin the position of director in December 1948, while moving the current director, Hinks, to the more secure post of representative in the Netherlands. Given Edwin's closeness to retirement age at that point, this could be seen as an appropriate appointment, but it does seem surprising and somewhat disingenuous, that no indication of its likely limited duration was communicated when the position was offered. Later, on 20 October 1949, after Edwin had been in post for almost a year, Bottrall wrote to 'Overseas Division "C"', that in contrast to previous 'adverse comments' from London officials visiting the Rome Institute, he was now glad to report that—

> during the last eight or nine months a great deal has been done to remedy these defects. The weekly programme is now extremely varied and the fact that 83 Air Force officers and 12 Naval officers are taking special courses at the Institute means that more men are seen in the building than women. The institution of a tea-room financed by Institute members, which is open from five to seven each day, has greatly increased the number of members regularly attending the Institute. A series of lectures in Italian has been arranged for the current term.

He then acknowledges that 'Mr Muir and his staff have all contributed to the improvement of the Institute which I now regard as probably the most successful in Italy.' A handwritten letter a few days later from the Director of S. Europe commented caustically 'Mr Bottrall's letter of 20/10 about the achievements of the Rome Institute is rather a funeral wreath, I fear, as on his recommendation we are

'1949–50: The British Institute Rome Saga'. There is little mention of Edwin Muir's directorship in either BW 40/30 or Pocock's account, nor does Pocock mention the petition of over a hundred signatures sent to London in support of the institute by users and supporters protesting against its closure.

now signing the Institute's death warrant'; to which a comment written in another hand added 'There is nothing like a death-warrant for bringing home the virtues of the condemned.'[21] And so the Rome Institute was scheduled for closure in the summer of 1950, as Bottrall had previously recommended, despite a petition of over a hundred signatures being sent to London by Italian members of the institute. Edwin himself sent a letter of 12 May 1950 to the representative, recommending that serious consideration be given to an offer from a wealthy Roman, Advocato Coppa, to pay for the continuance of the institute on its present British Council lines. At this point Edwin could write without any personal interest because he had been invited to become warden of the recently reopened Newbattle Abbey, a residential adult education college in Edinburgh. Nevertheless, the offer from Advocato Coppa was rejected and the institute closed at the end of June. So it was that Edwin and Willa, with regret but also some excitement, left Rome for their new adventure in Newbattle Abbey on the outskirts of Edinburgh.

---

[21] British Council BW 40/30, National Archives, Kew. See also Pocock, p. 41.

17
Newbattle Abbey 1950–1955

> We do not clamp down any ideology on our students; we lead them to use their own minds and think for themselves. A people thinking independently is necessary for the working of a democracy, as the opposite is for the existence of a dictatorship.
>
> Edwin Muir, Newbattle Information Booklet

Edwin was especially attracted to Newbattle Abbey College because he would be working with students like himself who had not had the opportunity of a higher-grade school or college education. Willa had her own reasons for looking forward to Newbattle, even if she still had some misgivings about living in Scotland after their unhappiness in St Andrews. Edwin was now 63 years of age and she was 60. They had not had a permanent home since their marriage in 1919, having led a peripatetic existence in Europe and the British Isles. This had been exciting and mostly enjoyable when they were younger, but Willa wanted a settled home now, and began to hope that Newbattle might provide it. She was so excited at the prospect that she and Edwin—and it is most likely that Willa was the driving force here—took a taxi to Newbattle shortly after they arrived in Edinburgh, without contacting the college housekeeper to check whether a visit was suitable. They knew that Newbattle Abbey had been one of the family homes inherited by Philip Kerr, who had become 11th Marquess of Lothian in 1930, and that on his death a decade later it had passed to the foundation he had set up to create a residential adult education college. What they had not expected was the fine, spacious country house that met them as they drove up its tree-lined driveway—a house, which was as impressive internally as externally set in 125 acres of garden and parkland (Figure 17.1). As the glass door at the top of the steps was open, they walked into a spacious hall with a fine wooden staircase rising to the focal point of an eighteenth-century marble roundel before branching left and right. Two smaller sets of steps led down to what they would later discover was the crypt. As they stood looking at this unexpected grandeur, the sound of footsteps brought into sight what Willa described as a smallish man and a tallish woman who told them that the abbey was not open to visitors. Then the housekeeper arrived, amazed when Edwin confessed that he was the new warden. They were made aware that their unauthorized arrival was a breach of decorum that had to be overlooked. A summer school was about to begin in the abbey the next day—hence the presence of the smallish man

Figure 17.1 Newbattle Abbey
Source: National Galleries of Scotland. Collection of Mrs Catherine Clark, gifted by her sons Sandy, David and Peter in her memory, 2008

and tallish woman who were respectively a City of Glasgow Bailie and the Head of a Glasgow Pre-Nursing College, who had come to check arrangements for the summer school. The warden's flat could not be inspected since it was locked up, with the key in the pocket of the caretaker who had gone to Fife for the day. It was all most unfortunate. Willa felt that it was indeed unfortunate that they had forgotten that Scotland was not Rome, where their impetuous behaviour would have been indulged. They were, however, able to look over the spacious college grounds and the other apartments in the abbey, including the library with its 'pastiche 17th-century woodwork and Morris & Co. fireplace tiles' and a magnificent drawing room, recently described as 'still one of the most remarkable 19th-century interiors in Scotland despite the loss of most of the pictures that were its *raison d'être*'.[1] They inspected the bedrooms, including the student bedrooms, and by this time the 'thin film of social ice' had begun to thaw. The Glasgow Bailie 'grew facetious' about the state bedroom, once prepared for Queen Victoria, the floor of which 'seemed to heave as one looked at the blue-ribboned bouquets of lily of the valley that ran diagonally from corner to corner'.[2] Edwin laughed at the Baillie's remarks,

---

[1] Michael Hall, 'Newbattle Abbey, Lothian', article in *Country Life*, 8 July 1993; reproduced by Principal and Governors of Newbattle Abbey College as an information leaflet with permission of *Country Life*.
[2] *Belonging*, p. 267.

they approved the students' bedrooms, and ended up having afternoon tea with the others in the crypt. When tea was finished, they were escorted into the Knot Garden at the back of the house so that they could look from the outside at the windows of what would be their drawing room and Edwin's study. The awkward beginning had ended well and taught them a social lesson that would prove useful in their later dealings at the abbey.

Philip Kerr, who became Marquis of Lothian in 1930 and whose family had owned the Newbattle Abbey Estate since the late sixteenth century, was a politician and diplomat, who served as private secretary to Prime Minister Lloyd George between 1916 and 1921. From 1939 until his unexpected death in 1940, he was Ambassador to the United States, where he was considered to have made a significant input into winning America's support for the British war effort, especially in relation to the Lend Lease legislation that was passed by the American Congress after his death. Kerr was an idealist about education and social reform and was a leading figure in the British parliamentary campaign during the 1930s to allow the owners of historic houses to pass over their estates to the National Trust and the National Trust for Scotland. He himself had inherited '32,361 embarrassing acres'[3] on his cousin's death in 1930, consisting of the estates of Newbattle in Lothian, Monteviot, and Ferniehirst, both near Jedburgh, and Blickling in Norfolk, and he planned to extract what public benefit he could from these properties. Newbattle Abbey was the original family home of the Kerrs, who at the time of the Reformation had acquired the buildings and land from the Cistercian Abbey in the area. It later became the family's principal Scottish estate, but Philip Kerr, who was unmarried, did not plan to live there, and as early as 1931 he declared his intention to pass the house and its 125 acres of gardens and parkland to the Newbattle Foundation as an adult education college. After a long campaign to raise the necessary finances, his plan came to fruition in 1937 when the first students arrived to spend a year at the college.

Kerr's idealism extended to the nature of the college he envisaged. It would be a 'second chance' college for men and women who for reasons of social, financial, or personal circumstances had not had the opportunity to study and develop their talents. The abbey house and its fine gardens and grounds would offer its students an educational year free of the usual academic hurdles and examinations. There would be no leaving certificates to categorize performance, and the subjects to be studied would be selected by the students themselves from a varied set of options, under the guidance of lecturers and tutors. This was a pattern that spoke strongly to Edwin's own experience. He knew how valuable it could be to have time away from work and the pressures of daily living, in order to allow oneself to think and explore and to talk with others who were similarly minded.

---

[3] Hall, *Newbattle Abbey pamphlet*, referring to letter from Philip Kerr to Lloyd George relating to his inheritance.

Not everyone saw it his way, however. Bernard Bergonzi, who would become a prestigious literary scholar and critic, was one of Edwin's students at Newbattle, but he disagreed with the open-ended curriculum and its lack of assessment. In an unpublished memoir, he wrote that Newbattle was 'an aristocratic gesture that was both generous and condescending, and ultimately impractical'.[4] Edwin would later find that this view was shared by the trade unions, who preferred the idea of practical weekend and day-release short courses. But Kerr was right to recognize that Newbattle might fulfil a real need for wider educational experience in the late 1930s, and again at its post-war reopening in 1950. Nor was there any condescension or sloppiness in its teaching programme, and Edwin's students would comment on his 'insistence on the importance of grammar, impeccable spelling, clear expression, intellectual honesty, industry and craftsmanship'.[5] Indeed, the number of students who achieved entry to Cambridge, Oxford, Edinburgh, and other universities on the basis of extended essays submitted at the end of their residence at Newbattle (including Bergonzi himself), is a testament to the success of its educational approach. On the creative front, poets and novelists such as George Mackay Brown, Tom Scott, and Archie Hind owed a lot to Edwin and their time at Newbattle.

The educational approach written into Kerr's Newbattle Foundation was very close to Edwin's heart when he took up residence in the summer of 1950. Numbers were always quite small, however, and did not rise much during the five years in which he was warden. Not all the students were Scottish, and in this first year, they included a man from French Togoland who had been sent by the Colonial Office to learn English so that he could train as a teacher at Moray House College of Education. He had been sent to Newbattle because he was having difficulties with the lectures at Moray House, but after a term at Newbattle he was sufficiently fluent to talk animatedly with the other students and particularly with Bob, his metalworker friend to whom his regular request became 'Gie's a fag, Bob'.[6] Bob returned to Newbattle for a second year and was later accepted at Cambridge University after submitting an essay to the Cambridge Extramural Delegacy, which offered access for those who had not come through the normal academic routes. Another non-Scot in Edwin's first year was a Dutch trades unionist who came to improve his English and learn about British trade unions.

By spring 1951, the Muirs were enjoying their residence in Newbattle despite their growing realization that not all trades union representatives connected with the college were fully supportive of its educational aims. The gardens and the garden walks in the grounds of the abbey were a special joy, especially in the springtime when the plants and trees were coming alive again. Internally, the abbey

---

[4] Bernard Bergonzi, quoted by Maggie Fergusson in *George Mackay Brown: The Life* (London: John Murray, 2006), p. 102.
[5] James D. Young, 'A Socialist's-eye View of Edwin Muir', *Chapman* 49, Summer 1987, p. 23.
[6] *Belonging*, p. 270.

gave them the space to put all their books on display for the first time and to make provision for keeping papers rather than discarding them. In addition, Willa turned the wide upstairs corridor that led to their bedrooms into a private dining room so that they could have some meals on their own away from the students and also invite friends and other guests to dinner. She engaged a personal maid who cooked for them and slept in their spare bedroom. Edwin was busy organizing the newly opened college during that first year, but he lectured on literature three times a week and was available to talk and discuss essays. He continued to write regular reviews for the *Observer* as well as working on new poetry. Most of the poems published in his 1956 collection *One Foot in Eden* would be written during his years at Newbattle, although many were inspired by his experience of Rome. He also returned to his 1940 autobiography, *The Story and the Fable*, following an invitation by Hogarth Press to bring it up to the present. Another literary development was the visit of a young man, John Hall, who had written an extended essay on Edwin's poetry in *Penguin New Writing 38* in 1949. Hall proposed that it was now time for a collected poems, and when Edwin, after a considerable delay, said he had no free time for the task, Hall offered to do it himself. Accordingly, he visited Newbattle to discuss the matter in early 1951, and the eventual result was *Edwin Muir: Collected Poems 1921–1951*, published by Faber in June the following year.

In contrast to such positive experiences, some trouble arose in the second term of that first year to do with a young Philosophy lecturer that Edwin had interviewed in London and recommended for appointment. A group of students, including some of the most able and reliable, complained that this lecturer was directing their studies towards Marxism and trying to make converts of them. They reported dissension within the college, and claimed that the bursar, who was friendly with the lecturer in question, was canvassing students to support him. Edwin, although socialist in his political thinking, was no friend of communist activity, especially after what he had experienced in Prague. He interviewed both lecturer and bursar and concluded that there were no real grounds for concern. But student unrest continued, with claims of favouritism and a report that the lecturer had been overheard to say he would be satisfied with his work 'if he made one Communist a term'.[7] Edwin advised the lecturer to avoid the appearance of bias, who promptly offered to join the Labour Party or the Fabian Society if this would help to reassure the complaining students. It proved difficult, however, to defuse the hostility that had arisen in the enclosed environment at Newbattle,

---

[7] See reference to Edwin Muir's 'confidential report' in Neil Kevin Hargreaves, 'An 'experiment in the wilderness': Newbattle Abbey College and the idea of residential adult education in Scotland 1931-1955', *History of Education*, 3 April 2009, pp. 1–20 (p. 15). Online access to this article: DOI: 10.1080/00467600802635220. This is an important article for information about the Newbattle experiment more generally, and I am grateful to Neil Hargreaves of present-day Newbattle for bringing it to my attention.

and Edwin came to the reluctant conclusion that the Philosophy lecturer and the bursar would have to leave. The executive committee agreed with his decision for the good of the college, and when the governors reported the matter to the Scottish Education Department they were at pains to point out that while the behaviour of the staff concerned might be acceptable in a large university institution, it made them 'temperamentally unsuitable' for teaching in a small closely knit residential community such as Newbattle.[8] This incident heralded future difficulties at the college, whose nature and organization had been a cause of dispute among trades union representatives and some educationalists long before Edwin was appointed warden.

After this unfortunate episode in an otherwise stimulating and successful first year, Edwin and Willa spent much of the summer of 1951 in Orkney, relaxing and seeing old friends. They also met with George Mackay Brown, a young man from Stromness who had expressed interest in studying at Newbattle (Figure 17.2). In a short memoir of his time at the abbey, Mackay Brown would describe how his interview was carried out over afternoon tea with Edwin and Willa at Stromness Hotel. His strongest memories were of Willa and what he described as the flow of her talk and laughter. It seemed to him that she 'loved life and the masquers in the pageant of life and chiefly the amusing ways they behave'. Edwin was a quieter presence, 'smiling and smoking cigarettes for the most part'. But he told George, 'kindly', that he had read one of his short stories in the *New Shetlander* and that on the basis of this he would be happy to enrol him as a student at Newbattle when the new session began in October.[9] In later life, as an established poet and prose-writer, Mackay Brown was noted for his reluctance to leave Orkney, even to promote his own writing. So his departure for Newbattle in the autumn of 1951 was something of an adventure for him, as he prepared to fly from Orkney to Aberdeen and take the train south to Edinburgh. Characteristically, Edwin himself met the train at Waverley Station and took Mackay Brown by car to the abbey where, coming from a relatively treeless Orkney, George was struck by its trees, 'rich with autumn'. When snow came, he wrote that he had never known 'such an intense preparatory frost' in Orkney, and in January when the students returned to Newbattle after the Christmas break, he remembered 'a great storm that blew down the ancient beech tree beyond the garden'.[10] A different kind of life caught his attention on one of his first expeditions beyond the abbey to Dalkeith. He wrote to his friends the Marwicks in Orkney, 'When you walk through the streets [...] and see the grim dour look that everyone wears, you might imagine you were on the outskirts of Purgatory.' And he added (in a way that matched Edwin's *Scottish*

---

[8] Ibid.
[9] George Mackay Brown, 'Edwin Muir at Newbattle', *Edwin Muir: Selected Prose* (London: John Murray, 1987), p. 204.
[10] Ibid., p. 207.

Figure 17.2 George Mackay Brown
Source: Orkney Library and Archive

Journey comments fifteen years earlier) 'There is something bad and rotten about modern industrialism to give people such hopeless harsh faces.'[11]

George gradually became settled at Newbattle, especially enjoying the Cistercian roots of the abbey and a sense of its history. He made friends with the other students, men and women of different ages, nationalities and backgrounds. One young woman from Yugoslavia, a former interpreter, had experienced both Nazi occupation and post-war communism. She was financially very poor, but her time at Newbattle resulted in her being accepted for Cambridge University. One of the male students came from a family of refugees from Kashmir and arrived at Newbattle with possessions that consisted of one light suit, two pens, and a *Concise Oxford English Dictionary*. Newbattle was good for him as well, taking him to Edinburgh University and a PhD in Victorian fiction. George's special friends at Newbattle were Scotsmen close to his own age, a clerical worker from Larbert, a post office worker from Stornoway, a miner from West Lothian, and a metalworker

---

[11] George Mackay Brown, letter to Ernest Marwick 5 November 1951, quoted in Maggie Fergusson, *George Mackay Brown*, p. 104.

from Airdrie. The clerical worker and the post office worker both went on to Edinburgh University to study English. The metalworker, Bob, won a scholarship to Cambridge with an essay on Milton's *Paradise Lost*, and the miner did the same with an essay on Kant. Both eventually taught English in Scottish schools.

Mackay Brown's own poetry developed strongly during his time at Newbattle, and Edwin was later instrumental in sending a collection of his poems to Hogarth, which became *Loaves and Fishes* in 1954. It was, however, the friendship among the students that remained most strongly in George's mind as he thought back on these years. 'I have not, before or since, known such friendship', he wrote in his memoir of Newbattle, adding 'In the Justinlees bar a mile up the road, at Eskbank, beer never tasted so good.' He was equally positive about Edwin's lectures, admiring his capacity to open up a topic gradually, with exploration and illustration; admiring also his mingling with the students in the crypt of an evening, listening to what was going on but not attempting to be the centre of discussion himself. He was fond of Willa too, appreciating her liveliness and her gossip. He wrote that Willa's presence was felt everywhere in the college—

> cheerful, kind, delighted especially if she succeeded in slightly shocking someone. But there was never malice in her laughter. She was the most generous woman I have ever known. She would tutor this student and that in Latin (for no reward, I'm sure). Once I was unwell, and she installed me in the guest bedroom of her flat, so that I could recover with delicious meals and peace and laughter and good books.

And he added 'Yet all the time we were at Newbattle she herself was far from well, with arthritis; she toiled along laboriously on a stick.'[12]

Another Newbattle student in 1952 was Tom Scott, who would later become one of Scotland's important new poets, going on to achieve a first class degree and a doctorate on the work of the medieval Scottish poet William Dunbar. In fact, Scott had known the Muirs when he was a young man in St Andrews, having left school at 15 to work as a labourer in his grandfather's building firm. His trades union father had joined the discussion club set up by the Oesers and Muirs in St Andrews, and Tom himself formed a literature club that met in the Muirs' house where Edwin predicted that Tom was the member most likely to do something important. War service and a period in London, where he met and interacted with G. S. Fraser and W. S. Graham and other poets then associated with the New Apocalypse movement, had shown Scott a way forward in literature, especially poetry, and eventually led him to Newbattle. His view of Willa at Newbattle was that she seemed to have controlled the more flamboyant aspects of her character and taken on a mothering role. That impression would certainly fit with George Mackay

---

[12] Mackay Brown, 'Edwin Muir at Newbattle', p. 207, p. 206.

Brown's memories, but others who had not previously known her could find it difficult to come to terms with her personality. One of these was James D. Young, who studied during the 1952–53 session before gaining a scholarship to Ruskin College and then becoming a lecturer in History at Stirling University. Young was a strong socialist, and his memoir of Edwin, published in *Chapman* magazine's 1987 centenary issue on Muir, is titled 'A Socialist's-Eye View of Edwin Muir'. As with Mackay Brown's experience at Waverley Station the previous year, when Young arrived at the main gate of Newbattle for his interview, he found Edwin himself waiting for him. Edwin took him for a long walk along the banks of the Esk, asking questions and listening to the answers of what Young in retrospect admitted was 'a very angry young man'. Young did not realize Edwin's own socialist background at that point, nor did he know that in 1915 he, too, had been described by one of his associates in the Glasgow Branch of the National Guild League as 'an angry young man'.[13] He was surprised, therefore, to find how democratically socialist Edwin was in his thought and in his interaction with his staff and students. On the other hand, Young found Willa more difficult. While he accepted that she was 'witty, entertaining and charismatic', he thought her to be 'often domineering, mischievous and somewhat dictatorial'. He believed that she was probably responsible for the 'erroneous general impression that Edwin had ceased to be a socialist' because of her constant criticism of Hugh MacDiarmid, James Barke, and Lewis Grassic Gibbon—all three strongly socialist, even communist, in their writings. He did not know that Willa had once been friendly with Grassic Gibbon and dedicated *Mrs Grundy in Scotland* to him. Barke and MacDiarmid presented a different case. Young records that Willa was responsible for blocking the student council's wish to invite James Barke to Newbattle to talk about his novels and politics, on the basis that neither she nor Edwin approved of his Marxism nor his use of language in his novels about the life of Burns. And she vetoed the suggestion that Hugh MacDiarmid should speak to the students, insisting 'MacDiarmid is not coming here. If he did, he'd drink all our wine, be sick all over the carpets, then go away and write nasty verses about the Muirs.' Bernard Bergonzi, who had been sceptical about the whole Newbattle venture, also had difficulties with Willa, describing her as 'the most malicious woman' he had ever met, while Donald Gordon, who had replaced the controversial Philosophy lecturer, admitted that he was never sure whether Willa liked him or not, and it was only after her death, when he found some letters she had written to him, that he realized she had indeed included him in her obvious fondness for his wife and children.[14] Willa's personality therefore continued to be a complicated one, especially for those who did not know her well. Her capacity for holding the stage in public, and her enjoyment and employment

---

[13] James D. Young, *Chapman* 49, 1987, p. 21, p. 23; also 'Hugh MacDiarmid, the Muirs and Grassic Gibbon' in *Cencrastus* 65, 2,000, p. 19.

[14] Bernard Bergonzi, quoted by Maggie Fergusson in *George Mackay Brown*, p.113; also Donald Gordon in an interview with Kirsty Allen, St Andrews doctoral thesis on Willa Muir, p. 452.

of scurrilous gossip and extravagant humour, demonstrated one side of her, but this could conceal a more fragile private identity. She was suffering with arthritis at this time, as George Mackay Brown observed, but she seemed to enjoy her 'mothering' role in the early years of Newbattle, presiding over the dining table, and tutoring students in Latin and at one point German to help with their university entrance.

The more vulnerable part of Willa's personality is shown in her journal writings. As in Prague, Willa kept a journal for a large part of their stay at Newbattle, and it begins in early January 1951 with a complaint about 'how much more lucidly I feel and reflect upon things before rising out of the horizontal. Getting up muddies the waters in some way'—a comment many readers might endorse, even without having to suffer arthritis. Edwin was more cheerful, and on one particular morning Willa recalls him 'gaily', reading the Scottish P.E.N. Club newsletter humming 'The Pen Club, the Pen Club, what though the rooms are wee?' as he mused 'Not worth going to, but equally not worth withdrawing from' before deciding to pay his subscription. Her journal recalls one of Edwin's visits to the Women's Guild in a church at Newtongrange, a mining village in Midlothian not far from Newbattle. In the 1890s this was the largest mining village in Scotland, but with coal in decline, it seemed a grim place indeed, and 'the ugliness, the bleakness of the hall struck [Edwin] painfully. The only concession to comfort was that the benches had backs.' Willa continues 'Long rows of dreary women drearily knitting: he found it difficult to raise a smile from them at all.' The only note of decoration in the hall was to be found in 'the markers stuck in the outsize Bible which lay on the table before the President: markers like garish Christmas cards'; while 'two fires in the top corners of the hall were supposed to give out heat, but didn't.' Then, 'after a hymn, woodenly thumped on a bad piano, and a Bible reading, Edwin gave a talk on Italy.' After his talk, 'there were soloes. *My ain folk*, dripping with sentimentality.' Whereas Mackay Brown had seen 'hopeless, harsh faces' in the industrialized Dalkeith, in her description of Newtongrange Willa muses how 'sentimentality seems inevitably to accompany a grim life of violence and oppression', something she believes to be 'true of Scottish coal towns, evidently.'[15] This was a far cry from the grand environs of Newbattle Abbey or their recent sojourn in Rome.

Willa's next journal entry on 13 January is very different in tone, telling how she was 'penetrated by thoughts of death, because of Lizzie's sudden death'. Lizzie was Edwin's older sister, and both Edwin and Willa had kept up a relationship and correspondence over the years with Lizzie, her husband George Thorburn, and daughters Ethel and Irene. George had died before the outbreak of the Second World War, and now Lizzie had followed him. Willa writes 'I feel she is blown out, extinguished, and that so will I be and Edwin, when we come to die.' She deliberately misquotes Yeats, turning 'love's bitter mystery' to 'life's bitter mystery', and

---

[15] Willa Muir, Newbattle Journal, 12 January 1951, UStA, MS 38466 5/5.

continues 'Death's bitter mystery is life. Why are we alive at all?' She thinks of the Church's belief in resurrection and how there are people she herself would not wish to meet again in the afterlife, including her brother Willie, with his mental health problems, her 'ex-fiancé Cecil', and surprisingly and seemingly unkindly, she adds 'Lizzie, too. She was becoming a trial to everyone, with her persecution mania. She is better gone.' Without knowing the circumstances of Lizzie's health in her last years, this appears a harsh judgement, but her death had clearly upset Willa's equilibrium in regard to her own—and Edwin's—mortality. She asks herself 'Does some[thing] of us live on in our ambience? If so, it is something very tenuous', then she continues—

> Edwin's poems will live. But of himself only a legend. Of me, only a very distorted legend. Anyone who dies is present only in memory, and only while the memories are alive. Is it a complete disappearance of all that made a personality? And we don't even know the extent and effects of our own personalities, while we have them. I doubt if we should recognise ourselves in other people's memories of us.[16]

There is just over a year between this despondent entry and the continuation of Willa's diary in February 1952, a delay which she explains was caused 'because I began my book again and have written nothing else. It is finished, but not revised.' The book in question was 'The Usurpers', her fictionalized account of life with the British Council in Prague before, during, and after the communist Putsch of February 1948. It may be that John Hall's visit about Edwin's *Collected Poems* the previous year had spurred her to take up her Prague novel again. She is clearly excited at completing the first draft, writing 'I think, whiles, it's very good; surprised that I could have thought it out at all; then, whiles, that it's disjointed, ill put together, lacking proportion and style.' Edwin let it 'lie for days before reading it'—

> I know he was tired and busy, but I had wanted him to show enthusiasm & interest; he never said a word about it [she underlines each word heavily], not even regretting that he couldn't read it, because his eyes hurt, or he had other work, or what not.

She continues—

> Had he regretted not reading it, had he said: 'I'm sorry I can't get at it yet', I should have been appeased, for I think I am reasonable. It was his apparent utter indifference that got me down; I could see how little value he attached to the expectations he might have of it, how little real importance he felt it would have. Perhaps

[16] Ibid., 13 January 1951.

he is right; this book I have been dreaming myself into, with such enthusiasm & delight, is really a very second-rate production: it won't matter to anyone. It made me suicidal for some hours, until I got the better of it.[17]

This is a distressing entry, for it shows how alone and despondent Willa was feeling within herself despite her usual ebullience. Since their translation work came to an end, she must have had a large hole in her working life, with no ideas for creative writing projects of her own, while Edwin seemed to be forging ahead with new poetry collections and increased interest in his literary reputation. In contrast, she was struggling with ill health and increasing immobility, with nothing to remind readers of her previous identity as a creative prose writer and translator. So when she turned to the draft of 'Usurpers', Willa was once more choosing 'to depend on myself', making necessary revisions by 'cutting out my excess of emotional statement: all the "alls" and the "veries" and some of the descriptive adverbs; more important, I excised bits here and there that weren't strictly necessary. The result, I think, is shapely.' When Edwin did at last get around to reading it, 'he had no suggestions to offer; I had done what he thought needed doing.'[18] Willa's troubles with 'The Usurpers' were not ended, however. She took the manuscript with her when she and Edwin went on a short Easter holiday visit to Flora Grierson and Joan Shelmerdine in Woodstock, hoping that Flora would read it. But Flora was suffering from a bad cold and said she couldn't be expected to read 'handwritten stuff', so Willa again felt aware of 'how little importance other people expect to find in anything I write.' The book was rejected by the three publishers to whom she sent it—Macmillan, Hamish Hamilton, and Chatto & Windus—and in October 1952 she finally withdrew it from attempted publication. She wrote in her diary (most probably ironically given their history) 'I shall try to write a book abt. my mother.'[19]

While Willa's typescript may well have needed further work, she should have realized that her subject matter was still too close to the events in post-war Prague, leading perhaps to fears of libel on the publisher's part, not to mention fears for the safety of some of the people caught up in that dangerous time. Indeed, Lumir Soukup would ask Edwin to cut some of the information he had included in the first drafts of his own memories of Prague in the expanded autobiography. Perhaps Edwin should have pointed these dangers out to Willa in his turn. As with the unpublished 'Mrs Muttoe and the Top Storey', Willa seems to have needed a life-writing source to work with in constructing her fictional narratives, and this has potential drawbacks.

[17] Ibid., 22 February 1952.
[18] Ibid.
[19] Ibid., 15 April 1952, 14 October 1952.

Willa's disappointment about 'Usurpers' produced another year-long gap in her journal which does not restart until 18 August 1953, under the disturbing heading 'What a mess I am.' This time the immediate problem lay with her son Gavin, who was living with them after graduating from St Andrews, but had not yet been able to find satisfactory employment. Although he was talented in music and graduated in mathematics, he seems to have been remembered by classmates at St Andrews as a rather lonely young man. By the time the family was at Newbattle, he appeared to be suffering from deafness, a condition that would end any hopes he might have had for a career as a pianist. His parents had supported him in this, with Willa in particular encouraging him to play in public and praising his performances, even if she was not so happy when he changed his repertoire from classical to jazz. Some observers, and eventually Willa herself, thought that Gavin's deafness could be a psychosomatic condition, as it varied in its presence or severity. Despite this, and early rejections, he was still encouraged by his parents to keep trying for an L.R.A.M. Performers Diploma from the Royal Academy of Music in London, which could be taken as an external music student.

Gavin's psychological situation seemed to have worsened in the summer of 1953. Newbattle students at this time were somewhat wary of him and spoke of his wandering around the upper levels of the abbey, or playing loudly on the grand piano in the drawing room. He appeared at times to be 'at war' with his parents, especially with his mother, and at others almost hysterically dependent upon them. Willa's August diary tells of him coming to her room in the middle of the night, sobbing on her shoulder, apologizing for being unable to show his love for her, while she comforted him by 'cuddling, soothing, babying' him until he slept. A day later he turned up at the college grounds, where she and Edwin were sitting on a seat by the river, and squeezed between them aggressively, telling Willa not to be 'so *possessive*'. Her response was a psychological lecture in which she emphasized that 'love is clean away from the dominant/submissive world.'[20] In September he made another attempt at his L.R.A.M. Diploma in London. Willa had to remedy his failure to book accommodation for his stay by getting in touch with a former Prague friend, Mary Bosdĕt, now resident in the city. Unfortunately, this attempt also ended in failure, but what communicates uncomfortably to the reader of Willa's diary is the fact that she herself opened the results letter from London, instead of leaving it for Gavin to open. She wrote in her diary, 'I couldn't resist opening the envelope, addressed in his own handwriting, because I knew it must be the result of his exam, and I was instantaneously depressed.' She added 'He took it "well"; that is, he did not make any demonstration and said it must have been a "close shave". Perhaps it would have been better had he burst into tears and let something out.' She continued, 'Unless Edwin and I are completely out in our estimates of his ability,

---

[20] Ibid., 19 August 1953.

he is well above the standard needed, and only his nervous instability must have frustrated him.' Others who heard Gavin play, however, commented on a lack of subtlety, with an over-loud dynamic and a limited repertoire. Gavin did take piano lessons, but there is nothing in the memoirs of either parent to suggest that these lessons were at a high professional level. Willa's diary entries on Gavin end at this point, with his going to an appointment at a psychiatric clinic in Edinburgh in the hope that some way might be found 'to harmonise his conflicts'.[21]

Willa continued to have her own conflicts in this 1953 section of her journal, continuing her self-examination in August under the heading 'Why I am to be described as a mess'. This time she is concerned with Edwin's expansion of the autobiography, which involved him going back in time to their post-Prague residence in Europe, and their subsequent years in England and Scotland. As they were walking in the Newbattle garden, Edwin confessed that he was having difficulty writing about their first visit to Italy in 1923. Willa replied that this was probably because he was going to leave out so much of it, especially what she called the 'Gerda episode'. Not surprisingly, Edwin replied, 'Yes, indeed he would', a response that made Willa feel all over again 'the dull misery behind these brilliant blue days in the white powdery dust'. She reminded Edwin how his behaviour at that time 'had poisoned my pious pilgrimage to Catullus's Sirmione', and asked 'What *did* she do to you?' continuing, 'She must have felt your emotional state was vulnerable, and launched a shaft of power into it', to which Edwin somewhat limply replied 'Something like that'. Clearly Willa never knew the whole story behind Edwin's relationship with Gerda, especially his letter to say he would come to her in Hellerau if she wished him to do so. Others in the know, such as John Holms and Hugh Kingsmill, seem to have kept it to themselves. Yet it affected Willa so strongly that she was still able to recall every detail of that day on Lake Garda. Revisiting the experience in her Newbattle diary is another marker of how insecure she could be, under a seemingly confident public persona. The diary reopens her dislike of John Holms and how he seemed to her to drive a wedge between herself and Edwin. Every little 'belittlement' she had felt during their European travels rose again to the surface of her mind, along with Edwin's indifference to her 'Usurpers' novel. She wrote 'I really did let them all out. Edwin said, once, when we came back to the house: "I don't think we should say any more about it"; but I felt that these things *should* be talked out, to prevent their festering inside.' The encounter ended with Edwin, in a characteristically non-combative way, saying, 'I'm afraid, you know, that I haven't got much sense.' His wife's diary adds, 'Which is true of both of us.'[22]

Willa's sense of grievance could not be so easily controlled, however, and the diary revisits their work as translators.

---

[21] Ibid., 30 September 1953 (Gavin's LRAM exam failure).
[22] Ibid., 20 August 1953 (section 'Why I am to be described as a mess').

And then I told him that even the translations I had done were no longer my own territory, for everyone assumes that Edwin did them. He is referred to as 'THE' translator. By this time he may even believe that he was. He has let my reputation sink, by default; so now I fear that if the Feuchtwanger publishers are told that *I* am prepared to do his beastly novel, they will refuse unless Edwin engages to do it, or to put his name to it.

She continues—

And the fact remains: I am a better translator than he is. The whole current of patriarchal society is set against this fact, however, and sweeps it into oblivion, simply because I did not insist on shouting aloud: 'Most of this translation, especially Kafka, has been done by ME, Edwin only helped.' And every time Edwin was referred to as THE translator, I was too proud to say anything; and Edwin himself felt it would be undignified to speak up, I suppose. So that now, especially since my break-down in the middle of the war, I am left without a shred of literary reputation. And I am ashamed of the fact that I feel it as a grievance. It shouldn't bother me. Reputation is a passing value, after all. Yet it is now that I feel it, now when I am trying to build up my life again and overcome my disabilities: my dicky back-bone, for instance. Because I seem to have nothing to build on, except that I am Edwin's wife and he still loves me. That is much. It is almost all, in a sense, that I could need. It is more than I deserve. And I know, too, how destructive ambition is, and how it deforms what one might create. And yet, and yet, I want to be acknowledged. That is why I say: 'I am a mess'.[23]

After such *angst*, the atmosphere in the diary is lightened a little by Willa recounting one of her frequent, vivid, and inventive dreams, this time about Edwin and herself killing two soldiers in scarlet coats and being troubled about how to dispose of the bodies. They had chopped off their legs 'neatly' and put the bodies under their sofa so that anyone passing their windows and looking in would not see them. But there were children outside who 'came sliding down a kind of mill-lade, or waterfall, face down, under the water, and landed in our garden. How could we prevent their watching us, if we tried to dig the bodies in, somewhere in the garden?' The problem was still unresolved when she woke up to tell Edwin about the dream—'What on earth could make me dream such a dream? Why should we be murdering soldiers in scarlet coats?' she asked him. 'Well', came Edwin's reply, 'they were obviously a couple of Reds!'[24]

Late summer brought the annual Edinburgh Festival of music and drama, now well established after its inauguration in the immediate post-war years, along with

---
[23] Ibid.
[24] Ibid., 21 August 1953.

the chance to catch up with old friends and make new acquaintances. A. S. Neill was a visitor in 1953 'still fascinated by Lesbians, masturbation & sexual perversities, as he always was', according to Willa's diary. At the festival they saw T. S. Eliot 'for a moment', looking, according to Willa, 'very *old*'. He said 'I hope you'll like my play better than I do', but an acquaintance, Nigel McIsaac, told them he thought it was 'Oscar Wilde with water'.[25] On another evening they met Henry Sherek, Eliot's theatrical producer, described by Willa as 'a large, surging, rumbustious man, very likeable', and she saw the violinist Isaac Stern at the same event. Then, in her diary for 2 September, she writes that at a BBC cocktail party she met the Scottish historical writer Marion Lochhead, who told her that Helen Cruickshank, former secretary of Scottish P.E.N. and a fine poet herself, had been ill with rheumatism and was now in a nursing home for former civil servants. In earlier days with Scottish P.E.N. Willa had been on good terms with women writers such as Cruickshank and Lochhead, but she is dismissive in her diary about this more recent encounter, writing 'These dim, well-meaning, intense & serious women!' The outburst would appear to have been occasioned by Marion Lochhead telling her that 'reading Edwin's poems had been a spiritual experience—not only an intellectual pleasure', and Willa continues, 'I had to stave her off from inviting us to her house for an afternoon.' Florence McNeill, who had once helped Willa in her search for a gynaecologist, receives equally short shrift in the diary—'And now today, Sep.3, Floss on the telephone. Wants to bring a lady from Cairo, "a wealthy lady", to see us tomorrow. I said, unwillingly; all right, come to tea. What Edwin will say, I dread!' She continues 'Floss McNeill is another of these dim and faintly pleeping figures: she wraps herself round one like a large jelly-fish. We can't kick her quite off; she clings and recurs. And Floss, & Marion Lochhead, and Helen Cruickshank, are all "literary" figures in Edinburgh!' It may well be that it was Willa's anxious sense of her own lack of achievement, and of her own ageing and arthritic appearance, that brought her to speak so unkindly of her acquaintances, similarly ageing, who had contributed so much to Scotland's early twentieth-century literary revival. Ironically, Floss's wealthy lady from Cairo, suitably named 'Mrs Flower', proved to be 'a very nice, gay, intelligent woman' who later invited Willa to accompany her to an Usher Hall concert by the Vienna Philharmonic, a Brahms evening where Willa enjoyed the orchestral part, but not the choral *Requiem* that followed. Willa willingly gave the non-pleeping Mrs Flower 'a snack supper afterwards'.[26]

Edwin had taken the car to that BBC cocktail party, and Willa's diary tells how apprehensive she felt when he was driving in town, where the press of traffic and the difficulty in parking could bring on what she called 'his chest pain'. She worried,

---

[25] Ibid., Eliot's *The Confidential* Clerk, his penultimate play, was premiered at the Edinburgh Festival in 1953 and this, presumably, is the play referred to by Willa.

[26] Willa Muir, Newbattle Journal 1952ff, UStA, MS 38466 5/5, relating to Edinburgh Festival 1953.

too, that her own tension was making Edwin even more nervous in traffic. Soon they had to drive to Edinburgh again, to visit a friend who had loaned Edwin a morning suit to wear at his recent investiture in London. Central Edinburgh was busy, and at the corner of Hanover Street Edwin's car was held up by traffic and 'hemmed in by a flock of pedestrians crossing his bows'. Thinking the way was clear, Edwin started to move, but knocked down one woman who fell against an elderly woman, who was knocked down in her turn. Shaken rather than hurt, they were taken into a nearby shop to recover. Equally shaken, Edwin hurried after them only to experience the return of his chest pains. The incident passed over and Willa thought they might hire a chauffeur in future, but neither seemed to realize that this pain could be related to heart trouble, and that it was time to consult a doctor.[27]

Edwin was under increasing pressure at Newbattle. He had been working hard at his own writing, with his extended autobiography scheduled for 1954 and a considerable number of new poems to be written. He enjoyed teaching at the college and the staff worked well together, but it was becoming increasingly clear that there was a powerful group on the executive committee, led by trade union members, who felt that the college would do better to offer day release and short-term courses that were more relevant to the working life of the students. Edwin had not been informed about these arguments and the running debate within the Scottish Education Department when he was interviewed for the post. The issue had raised its head again during the problems with the Philosophy lecturer, and it was becoming clear that not all educational sources in Scotland were as supportive of the ideas behind Philip Kerr's bequest as Edwin was, or John Macmurray of Edinburgh University, who had initially recommended him. Edwin had delivered a splendidly effective speech about the college's values at a Scottish Educational Conference in Dunblane at Easter 1952, but he was never free from anxieties about the ethos and the financial future of Newbattle. Short term weekly courses for miners were set up in an attempt to bring in more money. The residential students accepted this new cohort and socialized with them in the crypt of an evening, but the vocational courses still did not solve the residential college's money problems.

Edwin's increasing frustration with these arguments at executive committee meetings led him to drive angrily out of a side street in Edinburgh directly into a tram coming downhill. This time the accident was clearly his fault, his licence was endorsed, and his chest pains increased. Then in the spring of 1954, Willa herself became seriously ill and was taken to hospital to be operated on for the removal of non-cancerous bowel tumours. Edwin wrote to his old friend Joseph Chiari in June, apologizing for his late response to Chiari's request for a testimonial in relation to employment problems of his own.

[27] Ibid., concerning Edwin's car accident on 4 September.

Do forgive me. I've been very worried for a long time about Willa's health, and last February she at last agreed to go into a hospital in Edinburgh. There the surgeon operated on her, but found that he had to make two operations instead of one: an older growth behind the one shown by the X-ray. Two days later internal bleeding was still going on, and another operation had to be made to stop it. For some days she hovered between life and death, but then gradually began to recover. Then pleurisy set in, throwing her back again, but at last she began to come to life.

Willa had been back in Newbattle for several weeks by the time Edwin wrote to Chiari, but he tells him that, although improving, she is still weak and unable to make much effort. The operation had been 'the last phase of a long illness, which has cast anxiety over her and me', but now that it had been successfully carried out, he believes that 'she will be in better health than she has been for years.' He adds, 'I feel as if we were beginning to emerge out of a long dark fog of anxiety into light again.'[28]

The 'light' was still some distance off, however. Edwin would write to Kathleen Raine in December that it had taken him 'quite a long time to recover from the thought that Willa might die (she was very near it), and I'm still very tentatively, and slightly fearfully, attempting poetry.'[29] Back in Newbattle, rumours continued about the need for short-term vocational courses, a change increasingly canvassed by the executive committee, but not yet agreed by the governors. For Edwin, the final blow came when he discovered that a member of the committee, whom he had believed to be among his early and continuing supporters, was in fact one of the leaders in the attempt to replace him with a younger warden more sympathetic to change. He told Kathleen Raine in his December letter that things were 'very difficult' at Newbattle—'A Party in the Committee (this is private) have been trying to get rid of me for some time, and to turn this into a short-term college: courses for week-ends, or weeks at most.' He said that while he liked the work with the students, the perpetual infighting had spoilt things: 'I've got tired of fighting back (successfully so far); I hate fighting. That is why I've been thinking for some time of throwing the whole thing up: the worry and dissension gives me pains in the chest at the least occasion, and all sorts of other silly complications.'[30]

On the brighter side, Edwin was pleased with the positive reviews of his expanded autobiography, including one by Kathleen Raine in the *New Statesman* of 17 November. His confidence had been further boosted by the Heinemann Award from the Royal Society for Literature for the *Collected Poems*, and the award of a CBE in the Coronation Honours List for 1953. But his success as a poet carried little weight with those who wanted Newbattle to become a vocational resource for

---

[28] Edwin Muir, letter to Joseph Chiari, 7 June 1954, *Selected Letters*, p. 168.
[29] Edwin Muir, letter to Kathleen Raine, 6 December 1954, *Selected Letters*, p. 171.
[30] Ibid.

working men—it was always 'men' in such debates. By the end of December both Edwin and the still recovering Willa felt so exhausted that they deserted the abbey and spent Christmas in a small hotel in Edinburgh. In January, Willa confessed to Edwin's niece Ethel that they used the hotel as a 'nursing home: i.e. we just ate and slept and ate, sleeping every afternoon, most evenings, and all the nights'.[31] Gavin joined them, but went out on his own over the Christmas period, while his parents recuperated in their room. This period of rest allowed them to review their situation. Willa told Ethel that what she called 'Edwin's nervous pain' had subsided, 'partly because he has quietly made up his mind to leave Newbattle this summer'. She tells her that he can no longer 'stand the strain of coping with Lord Greenhill and W. D. Ritchie', his main opponents, and will give the college three months' notice in June. She goes on to explain that in the current year they have had only twenty students in residence although over seventy had applied. The problem was that the local authorities and the unions refused to give grants to residential applicants, and without such support, no one could afford a year at Newbattle. As for themselves, they have no idea where they might go or what they might do, but it would have to be somewhere, most probably in or near London, where Edwin could be in touch with literary people and opportunities for making a living by writing.[32] Although Willa did not know it, their problems were about to be solved by a most unexpected opportunity, when Edwin was invited to become the next Charles Eliot Norton Professor of Poetry at Harvard University for the session 1955–56.

The content and tone of Edwin's final letters from Newbattle reflects this happy change in their fortunes. Writing to T. S. Eliot in July, he agrees with Eliot's suggestion to stay with *One Foot in Eden* for his next collection (Edwin had suggested 'The Succession' as an alternative) and he is happy to agree to Eliot's request that he should write something about Djuna Barnes' new play, 'The Antiphon'. Like Eliot himself, Edwin had been an admirer of Barnes' novel *Nightwood* and met her when he was living in London many years previously. Now he looks forward to her new play and hopes to see her in America. He tells Eliot that he feels sure his time at Harvard will be 'very interesting and enjoyable and surrounded with kindness', and hopes to be able to write some poetry there, for 'here, I have very little time for it.'[33] A final letter to Kathleen Raine is equally cheerful. She had suggested he might be awarded a fellowship by the Bollingen Foundation and offered to support an application on his behalf. He tells her that the idea appeals to him and looks forward to meeting up in London. He takes time to send his Harvard address to the poet Tom Scott, who seemed to be having some difficulties finding his way forward in his poetry, and invites further correspondence. In mid-August,

---

[31] Willa Muir, letter to Ethel Ross, 17 January 1955, NLS, Acc. 12592.
[32] Ibid.
[33] Edwin Muir, letter to T. S. Eliot, 8 July 1955, *Selected Letters*, p. 172.

Stanley Cursiter organizes a farewell party for Edwin and Willa at the Art Club in Edinburgh, before they travel south to spend a few days in London to meet friends and attend another party, organized by Kathleen Raine to mark their departure for the new world. On 26 August they duly left Britain by ship for their first visit to the United States.

PART V
A NEW WORLD

18
American Adventure 1955–1956

> We felt dazed for a moment to find ourselves in America instead of Vienna, and that was when we realized that we had had to come to America to find out how European we were.
>
> Willa Muir, Belonging (1968)

After the excitement of their farewell parties, the Muirs were exhausted as they boarded the Cunarder at Southampton en route for New York. Willa wrote that they were 'tired all through'—'We lay inert on day-beds spread out on a deck, glad of the rest and the mid-morning cup of broth, thankful, too, that we had opted for a sea-voyage instead of flying across the Atlantic.' They were older now and no longer felt the thrill of their first crossing to Europe in the 1920s. They had met many Americans during their travels, so the United States may not have seemed so very foreign to them. The first shock came when the taxi decanted them at New York's Grand Central Hotel, where they would stay before continuing their journey to Boston by train. The Grand Central's reception hall was more like a large Continental railway station than a hotel. There were many shops, including a hairdresser and beautician, a jeweller, a bookstall, and even a bank and a post office. They were unable to identify the reception desk at first, and when they found it, they were 'nearly knocked down by a hurrying phalanx of women in tricorne hats, sashes and badges announcing them to be Drake's Daughters'. Instead of meeting people just like themselves, it appeared to Willa that these 'far-out cousins' could be 'startling'. The feeling persisted next morning when their breakfast trays came with something called a 'Hottle'. These objects contained hot, excellent coffee, and Willa described them as 'rather like elaborate thermos flasks' with their 'absurd names' round their necks. 'Hottles! Drake's Daughters! We might as well be on the moon', they told each other.[1] The 'moon-feeling' continued next day during the train journey to Boston. The coaches were very different from the individual compartments found in British trains in the 1950s, although similar to what is customary today, with two long rows of swivel chairs running down the length of the coach with a gangway in the middle. There was no restaurant car, and since it was Labour Day in America, there was no 'labour' to serve meals in the coaches. The problem was solved when food-sellers came on board at a stop halfway to Boston with hot dogs and other picnic foods, so in the end they did not starve as they had

[1] *Belonging*, pp. 284–5.

feared. Then they found that they had to go to what was called the 'club car' at the front of the train in order to smoke. This turned out to be a good move, however, since the club car had an observation window as well as small tables at which drinks, although not food, could be served. They stayed there for the remainder of the journey, duly observing the countryside.

> A succession of inlets from the sea ran past us, with pleasant wooden houses among stretches of young scrub, much of it birch. There were no woods as the English understand woods, with well-grown trees and a deep look of permanence, only these provisional stretches of spindly young trees and random wooden houses, which also seemed provisional. Every now and then one came to a town apparently full of parti-coloured beetles.

Although they were now in 'New England', what they were finding was 'not at all like England'.[2]

Things changed when they reached their hotel in Cambridge, the home of Harvard University and Edwin's Norton Professorship of Poetry. The Hotel Continental looked just like the kind of family hotel they were familiar with, and the 'housekeeping suite' they had booked, without being certain as to what it might consist of, was exactly what they needed—a sitting room and bedroom which Willa thought might have belonged to any simple English hotel, together with a small kitchenette and a shower. She was particularly happy with the shower, which was much easier to use with her arthritis than a bath would have been. They had unwittingly booked themselves into a pleasant, private little flat with the wider facilities of a hotel to draw on if they wished to do so. This Cambridge already appeared to be promising a happier stay than its English counterpart had offered, when they fled there in distress after their problems in post-war Prague. The town was attractive, with large old trees and common land surviving from the horse-and-carriage age. The university was composed of what Willa called 'Georgian-style houses in warm red brick with white trimmings and a few stately pillared structures in its Yard', and indeed Harvard Yard, with its ancient trees, was a pleasant place for a stroll. People associated with the university tended to live in close proximity to each other and it was easy to walk to invitations to tea or evening events. Similarly, it was easy for members of the university staff or visiting poets and lecturers to drop by their Continental Hotel flatlet. Willa describes one occasion—and there were probably more than one—when the sitting room had to be cleared up in a hurry when an unexpected visitor was announced. The poet Robert Frost was one such visitor, for Amherst College kept a room ready for him during the winter months and so he was often to be found in Cambridge of an afternoon. Willa remembered

[2] Ibid., p. 285.

that he told them his mother had been an Orkney woman and that he would tease Edwin whenever they met by repeating 'We Orkney-men'.³

Nearby Boston surprised them in the way it was connected to Cambridge by 'dull lines of factories and business buildings', but they liked the town and the fact that its streets were not organized in a right-angled grid like New York, but were more humanly irregular in their pattern. It seemed to offer links with past history too. They were invited to tea by the very elderly daughter of Charles Eliot Norton, the founder of the Poetry Professorship at Harvard, and the tea she gave them 'might have come out of an Oscar Wilde play, even to the wafer-thin cucumber sandwiches'. The most fashionable shop for men in the town, called 'Brooks Brothers', had a large portrait of the English King Edward VII hanging on its wall, and Willa tells how they went there 'for fun', and Edwin bet her that if he asked the assistant for 'galluses' the assistant would not know what he meant. Edwin had forgotten, however, that 'galluses' was an Irish word that had been imported to Glasgow along with the many historical waves of Irish immigration, and that there had been Irish immigration to Boston also. So the counter assistant 'did not blench' at Edwin's request, and 'produced braces at once'.⁴ A less successful shop experience occurred when they were still acclimatizing themselves. Edwin went to a watchmakers in Cambridge one morning in order to collect Willa's watch, which had been left for mending, and paid by cheque. They spent that afternoon and evening with two new young friends, Richard and Charles Wilbur, who took them out in their car into the New England countryside and then to tea with Mrs Wilbur's mother in her old house in Wellesley, described by Willa as 'full of lovingly tended old furniture and brasswork'. They came home at night tired but pleased with their day. The next morning, however, Edwin awoke in a panic convinced that in his unfamiliarity with American currency he had written a cheque for six hundred and fifty dollars as opposed to the six dollars fifty cents that the shop owner's request for 'six fifty dollars' had intended. Willa describes Edwin's repeated cry of 'I have done an awful thing' as they took a taxi to the shop, asked the man if Edwin had indeed written his cheque for six hundred and fifty dollars, and waited in agitation until he looked through a large envelope containing the previous day's cheques which he had not yet examined. And there he found, as Edwin had feared, the watch-mending cheque for six hundred and fifty dollars, both in writing and in figures. The shop owner laughed, saying, 'I sure would like to do business with you.' Edwin tore up the cheque, but remained upset at how 'abysmally stupid' he could be. This story is told in Willa's unpublished journal of their early months in Cambridge but does not appear in *Belonging*. Her journal entry for the next day, Friday 30 September, calls it a day of celebration because they had 'saved such a magnificent sum of money'.⁵

---

³ Ibid., p. 290.
⁴ Ibid.
⁵ Willa Muir, Harvard Journal, UStA, MS 38466 5/6.

Edwin's first official poetry lecture was not scheduled until Wednesday 9th November, so they had plenty time to become familiar with their new surroundings and with the many Harvard staff, visiting poets and lecturers, and Cambridge residents who visited them, invited them to dinner and tea parties, and generally helped them to feel at home. Willa especially enjoyed this kind of celebrity socializing, which had been to a large extent absent in her life since they returned from Rome in 1950. Edwin, on the other hand, sometimes protested that he did not want to meet any more people. Willa's journal gives a lively account of their new acquaintances and experiences, including being driven into the surrounding countryside in the cars of new friends such as the Wilburs, who took them to Concord, Lake Walden, Lincoln, and Wellesley on 29 September. Willa describes how 'the wooden "frame" houses, some of which, especially in Concord, are both charming & elegant, nestle among the woods, here and there along the roads, not cut off by fences or hedges, with trees around them, and cylindrical metal post-boxes stuck up beside the road with the owner's name painted on each'. She is not so attracted to the little towns along the road.

> Every now & then the houses clot into a town. The residential streets are lined with trees; the 'shopping centre' has no character, for it is made up of single-storey buildings on a standardised pattern (Esso Servicentre; Mobilgas; Jenney's). Since no one lives above these shops, they don't look as if they were an integral part of the township; they look like rows of booths knocked up for a fair, quite provisional, to my eye, at least.

These scattered townships are then 'woven together by magnificent main roads, with "clover leaf" junctions and "fly-overs", only the side roads are really rustic'. And although they found that 'outside Lincoln there were low stone dykes along the dirt road, and one might have been in Britain somewhere', it was clear that this new world was 'a motor-car civilisation'. She would love to live in one of the frame houses among the woods but 'alas! A car would be a necessity'. On the other hand, the beauty of a New England autumn was something that would live long in her memory.

> The maples in especial take on amazing pink colours before they turn scarlet. The trees, apart from scrub, are mostly maple and elm; there *are* oaks, more elegant than ours, their leaves of finer texture & more finely cut, their structure not so gnarled, and there are some poplars, too. The biggest difference lies in the scrublands, overgrown with sumach & wild vine and golden-rod. Golden-rod is as common, and blazes as golden, as gorse in parts of Scotland.

Unlike the scattered townships, this natural landscape was not an alien one, 'we feel very much at home in it, unsurprised by it, delighted.'[6]

---

[6] Ibid.

Their social life was busy. Archibald MacLeish, the poet and professor at Harvard who had invited Edwin to come to America, made sure, with his wife Ada, that they were well looked after. Edwin described them to Kathleen Raine as 'a really warm and human pair: I feel a great affection for them.'[7] The first social occasion after they arrived in Harvard was a memorable invitation to tea with the MacLeishes. At first Edwin and Willa were the only guests. Once the teacups had been cleared away, however, drink trays and savouries appeared, and other guests began to drift in. They soon found themselves launched into a cocktail party in which the liquid in their iced tumblers was much stronger than their usual martinis. This was their first introduction to Harvard hospitality and Bourbon on the Rocks, which Willa describes as having lit them up 'until our tongues wagged very gaily and we laughed a lot. Edwin was already calling Archie "Archie" as everyone else did; it took him only a little while longer to get round to calling Ada by her first name.'[8] Not usually in need of strong drink to set her tongue wagging, Willa's performance must have been especially lively. She wrote later that 'American dons clearly enjoyed the company of women and expected them to join freely in the talk, so that there was genuine social intercourse at this blissful party.'[9] Neither she nor Edwin had expected such social and academic freedom, and Willa was delighted to discover that one of the basic assumptions underlying American life was that it was 'one's duty to be a Good Mixer, unfettered by protocol, free to take off in any direction.'[10]

In addition to Robert Frost, Edwin's 'fellow-Orkneyman', they met the critic I. A. Richards, one of the founders of the New Criticism movement in literary theory. Edwin would later write in *The Estate of Poetry*, the published form of his Harvard lectures, that the methodology of New Criticism 'gives me a faint touch of claustrophobia, the feeling that I am being confined in a narrow place with the poem and the critic, and that I shall not get away until all three of us are exhausted.'[11] Perhaps unsurprisingly, they did not get to know Richards quite so well as some of the other poets and academics they met, such as Harry Levin, Professor of Comparative Literature at Harvard whom Edwin described as a 'gentle, sensitive creature with a razor-sharp intelligence' and for whom, as for Archibald MacLeish, he felt 'a great affection'. Young Karl Miller, a Midlothian scholar who was visiting Harvard to research Scottish literature, became a regular visitor to their little flat. Willa found him initially 'disgruntled about things and people—the chip on the shoulder—but softened and became human as the evening wore on'. He was a supporter of F. R. Leavis, 'fierce in his defence', and said he had left Edinburgh for Cambridge to take his degree because he couldn't 'stomach' the professors at Edinburgh.

---

[7] *Selected Letters*, p. 185.
[8] Edwin Muir, letter to Kathleen Raine, 10 April 1956, *Selected Letters*, p. 185.
[9] *Belonging*, p. 288.
[10] Ibid., p. 289.
[11] Edwin Muir, *The Estate of Poetry* (London: Hogarth Press, 1962), p. 69.

He had never thought of himself as being 'conditioned' by Scottish attitudes, but since he had moved to Cambridge, he had realized that 'he had Scottish attitudes after all.'[12] He told them he hoped to take up a post in the civil service and to be able also to do some writing, since he did not think any good writing had been done by British academics for years. Miller also brought them news of Pegeen and Sinbad, the children of Peggy Guggenheim. He had met them in Paris, heard much about Peggy and John Holms, but had not met Peggy herself. Miller returned to Britain to become a leading critic, essayist, editor, and biographer and was a founder member of *The London Review of Books*. There must have been much good home-bred gossip in Miller's visits to counterbalance their discoveries in the New World.

There were other attractions in Cambridge besides tea parties and visiting. There was the Widener Library, which Edwin found useful for research, but got lost in more than once. Willa commented 'What a pity Kafka didn't know about this library! How he could have used it to "wander" his hero in!'[13] There was the Lamont Poetry Library, where they were always made welcome. This was a small building, separate from the Harvard complex, with reading desks and quiet alcoves for browsing. It was comprehensively stocked with poetry from all periods and places as well as recordings of poets reading their own work. Jack Sweeney, the librarian, asked Edwin to record some of his poems, which he did, if a little unwillingly. He had broadcast his own prose scripts for radio programmes while living in St Andrews and Edinburgh, but reading his own poetry was something he was still hesitant about. Jack Sweeney also asked Willa to read one or two of Edwin's poems and she readily agreed. But when she began to read 'In Love for Long' from the 1946 collection *The Voyage*, and reached the third verse with its words 'Being, being, being, / Its burden and its bliss', she found herself in tears and could not read on. Written at Robert Louis Stevenson's Swanston, just outside Edinburgh, 'In Love for Long' is not a conventional love poem about love between two people; it is, rather, a love poem to the sense of being alive, to life itself in spite of its difficulties and sorrows. Willa had experienced enough of life's difficulties with poor health over many years, but in Harvard, she recovered much of her old *joie de vivre*, even if her arthritis was still troubling her. The reading of that particular poem must have reminded her of darker times.

A cultural institution in Cambridge was the Poets' Theatre—a very small venue that could accommodate only about eighty people, but which had all the necessary accoutrements of a proper theatre such as stage, wings, and footlights. Performances took place in the evening and the actors were students. *Belonging* records that Willa and Edwin 'came upon T. S. Eliot and Djuna Barnes at a performance of Dick Wilbur's translation of Molière's *Misanthrope*' at the Poets' Theatre one

---

[12] Willa Muir, Harvard Journal, UStA, MS 38466 5/6.
[13] Ibid.

autumn evening, shortly before Edwin was due to give the first of his Norton lectures. She writes that neither she nor Edwin had met Djuna Barnes before, but they were 'drawn to her on sight: a tall, gallant, high-spirited woman with a faint suggestion of rakish adventure and fun about her'. She found that in Djuna's company Eliot 'seemed to have shed some English drilling and become more American'.[14] But Willa's memory would appear to have played her false regarding the dating and details of this encounter. Her Harvard journal certainly mentions a performance of *Le Misanthrope* in late October just after they had returned from a visit to Edmund Wilson's home at Cape Cod, but Eliot and Barnes did not arrive in Harvard until May of the next year. And the reason for their visit was not *Le Misanthrope* but a reading of Barnes' as yet unpublished new play *The Antiphon* which Edwin had agreed to read for Eliot before they left Britain. And, contrary to Willa's memoir, Edwin had in fact already met Djuna Barnes in London some years previously, as he mentioned to Eliot in a letter of July 1955—

> I am very glad that Djuna Barnes has written something again. I admire her book *Nightwood* very much indeed, and would like very much to read her new play. I met her once in London many years ago, and I think I shall try to see her in America when I go there; I liked her very much. I think anything she writes must be remarkable … . So I am looking forward very much to seeing the play once it is in its final form.[15]

The days before Edwin's first series of lectures in the late autumn of 1955 continued to be full of activity. On 28 October they went to spend a weekend at the Cape Cod home of the literary critic and essayist Edmund Wilson and his wife Elena. Willa wrote—

> No words can do justice to this weekend: it was utterly delightful. To begin with, weather soft, warm, clear Indian summer, all Friday & Saturday. Cape Cod wildish woodland, as usual, with houses & little townships tucked into it, all wooden frame houses, of course, but wilder, sandier, more remote than round Cambridge. Soft-needled scrub pines everywhere, sand dunes on the "ocean" as they call it, (incredibly deep blue in colour), bright skies, silvery light like Orkney.

The Wilsons' house was at a road junction and there was an additional house of two rooms and a bathroom for guests on the opposite side of the path, 'with lovely views of trees and hills on all sides'. The house had 'bare wooden floors, kindly old furniture, and such a welcoming, home-like feeling about it all'. They got on well together—'Both Edmund & Elena are remarkable and lovable. We had a great

---

[14] *Belonging*, pp. 294–5.
[15] Edwin Muir, letter to T. S. Eliot, 8 July 1955, *Selected Letters*, p. 172.

spate of intelligent talk, mostly but not entirely literary.' Edmund Wilson, author of the influential *Axel's Castle*, was one of the foremost American critics and had a reputation for being 'feisty' in defence of his literary views. For Willa, 'Edmund when obstinate has a look of Winston; impressionable, prejudiced, understanding, intuitive, and most lovable, besides being a "magician".' Their journey back to Cambridge was less pleasant—'a long trek in car to train, long, slow trek in train, brought us here quite exhausted.' Not too exhausted, however, to miss that Tuesday evening's performance of *Le Misanthrope* at the Poets' Theatre. Willa comments in her journal that it was 'very good'.[16]

Two days later, on Thursday, they went to Boston to a radio recording studio where Edwin read of a number of his poems. Jack Sweeney of the Lamont Poetry Library in Cambridge, whom Willa described as 'a gentle, sensitive, *comforting* man', took them there, and kept an eye on them during the recording. It was hot in the studio and after a time Edwin's eyes and his head began to ache, so Willa read one or two poems to complete the session. Again, as in the Lamont Poetry Library, she reports that she 'made a fool' of herself by nearly sobbing over the last ten lines of 'The Transfiguration'. She had 'hard work of it' to keep herself from breaking down altogether, as tears kept blurring her eyes during her reading of the second poem, 'The Combat'. Willa was a little shaken to discover how 'near the edge' her control of her emotions still appeared to be.[17] She was still not the old Willa who was always ready for a challenge. Edwin lay down in the dark to rest when they got back to their flat, while she cleared up their sitting room and made snacks for yet more visitors. On Friday they heard that the television Channel 2, which hosted cultural and serious news programmes without advertisements, wanted to record Edwin's forthcoming lecture on 9 November. Later that day they went to tea with a family called Guérard. Mrs Guérard was a Southerner unaccustomed to the rituals of tea, but her mother-in-law, who came from a Glasgow family and had married a Frenchman, explained how to produce a spread for her Scottish visitors. Willa was able to cope with the fingers of toast spread with Scotch marmalade and buttered slices of ginger bread, but she was defeated by the mother-in-law's adoption of what she called 'all the social pretensions and conversation of the Edinburgh middle-classes'. This resulted in 'prestige conversations' along the lines of 'Have you been to Old Meldrum? Dunfermline Abbey? Who founded that? do you know …? do you know …?'; to most of which Willa answered with 'a flat No', adding 'It was very tiresome, not unlike a Mrs Calder tea-party in Edinburgh.'[18] She would have preferred to meet the younger generation Guérards on their own. Tired after her ordeal, Willa went to bed, leaving Edwin to go on to meet Karl Miller by himself. This was the kind of visiting he enjoyed, since there were two tutors from

---

[16] Willa Muir, UStA, MS 38466 5/6.
[17] Ibid.
[18] Ibid.

Leverett House there, with red wine and good talk. Their weekend was equally busy, with a punch party at Leverett House on Saturday and on Sunday a visit to the Boston flat of a young couple of Irish extraction called Jack and Moira Sweeney. The Sweeneys' flat overlooked the river, with Finnish furniture and 'large Picassos on the walls' about which Willa's journal could only record 'very decorative'. The appreciation of visual art was clearly not among her talents, nor among Edwin's either. Their Prague friend Lumir Soukup had often said that if they had had any understanding of the visual arts then they could have purchased—and saved— some of the important works available at little cost in post-war Prague. At the Sweeneys' flat, Willa was more interested in their Finnish furniture—'in excellent condition, unlike ours'.[19]

Soon, however, it was Wednesday 9 November, and time for Edwin's first lecture which Willa had gone over very thoroughly with him the previous Sunday. She describes herself as being very tense and nervous, writing that her back was 'aching' and that 'during the lecture I had to struggle against and overcome a tendency to the tickly nervous cough I used to have when I first went to Prague in 1945'. Edwin, on the other hand, seemed very composed and spoke slowly and calmly. Willa thought he looked 'spiritual' but worried that his soft Orkney voice might not carry to people at the back of the hall.[20] The microphone worked well, however, people were attentive, and as Edwin reached the part of his talk where he quoted from the ballads, Willa began to relax. She had not had many opportunities to listen to Edwin lecture, for she did not attend his classes in Prague and not many, if any, of his British Council talks in Rome. But he had become a confident and communicative speaker who caught and held the attention of his audience. In his foreword to *The Estate of Poetry,* the published collection of Edwin's Harvard lectures, Archibald MacLeish wrote—

> American reviewers of his books had prepared the Cambridge audience for a Celt and a mystic, but to the astonishment of everyone Muir devoted his six lectures to an effort 'to measure the gap between the public and the poet and to find some explanation why it is so great'.

MacLeish continued,

> Mystics and Celts are not supposed to care about the public or to know that it exists, but here was Muir taking issue with those of his contemporaries who had resigned themselves to the defeated notion that poets write only for other poets and establishing his own position in the great tradition of the Scottish ballads which had a whole nation for audience—not to say a world.[21]

[19] Ibid.
[20] Ibid.
[21] Archibald MacLeish, Foreword, *The Estate of Poetry,* p. xvi.

Edwin's second and third lectures were also well received, although he had difficulties in the second talk when what Willa called the 'necklace mike' did not work well, prompting Archibald MacLeish to keep jumping up and down from his seat to boost the volume. Willa worried that people might not have fully heard the first fifteen minutes and was concerned that Edwin seemed 'tired' and did not 'lay it off' as well as he might have done. 'A brilliant lecture, but not brilliantly performed' was her verdict.[22]

Reading the 1962 published versions of the lectures, however, one might suspect that the problem, if there was one, with lectures two and three (on Wordsworth and Yeats respectively), had less to do with performance than the fact that their subject matter did not have the freshness of approach to be found in Edwin's first talk. Here he had opened up the question of what he called 'the estate of poetry', 'the actual response of a community to the poetry that is written for it; the effective range and influence of poetry', focusing on the earliest oral forms of poetry such as the ballads.[23] He returned to this theme in the three lectures he gave in the spring term, which explored the relationships between criticism and the poet, poetry and the poet, and the public and the poet. There is a freshness to these talks that is missing in his more conventional approaches to Wordsworth and Yeats. The hectic social life they were leading, right up to the date of the first lecture, might have had something to do with this. In a letter to George Mackay Brown in April 1956, Edwin confessed 'Forgive me for not writing sooner. I have been in the stress of writing out and giving the last three of my lectures, and I have been entangled as well in a web of hospitality, not really insistent, indeed so kind and considerate that it was impossible to escape.'[24] The autumn and Christmas seasons were certainly busy for the Muirs, and in the early months of 1956, Edwin's letters to friends and colleagues such as Mackay Brown, T. S. Eliot, and Kathleen Raine all begin with apologies for his long silence.

In addition to the Norton lectures, Edwin was expected to take his professorship on the road to give talks and readings beyond Harvard. Neither he nor Willa felt inclined to be ambitious in exploring more distant areas such as New Mexico, Arizona, or California, so they preferred to keep their travels within New England. They visited New York in January 1956, where Edwin was booked to give a Poetry Reading at the Metropolitan Museum of Art. This time they forsook the Grand Central Hotel for what Willa called 'the charming flat of the van Dusens, belonging to the Union Theological College, which gave us the chance of feeling more at home'. They had met the van Dusens at one of Cambridge's many dinner parties and their hosts treated them kindly, with every effort to make them feel at home. But neither Edwin nor Willa could feel at ease in New York, with

---

[22] Willa Muir, Harvard Journal, UStA, MS 38466 5/6.
[23] *The Estate of Poetry*, pp. 1–2.
[24] Edwin Muir, letter to George Mackay Brown, 9 April 1956, *Selected Letters*, p. 183.

its skyscraper buildings and numbered avenues and streets where Willa felt as if they were 'walking about on a squared-paper graph'. On the other hand, Edwin's reading at the Metropolitan Museum went well, with Willa referring to an 'appreciative' audience.[25] Edwin arranged to visit Djuna Barnes to discuss *The Antiphon* with her and then report back to T. S. Eliot. At this point Willa had not met Djuna Barnes, nor had she been able to make anything of the manuscript of the play. In her journal for the previous October, Willa had confessed, 'I tried, several times, to read Djuna Barnes' verse play, but I cannot and I cannot. It sickens my stomach. I fled from it to darning my vest & Edwin's socks!' Not surprisingly, she did not accompany Edwin on his visit to Barnes, but took herself off to Fifth Avenue instead, where she bought 'a dinner-dress for our Cambridge engagements to vary the solitary black silk outfit from Rome in which I had been appearing', along with 'two becoming summer frocks in a fine, drip-dry fabric'. New York might have some advantages after all, to counter its graph-paper streets.[26]

On their return to Cambridge, they were due to make a visit to Chicago for Edwin to give a lecture and read some of his poems at the University. After their pleasant autumn season in New England, they had not expected winter to be quite as severe as they found it by the Great Lakes. This was in the early months of 1956 when the blizzard season began. Traffic was disrupted and flights were impossible, so Edwin would have to travel by train, a journey lasting nineteen hours. Willa had planned to travel with him, but her arthritic back meant that in the end Edwin went alone. He did not enjoy the experience, writing to George Mackay Brown, 'I undertook an expedition by myself to Chicago, an unspeakable place, flung down in every conceivable style, all of them bad, on the border of a great lake. I won't return there again.' More enjoyable were his visits with Willa to Washington, 'a really handsome, I'm tempted to say beautiful city'; and to 'Bryn Mawr, a woman's college near Philadelphia'.[27] They made a second visit to New York and Edwin again gave readings of his poetry. Since his earlier discussions with Djuna Barnes, she had sent a new version of her play to Eliot, and Edwin wrote to Eliot in March to say that he had 'taken the liberty of speaking about the play to the people who run the Poets' Theatre here in Cambridge, and as they are young and eager I think they would love the chance to put it on.' He adds 'I wonder if it would encourage Djuna, or perhaps make her see the need to alter or omit some things in the play, if she were to see it on a stage.'[28] Accordingly, a first reading of *The Antiphon* was arranged in May, supported by the Poets' Theatre group. This was to take place in the library of a house belonging to the Phillips family, who had not yet moved into it, in Berkeley Street, Cambridge. Mrs Phillips' note of the attendees at the reading includes Djuna Barnes herself, Eliot, Edwin, I. A. Richards, and Robert Lowell, but

---

[25] *Belonging*, p. 295.
[26] Ibid., p. 296.
[27] Edwin Muir, letter to George Mackay Brown, 9 April 1956, *Selected Letters*, p. 183.
[28] Edwin Muir, letter to T. S. Eliot, 13 March 1956, *Selected Letters*, pp. 180-1.

there is no mention of Willa, who was to meet Barnes at a later performance in the Poets' Theatre itself. Mrs Phillips remembered, 'it seemed a torrent of language to my husband and me', adding that at that time 'we were ill-equipped to cope with her Elizabethan style or her family revenge themes.' The literary audience 'seemed stunned. Applause was muted; Djuna Barnes left rather abruptly', and the Poets' Theatre people felt 'that she had not been gracious in her thanking of them' for arranging the reading. Mrs Phillips remembers only two comments from Eliot— 'no sugar' for the coffee at the interval, and 'bit long' in relation to the second act.[29] In a later letter to Eliot, Edwin would express his pleasure that Eliot had 'managed to get Djuna's play into reasonable shape at last'; adding that 'it has been a long struggle' and that it was the reading supported by the Poets' Theatre that had made him 'realise that in my repeated readings of the play I had remained quite unaware of quite obvious impossibilities; I suppose I was beguiled by Djuna's imagery.' In relation to Willa's earlier comment that Eliot was much less stiff when they met him in the United States than he tended to be in London, it is interesting to note that Edwin addresses him informally as 'My dear Tom' and ends 'Yours ever, Edwin.'[30]

At the time of Edwin's March 1956 letter to Eliot about the Djuna Barnes play, he had decided to apply to the Bollingen Foundation for a grant in order to research and write a book on the Ballads, a topic that had long interested him, and the principal subject of his first Harvard lecture. It was Kathleen Raine who first told him about the Bollingen Foundation, and now he was in the process of putting together an application with Eliot as one of his supporters. With such future projects in mind, and with the Norton Lectures drawing to a close, Edwin and Willa's thoughts were turning to Britain again. Much as they had enjoyed and appreciated the hospitality and friendship of the Cambridge and Harvard community, staying on in the United States—as some of their new friends had tried to persuade them to do— was not a possibility that attracted them. Edwin's principal wish was to make for Orkney as soon as possible, while a chance visit with an elderly Austrian couple, who invited them to coffee in their Cambridge flat, confirmed the Muirs' sense of how European, as opposed to American, they were. They did not know at the time of their visit to the Austrian couple that their host, Dr Weisskopf, was a distinguished nuclear scientist, but they did know that they were immediately at home with him and his wife as they talked about shared experiences. Willa wrote later of what she called 'one of the most comfortable afternoons we had had for a long time'.

> It was comfort in depth, arising from a background of common feeling and common knowledge among the four of us. Naturally enough, we talked about Hitler,

---

[29] Sayre Phillips Sheldon, 'A Cambridge Literary Footnote: First Performance of "The Antiphon"', *Harvard Review* 15, Fall 1998, pp. 141, 143. http://www.jstor.org/stable/27561155. Accessed 28.02.2018.

[30] Edwin Muir, letter to T.S. Eliot, 17 October 1956, *Selected Letters*, p. 188.

and there we were at one. Hitler led on to mention of Broch, and we did not have to explain Broch to our hosts, for they knew about him. They agreed with Broch's conclusions as far as Austria was concerned; Austria, they said, had been shaken to pieces. Remembering Prague, and how Czechoslovakia had been shaken to pieces, we knew what they meant; they did not have to explain it to us.

The couples discovered also that each of them (although not at the same time) had 'enjoyed *Cosi fan Tutte* in the small theatre of the Vienna Hofburg'. Willa added that when they came out of the Weisskopf's flat into the street they 'felt dazed for a moment to find ourselves in America instead of Vienna, and that was when we realized that we had had to come to America to find out how European we were'.[31] In May, they said goodbye to the many friends they had met in the New World and returned to Britain.

---

[31] *Belonging*, pp. 303–4.

19
Swaffham Prior 1956–1959

I would like to come up to Orkney next summer with Willa, if that is possible:
I long to see it once more at least.

Edwin Muir

Edwin's compass, as so often, continued to point to Orkney, and he would have liked to travel there immediately, but their first priority was to find a permanent home. If possible, this would be reasonably close to London since in future they would be dependent on freelance writing activity to keep themselves solvent, now that Edwin would be without salaried employment for the first time since the early 1940s. Willa had loved Hampstead in the 1930s, but Hampstead and their former Downshire Hill house was now well beyond their means. Edwin had written to Nora Smallwood of Hogarth Press before leaving Harvard, saying that John Holloway suggested they should live somewhere near Cambridge where he was lecturing and had promised to keep an eye open for possible suitable places. Attractive cottages at an affordable price were not easy to find, however. Edwin was impatient and all for going to Orkney and worrying about a cottage later. But Willa was conscious that their trunks and books were parked near Victoria, their furniture was stored in Edinburgh, where Gavin was also, and their old car was still at Newbattle Abbey. She was troubled that the dispersal of their belongings might suggest a dispersal of their personalities, and she wanted to get them all under the same roof before they left for the north. She was not afraid on this occasion, as she had been in the 1930s, that Edwin would want to settle in Orkney. He recognized that the damp, dark winter and Orkney's distance from specialist treatment on the mainland would not be good for either of them. But he was anxious to spend the summer there, and had been negotiating with the BBC in Scotland with a view to a future broadcast on the topic of revisiting Orkney. In the end they took John Holloway's advice, supported by Kathleen Raine, and found an affordable freehold cottage in the village of Swaffham Prior that seemed to be exactly what they wanted. The cottage was on the main street of the small village and its front windows looked out on two churches, one on either side of a hill, and both with ruined towers. In a letter to his friend Ernest Marwick, a folklore collector and at that time a journalist on *The Orkney Herald*, Edwin said the towers reminded him of the castle on his home island of Wyre in the Orkneys.

The front door of the cottage opened directly into a spacious sitting room that had been converted from two smaller rooms, while the back door led to a walled garden with a garage attached. They decided this was exactly what they wanted and booked it immediately, without having a survey done, just as they had done in Hampstead. This time, fortunately, there were no disasters pending. Priory Cottage had been constructed out of three smaller cottages by the local owner of a large manor house who, for financial reasons, proposed to let out the manor and live in the converted building. So the refashioned cottage had been finished to a high standard inside and outside, with its own cesspool, a significant advantage in a village where there was no sewage system. Another benefit was that the village shop was easily accessible, right next to their cottage, and the garden soil was rich, a good soil for roses, with a small crab apple tree. They bought the cottage, with entry on the first of August, collected Gavin from Edinburgh, and set off for Orkney.

On this visit they stayed at the Royal Hotel in Kirkwall for three weeks at the BBC's expense. Ernest Marwick hired a car and took them to farmhouses where there was playing of fiddles and accordions and singing of old songs by the people gathered there. Sometimes they visited Edwin's second cousins in Kirkwall, or went to Deerness, to a cousin's farm at Skaill where he had often spent holidays as a young man working as a clerk in Glasgow. They visited Stanley Cursiter and George Mackay Brown in Stromness, and sometimes they just sat on a bench in Kirkwall, opposite St Magnus Cathedral, watching the people go by. They were, however, worried about Gavin, who still appeared to be suffering from the deafness that had suddenly manifested itself around the time he left university. Concerns about Gavin had often featured in Willa's Harvard journal—'No letter yet from Gavin', or less often, 'a letter, a good letter, from Gavin', and on one occasion, 'A letter at last from Gavin. He has failed his exam, but seems to be on an even enough keel: says they didn't seem to think him mature enough & "probably they were right". Says he will try again.'[1] Having given up the idea of being a concert pianist, Gavin, who would be 30 on his next birthday, had enrolled at Moray House College of Education in Edinburgh in order to train as a teacher. While his degree in Mathematics would have given him the written qualification to undertake teacher training, his actual performance on the course was not satisfactory, as Willa acknowledged, 'after a while they rejected him. For the time being the bottom was fairly knocked out of his universe.'[2] So Gavin was free to accompany them on their summer holiday and went with them, too, in August to their new cottage in Swaffham Prior. He found it difficult to obtain satisfactory employment, and was often seen striding over the fens, 'tall and dark, with a dour look', as one young woman described him. This particular young woman was the

---

[1] Willa Muir, Harvard Journal, UStA, MS 38466 5/6.
[2] *Belonging*, p. 306.

daughter of a neighbour who, in an unspoken alliance with Willa, seemed to think it would be a good thing if her daughter Mary and Gavin could become friendly with each other, being of a similar age. The daughter herself was not at all keen on such a relationship. Before Edwin and Willa had their piano installed in Priory Cottage, Gavin had been given permission to practise on the piano in her mother's house, and in her memoir of the Muirs at Swaffham Prior, Mary remembers how Gavin 'would appear, louring in our doorway, and without a word invade the living room'. She thought that because of his deafness he 'played very loudly, and to my mind mechanically', adding, 'though I'm sure he was a very knowledgeable musician'. She tells of one evening, 'when he had tired of thumping the keys', that he sat with her and her mother until it was very late. Her father had already gone to bed and her mother was 'visibly drooping', with the only sound in the room now coming from Gavin's hearing aid which made 'strange growling and whining noises'. It did not appear to be a particularly effective hearing aid, and one consequence of wearing it seemed to be that Gavin 'occasionally thought aloud, without realising that he had spoken'. On this particular occasion, when the village church clock struck eleven, he apparently said 'quite clearly, and with feeling: "I wish her mother would go to bed"'; at which point the girl's mother came fully awake 'and firmly showed him to the door'. The daughter does not say whether this ended the invitation to use the family's piano.[3] By Christmas 1957, however, Edwin was able to write to Ernest Marwick that 'Gavin has lately been given a really good hearing aid by Addenbrookes Hospital in Cambridge, as well as lessons in lip-reading; and he is far better in every way than when you saw him last.' And Edwin hopes that this will help him towards 'a position to hold up a job and strike out for himself'.[4] In May 1958, in a letter to the poet Norman MacCaig, who was working as a teacher in Edinburgh, this hope seems to have been fulfilled, for Edwin reports that Gavin 'has made a great deal of genuine progress in the last year' and had now obtained a tutoring appointment with Wolsey College in Oxford. Wolsey was a correspondence college and so Gavin could work from home, 'correcting mathematical papers and sending them off'. Edwin believes that 'this job will mean a great deal to him, and give him hope, which he had little of before.'[5]

Edwin and Willa themselves soon settled in Swaffham Prior to become what Willa described as 'villagers *de luxe*'. They had a study upstairs lined with books, and downstairs, once their own piano arrived, they had 'a piano, a big radio-gramophone and plenty of records housed on a home-contrived arrangement of shelves'. She told how, as in St Andrews with their visits to and from the Oesers, 'Edwin passionately enjoyed listening to music.' As other friends had mentioned over the years, he had a light but 'true tenor voice' and as a child in Orkney had

[3] Mary Hubble, 'Among the Immortals: memories of Edwin and Willa Muir', *Cambridgeshire Life*, October 1990, pp. 26–7.
[4] Edwin Muir, letter to Ernest Marwick, 24 December 1957, Orkney Archives, D31/31/6.
[5] Edwin Muir, letter to Norman MacCaig, 22 May 1958, *Selected Letters*, p. 204.

apparently learned to play the accordion. Willa had taught him to read music when they were in Dresden, and to play it on the piano. Nevertheless, with Gavin in the house as 'such a brilliant pianist', neither of them thought to play when he was able to do it so much better. In compensation, they now 'had the joy of listening to orchestras and operas' on their radio-gramophone which had 'a first-rate sound chamber'; and in addition they occasionally had a Saturday afternoon performance of the bell ringers practising in the tower of the right-hand church opposite the cottage.[6] They also had regular visits from friends from Girton and Queens College. Kathleen Raine, who was a fellow of Girton and who had helped them previously in so many ways, encouraged the College to hold a welcoming reception for the Muirs when they first arrived in Swaffham Prior, and they were delighted to meet Bob, the ex-metalworker from Newbattle who had won a place at Cambridge with his essay on *Paradise Lost*. He had just completed his degree studies but had stayed on for a few days in order to attend the reception and meet Edwin and Willa again. Girton continued to be a friendly place for them and they met up with Harvard acquaintances such as I. A. Richards and his wife, who returned from Cambridge New England to the old English Cambridge every summer. On one special occasion Edwin was invited to give a poetry reading at the College and he and Willa were accommodated overnight in a suite which, according to Willa, was 'specially kept for the bishop who was the College Visitor'.[7]

A new acquaintance whose visits to Priory Cottage must have resulted in reawakened memories of Prague was Muriel Bradbrook, a notable Shakespearean scholar and, like Katherine Raine, a Fellow of Girton. Bradbrook had earlier befriended Bohuslava, a young Czech woman who had been one of Professor Vočadlo's students in Prague, in the years immediately after the Putsch that ended Edwin's connection with Charles University. Professor Vočadlo continued to supervise this student's doctoral dissertation privately after he was dismissed from his university position, until 1952 when she joined some friends and managed to make a hazardous escape from Czechoslovakia. She spent many difficult months in refugee camps in various zones of occupied Germany, before eventually obtaining permission to travel to Eire to take up a teaching post. Muriel Bradbrook had become involved in the refugee situation when the young woman sent an enquiry to Girton College about whether a scholarship Professor Vočadlo had told her about was still open to applicants. This was on behalf of another Czech student, and the scholarship was no longer available, but the girl's letter resulted in Muriel Bradbrook and her Girton colleagues taking an interest in the plight of young graduate refugees stranded in Germany, an interest that eventually resulted, not only in the young Prague woman's coming to Cambridge in 1953 en route for Eire, but also in her later marrying Bradbrook's brother. Bohuslava Bradbrook,

[6] *Belonging*, pp. 308–9.
[7] Ibid., p. 309.

now Muriel's sister-in-law, went on to become a distinguished literary academic, publishing on Czech literature and the writings of Karel Čapek.[8] The Muirs would have had much to talk about with Muriel and their connections to Prague, including Professor Vočadlo who was a friend of Bradbrook's and Edwin's sponsor at Charles University in the late 1940s. Unfortunately there seems to be no record of any meeting between Edwin and Willa and Bohuslava herself, perhaps because she had a scholarship for further research that took her to Oxford around the time of the Muirs' arrival in Swaffham Prior.

Having completed a successful year as the Charles Norton Visiting Professor at Harvard, and as the recipient of the Russell Loines Award from the American Academy of Arts and Letters in May 1957, Edwin's reputation as a critic and poet meant that he was well received in Cambridge. He was made a member of John Holloway's College, Queen's, so that he could borrow books from the University Library. David Daiches, then at Jesus College, visited Priory Cottage and invited Edwin and Willa to what Willa described as a 'sumptuous luncheon' in his rooms at Jesus, 'with the College speciality, *crème brulée,* to crown the feast'. She added that she got the impression that Cambridge dons 'lived very comfortably by our standards, for they could entertain people well without much effort'. The Muirs' own standards could not compete now that Willa was both cook and housekeeper, situations for which she had always employed paid help in the past. And having to 'do everything while hobbling about on a stick' made offering more than a cup of tea a rare activity.[9]

One Foot in Eden had been published to critical acclaim in March 1956, although Edwin had had doubts about the proposed title just before leaving for Harvard. He worried that it may seem overly religious, but fortunately Eliot persuaded him that the original title did more justice to the thematic and artistic richness of the individual poems in the collection. And, as Willa pointed out, the title could equally imply that the author had his other foot—and one could argue it was the dominant one—'firmly on earth': a 'difficult country, and our home', as 'The Difficult Land' poem in the collection argues.[10] In the essay 'Burns and Popular Poetry' from his *Essays on Literature and Society* of 1949—the year also of his poetry collection *The Labyrinth*—Edwin had written that 'a myth is endlessly adaptable'; and this idea is illustrated and substantiated in the *One Foot in Eden* collection as it had been also, if in different ways, in *The Labyrinth*. In the later collection, the adaptation of Greek myth, which he had tentatively begun to use as early as 'The Ballad of Hector in Hades' from *First Poems* of 1925, is used

---

[8] See Bohuslava Bradbrook, *Karel Čapek: In Pursuit of Truth, Tolerance, and Trust* (Brighton: Sussex Academic Press, 1998); and *The Liberating Beauty of Little Things: Decision, Adversity & Reckoning in a Refugee's Journey from Prague to Cambridge* (Brighton: The Alpha Press, 2000).
[9] *Belonging*, pp. 309–10.
[10] Ibid., p. 276; Edwin Muir, letter to T. S. Eliot, 8 July 1955, *Selected Letters*, p. 172; *Complete Poems*, pp. 220, 219.

confidently alongside a new approach to the use of the biblical stories which had often provided the imagery for his early poetry. As the literary scholar Graham Hough would argue in his book *An Essay on Criticism*, published in 1966, a decade after *One Foot in Eden*, biblical myth is not as readily adaptable for literary purposes as Greek myth since it is perceived in a different way as being 'God-given'. It is perhaps not surprising, then, that although the ratio of biblical myth to Greek myth poems in Part I of *One Foot in Eden* is 2:1, on the whole it is the poems deriving from the legends of Greece that make the strongest impact—poems such as 'Orpheus' Dream' which reworks the story of Orpheus and Eurydice to show the power of love in the face of adversity, and ends with Pluto being the one who is left, with the 'ghost' of Eurydice sitting in his 'empty' hall. In 'Telemachos Remembers', the son of Penelope and Odysseus recalls the apparent futility of his mother's weaving and unweaving when he saw it as a child, compared to his adult understanding of its significance. 'The Grave of Prometheus' reflects on what is lost but cannot be forgotten, with its strongly visual and enigmatic closing lines, 'And made his burning body a quiet mound, / And his great face a vacant ring of daisies'. 'The Other Oedipus' is an equally enigmatic reflection on the original myth as wandering Oedipus seems to have found peace in a happy loss of his mental capacities: 'quite storyless and had clean forgotten / That memory burning in another world'.[11]

Part I of the collection also contains the biblical myth poem 'The Annunciation' which derived from Edwin's coming upon the plaque of the angel and girl on a building in Via degli Artisti in Rome. His description of the plaque in *An Autobiography* and his recreation of it in 'The Annunciation' both focus on its being 'the perfect earthly symbol of the love that passes understanding'. 'The Annunciation' comes closest to Edwin's use of Greek myth in the tautness of its form, the vitality of its enigmatic imagery and the directness of its eroticism—'Immediacy / Of strangest strangeness is the bliss / That from their limbs all movement takes. / Yet the increasing rapture brings / So great a wonder ....'.[12] What Edwin found in the representation of religion in Rome, compared to the contrasting legacy of Scottish Calvinism, is presented in 'The Incarnate One' with its angry, atmospheric opening lines, 'The windless northern surge, the sea-gull's scream / And Calvin's kirk crowning the barren brae'. This poem is not adapted from a biblical story but from Scottish religious history and what the poet sees as the betrayal in Calvinist doctrine compared to the 'word made flesh' in Giotto's paintings, which brought the gospel stories to an illiterate public, and the 'iron pen' of 'King Calvin', which reduces 'God' to 'three angry letters in a book'. And then, as so often in Edwin's prose writings, Calvin's bending of 'the Mystery' into 'an ideological instrument' transfers itself to the idea of the 'cold empire' of the 'abstract man', which he

---

[11] *Complete Poems*, pp. 200, 201.
[12] 'The Annunciation', 'One Foot in Eden', *Complete Poems*, p. 206, pp. 212–13, also *An Autobiography*, p. 278.

believed was to be found in communism, leaving the future tale uncertain, still to be told.[13] 'One Foot in Eden', the title poem of the collection, is placed towards the end of Part I, immediately before 'The Incarnate One', and so it acts as a kind of end piece to the theme of reconciliation which characterizes this first part of the collection, and is present in the scenarios of the religious myth poems as also in those which adapt the stories of Greece. The new understanding of an earthly 'Incarnation', that had come to Edwin in Rome, replaced the despair he felt in Prague with the realization that—as he expresses it in the title poem—'Strange blessings never in Paradise / Fall from these beclouded skies'.

'The Horses', positioned in Part II of the collection and first published in *The Listener* in March 1955, was written in the context of a growing concern about the possibility of nuclear war between the West and the Soviet Union, and is now one of the best known of Edwin's poems. In keeping with the dual nature of the themes in Part II, its scenario imagines the aftermath of a nuclear war in which there are areas that have escaped complete devastation—as was believed could be possible, in the earlier stages of thinking about nuclear war and 'theatres of conflict'. From the images in the poem, it seems that the survivors could be islanders in a place such as Orkney and, as they contemplate their new situation, they realize that it has been their unthinking adoption of technology, and their rejection or their forgetting of human values, that has brought them to this present disaster. In keeping with the overall thematic context of the *One Foot in Eden* collection, they are given a second chance by the arrival of the 'strange horses', and the opportunity to renew a 'long-lost archaic companionship' between animal and human life. 'Their coming [is] our beginning.' This poem has been criticized by some readers as presenting too easy an escape from the devastation that nuclear war would bring, but an answer to such criticism—if it needs one—is to be found in Edwin's later poem 'After a Hypothetical War', written after he went to Harvard in the summer of 1955, and first published in *The Listener* in January 1956 under the title of 'The Bad Lands'. Edwin had written to Kathleen Raine from Harvard that he had 'been writing some very queer poetry since I came here, with a good deal of new horror in it'. This comment is very applicable to 'After a Hypothetical War', which acts as a companion piece to the earlier 'Horses' but with a very much grimmer picture of human society fallen into post-nuclear savagery. There is no saving myth here, only a 'chaotic breed of misbegotten things, / Embryos of what could never wish to be'. Read together, these two poems dramatize the possibility of the destruction of life on earth, and the choices facing human beings in a machine age that has run out of control—a theme that also appears in Edwin's late critical writing.[14]

[13] 'The Incarnate One', *Complete Poems*, pp. 213–14.
[14] Edwin Muir, letter to Kathleen Raine 20 April 1956, *Selected Letters*, p. 185; 'The Horses', *Complete Poems*, pp. 226–8, 'After a Hypothetical War', p. 243.

When Edwin took up residence in Swaffham Prior in August 1956, his reputation in both poetry and critical writing was at a peak, with many ideas for future work. He had been successful in his application for a Bollingen Foundation grant, for three years to work on a book on the Ballads, and he was in the process of preparing his Harvard Lectures for publication with both Harvard University Press and the Hogarth Press. Hogarth had been supportive over the years when publication had been more difficult for him, and he was happy to get an agreement with Harvard that Hogarth could publish the Norton Essays instead of Harvard's usual connection with Oxford University Press. He was also keeping together a group of late poems, which he had not included in *One Foot in Eden*, telling Eliot that he wanted to hold on to them to be published in a separate collection of 'Late Poems'. Edwin's plans were not helped, however, by his steadily weakening physical condition. When they were in the United States both he and Willa had consulted Harvard Medical School doctors about their respective ailments. Willa had been advised that her back pain was caused by a cyst at the bottom her spine, 'usually a young woman's affliction', which would clear up in time. The arthritic pain in her hip joints was a different matter and could and should be attended to, but this would involve being on crutches for a time, which did not seem feasible while they were on Harvard duties. Edwin had been told that he had 'the arteries of a young man' and that his chest pains came from 'a false angina', but this was a sadly inadequate diagnosis, as future events would show. In Swaffham Prior he felt increasingly tired, but without a regular income to depend on he had to keep up his regular reviewing commitments with the *Observer* and *Listener*. In May 1957 he went north to Edinburgh to the School of Scottish Studies, to consult the staff and research ballad material for the Bollingen book. While there, he managed to spend an enjoyable evening with former Newbattle students, but the trip and its various meetings brought on his chest pains once more, and he found he was having difficulty in breathing. Shortly after his return to England, his Harvard friend, the poet Robert Frost, was awarded the honorary degree of Doctor of Letters from Cambridge and Edwin was invited to the ceremony. He did not feel able to attend, however, and gave his ticket to Mary from Swaffham Prior, who had suffered Gavin's 'thumping' on her family piano. In her memoir of the Muirs, she wrote that she 'felt a fraud' when conducted to a seat in the Senate House 'reserved for the great poet, Edwin Muir'.[15] Edwin himself would be awarded the same honorary degree from Cambridge the following year, and this time he was strong enough to be there in person.

But he continued to feel tired and often unable to concentrate, and early in 1958 a local doctor who was called in to examine him prescribed what Willa called 'a regimen of tranquillizers'.[16] At first this appeared to alleviate the situation, so that

---

[15] Mary Hubble, 'Among the Immortals', p. 27.
[16] *Belonging*, p. 312.

he felt able to go to Bristol in mid-February to give the newly founded Churchill Lectures at the University. He was in Bristol for a month, giving lectures that focused on his preoccupation with the theme of imagination and the continuing need for it in the modern world. He also spent a good deal of time resting in bed. The lectures were a success with the students and academics who had invited him, but unfortunately no one thought to record them, and Edwin, as so often, did not have a fully developed written script. Regular letters sent between him and Willa when he was in Bristol show their continuing loving relationship after so many years together, but they also reveal tensions in their life at Swaffham Prior, perhaps inevitable in the case of two people with illnesses, little domestic help, and limited intellectual stimulus, living in a small house with an adult son who had health and employment problems of his own. When Willa wrote to Edwin in Bristol that she had had 'a wonderful night's sleep and felt all the better of it', he replied that he too had been sleeping well, and was feeling 'more myself as I used to be'. He admitted that 'a double set of ailments in one house has been getting us down', but now he was not 'bothering nearly so much about myself' and was 'unwinding quite a lot'. He added 'I only realise now how great a trial I must have been to thee, poor lamb, in all these months. Forgive me. I don't know whether I'm a domestic animal or not; I've certainly been worrying a lot, and needlessly, and worrying thee too, my poor poor lamb, more than I can bear to think of.' As for Willa, she replied that she was 'doing quite well', and added that 'this Saturday morning I got up and opened the house and got the cup-parcel from the postman, and paid the milk and the papers, all with much more competence than I would have shown once.' She thinks that she had 'muted' herself too much, for fear of upsetting Edwin's 'solar plexus', and warns him she is 'not going to be so muted in the days to come'.[17]

Back at Swaffham Prior, Edwin was busy 'taking notes' for the Ballads book, and writing to Norman MacCaig in April that he hoped to return to Edinburgh in the summer to make more enquiries. He had been very impressed by MacCaig's 1955 collection, *Riding Lights*, writing to Norah Smallwood of Hogarth Press, before he left for Harvard, that he considered it 'the best book of new poetry to appear since the war'. He also suggested that he might take some copies with him to Harvard, having already sent a copy to John Hall in the hope that he might be able to publicize it via the BBC. Now, in April 1958, he was writing to MacCaig telling him that he was full of 'friendly envy' at seeing poems by him 'everywhere', adding 'How lovely to have the spring flowing freely (you are really to be envied) and not monotonously either, but with more variety than ever before.' Then he confesses that he has been 'rather daunted in the last year or two by the fear that I am keeping on writing the same poem, and I fear that it has inhibited (horrible word) the

---

[17] Letters between Edwin and Willa, 20 February 1958 and 1 March 1958, *Selected Letters*, pp. 199, 200.

flow'. He tells MacCaig that he has written very few complete poems lately, 'but many parts of poems which ceased when they seemed to be taking the same old course'. He thinks that 'perhaps the best thing I could do with them would be to integrate (another awful word) them in a longish poem: I don't know; that may be what they are best suited for. Time will tell.' And he adds the provocative comment, '*The Waste Land* was made out of splinters.'[18] In fact, Edwin's 'splinters' eventually came together in the poem titled 'The Last War', one of a group of late poems which, far from 'taking the same old course', continued to urgently investigate the theme of 'how we live together' in an increasingly dangerous and depersonalized modern world, a theme prophetically relevant in the decades to come.

Unfortunately, Edwin's health did not show the resilience of his late poetry. Cambridge awarded him the honorary degree of Doctor of Letters, in June 1958, and he was paired in the procession with Dag Hammerskjöld, Secretary-General of the United Nations. Willa remembered Edwin and Hammerskjöld 'talking eagerly together, apparently getting on well with each other', as the procession passed her in the street, adding 'as usual when animated Edwin looked less frail.' However, when it came to his turn at the ceremony, Willa saw how fragile he looked in the light of a nearby window, and wondered if he would be able to see it through to its end. He did, and after lunch Edwin told Willa that he had been talking to Hammerskjöld mostly about Djuna Barnes, whose work he much admired, and which he was planning to translate into Swedish, although the pressure of his life left little time for literature. This degree ceremony would be Edwin's second last public appearance in the Cambridge area. His last outing in public was also in June, when he gave a talk at the college in Bottisham Village, situated between Cambridge and Newmarket. Halfway through the event, however, he felt that his breath was giving out and he had to excuse himself from continuing. Clearly distressed, Edwin was taken home, the doctor called in, and fluid in the lungs diagnosed. Neither Willa nor Edwin seemed to realize that this indicated a failing heart, and previous doctors, including the Harvard medical team who had investigated his chest pains, would not appear to have considered heart failure as a possible diagnosis. Or if they suspected it, they did not tell the patient. Edwin did not want to stay in bed, but preferred to lie in the long chair in their summer garden, close to the lavender and in sight of the apple tree. This was a situation uncannily apposite, in setting and tone, to two poems from *One Foot in Eden* which had been written in the early fifties—'The Late Wasp' and its companion 'The Late Swallow'. George Mackay Brown, remembered telling Willa how much he admired 'The Late Swallow', which looks back to Henryson's 'Preiching of the Swallow' in its warning that it is time to 'Shake out your pinions long untried / that now must bear you there where you would be', and Willa replied, 'It is Edwin's epitaph.'[19] So Edwin

---

[18] Letter to Norman MacCaig, 23 April, 1958, *Selected Letters*, pp. 202–3.
[19] George Mackay Brown, 'Envoi', *Edwin Muir: Collected Prose*, p. 210.

convalesced in his garden, waiting for the district nurse to come to the cottage to 'dehydrate' him, as he called it, and after such sessions he would feel able to take a short walk up the hill to the two churches of Swaffham Prior. Around this time he wrote to a correspondent apologizing for a late reply and saying that he had been 'ill with water on the lung', had been having injections to draw off the water, and that he had been ordered to rest.[20] In August he wrote to T. S. Eliot, with whom he had been corresponding about a proposed *Collected Poems*, saying that he was 'taking care to follow the doctor's instructions', having been 'almost a model patient for the past few weeks'. Nevertheless, however, he was clearly not well, telling Eliot that he had to go for another X-ray on Tuesday, 'to test my lungs for water again', and adding, 'I have been breathing almost freely for more than a fortnight, and I had not realised for quite a while that breathing could be such a pleasure.' Eliot would seem to have been giving him advice about breathing, for Edwin tells him in a letter of 19 September that he was much interested in what he had said, and that he feels that he had 'never breathed in the right way all my life—a curious habit of holding my breath at the most trivial effort, tying my shoes, for instance'[21] and he intends to consult the doctor about breathing exercises. He also reports that the putting together of a *Collected Poems* is progressing, with much of the material to be included now decided, except for *The Narrow Place* of which he did not appear to have a copy. Eliot sent one more or less by return, and Edwin wrote on 24 September saying that he wanted to include it all, 'except for 'Isaiah', at the same time wishing Eliot 'a happy seventieth birthday, long life, continued happiness, and all that you most set your heart on'.[22]

Edwin's own heart was failing. He became more and more easily tired, and unable to work. Yet in October he was still able to write optimistically to a correspondent, 'I think in a few months I shall be in better health than I have been for years.'[23] But he had to take to his bed again, and people who came to see him had sometimes to be sent away. Two days after Christmas he was taken to Addenbrookes Hospital in Cambridge. Two incidents from these last weeks remained in Willa's mind; one was when, troubled as he was so often about the state of the world, Edwin suddenly sat up in bed one day and said insistently to her 'There are no absolutes, no absolutes'—a return to the topics of his early debates with John Holms in Glasgow. Willa did not understand what he meant by this, but reassured him by agreeing that there were 'no absolutes at all'. The second incident occurred shortly before he was taken to hospital when Willa was leaning over his bed, smiling to him. He smiled back and said to her, 'My lamb, how *nice* thu looks.' She wrote that at that time she was 'haggard and exhausted' and that 'only the eye of

---

[20] Edwin Muir, letter to Derek Hawes, 7 July 1958, *Selected Letters*, p. 205.
[21] Edwin Muir, letters to T. S. Eliot, 1 August 1958, *Selected Letters*, p. 206, 19 September 1958, p. 208.
[22] Edwin Muir, letter to T. S. Eliot, 24 September 1958, *Selected Letters*, p. 209.
[23] Quoted by Peter Butter in *Edwin Muir: Man and Poet*, but no provenance given.

love could have seen me as looking "nice" at that moment.'[24] Yet even then, she did not seem able to believe that Edwin's life could really be coming to its end. Others did, however. On 24 December, Professor L. C. Knights of Bristol wrote to Ian Parsons of Chatto & Windus thanking him for his 'sympathetic response' to his appeal for funds to assist Edwin. Knight had written to a number of literary colleagues to see if they would be willing to contribute to a fund that would help the Muirs out of their current financial difficulties, caused largely by Edwin's illness and his inability to complete the ballads project or earn fees by reviewing. Knights wrote to Parsons that he had tried to contact Eliot, 'but he was not at the office, and—as I expected—they wouldn't give me his private phone number. So I am writing to him explaining the circumstances.' He added, 'It seems to me a terrible thing that someone like Edwin should be so ill, and at the same time distressed, as he must be, about money.' In this regard, an application had been made for a Civil List pension, which seemed likely to be successful, but any decision would not be announced until February of the next year. Knights' writing to Parsons had a successful and early outcome, however, for by 29 December Willa—who had known nothing about Knights' plea for help—was thanking Parsons 'for the cheque that arrived so miraculously this morning'.

> Edwin cannot write, I am sorry to say; he is very gravely ill and was taken into Addenbrookes hospital in Cambridge two days ago. Apparently he has congestive heart trouble. The doctors think he has a chance, & I think he has more than a chance of recovery, to some extent at least. But he will never be able to *work* much, only to do what his spirit moves him to do.

She tells Parsons that she has been 'cashing cheques without asking our bank in Hampstead if we have any assets left'. And she ends 'Bless you & Norah Smallwood.'[25]

Despite Willa's hopes, Edwin died in hospital on 3 January 1959, just after answering the visiting doctor's morning greeting. He never did manage to see Orkney, 'once more at least', but is buried in the Swaffham Prior churchyard close by the two towers that reminded him so much of his Castle on Wyre.

---

[24] *Belonging*, p. 315.
[25] L. C. Knights, letter to Ian Parsons of Chatto & Windus, 24 December 1958; and Willa Muir, letter to Ian Parsons of 29 December 1958, Hogarth/Chatto & Windus Archive CW 166/14 (1955–58), University of Reading.

20
Willa Alone 1959–1963

> Ich weine viel in meinen Einsamkeiten,
> Der Herbst in meinem Herzen währt zu lange,
> Sonne der Liebe willst du nie mehr scheinen,
> Um meine bitter'n Tränen mild aufzutrocknen?
> Gustav Mahler, 'Der Einsame im Herbst'
> (*Das Lied von der Erde*)[1]

My dear Violet,

> How did you cope with your grief when Sydney died? I try and try, but mine still rises and suffocates me. I *must* get more control over myself, because I have to earn a living somehow, especially if I am to go on staying in this cottage, which I want to do. It is so full of Edwin, and his grave is within three minutes' walk of it […] I must get a grip on myself and sit down to work. But I can't do it yet; and there are moments when I feel as if I never will be able to do it.

Willa poured out her grief to Violet Schiff shortly after Edwin's burial in the Swaffham Prior churchyard. As she thanks Violet for her letter of condolence to 'a very desolate Willa', she ends 'What does one do? How to keep under control the turbulent emotions that come up, without one's volition, when least expected. Perhaps time will do it?'[2] Violet knew about grief, for she had lost her husband Sydney to a heart attack in 1944 at the age of 75.

Willa might have been comforted by the many personal letters she received from friends and literary colleagues, and by the positive obituary notices of Edwin, the man as well as the poet, which were immediately published in newspapers and journals from Orkney to London. Initially, however, she was inconsolable. Kathleen Raine described Willa as 'absolutely shattered' at Edwin's funeral, unable to look towards Gavin who played the organ at the service.[3] Edwin's death had come too suddenly for her. *The Manchester Guardian* lamented 'a poet of rare genius' and one who, although his most recent collection of poems had been titled *One*

---

[1] 'I weep much in my loneliness, the Autumn in my heart lasts too long, Sun of Love, will you never again shine and gently dry my painful tears?'

[2] Willa Muir, letter to Violet Schiff, 18 January 1959, Schiff Papers, BL, Add MS 52920.

[3] Kathleen Raine—in response to a series of questions by Dr Kirsty Allen when working on her doctoral thesis on Willa Muir at St Andrews University in the early 1990s. I am grateful to Dr Allen for giving me a photocopy of these unpublished questions and answers.

Foot in Eden, had his other foot 'firmly upon twentieth-century earth'.[4] The notice in the *London Times* gave a strong overview of his career as poet and critic, commenting that 'he became at 70 perhaps the foremost poet in English to be writing actively week by week'. And, having started to write poetry later in life, his dying at the advanced age of 70 'was his prime. Old age and declining powers were things that he did not experience'. The *Times* obituary also drew attention to the early criticism of *Latitudes* in 1924 and *Transition* in 1926, finding the latter remarkable for 'among other things, almost the first wholly outspoken recognition of D. H. Lawrence as the major genius of his generation'. This was a perceptive comment, for although Edwin had struggled against Lawrence's social and philosophical ideas, as well as his manner of expression, he recognized that there was something new and significant in his work and its engagement with a disturbing and complex new age. Edwin's contribution, along with Willa, to the translation of modern German literature was seen to be especially significant, for 'before their appearance Kafka was almost unknown in Britain', and 'the Muirs virtually created his literary reputation among us'. The *Times* obituary closed not only with a recognition of the several honorary doctorates Edwin received but even more importantly with a reference to *One Foot in Eden*, and to 'late substantial poems (like "The Last War") that had been published in periodicals up to within a few months of his death', thus substantiating the opening comment about Edwin dying 'in his prime', even if this was also at an advanced age.[5] The *London Times* obituary was followed a couple of days later by a letter from T. S. Eliot, congratulating the newspaper on an obituary which 'does justice both to the man and to his work, and requires neither supplement nor correction', and asking leave to add his own personal tribute. Edwin had not been kind to Eliot's poetry in his early *Transition*, although he had always respected and been influenced by Eliot's criticism. In his turn, Eliot had not paid much attention to Edwin's early poetry—so different from his own ideas about what poetry could be, and still, perhaps, immature. Now, late in life, both writers had come to admire and respect each other's poetry and their criticism, too. In his *London Times* tribute, Eliot acknowledges that while Edwin's literary criticism 'had always seemed to me of the best of our time', it was only 'more recently that I came to regard his poetry as ranking with the best poetry of our time'. Eliot maintains that, as a late starter, some of Edwin's 'finest work—perhaps his very finest work—was written when he was already over 60', and he believes that his two most recent volumes of verse, *The Labyrinth* and *One Foot in Eden*, 'contain more of his best work than any other', while the 'still more recent and as yet unpublished poems which I have seen show no falling off in quality'; and he compares this late development with that of the 'later poetry of Yeats', recognizing in both cases, 'a triumph of the human spirit'.[6]

[4] *Manchester Guardian*, 5 January 1959.
[5] *London Times*, 5 January 1959.
[6] T. S. Eliot, *London Times*, 7 January 1959.

This south-of-the-border recognition of Edwin's achievements was not so evident in the obituary notices from Scotland, which tended to show a lack of detailed knowledge about his writing career. Surprisingly, *The Orcadian* of 8 January simply reprinted sizeable sections from the *Scotsman* obituary of 5 January, citing his career appointments with the British Council, Newbattle, and Harvard, and working these into its own slighter commentary. This included Edwin's 'years of drudgery in Glasgow', together with the statement that his life being such an 'interior one', he needed 'the guiding hand' which his marriage supplied.[7] This was a clichéd and (as many friends and acquaintances knew) an untrue comment on a marriage where Edwin was actually the stronger and more organized partner upon whom Willa greatly depended. For his Orkney boyhood, where one might have expected some insightful detail, the reader was merely referred to Edwin's own autobiography. Fortunately, a first-hand and livelier character account of the poet's character was given in appreciations by his close friend Stanley Cursiter and two other Orkney-born acquaintances. *The Orcadian* was not alone in its Scottish obituary awkwardness. *The Scotsman* characterized Edwin as 'a metaphysical poet', suggesting that it had been claimed he was the 'first Scottish poet of his kind', before quickly moving to the fact that he was not part of the Lallans revival but 'wrote solely in English'. His European connections were recognized, with references to Hölderlin and Rilke (although the latter was never really an 'influence' on Edwin), and influences from Yeats and Eliot were also mentioned. There seemed to be little first-hand knowledge of Edwin's poetry itself, when the reader was told that 'some of his early verse was descriptive and little more', although 'with each successive volume' it grew 'richer and more profound as a result of the invention of new symbols'. The notice ended, somewhat parochially, 'Last year he was elected an honorary member of the Scottish Arts Club.'[8] *The Scotsman*'s rival paper, *The Glasgow Herald*, concentrated almost entirely on Edwin's reputation as critic, seeing him as 'a product of an age of transition.' The many honours awarded him in later life were listed and linked solely to his critical career and his work with the British Council. Only in the last paragraph was there a mention of Edwin the poet—'Muir wrote several small volumes of poetry of which "The Narrow Place" was maybe the most significant.' And the article added that 'at its best his poetry has a visionary quality that equals some of the Border ballads', although it considered also that 'his imagination is obsessed by time, and his images tend to have a heraldic, static, character.'[9] As with other Scottish newspapers, the piece had little to say about Edwin's career as a poet in the wider world. It seems that his comments about Scottish literature in *Scott and Scotland* may have cast a long shadow. In a lively and appreciative column in the *News Chronicle* for 9 January 1959,

---

[7] *Orcadian*, 8 January 1959.
[8] *Scotsman*, 5 January 1959.
[9] *Glasgow Herald*, 5 January 1959. All obituary references from Orkney Archives, reference D31/31/4.

Douglas Young wrote that Edwin himself 'had a phrase about Scotsmen carrying somewhere inside "a broken image of the lost kingdom"'. And he suggested that 'in memory, Muir, too, will become part of that broken image of the Scottish heritage.' This comment seems particularly appropriate, given that the Scottish obituaries had showed so little appreciation—or awareness—of what Douglas Young went on to describe as 'his critical insight, his poetic creativeness, and the kind humorous personality he had'.[10]

When Edwin died, T. S. Eliot was already in the process of preparing a collection of his poetry for publication by Faber, and this would be the comprehensive volume that Edwin himself had supervised when he was unwell, with the help of John Hall. Working on this collection helped Willa find the strength to go forward again after the loss of her husband, as did her involvement with other projects that he had not been able to undertake. In a letter to Violet Schiff, she stressed her determination to 'go on living in this cottage, which is so full of Edwin'; and her recognition that doing so would mean finding some way of earning a living. 'I shall be forced to pull myself together, and cease being a decrepit wreck' she adds, in a manner more typical of her lively self-deprecating style. For the new collection of Edwin's poems, she told the Marwicks that she wanted it to include 'all the stray poems in various periodicals since his last collection', asking them if they knew of any, since Edwin had left no lists or files of these in the cottage. She concluded, 'Edwin died with so many unwritten poems in him. My dear, dear love: he should have died hereafter, not now' and signed herself, 'Yours Willa (rather desperate)'.[11] In March, however, she could write again to Violet Schiff, 'My dear Violet, This is a more cheerful letter from me. I have begun to pull myself together a bit and am learning to live with grief and not break down; a hard lesson, as you know, and a horrible one.'

Several pieces of good fortune helped Willa's recovery. From a financial perspective, the Civil List pension Edwin had applied for was awarded to his widow. This amounted to £250 a year and meant that she could continue to live in Priory Cottage, 'with my memories'. Gavin succeeded in obtaining (with some help from Kathleen Raine) a position in Kew Observatory measuring earthquakes that would pay him £550 a year and allow him to be self-supporting. The Bollingen Foundation agreed to transfer the grant awarded to Edwin to Willa, so that she could 'finish' his work on the Scottish Ballads, although, as it turned out, Edwin had hardly started, so the completed book would be very much Willa's own perspective on the topic. And since Edwin's illness had hindered the preparation of his Harvard lectures for publication, Willa worked on these for Faber along with the collected poems. She wrote to Violet, 'I have work, you see, and an income, and

---

[10] Douglas Young, '"He sailed strange seas of thought". My Scottish Diary', *News Chronicle*, 9 January 1959, Orkney Archives D31/31/4.

[11] Willa Muir, letter to Ernest and Janette Marwick, 9 February 1959, Orkney Archives, D31/31/6.

although in a sense Edwin's wife died with him I am going to recover my old self, I hope, and be like the woman he fell in love with forty years ago.'[12] Friends of many years' standing rallied to her cause. These included her cousin Dora, who came to Swaffham Prior from Cambuslang near Glasgow at the time of Edwin's death and 'stood by me'; Mary Bosdêt, a friend from Prague days, offered to come with her typewriter to help Willa answer letters of condolence; Sylvia Lehfeldt, one of her friends from student days and now a civil servant in London, advised Willa and Gavin about lodgings for his new appointment at Kew, and met him at the station when he arrived there. And the Marwicks of Orkney, Ernest and Janette, were regular correspondents, always ready to listen to problems and suggest possible ways forward.

Willa's later life bravery in the face of an uncertain future was reminiscent of the optimistic young woman who extracted an overcautious Edwin from his safe but dull clerking job in Glasgow, just as she had encouraged him to try his luck in London, and then to go adventuring in Europe. On the other hand, she was a woman now approaching 70 years of age, and crippled with arthritis. Lumir Soukup was shocked when he went to visit Willa after Edwin's death, not having met her for some time. He wrote in his memoir of their friendship that when he went to see her at Priory Cottage, his first impression was the sound of her familiar hearty voice shouting to the hesitant daily maid who was asking his name, that 'of course he could come in—did the maid think he was going to rape her!' Lumir continued—

> I was pleased, this was the old Willa, but a few minutes later I was shocked by her appearance: an old, old woman was struggling to get up, moving with difficulty with the aid of two sticks, each step bringing stabs of pain—at first she was so bent that her face was hidden, all I could see was her hair, previously so smooth and well kempt, now slightly ruffled and untidy.[13]

Her fingers were stiff and as she poured the tea made by the maid, holding the teapot in both hands, he could see that her knuckles were swollen and distorted, and that her index finger would not bend, giving her pain. Yet she managed to accompany Lumir to the churchyard to put a bunch of violets on Edwin's grave. In the months after Edwin's death, she would alternate between moods of hopeful determination and more negative feelings of uncertainty. At this early period, the Marwicks of Orkney were important listeners as well as supportive friends, and in early April, feeling 'lonely, sometimes very lonely, with no one here but myself and the pussy-cat', Willa told them that she had given herself two years to remain in the cottage, 'partly because I can't look forward too long, and partly because it costs a lot to keep on this cottage: mortgage, electricity, rates etc., so that I have to earn

---

[12] Letter to Violet Schiff, 1 March 1959, Schiff Papers, BL, Add MS 52920.
[13] Lumir Soukup, Memoir of Willa and Edwin Muir, NLS, Acc. 12007, p. 166.

extra money to do it.' Edwin had been the one to keep an eye on their living costs in the past, just as he had been the one to check the Edinburgh British Council accounts when things went wrong, but now she is on her own. In two years, Gavin might 'be married and settled', she would no longer need to keep a home for him, and could look for somewhere more suited to her pension. She wonders if the Marwicks might find an economical house in Kirkwall, 'something small, not needing much upkeep, because I should have to have at least a daily maid to do the chores I cannot do', and she asks if Orkney, 'being a moist place', might be 'very bad for rheumatism'.[14] The Marwicks must have sent her an encouraging letter in return, for by 21 April she was replying in the guise of what she called 'the advocatus diaboli', listing all the possible difficulties of such a move. Her arthritis, for example, is especially bad.

> I have it in both hip-joints & in the base of my spine. I can't walk very much: I hirple from room to room. I can't stoop or bend except with difficulty. So I need to have domestic help. I can't sweep and clean and carry coals and dustbins. I can only just poke a fire. I can't easily lay it. I can wash up dishes if I sit on a stool at the sink, but trotting back & fore from sink to stove does me in. It's physical movement that is so difficult for me. I have done all the cooking here for the past 2 ½ years only because there was no help for it: anyhow the kitchen adjoins the dining-room and there's a hatch for pushing dishes through. As it was, I usually had to lie down after dishing up a midday or evening meal. (I cooked 2 square meals daily!)

She concludes, 'So I need a stout, energetic woman to do all the things I can't do: and I would need her *every* day, Sundays too. If I get any more decrepit, I should need a resident keeper!' By the time Willa gets to the end of this letter, with its additional examples of her helplessness 'for all ordinary chores', her need of electricity for her electric blanket, and her uncertainty about 'managing oil lamps' or coping with coal fires, her inability to go shopping and so her need to be close to a shop, or to have someone to 'fetch and carry for me', the feasibility of moving to a very different lifestyle in Orkney becomes more and more doubtful. She can still 'write and read and talk'—although she cannot talk very much without getting tired—but having let her friends 'see what kind of decrepit old hulk it is that you are encouraging to come to Orkney', she ends by saying 'I'm not at all sure that it can be done.'[15]

By early May Willa had recovered her spirits and was writing to the Marwicks to apologize for writing 'such a desponding letter' and advising them that she thinks she has now 'gained a spiritual victory over my baser self'. She continues, 'I am no

[14] Willa Muir, letter to Ernest and Janette Marwick, 6 April 1959, Orkney Archives, D31/31/6.
[15] Ibid., 21 April 1959.

longer sorry for myself. I have been mourning Edwin, in appearance, but it was really myself I was grieving for. I shall be all right now.' And by July she appeared to be much stronger in body as well as spirit. Thoughts of moving to a moist Orkney had disappeared, although the Swaffham Prior summer weather seemed 'as bad here as Rome in July or Washington in a heat wave'. With the security of the Bollingen grant transferred from Edwin to herself, she was looking forward to working on the Ballads project, telling the Marwicks that the Foundation had said 'they did not care how long I took to do the work, and that I was to go ahead with a light-heart'. She had also received a prize award of 3000 marks from the German Academy of Language and Literature for the Kafka translations, and although her arthritis prevented her from travelling to the event, the Academy suggested that she write a speech to be delivered by a delegate at the award ceremony. She was now more secure about staying in Swaffham Prior 'for the next few years', and the success of the new chloroquin medicine made her feel that she was 'growing younger and abler every day', adding 'to climb on to a bus is now the goal I have set myself to reach by September.'[16] By November and December it is a much more cheerful Willa who is busy with her projects and replying to letters from Violet Schiff and the Orkney Marwicks. Violet had sent her a copy of a publication titled *Adam*, an international review that contained an account of the Schiffs' life together, which would appear to have been contributed by Violet herself. Willa wrote, 'What a multitude of interesting encounters you have had in your life!', before confessing 'I don't think either Edwin or I realised when we first met you what a predominating influence you and Sydney had been in so many people's lives: we were very ignorant.' She had 'particularly relished' Violet's 'sober account' of a meeting between Proust and Joyce in Paris (they did not get on) and Max Beerbohm's 'delightful caricature' of her husband Sydney. She also tells Violet that she has been correcting the proofs of Edwin's *Collected Poems* and has been comforted by them, although when Edwin died, she 'would have given all the poetry in the world to get him back, himself'. Now she has discovered that 'the essence of him' is in his poems, and so she is lucky to have them as well as her memories of their life together. And she thanks Violet once again for her 'patience and kindness' to her when she was so grief-stricken and 'sending you wild outpourings'.[17] On the practical side, Willa continued to receive regular help from her Prague friend Mary Bosdêt, who came with her own friend Hetty during the summer and autumn to tidy up Willa's garden, presenting her with a dandelion-cutting gadget called a 'Killa-Kane', something Mary considered a much more appropriate gift than Willa's preferred option of Virginian cigarettes.

Willa's December letter to the Marwicks tells of her gradual reintegration into literary society. Although unable to walk very far, she had managed to go up to

---

[16] Ibid., 4 May 1959 and 8 July 1959.
[17] Willa Muir, letter to Violet Schiff, 20 November 1959, Schiff Papers, BL, Add MS 52920.

London for the presentation of the Guinness Poetry Award, given in 1959 to Edwin for his poem 'Impersonal Calamity'. She writes that 'the Guinness people kindly sent a car to take me there and back again, so as I didn't wish to seem ungracious, I gave in, and went.' And her going was 'worth it'. She 'got through the evening very well on champagne' and she read Edwin's prize poem 'without breaking down as I had feared I might'. She met many people she was 'glad' to see again, and had conversations with 'John Lehmann, Day Lewis, Nora Smallwood of Chatto's, Louis McNeice (*not* such a pleasure) and of course, the arch-witch Edith Sitwell, who had the nerve to tell me I hadn't changed in thirty years!' She tells the Marwicks that of course she paid a price for her visit to London, which was duly followed by weekend visitors, including Gavin. Then, sitting up late over some literary work, she forgot the time until she heard midnight striking, and found herself 'crawling on two sticks' again the following morning. She writes that she has 'learned my lesson: I am again taking chloroquin, which I had given up; and I am *never* going to try to do so much again.' Meanwhile, a New Zealand professor is coming to tea in the afternoon 'to talk about Hermann Broch on whom he is writing a monograph', but at least she can ask him to post her letter to the Marwicks.[18]

Edwin's *Collected Poems* was published in April 1960. It was dedicated to Willa, and a final section 'Poems not Previously Collected' was added by Willa and J. C. Hall. This contained poems published individually in journals, together with unpublished ones that Edwin had intended for a separate collection. These late poems included 'The Last War', which had been mentioned in the *Times* obituary, and 'The Refugees Born for a Land Unknown', which even in its unfinished draft condition seems uncannily evocative of the unsolved refugee problems of our own times.

> I have fled through land and sea, black land and sea,
> Because my house is besieged by murderers,
> And I was wrecked in the ocean, crushed and swept
> Spilling salt angry tears in the salt waves.[19]

It is much to the credit of John Hall, and of Willa especially, that even in the midst of their mourning for Edwin, they took the time to search out such uncollected and even unfinished poems to make the *Collected Poems* of 1960 truly representative of Edwin's writing in the last years and even his last months.

Although Willa would never get over her feelings of loss, she would appear to be regaining a sense of her own creative possibilities, qualities that had been marginalized to some extent during her illnesses but also during the years when she had supported Edwin's public career in Europe, Newbattle, and Harvard.

---

[18] Willa Muir, letter to Ernest and Janette Marwick, 17 December 1959, Orkney Archives, D31/31/6.
[19] *Complete Poems*, p. 272.

During a particularly insecure period in post-war Prague, she had written a short aphoristic poem in her diary which ran, 'It is long since bulbs were set in me / So I shall plant bulbs in my front garden / As a wishful sign, / Hundreds of them'.[20] These lines seem to point to a need for creativity and a hope that she herself would imaginatively grow and flower again, as she had when she was writing her novels. Now, in the spring of 1960, there are signs that the old Willa is beginning to re-emerge. Letters to the Marwicks and Violet Schiff refer to the critical success of the *Collected Poems* and to Kathleen's Raine's customary thoughtfulness in raising subscriptions from a number of poets to inscribe a headstone for Edwin's grave at Swaffham Prior. His Orkney friends were also planning a memorial plaque in St Magnus Cathedral in Kirkwall. With Edwin's estate finally settled, 'at long last I have got the executors off my back', future royalties on the *Collected Poems* would now come to her. Another cause for happiness is that Gavin is well and going to be married at the beginning of September—'to a golden-hearted girl, a trained nurse and midwife, whom he has known for nearly nine years'. The ceremony will be in Swaffham Prior church so that Willa can be at the wedding. She is especially delighted that when she herself dies, she can 'safely leave him in his Dorothy's capable and loving hands'. Then, in characteristic self-reflexive Willa fashion, she adds in parenthesis '(I may be a grandmother yet!)'[21] The pair had first met at Newbattle in the early 1950s when Dorothy was employed as a nursemaid to the children of the folk singer Ewen MacColl, who was directing a summer school at the Abbey. Her schoolmaster father's opposition prevented their friendship developing until they met again in later years. Dorothy had trained as a nurse, specializing in midwifery and had a part-time post in Queen Charlotte's Hospital, the hospital where, according to Willa, the upper classes had their babies. Edwin and Willa had been long concerned by Gavin's unexplained deafness, his difficulties with employment and personal relationships, together with a nervous disposition that had persisted over many years. Now it would appear that he had achieved steady employment that drew on his mathematical skills, and a personal relationship with someone he had known and been attracted to over many years. His mother could take a back seat so far as his welfare was concerned and concentrate on her own interests more freely.

That Willa was determined to make something of a writing life for herself again is shown by her plans for a feminist essay or booklet to be called 'This Lopsided World'. Writing to Mary Bosdêt, on 14 January 1960, she announces 'My little book is at its last chapter: its last gasp. But I do hope it will find a publisher, since it seems that my Bollingen subsidy is now at an end, although the work isn't.' And by 2 February David Higham of Agents Pearn, Pollinger & Higham Ltd (whom she

---

[20] Willa Muir, Prague Journal, 14 January 1947, UStA, MS 38466 5/3.
[21] Letters to Ernest Marwick, 30 April 1960, Orkney Archives D31/31/6; and Violet Schiff, 23 May 1960, Schiff Papers, BL, Add MS 52920.

appears to know personally, since they address each other by their first names) is writing to Willa to acknowledge the receipt of her essay. He writes, 'I took this straight home last night and read it with very considerable enjoyment. The difficulty about selling it is, of course, going to be its length. 22000 won't make much more than a booklet.' Another problem is that Willa has chosen the somewhat odd pseudonym of 'Anicula' as opposed to using 'Willa Muir', which Higham rightly suggests would be 'distinctly a factor in its acquiring readers'. Seeking a publisher, he suggests that 'in the normal course of events the Chatto/Hogarth people would be much in my mind, simply because of having published Virginia Woolf whose views weren't by any means dissimilar and for whom they published in this booklet sized form.' Higham must have been thinking here of the Hogarth Essay series, inaugurated in 1924 with Virginia Woolf's *Mr Bennett and Mrs Brown*, followed in 1925 with Willa's own *Women: An Inquiry*. Indeed, 'This Lopsided World' was no less than a return to the investigation of the place of women in society, although now in 1960, her principal interest was to be the situation of old women. Willa replied to David Higham to say that she had looked through 'This Lopsided World' again, and he was 'quite right about its being short'—something that had apparently not struck her previously.

> But what can I do? I am not only an old woman, I am a rather decrepit old woman; and it took me months to concoct even this much. I started it by way of practice, since I was in a very incompetent state and I wanted to exercise my faculties, such as they are; well, I am now much better than I was, and perhaps I could put in a chapter or two: but I don't like padding, and I have pretty nearly said what I wanted to say. I had a notion of sending out a vibration or two into the climate of public opinion, that was all.

So far as anonymity is concerned, she tells Higham that, should a publisher be found, she does not want 'Edwin's name associated with any rancour caused by my speculations: that is why I picked a nom-de-plume'. She accepts that the essay may be difficult to place, 'now that I have looked at it with a more detached eye', and adds 'But it's good middle-brow journalism, isn't it? I don't think it has any literary value—I am not Virginia Woolf. Still, it has tickled my own peculiar sense of humour, and lots of women might enjoy it, and some men as well.'[22]

In her attempt to practise and exercise her literary faculties again after such a long silence, it is interesting that Willa should have returned not to fiction as with *Imagined Corners* and *Mrs Ritchie*, but to the essay form of *Women: An Inquiry* and *Mrs Grundy in Scotland*. She had made another plea for the voice of women to be heard in public life with 'Women in Scotland' published in 1936 in the

---

[22] Willa Muir, letter to Mary Bosdêt, 14 January 1960, Orkney Archives, D51/1/2; David Higham to Willa Muir, 2 February 1960; Willa Muir to David Higham, 3 February 1960; Willa Muir/Higham correspondence from Harry Ransom Centre Archive, University of Texas, HR 234-25; 127–8.

Left Review. In fact, 'This Lopsided World' is almost a later-in-life addition, to 'Alas! We Females', which was an extended feminist essay written jointly, but never published, with her friend Flora Grierson, daughter of the Renaissance scholar Sir Herbert Grierson. Willa may have told David Higham that she was 'not Virginia Woolf', but this does less than justice to her two published novels where her descriptions and dramatic dialogue have significant literary value. On the other hand, and despite her degree from St Andrews University, the intellectually discursive or ironically polemical essay was not her best medium, however much she attempted to employ it in the investigation of issues relating to the nature and status of women in society.

David Higham tried hard to find a publisher for 'This Lopsided World' throughout 1960, but with no success. It was rejected for various reasons, and sometimes for no stated reason, by *The Spectator, Encounter*, and *Twentieth Century* as well as by publishers Victor Gollancz, Philip Toynbee, and Cresset. By 25 September, Willa was asking Higham to return the manuscript, since it 'doesn't seem to cut any ice', and it duly arrived on 2 December 1960.[23] By then she was fully involved with the Bollingen Ballads project, reading and thinking about her approach to the topic and becoming more and more imaginatively involved with it. 'This Lopsided World' was permanently laid aside. Translation work came her way again when Michael Hamburger asked her to translate Hugo von Hofmannsthal's *Der Schwierige—The Difficult Man*—a comedy Edwin and she had enjoyed during their European travels in the 1920s. Hamburger wanted to include the play in a collection of dramas and libretti he was editing for a new Bollingen edition of Hofmannsthal's work, and despite an attack of gastric flu—described to Mary Bosdêt as 'a village epidemic'—Willa was prepared to put the Ballads aside to reacquaint herself with the Hofmannsthal, which she finished 'at top speed' just before Gavin's wedding. And shortly after the wedding she 'wiped something else off the slate—a couple of Kafka fragments: contract signed by Edwin but translation never done: now done and posted'.[24]

Gavin and Dorothy's wedding was the big event of Willa's autumn, taking place at the Swaffham Prior church on 3 September. She gave good accounts of the day to several friends, writing to Mary Bosdêt that it was a 'slap-up success', with a 'beano in the cottage', although she had worried about the wedding feast. The bride, bridesmaids, and 'a handsome best man' (chosen by Willa from former Newbattle students) were all one could have wished for, although Gavin's old blue suit had to be pressed into service (literally) because his planned wedding suit 'arrived first thing on the Monday after, just in time to be too late'. As a 'special indulgence' to herself, Willa had invited her old friend A. S. Neill of Summerhill

---

[23] Willa Muir, letter to David Higham, 25 September 1960, HRC Archive 114.
[24] Willa Muir, letters to Mary Bosdêt, 26 March 1960; 25 September 1960; 16 November 1960, Orkney Archives, D51/1/2.

School, and 'succeeded in keeping him apart from Dorothy's father—who is an elementary school headmaster in Manchester, and, if he had heard of Neill, regards him as a horned and tailed monster'. Willa confessed that she had been 'a bit terrified myself at meeting Pa Hargreaves, for he had already written me the kind of letter headmasters write to Education Committees', but 'under the influence of excellent Riesling (I didn't rise to champagne) Pa Hargreaves became a simple human being enjoying himself no end. Ma Hargreaves, having become too excited, had been prostrated by diarrhoea and didn't come.' In short, the day was a great success. A. S. Neill stayed until the next day, 'but as soon as he was gone I fell into bed and stayed there more or less for nearly a week.' When the wedding photographs arrived some time later, clearly addressed to Gavin and Dorothy, Willa cheerfully tells Mary that '*of course* I steamed open the envelope, had a good look, and made and ordered my selection before eventually sealing the whole up and sending it to the honeymooners when they get back from the Mystery Coach tour of Bavaria.'[25]

Willa shared Christmas 1960 with a friend from the village, since Gavin and Dorothy were spending Christmas with her parents, but would come to Willa for New Year. She had written to Mary Bosdêt shortly before Christmas telling her that she prefers a 'gossipy letter' to Christmas presents. But since her Christmas present had been a 'patent Kleen-e-ze brush to remove cat hairs from my garments' she is now beginning to wonder 'how I look to my friends'. Since her Bollingen grant is scheduled to stop in June, she is trying to get the Ballads book finished by then. She half-promises that she will then 'try to cut down on cigs', a habit Mary strongly disapproved of and regularly tried to make her give up. The Ballads book is progressing well so far as her research is concerned—'I have got it all in my head ... but it will have to be written down, and well written so that it doesn't disgrace the memory of Edwin.'[26]

Willa continued to be much preoccupied with the Ballads throughout the spring, although she also wrote regularly to Mary, telling her in one letter that 'yesterday I had a thrill of pure happiness when I read what I had written, and found it good.' She added, 'This was such an unfamiliar feeling that at first I hardly knew what to do with it.' By this time, Mary was herself looking for a new house after the death of her difficult father. Thinking of the prolonged problems her friend had experienced with old Bosdêt, Willa wrote, 'I hope I don't out-live myself entirely', before adding, 'Although I begin to believe that I have the vitality and persistence of a weed—a dandelion, say—and I may well live too long.' Mary and her friend Hetty were coming to Willa in May to tidy up the garden (and no doubt remove the dandelions), but Willa herself was still 'striding forward' with the Ballads, reporting

---

[25] Willa Muir, letters to Mary Bosdêt, 25 September 1960; 16 November 1960, Orkney Archives 56/1/2.
[26] Ibid., 20 December 1960.

that, 'I really do have some good and exciting ideas, if I can get them all down coherently.'[27] She is sorry that she won't be able to travel to Orkney for the unveiling of Edwin's plaque in the cathedral, but the Ballads are going well and Edwin's Harvard Lectures, will be ready for the publishers in the summer. As well as keeping in regular touch by letter with the Marwicks, Mary Bosdêt, Edwin's niece Ethel, and many other friends, Willa had also re-established contact with earlier Newbattle students such as Tom Scott who had found success in both his university studies and his poetry. In October she is thanking Mary for the gift of new shoes.

> I am wearing them with delight. No pinching, no pressing *anywhere*; they really do fit like gloves; and I can put them on without untying the laces and without trying to use a shoe-horn. I thought that never, never in my life, would I have nice shoes again, and so I am extremely happy. I cannot thank you enough for your kindness.

She adds, 'Gavin is coming tonight, and on Wednesday Kathleen Raine is coming to stay for some weeks; so I shan't be starved of companionship. She and I will fit together very well: she working up-stairs, I down.'[28] At this point, in the autumn of 1961, Willa does seem to have recaptured the spirit of her old self after the despair of Edwin's death. Settled in Priory Cottage, with a routine that works and good friends around her, she had come a long way since the dark days of early January 1959.

Then, unexpectedly, her life took another turn. When Gavin and Dorothy arrived in the late autumn, they suggested that they should come to live with her in Priory Cottage. In fact, the cottage was initially purchased in the joint names of Edwin, Willa, and Gavin, and so after Edwin's death Gavin's request could not be easily denied. Writing in November, to Edwin's niece Ethel, with whom she had become close since Edwin's death, Willa explained, 'It will be less expensive for all of us; at least that's the theory.' Gavin was 'trying to get a job in some Cambridge lab programming computers' and was taking a course in London in preparation for this, and she believed that Dorothy would easily obtain a midwifery post in the Cambridge area. Speaking frankly to Ethel, she continued, 'I shall do my best to make room for them, with grace and generosity, I hope; although by now I am so used to being by myself I may find it queer at first, even a bit cramping if they don't leave me freedom to get on with my work', adding, 'Their world is so different from mine.' Willa also wrote to Mary Bosdêt in November, saying, 'Did I break the news to you that Gavin and Dorothy are coming to live here with me? It was their proposal, not mine, for I regard the prospect with mixed feelings: but they are coming on Dec. 22 as ever is, after which I shall not be alone and can at least

---

[27] Ibid., 3 March 1961.
[28] Ibid., 7 October 1961.

expect to have my fires stoked for me.' Then she pronounced emphatically, 'I shall guard my privacy like a tigress, for I must be left in peace to finish my Ballad book, which is now moving well along.'[29]

The new living arrangement seemed to work reasonably well as they moved into the spring of 1962. Willa wrote to Mary 'learning to ad-just myself' has left her tired. Furthermore, a pipe had burst and flooded the cottage on the day the couple arrived, revealing more problems, prompting the refurbishment of the kitchen with a stainless-steel sink, Dorothy's washing machine, and a complete repainting. Willa tells her friend that, 'it now looks like something out of a Woman's Magazine', and adds—

> But, O! the upheavals I have had to suffer! My bedroom has been painted too, so that it is less slum-like. Every cupboard and bookcase in the cottage has been tidied within an inch of its life: but my writing table, in a corner of the sitting room, is still a fertile compost-heap and will remain so. I can find anything I want on it, and I can't find *anything* I want in any cupboard.

By this point, Gavin had found temporary, if 'ill-paid' employment in the Cavendish Laboratory in Cambridge, and Dorothy had become a Maternity Ward Night Sister in Newmarket Hospital, working three nights a week. This meant that Willa had 'peace all day' to get on with her writing, since Dorothy slept during the days she had night duty, and Gavin was at work all day. But there are clearly tensions between their different living styles, since Willa tells Mary that she can 'retire to my bedroom and work there, if my children want to turn on their T.V.'[30]

By summer the Ballads book was 'heading towards chapter X', and she tells Mary that 'there are days when I am very pleased with it.' One advantage of having Dorothy and Gavin staying with her is that 'I now share in a good supper every night and so have enough to eat.' (Willa was never much of a cook and Mary Bosdêt had introduced her to the packet soups that were new to the market, often sending her several in the post.) But there were disadvantages, too, especially 'the need to keep Dorothy Compulsive, rash creature, from altering things in the house without consulting me at all; but I am learning to undo her nonsense without getting unduly irritated'.[31] Unfortunately, neither Gavin nor Dorothy were gardeners, and the Priory Cottage garden was becoming 'neglected' and 'hard as iron', with the weeds 'vulgarly healthy'. Edwin's grave was being tended by a Mrs Hewitt from the village.

---

[29] Letter to Ethel Ross, 20 November, 1961, NLS Acc. 10557/2; and to Mary Bosdêt, Tuesday Nov. ?? [1961 added in smaller hand, perhaps later], Orkney Archives 56/1/2.
[30] Letter to Mary Bosdêt, 1 February 1962, Orkney Archives 56/1/2.
[31] Ibid., 3 July 1962. 'Dorothy Compulsive' seems to be the nickname Willa has given Dorothy at this point.

Willa is more circumspect when she restarts her correspondence with the Orkney Marwicks, which had lapsed a little as a result of all the changes in her situation. She tells them that she is now 'sharing a proud supper' every evening with Gavin and Dorothy, and that 'G. and D. are fine—both tall, upstanding, handsome & happy: it's a good marriage.' The Ballad book would be finished by Christmas, Edwin's Harvard lectures will be published in September as *The Estate of Poetry*, and she is expecting a visit from the academic Peter Butter, who has 'just done a small book on Edwin for Oliver & Boyd which should come out in the autumn'. Apparently, Peter Butter 'now wants to do Edwin's biography' and is coming to talk to her about it. On the other hand, Kathleen Raine has suggested that Willa should write her own memoirs, and she is 'thinking it over'. She tells the Marwicks that she will not say anything to Butter about the possibility of writing her own memoir of her life with Edwin; and she warns them not to tell anyone outside Orkney, 'for it may mean that I shall keep to myself a lot of material and not pass it on to Peter Butter at all!' 'Anyhow', she continues, 'no one else has my memories or could write the book I might write. But if Peter B. wants to produce an academic work about Edwin he is welcome to do it. Mine wouldn't be academic!'[32] She sends Butter's small paperback to the Marwicks in December together with complaints about her arthritis, which seems to have become much worse again, probably with the winter weather. Gavin is now a research student at St John's in Cambridge, with the idea of taking a PhD, which Willa thinks will be good for his career. He has started playing the piano again, since his in-laws have presented him with 'a decent piano' with a rich tone, despite it being only an upright—inferior to a grand piano in Willa's view. So now they could have music in the evenings as a diversion from the television, with a special musical evening to celebrate the new instrument. A local farmer brought his French horn, so that they had horn and piano concertos. Dorothy played the recorder and sang with 'a sweet and true soprano voice', accompanied by Gavin. They were not without visitors, for Michael had been to tea on the Friday, before the concert, and two young men from Gavin's class at school arrived for tea on the Saturday. Then she had had 'a B.B.C. man for 3 hours on Monday afternoon, discussing the possibility of recording my reminiscences on tape, in about 10 days' time', all of which activities had left her exhausted. Willa told the Marwicks that she believed that Gavin's return to piano-playing showed that he was happy, while she herself was not unhappy, 'but oh! So decrepit', adding that 'it was the whole weekend that did me in.'[33]

The new year began well, with Willa writing to Ethel that she had reached chapter eleven of her Ballad book. By the end of March, however, she was recovering from bronchitis and congestion of the lungs after a bout of gastric flu, so the

---

[32] All refs in this paragraph from Willa's letter to Marwicks 16 July 1962, Orkney Archives, D31/31/6.
[33] Letter to the Marwicks, 3 December 1962, Orkney Archives D31/31/6; letter to Mary Bosdêt 7 November 1962, Orkney Archives 56/1/2.

Ballads had one and a half chapters still to go. Writing to Mary Bosdêt in March, Willa tells her that Dorothy also has been unwell, with laryngitis, although Gavin and Popsy the cat are 'all serene, so far'. She herself is the 'worst offender, easily' in relation to illness, and she has given up smoking for a week 'so you can see that I *have* been ill!' She adds, 'I shan't smoke again if I can help it, but I may not be able to finish the book without cigarettes.'[34] Under the tensions of their various illnesses, however, things were coming to a head with Dorothy. Willa confided to her most trusted friends that when she was bedridden at Easter, her daughter-in-law 'went berserk and abused me at the top of her voice for two days, standing in my bedroom door'. When she felt strong enough to 'totter', Willa got herself driven to Chelsea to spend ten days with Kathleen Raine in her house in Paulton's Square. When she returned to Swaffham Prior, she found that 'all my doings, writing-table etc., had been crammed into my bedroom & the sitting-room turned into a parlour for T.V.' She continued, 'Ever since then I have been trying to make up my mind to go away: but where ... ?' Initially she thought that Dorothy's resentment at what she considered Willa's cluttering up of the sitting room with her table, books, and papers might lessen and the incident be forgotten, until she discovered that Dorothy might also have been intercepting her mail. She explained to Mary that she had been worried about having had no response from an old friend in Edinburgh to whom she had written when she was at her 'lowest ebb' at Easter, despite having sent additional little SOS messages to her and to her daughter. It was only when the friend telephoned in some distress to find out why she had had no reply to her own four letters that she began to suspect that Dorothy might have been intercepting them. Willa promptly arranged to have her mail from Edinburgh sent 'under cover' to a friend's address in the village, and accepted an invitation from Kathleen Raine to stay for a while in the semi-basement flat at Raine's house in Chelsea. This move was planned for September.[35] By August, Willa wrote to Ethel and the Marwicks to explain that Gavin and Dorothy will stay on in the cottage 'and will be much happier without me'. To the Marwicks she confessed, 'You see, Dorothy doesn't like me, and I don't think it's my fault. But I cannot live in an unfriendly ambience.' Now that the Ballad book is finished, however, she can 'make a get-away'. In describing Dorothy's abuse, she believed that her daughter-in-law had been 'over-working and under-sleeping and was having a kind of brain-storm'. Yet she recognized that newlyweds living with in-laws is never easy. Dorothy 'really wants to be Boss in the cottage and has already changed the atmosphere and the look of the interior; our sitting-room is now a shrine for T.V.' Willa concluded 'I don't want to be boss, but I won't be bossed.' To be fair to Dorothy, on the other hand, it could not have been so easy to live with Willa's constant smoking, her mobility difficulties, and all the books and papers that must not be moved or cleared away. Nevertheless,

---

[34] Letter to Mary Bosdêt, Sunday March 17 [1963], Orkney Archives 56/1/2.
[35] Ibid., 6 July 1963.

it was Edwin and Willa's first home of their own, and it was a sad parting. Willa does not mention in her letters any conversation with Gavin on the subject, but she admitted to the Marwicks that Gavin was 'very much in love' with his wife, and 'does whatever she says', and she 'wouldn't come between them, for worlds'. So she was 'clearing out, although with a heavy heart'. In compensation, she knew that she would not be lonely with Kathleen Raine in London. Her letter ends, 'I am sorry to bother you with this news, but I wanted to let you know. And why haven't I written sooner? Frankly, because I've been in hell, as well as ill. Wish me luck, Love from Willa.'[36]

---

[36] Willa Muir, letter to Ethel Ross, 9 August 1963, NLS Acc. 10557/2; and to the Marwicks, 11 August 1963, Orkney Archives D31/31/6.

21
Last Years 1963–1970

Well, here I still am, no' deid yet.

Willa Muir, May 1969

In August 1963 Willa was preparing to move to Paulton's Square in Chelsea, and packing the books she wanted to take with her. She was not helped by the fact that her daughter-in-law had engaged an old man who lived nearby to varnish the sitting room floor with a substance that was making it 'sticky'. She tells her niece Ethel that she thinks Dorothy 'has a spite' against her, which she explains by 'thinking it her duty as a midwife to deliver Gavin from an over-powering mother', which she insists she 'never was, nor am now', conceding 'at least, I never meant to be.' When her books were collected by Pickfords she left Swaffham Prior with the 'Fish' (her local fishmonger), who kindly offered to drive her to Chelsea—'but not in the fish van'. She took Popsy the cat with her, 'because Dorothy is determined not to keep her'. After Christmas, on 27 December, she writes to Ethel again to say she is 'very snug here, with plenty of friends at hand and no lack of intelligent conversation'. She reports that *Living with Ballads* is to be published by Hogarth Press, who have said that 'it's a first-class book'. And she has started another book, 'really my memoirs' and is thinking of calling it 'Belonging'—'it will be all about me & Edwin, utterly personal and so not infringing on Peter Butter's.' In her new home and with a new project she is 'as content as Popsy'.[1]

Willa's move to Paulton's Square brought her back into contact with literary people she and Edwin had known in the past, including her friend from student days Sylvia Lehfeldt, who had praised the Ballad book. Willa wrote to Sylvia in November telling of 'a kind of wild evening last Friday with T. S. Eliot & wife and wife's mamma: very exhilarating and unbuttoned (at least *I* was)'.[2] She had also dined with Stephen Spender, the American Allen Tate, and Herbert Read and their wives; and had lunched with the philosopher John Macmurray and his wife Betty, whom she had known during the Newbattle period, and also with two of her own former students, both now, like herself, widows. Every day, she tells Ethel, she and Kathleen Raine would have 'heart-to-hearts', while other people would 'pop-in', like her old friend A. S. Neill, and Michael Hamburger for whom she had translated *Der Schwierige*. 'I am not lonesome at all. Most of these people are good friends of mine

---

[1] Willa Muir, letters to Ethel Ross, 8 August 1963 and 27 December 1963, NLS, Acc. 10557/2.
[2] Letter to Sylvia Lehfeldt, 12 November 1963, UStA, MS 37237/17/1-54.

and *like* being in my company.' She adds, 'And in this house I know I am liked and wanted, whereas to Dorothy I was an incubus. So I am content. I do need to be liked.' Her basement flat in Kathleen Raine's house was very comfortable, despite its access down what she described as 'a brute of a wooden ladder below street level'. She had a sitting room, bedroom, bathroom and what she called 'a London "passage kitchen"', and a French window to the back of the flat opened out on a 'nice small garden with a paved bit for having tea on'.[3] Because of her arthritis, she was not able to go out and about, to shop or make visits, but she had daily help in her flat, and shopping could be delivered. Perhaps most important was the fact that she had now started on a writing project that would bring her close to Edwin again, as she recalled their life together. She admits that she would have preferred to continue to live in the cottage that was so full of Edwin, but is reconciled to her situation and, as she said to Mary Bosdêt shortly before her move to Chelsea, 'I feel like Martin Luther anyhow in one respect: Ich kann nicht anders' ('I can't do anything else.')[4] She felt the same in March 1964, when Dorothy and Gavin told her that they wanted to sell Priory Cottage because Dorothy had obtained a new post in Huntingdon that included 'a brand-new bungalow'. Willa told Sylvia that she wrote to say, 'I agree', adding, '(What the hell? What's the use?)' She asked Sylvia, who was a civil servant and knowledgeable about business matters, 'Now, if we got £5,000 for it, could I buy an annuity with half of that, which would be my share?' And then she reports, 'The Belonging book is in Chapter V. The Ballad book, they *say*, is coming out this autumn.'[5]

Waiting for the publication of *Living with Ballads* did not trouble Willa unduly, since she was wholly preoccupied with *Belonging*. In the spring of 1964, there was a series of three programmes on the BBC Third Programme devoted to Edwin's life and writing. The first programme consisted of memories of Edwin by various speakers, while the second featured a selection of Edwin's poetry, chosen by T. S. Eliot, who also commented on the poems. The final programme was primarily devoted to Willa's memories of her life with Edwin and had been recorded some time previously, when she was still living in Priory Cottage. The programmes were well received, and Willa was happy about her part in them, although taken aback by a later comment about the series. She wrote to Sylvia Lehfeldt on 14 May, 'I have just been given a body-blow in today's *Listener* by a man called Calder-Marshall, who says he used to visit us in Hampstead and disliked me because I smothered and covered up Edwin.' This seems to have been a common misconception about the couple's relationship, probably as a result of Willa's tendency to be extravagantly loquacious in public, even as she was very dependent upon Edwin in their private life. Her own account of that life, both private and public, absorbed her

[3] Letter to Ethel Ross, 27 December 1963, NLS Acc. 10,557/2.
[4] Letter to Mary Bosdêt, 6 July 1963, Orkney Archives D51/1/2.
[5] Letter to Sylvia Lehfeldt, 9 March 1964, UStA, MS 37237/17/1-54.

throughout 1964. Writing to Sylvia at the end of August she reported that the book was 'struggling on, I am now in Vienna.'[6] At the same time Willa was still in touch with the literary acquaintances who came to Kathleen Raine's evening parties and, writing to the Marwicks and Mary Bosdêt, she was kept up to date with their own activities and travels. She also corresponded regularly with her niece Ethel, who came to visit with her husband Iain, when passing through London, and she acted as a source of information for them when they planned a holiday on Orkney, with details of people to contact, and which parts of the mainland and the smaller isles they should visit, especially Edwin's childhood home of Wyre.

Living with Ballads was published on 11 March 1965, and 'thrown to the wolves, if not to the wolf-whistles', as Willa put it.[7] The book was generally well received. Elizabeth Jennings, whom Willa had much admired when she came to talk about her own writing at the British Council Institute in Prague, described the book as 'knowledgeable, lively, scholarly, and always thorough in its references'. Richard Church found it 'both historical and scientific' but added, significantly, that it was also 'enlightened throughout by a poetic sensibility to the sources of folk song and children's games in the inexhaustible reservoirs of racial emotion'. He found Willa 'fully aware of the significance of oral poetry and its effects upon the more conscious craftsmanship of sophisticated poets'. Ernest Marwick, the Muirs' journalist friend from Orkney whose view of the book Willa was most anxious to receive, wrote that, for him, her book 'succeeded on the plane of careful scholarship, and— which is so refreshing and heart-warming—the plane of imagination and deep human understanding'. He added, 'It seems almost as if destiny has had a hand in reserving this work for you at your greatest maturity of mind; for anyone who knows you well can discover in the book the treasures of a lifetime of study and acceptance of life's sorrows and joys.'[8] A week after its publication, there was also a spontaneous discussion of the book on the Scottish Home Service's *Arts Review* programme on 18 March, following a more formal review of it given by the poet Alexander Scott.

This was a time when there was a revival of folk song traditions taking place in the United Kingdom and elsewhere, and in the following decade there would be a revival of interest in the ballad tradition, especially the Scottish ballads, explored in studies such as David Buchan's *The Ballad and the Folk* of 1972, followed by his anthology *A Scottish Ballad Book* of 1973. Talking of the 1960s folk song revival in the BBC *Arts Review*, Alexander Scott had suggested that Willa was too pessimistic in her view that the ballad tradition could not continue under the changed conditions of later centuries, and that ballads necessarily grew out of a small community.

---

[6] Letters to Sylvia Lehfeldt, 14 May 1964; 24 August 1964, UStA, MS 37237/17/1-54.
[7] Letter to Mary Bosdêt, 19 February 1965, Orkney Archives D51/1/2.
[8] Review comments from Elizabeth Jennings and Richard Church on the book jacket of the Hogarth Press edition, 1965; Ernest Marwick, letter to Willa Muir, Easter Monday 1965, Orkney Archives D31/31/6.

David Irwin, a young lecturer in Fine Art at Glasgow University, who had come to Scotland from the south and was part of the panel discussing Willa's book, was inclined to agree with Scott. He believed that 'Mrs Muir has reached her pessimistic position as a result of her own rather self defining definition of ballads.' Other panellists such as playwright Robert Kemp and Forsyth Hardy, writer and documentary film administrator, also disagreed with Willa's belief that we have lost the 'closed community' that gave birth to the ballad tradition. Kemp wondered 'if there isn't always going to be a closed community even inside our world', while Scott claimed that for him, 'one of the most hopeful things today is the way that the young are reacting against mass communication and have gone back to the ballad and made it their own.' Nevertheless, there was strong praise from Kemp and Hardy for a book that 'comes out with her own stamp'. For Hardy, it was a 'fascinating' book, as Scott had also found in his more formal review of it, and Hardy referred in particular to how 'Willa Muir writes with remarkable warmth of her own days as a schoolgirl and expresses the meaning of these playground songs in a quite delightful and charming way—and that she takes space and time to do that gives the early passages of the book a very special appeal and character.'[9]

While Willa might have found Hardy's 'delightful and charming' a little condescending, it is true that the early chapters on 'Children's Singing Games' (reminiscent of early passages in *Mrs Ritchie* and the young Annie Rattray's, and probably the author's own, playground experiences) do indeed provide a lively and intimate introduction to the topic. More surprising, perhaps, is the way the argument moves from demotic singing games to the Assyrian story of Gilgamesh, Homer's *Iliad*, and the Norse sagas, which is territory not usually cited in discussions of the ballad form. Willa also made a lengthy attack on Scottish Calvinism as a negative force on the ballad tradition, as William Montgomery noted in his review for the journal *Scottish Studies*, and indeed Willa acknowledged that she had to write that particular section of her book several times, to bring her dislike of Calvinism under control. Montgomery's further comment that 'human nature is the subject of this book'[10] is insightful, for human psychology is indeed the theme that underlies all Willa's creative and discursive writings. Readers could enjoy the liveliness and human interest of her new book, even if scholars with a more informed awareness of literature, orality and the ballad tradition, recognized that the title *Living with Ballads* revealed a rather more personal approach to the topic. Flora Grierson commented, 'This book is Willa to the back teeth', to which Willa responded 'but, you see, my back teeth, alas, are false!'[11] It is true that consistency was not always one of Willa's qualities, but for someone who so insisted on her feminism, it is odd that it should not have occurred to her during her research that 'Anon' would so

---

[9] 'Spontaneous Discussion Following Alexander Scott's Review of "Living with Ballads" by Willa Muir', BBC Arts Review, Thursday 18 March 1965, SHS, UStA, MS 38466/8/B12/2.
[10] William Montgomery, 'Review of *Living with Ballads*', *Scottish Studies*, 9, 1965, pp. 221–14.
[11] Willa Muir, letter to the Marwicks, Easter Saturday 1965, Orkney Archives, D31/31/6.

often have been a female singer, or even the female initiator of a ballad. Instead, in her book (apart from the school playground scenarios) the male pronoun 'he' is regularly used in relation to the ballad singer,[12] while many of the ballads discussed are either male working ballads from the North East or ballads dealing with male disputes and activities. There is no mention of a ballad such as 'The Twa Sisters', nor of Anna Gordon, Mrs Brown of Falkland, one of the principal singers and early collectors who learned her ballads from the house servants and the working people around her and sang them—or recreated them—in the traditional way, with a strong focus on love, jealousy, death, and betrayal. *Living with Ballads* is indeed a fascinating book, but it remains an unconventional one in relation to modern studies of the ballad tradition.

By the early autumn of 1965, Willa's arthritis was becoming increasingly troublesome. She wrote to Ethel at the end of August thanking her for the 'lovely Orkney report' she had sent of her holiday there. She was writing on a bank holiday, and so she was alone in the flat, with no daily help coming in as usual. Kathleen Raine seemed to be away from home, and Gavin and Dorothy, with whom she was still in occasional contact, were holidaying in Yugoslavia for 'a week near Lake Bled & then a week on the coast'. And Ethel herself, of course, was just back from travelling in Orkney. Willa, in contrast, was house-bound and could travel nowhere. 'I am FED UP with being crippled', she wrote to Ethel, 'but otherwise all right. I haven't gone gaga yet, although I feel sometimes that the sands are running out.' On a more upbeat note, she tells her niece that Gavin has changed his job again. He is now 'going to be Senior Maths Lecturer in the new Huntingdon Technical College (in September)'. He has also succeeded in obtaining an A.R.C.M. music diploma—a less high qualification than the previous L.R.A.M. performer's diploma, which he had so consistently failed. Willa tells Ethel that he is now qualified to teach music if he wishes to do this and is 'already dreaming of becoming a Professor of Music somewhere'.[13] She does not say what happened to his plans for a doctorate in the field of earthquake studies. At Christmas, Willa is still fretting over her restricted situation, although delighted by a Christmas present from the Marwicks of 'three beautiful hyacinth plants [which] seem to have flown from Orkney into my sitting room'. 'Thank you very much for such a lovely present—an "imaginative present", she tells her friends, explaining that she said 'imaginative' 'because I suffer from silly relatives (by marriage) who think I am a Nice Old Lady and send me Nice Old Lady presents, like nylon caps or shawls'. She insists 'I am *not* a Nice Old Lady, but I do like hyacinths!' She continues, 'Next year, if I am still alive, I am going to be rude to my relatives-in-law and tell them, well before Christmas, that if they want to send me anything, let it be cigarettes!' Winter made

---

[12] See for example p. 158 where, even in a chapter dealing with 'matriarchal ballads', the ballad singer is referred to as 'he'.
[13] Willa Muir, letter to Ethel Ross, 30 August 1965, NLS Acc. 10557/2.

her basement flat less enjoyable. She tells the Marwicks that she is 'as dark as if I were in the dark tunnel of the Orkney winter—probably darker—and I have electric light on somewhere all day'. She also found the season 'unsettling', since she is 'smothered in angels" wings (Christmas cards) and odd parcels which have to be acknowledged, and people who drop in, and I can't write my book until the days get more normal again'. Not being able to write her book also troubles her, 'I need to feel every day I have done something to it'; and she adds in parenthesis '(This is what keeps me alive & young. Yes, young: it's only my legs & hips that think they are old.)' She also gives the Marwicks the news about Gavin, adding that he is going to try again for a L.R.A.M., and is thinking of taking an external Mus. Bac. from Durham University. On the whole, however, 'life has been quiet', except that she 'had a silver cigarette-box stolen (probably by a drunk) and got it miraculously returned, with the help of an Edinburgh Scottish voice on the telephone, AND the police'. She ends with good wishes to all, and the assurance that she is 'keeping warm, and my cat Popsy sleeps on my bed at night and keeps me warmer'.[14]

1966 opened cheerfully for Willa with the news of the publication of Archie Hind's novel *The Dear Green Place*. Archie had been one of Edwin's students at Newbattle, and one of several potentially good writers who had struggled to find a way forward. Willa wrote to Ernest Marwick (a Newbattle student himself) that the novel had arrived from the publishers the morning before, and she had been reading it 'ever since'. She tells Ernest that 'it has wound me up into a state of excited joy, because he has at last got it out on paper and it is so good.' She continues 'Edwin & I knew he had gifts of imagination but we almost despaired of him for a while.' She wishes that Edwin had lived to read the novel, which she feels 'is the best novel that has come out of Scotland since The House with the Green Shutters. Yes, better than Sunset Song!' And she hopes that Ernest, who broadcasts regularly for the Scottish BBC, may be able to get a copy for review. In a further letter to him she goes on to explain that the book is 'hardly a *novel*, it's more a fictionally-disguised autobiography. What Archie has done is to map, with extreme honesty, all the stages of the struggle a sensitive boy has, when he wants to be a writer in a city like Glasgow.'[15] It is not surprising, perhaps, that she could empathize with Archie Hinds' narrative, for this description could be applied equally well to Edwin himself, and his novel *Poor Tom* from 1932. Newbattle students had been much in Willa's mind around this time, for George Mackay Brown was now widely recognized as a poet and short story writer. With a bursary award from the Scottish Arts Council, his poetry collection *The Year of the Whale* was published to acclaim in the spring of 1965, and a collection of short stories had been accepted for publication by Hogarth Press. Tom Scott, too, was making his reputation as poet,

---

[14] Willa Muir, letter to the Marwicks, 22 December 1965, Orkney Archives, D31/31/6.
[15] Ibid., 27 January 1966.

while Ernest Marwick was increasingly successful as a literary reviewer, broadcaster, and writer. In the autumn of 1966, Willa would find herself congratulating him on his two chapters on Orkney traditions in a newly published *New Orkney Book*. It seemed to her that Edwin's strong belief in the creative ideals of Newbattle Abbey was coming to fulfilment, and she regretted that he was not alive to witness it.

In her autumn letter to Ernest Marwick about the *New Orkney Book*, Willa would apologize for not having written for such a long time, telling him that she had been 'saving what energy I have for my Memoirs'. She was now in the second last chapter, about Newbattle, and 'trying to keep it going with a flow and a glow, although it finishes in what amounts to defeat'. As for herself, she acknowledged that 'old age is really catching up on me: if I work for two hours I need to lie flat in bed, with a disprin, for anything up to an hour afterwards, before I can even make myself a cup of tea'. She adds wryly, 'I would need someone to *bring* me a cup of tea so that I could rouse myself to make a pot-ful!' She falls asleep in her chair sometimes and then wakens up 'not knowing where I am, with my spectacles on my nose and my mouth open. It's just ridiculous.' Willa was clearly at a stage of her life where she needed someone in residence to look after her. She had a pleasant daily woman who came for two hours in the morning and managed to do her shopping, but she still had to organize her own meals. When working on her book, she often forgot about the time, only to find her whole day 'somehow out of kilter—making lunch at 2 p.m. and tea at 6, and supper at ungodly hours like ten o-clock'. Then, with a recognizable Willa type of determination, she affirms, 'But I shall get the book done; it shouldn't take so long now.' She had encountered 'a Writers' Block' when starting the Newbattle chapter, feeling that she 'didn't want to come to that end of the story, not at all, nor the next chapter either. But I have got over it.' So far as the period at Newbattle was concerned, she found that she could 'remember very well what everyone else did, but myself', and asked Ernest 'Was it a Gilbert & Sullivan character who "did nothing in particular and did it very well?"' She adds, 'That was me, as I remember!'[16]

In mid-November Willa was still feeling tired. She wrote to the Marwicks 'I am simply no' weel, in a state of nervous depletion, and I have therefore asked Floris Chocolates to send out my Christmas gift boxes for me.' She tells them that they will get one of these boxes and they should think of it as 'coming with my love', although there will be no message attached to it. She admits that she is having 'to lie a lot in bed, just to keep going', adding 'I don't like it, but I can't help it at the moment.' Nevertheless, she has reached the final chapter of her memoir and it should be finished before Christmas, even although she does not really want to come to the end of it. She feels pleased with how it has turned out, saying that she thinks Peter Butter's recent book on Edwin does not have the 'drawing power' of

[16] Ibid., 1 October 1966.

her own. Butter's book is 'painstaking, mostly accurate' and with 'surprisingly good penetration of Edwin's poems (some of them)', but it 'lacks magic, or whatever one calls inspiration, or whatever it was one felt in Edwin himself'. She concludes 'There's no radiance in it, and he over-emphasises the religious motifs that matter more to him than the poetry. At least that's how I feel.'[17] By early January she was feeling a little better, writing to her niece, 'I am not keeping so bad' and being a little more generous to Butter's book, saying that she heard Ernest Marwick and George Mackay Brown reviewing it on the radio. This time she allowed, 'it's such a good book that it ought to be noticed, and it hasn't even been mentioned yet in any weekly or Sunday paper down South, not even the T.L.S.' She also liked the way that he and George conducted the review, 'speaking in clear, confident voices, and saying true things about Edwin'. She added 'I liked especially your story about him muttering "egotist, egotist". So like him!' On the other hand, she wished that Butter had not attempted to explain her in his book, 'for he just can't—at least, I think he can't.'[18]

By this time Willa was 'on the very last lap' of her memoirs, but worried about how to finish them 'for it makes me cry: it's just like yesterday, and I can't bear it.' She wrote to Ernest 'I shall have to cut it short.' This is a telling comment, for in *Belonging*, Edwin's death not only comes very suddenly, but there is nothing at all about the events immediately after his death, no mention of his funeral or where he is buried, no reference to the obituaries, nor to her own response to his death. Now, in January 1967, she was suffering from 'headaches, spine-aches, tire—all the symptoms of an unconscious very unwilling to contemplate the end of the Story. But I am hanging on by my eye-lashes', she tells Ernest, 'and it *will* be finished soon.' (Figure 21.1)[19] The Marwicks must have been concerned about Willa when they received this letter, for it was dated 16 January (a Friday) and by Monday 19th, Ernest was responding from Janette and himself. He wrote—

> You have our love and prayers in your gallant struggle to end your book. We can almost feel what you must be enduring. You have made many a 'fine fecht' and this is one of the bravest. You are turning your necessity to glorious gain. We are very proud of you.[20]

To which Willa replied—

> My dear Ernest, I cannot tell you how much you comfort me! It is good to get 'love' either by telephone or letter, when one needs it, and I did need it, and I

---

[17] Ibid., 17 November 1966.
[18] Willa Muir, letter to Ethel Ross, 11 January 1967, NLS Acc. 10557/2; letter to Ernest Marwick, 16 January 1967, Orkney Archives D31/31/6.
[19] Willa Muir, letter to Ernest Marwick, 16 January 1967, Orkney Archives D31/31/6.
[20] Letter from Ernest and Janette Marwick to Willa Muir, 19 January 1967, Orkney Archives, D31/31/6.

Figure 21.1 Willa Muir in 1967
Source: Orkney Library and Archive

thank you. I have had a mini-breakdown, bed for four days, and feel better now. I have been revising my book, raking out the ash and clinkers; I've done more than half, and will have finished it off by Monday, I think.

She continued, 'In low moods I stigmatise it as "High Prattle", in more positive moods I think it's interesting: whether it does the Muirs justice, I doubt. How can one *ever* catch life convincingly in a book?'[21] By late April, however, Hogarth Press had accepted the book for publication and Willa appeared to be recovering from what she had called her 'mini-breakdown'. She no longer feels as if she had been 'socked at the back of my head by a piece of lead piping'. Her neck tendons still ache, and she is still easily upset and 'flurried', but feels much better than she had been. She tells the Marwicks that Kathleen Raine has been writing her own autobiography, but 'dares not publish it until her parents are dead'. Willa does not say why it should be held over in this way, but adds that although

---

[21] Willa Muir, letter to Ernest Marwick, 16 February 1967, Orkney Archives, D31/31/6.

Kathleen's father is 87 years of age and her mother 85, they 'show no signs of coming to the end of their lives'; so she does not know when 'the book will be let out.'[22] Willa regrets this, for she thinks it is a 'unique book' and a 'candid account' of a woman's development as well as being 'beautifully written'. So far as the publication of her own book with Hogarth is concerned, 'early next year is what I can expect, I am told.' She sounds a little dejected about her own book in this letter, saying she wishes 'it were better than it is, but it's out of my hands now'. She has had to cut 12,000 words from its length, and although she accepts that the book '*was* much too long', the cuts included 'some pet bits I liked.'[23] She is moving on, however, and tells the Marwicks that once she feels able, she will sort out Edwin's papers for passing over to the National Library of Scotland. This must have been an arduous task in itself, but she completed it in 1967, while awaiting the publication of her own memoir of their life together early in the next year.

Willa had kept in touch with several of her Cambridge friends after her move to Kathleen Raine's flat. One of these was Lyn Newman, a journalist and writer, married to a Mathematics professor at the university. Lyn, who at an earlier period in her life had been close to Leonard and Virginia Woolf, had recently completed a biographical book *Alison Cairns and her Family* that told the story of the mother of her friend David Cairns, professor of Theology at Aberdeen University. Uncertain as to whether she would readily find a publisher for her book, and influenced, perhaps, by the example of the Woolfs, she had set up her own publishing and mail-order business *Monologue Books*, and intended to publish the *Alison Cairns* book with this imprint under her maiden name Irvine. According to Lyn in a letter to David Cairns, Willa was at first 'astounded' to hear of Lyn's plans for publication when she told her about them in the autumn of 1966, then 'very excited and sympathetic', saying that, 'it was something more authors should do to escape from the tyranny of the big sales and the commercial slant of the modern publisher.' Willa was at this point writing chapter eighteen of *Belonging*, with two chapters to go. She was intending to send the typescript to Hogarth Press to see if they would be interested in publishing it, but had told Lyn that she might follow her example if Hogarth turned it down. Lyn told Cairns of Willa's surprise and interest in her plans, before saying rather unkindly, 'I did not offer to do it for her, because I fear I am going to find it rather dull.' But she was wrong in her assumption, for Hogarth Press liked the book, and after its publication in January 1968 David Cairns would find himself writing to Newman (who had sent him a copy), 'What a splendid and handsome present. I have just read it (Sunday) from cover to cover, and I have

---

[22] Raine's autobiography was published as a series of three volumes, *Farewell Happy Fields* (1974), *The Land Unknown* (1975) and *The Lion's Mouth* (1977), later collected as *Autobiographies* (1991). Influenced as a poet by Blake and Yeats, she imposed a certain mythic patterning on her own life story.

[23] Willa Muir, letter to Ernest and Janette Marwick, 27 April 1967, Orkney Archives, D31/31/6.

been dipping into Edwin's own life.' He ended 'Now I must turn to Edwin's poems again. Thank you a thousand times!'[24]

David Cairns was not alone in his enjoyment and praise of *Belonging*. Willa was especially delighted by double reviews in *The Orcadian* by George Mackay Brown and Ernest Marwick, writing to Ernest that George had sent her the paper with the reviews in it and that 'they simply overwhelmed me'; and that she would 'never be able to live up to such testimonials'.[25] Reviews in other newspapers and magazines were equally encouraging. Elizabeth Jennings found *Belonging* 'a really important book' which was not only the testament 'of a really indomitable woman and wife' but one which also 'throws a hitherto shadowy light on a poet who must surely now be regarded of the first order'. Janet Adam Smith found that 'in journeying through the years with Edwin', Willa had 'written a book to stand by his *Autobiography* and *Collected Poems* as fitly as Helen Thomas's story of her marriage stands besides the *Poems* of Edward Thomas'. In the Scottish press, *Belonging* was reviewed by Cuthbert Graham as a Book Choice of the week, and Kay Dick described the book as 'a very interesting social memoir of the last 50 years'—an acute perception, since Willa's narrative is much more than the story of a marriage, being also a story of social and political change in Britain and Europe in the decades after the First World War. Philip Toynbee, on the other hand, was more questioning in his review, although he also found that the book described 'a remarkable marriage between two good and interesting people'. He regretted that Willa had deliberately avoided covering ground already explored in Edwin's *An Autobiography*, and felt that this approach had left us 'with only the scraps of their long, loving and productive life together'. In his opinion, *Belonging* was 'a very feminine book', with Willa's femininity 'established by the combination of excessive garrulity with a certain feyness in more important matters'.[26] It's not known if Willa read these comments, but it is not difficult to imagine her likely reaction. She was, however, pleased with the book's general reception, and particularly happy about the response of readers who spontaneously contacted her about it. She wrote to Mary Bosdêt at the end of January, 'Don't worry about me, at present. If I can judge from the letters I am getting, my book has given great pleasure to lots of people, and Jill Balcon has just moved me nearly to weeps by an enthusiastic tribute on the telephone.' And she added, in a very Willa-like ironic response, 'I shall make some money on it, after all!' before continuing, 'I do feel very humble when I get so much praise, for it was

---

[24] Letter from Lyn Newman to David Cairns, 22 September 1966, University of Cambridge, St John's Library/Newman L./Cairns, D.30; letter to Lyn Newman from David Cairns 21 January 1968, St John's Library/Newman L./Cairns, D/28.

[25] Willa Muir, letter to Ernest Marwick, 14 February 1968, Orkney Archives D31/31/6.

[26] All review notices from Orkney Archives D31/31/4. Janet Adam Smith review from *Listener*, 1 February 1968; Elizabeth Jennings from Hogarth Press advertisement in *Listener*, 1 February 1968; provenance and date are missing from cuttings of reviews by Philip Toynbee, Kay Dick, and Cuthbert Graham.

my Unconscious that inspired & wrote "Belonging", and *it* should get the credit, though I may pocket the royalties.'[27]

By late January 1968, Willa was beginning to think of making a move from Kathleen Raine's semi-basement flat. Her arthritis was making her increasingly immobile, and she needed someone to make meals and help her with general care. Mary had sent information about financial assistance for 'gentlewomen', but Willa did not think she would qualify for this, since the income cut-off point was £400, which was lower than the sum of her own pension and royalties. She also told Mary, ironically, that she had noticed that the Fund asked for one's father's profession or occupation, and she did not think her father's occupation—'a draper in Montrose' and 'a very bad shopkeeper, who gave credit to all the hard cases who asked for it'—would assist her to qualify as a gentlewoman. Instead, another friend was 'doing her best' to get Willa accepted at a home for educated women called Meadowcroft, near Swaffham Prior, where she wanted to be buried beside Edwin, and also near Ely where Gavin was now living. Meadowcroft was run by the British Red Cross, and if she were to be accepted for a place, then she would aim to make the move from London in June or September. One possible 'big snag', however, might be her cat Popsy—'probably not allowed'.[28]

Willa was eventually accepted for Meadowcroft but did not manage to move from London until February 1969. Her health was deteriorating and she was particularly concerned about her poor eyesight, something that is noticeable in the greatly increased size of the handwriting in her letters. For some time now, she had had a telephone extension in her flat, so she could talk to friends when her eyes were too tired for writing. Another problem that had been developing over the year came to a head in these months. Gavin and Dorothy did not seem to have learned from their experience of living with Willa, for after Dorothy's father retired from his headmaster's post, he and her mother came to stay with them. Dorothy's father was an ambitious man, proud of his educational status, with little time for the unsuccessful. Gavin's frequent changes of employment did not look like the kind of successful partner he had envisaged for his daughter. Serious tensions in the shared household would appear to have brought Gavin, now a man in his 40s, once more into a nervous condition, perhaps approaching a breakdown in his health. Willa wrote to the Marwicks to find if Gavin could visit them in Orkney for a short break, and she seems to have asked Ernest about the prospects for some kind of teaching employment in Orkney. Unfortunately, the Marwicks could not accommodate Gavin because their spare rooms were already taken, and teaching posts on the islands were in short supply. Willa gave Ernest more details about her son's situation. Apparently, Gavin's father-in-law had made it clear that he considered him 'a reproach, a disgrace and a failure, because he doesn't stand up to

---

[27] Willa Muir, letter to Mary Bosdêt, 30 January 1968, Orkney Archives D56/1/2.
[28] Ibid.

interviewing Committees', and this was driving Gavin into himself and sapping what confidence he might have. Dorothy, on the other hand, was now matron of a maternity clinic, and had just returned home after spending two weeks attending a midwifery conference in Hastings. She could not take time off from her responsible position to have a short break with Gavin, and Willa wrote, 'It wrings my heart to think of what Gavin suffers in that atmosphere.'[29]

Dorothy's father may have been harsh in his judgement of Gavin, but it may be that Willa was not entirely blameless, for how she and Edwin had repeatedly encouraged their sons' ambitions over so many years, when his skills and his temperament were never, perhaps, quite sufficient to match his musical ambitions, nor his intellectual abilities up to the work required for a doctorate. Willa's ambitions for her son may have blinded her to his fragility and his need for professional help. Gavin's nervous collapse at this point in Willa's life was particularly distressing for her because—as she wrote to the Marwicks—'I am so helpless.' And she did not have 'much money either to give Gavin, so that he is not dependent on his wife', who is, Willa adds in brackets, 'well-paid'.[30] She was grateful to Ernest, however, for suggesting employment in the tutorial college system, and for giving her the address of what he considered to be the best tutorial college—Basil Paterson and Ainslie in Edinburgh.

In early January Willa was corresponding with Tom Scott, who was thinking of preparing anthologies of poems by Edwin and the medieval poet Henryson. She told him that on 13 February she was moving from Paulton's Square 'to a Home for Educated Elderly Ladies (!) run by the British Red Cross', signing off, 'Wish me luck—Yours, very decrepit, Willa.' Willa was writing to Tom again in April, this time from a small private nursing home at Church Farm, Over. Explaining the move, she told him that she had been extremely ill with flu at Meadowcroft, but that 'the Matron was furious, being a martinet and understaffed, & kept repeating that Meadowcroft was not a nursing home, and that I was malingering.' Hearing of Willa's plight, Professor Lionel Knights (who had invited Edwin to give a series of lectures at Bristol University the year before he died, and had offered financial help when the poet was in hospital in December 1958), arranged for a doctor to visit her in Meadowcroft. When she was well enough, 'some superior authorities of the Red Cross simply shifted me here', to Church Farm, with her furniture.[31] By the end of April, Willa had recovered to some extent from her ordeal at the Red Cross Home and was writing to Ernest in Orkney to bring him up to date with her situation. Ernest told her that passages from *Belonging*, along with some of Edwin's poems, had been read from the St Magnus pulpit. She replied 'goodness, fancy my book figuring in a Cathedral pulpit!', adding, ' I am not so amazed at Edwin's poems

---

[29] Ernest Marwick, letter to Willa Muir, 5 December 1968, Orkney Archives D31/31/6; Willa Muir, letter to Ernest Marwick, 7 December 1968, Orkney Archives D31/31/6.
[30] Willa Muir, letter to Ernest Marwick, 7 December 1968, Orkney Archives D31/31/6.
[31] Willa Muir, letters to Tom Scott, 13 February 1969 and 19 April 1969, NLS, MS 19703.

doing so. You didn't tell me *which* poems—would you mind telling me?' She is 'learning to walk again with a "walking frame"—I never knew they existed—soon I shall be able to sit at the telephone in the hall and talk a bit', adding, 'But *not, not,* if it comes too expensive for you.' George Mackay Brown had been writing to her about Gavin, who had moved to Edinburgh and was now working at the Basil Paterson Tutorial College. Gavin seemed to be 'well and happy', and Willa thanked Ernest for his initial recommendation. Dorothy's comment on this new employment had been, 'a private college, no holiday pay, no pension', which Willa considered typical of the Hargreaves' general attitude. But Church Farm was close to where Dorothy lived, and when she came to visit, Willa assured Ernest, 'we are on good terms. I just won't interfere—I mustn't.'[32]

Willa settled in well to Church Farm, although she was worried as to how long her own financial situation would enable her to stay there. She was cheerful, however, and at the end of May is sending Ernest and Janette 'some bits of verses I made up before Christmas, thinking they would be a kind of farewell gesture to my friends, for I was sure I was just going to die soon. Well, here I still am, no' deid yet; indeed getting stronger every day. So I'll have to stand the consequences of having the verses in print!' These verses were *Laconics and Jingles*, with the laconics written in response to Edwin's death. She describes the collection, 'The laconics are sad, the jingles cheerful enough, the verses not bad, I hope.'[33] By the end of June, Willa was still improving in health and decided to take up an offer to stay with Lilias Chisholm, widow of the composer Eric Chisholm and daughter of Edwin's old friend, the musician F. G. Scott. Lilias—still known to most of her friends as 'Lovey Scott'—invited Willa to come to St Andrews and stay with her in her North Street house. This was the university town where Willa had been so successful and popular as a young woman, and she was worried about the costs of staying in the privately run Church Farm, so the offer of a home in St Andrews was particularly appealing. Willa wrote to the Marwicks and other friends, telling them of her coming removal, and towards the end of September she was making final preparations for the move north. She wrote to Ernest and Janette on 21 September, 'I am just in the throes of trying not to forget this & that when getting ready to go away tomorrow, and I am cast down by my own inefficiency!' After giving them her new address, she continues 'I can scarcely believe it: I am full of old-age-anxiety & hope I'll get to Leuchars all right.' She says she is 'seething' with 'plain incompetence and self-doubt', but also that Lovey Scott 'knows what I am like, for she came here to urge me to come & live with her, but no one else in Scotland is aware of how broken-down I am, & I fear they are all going to be disappointed'. Asking Ernest and Janette to 'forgive this little outburst', she tells them that she departs at 1 p.m. the next day, and will meet a former Newbattle student, Spike

---

[32] Willa Muir, letter to Ernest Marwick, 30 April 1969, Orkney Archives D31/31/6.
[33] Ibid., May 1969, Orkney Archives D31/31/6.

Mays, at Heathrow airport, who will see her on to the Leuchars flight. She signed off (as so often in this period of her life), 'Wish me luck! Much love from Willa.'[34]

Unfortunately, the move to St Andrews was disastrous. After only nine days, Lovey Scott told Willa that she had made a mistake in offering her a home, having previously promised to help a friend start up a tea room and small gallery in Falklands in Fife. Willa was forced to move into a hotel. On 9 October she wrote to Sylvia Lehfeldt, 'Sylvia my dear Edwin's niece is taking me in on Saturday (this hotel shuts for the winter on Sunday)'; followed by 'Lovey Scott (Mrs Chisholm) is not ill-meaning but stupid. Love Willa.' Later, on 24 October, she again wrote to Sylvia.

> The effects of the shock I got from Lilias Chisholm's treatment, my discovery that her offers of loving care and a home were bogus play-acting, are gradually fading, although I am still mostly in bed (shortness of breath & troubled heart). What a *fool* I am to have believed her, to have taken her transitory impulse for genuine good will! Shall I ever learn not to be so naive? It is a bit late to learn that now.[35]

Willa was full of good words for Edwin's niece Margaret, who had given her a temporary home in Dunoon on the Clyde Coast. She then moved to stay with Edwin's nephew Jim and his wife, also in Dunoon, in a house above the British Linen Bank. They themselves were planning to move to another house on Jim's retirement in June 1970, and promised Willa a home with them for the rest of her life. By early December, Willa felt strong enough to write to the Marwicks, thanking them for 'a golden box of cigs', telling them 'I am very comfortable here in Life Above Stairs; I think I shall stay here for months.' Her eyes, however, were 'still not good'.

At the beginning of January 1970, Willa wrote to Mary Bosdêt that the Asian flu now 'ravaging' Scotland had hit Dunoon 'a dreadful wallop', and she had had 'another (and unwelcome) brush with the enemy'. She ended her letter, 'My transistor needs no repairs at all. But, O dear, *I* do.' Yet she still had the spirit to write to Kathleen Raine in April 1970, 'I *might* get a small book done.'[36] Then, on 22 May, quite unexpectedly, but peacefully, Willa died. She did not have the time in Scotland to enjoy the care of Edwin's relations nor to meet with her former friends. She was cremated at Greenock Crematorium on 25 May, with a small number of relatives and friends at the funeral service. Gavin played some of her favourite music on the organ. Her ashes were scattered by Gavin on Edwin's grave in Swaffham Prior, where she had hoped to be buried beside him.

---

[34] Ibid., 21 September 1969, Orkney Archives D31/31/6.
[35] Willa Muir, letters to Sylvia Lehfeldt, 9 October 1969 and 24 October 1969, UStA, MS 37237/17/1-54.
[36] Willa Muir, letter to the Marwicks, 10 December 1969; to Mary Bosdêt, 2 January 1970; to Kathleen Raine, 5 April 1970, Orkney Archives D31/31/6, Orkney Archives D56/1/2, NLS MS 19703.

With Willa's death coming relatively soon after the publication of *Belonging*, it was almost inevitable that obituaries would focus on her life as Edwin's partner. Nevertheless, the *Glasgow Herald* of 27 May 1970 described her as 'a writer of distinction' and 'an equal partner in many ways' to her poet husband. Compared to the somewhat dour and limited nature of its obituary on Edwin, the *Herald*'s remembrance of Willa—perhaps helped by the information in *Belonging*—gave prominence to the importance of the Muirs' work as the translators of Kafka, introducing his writings to the English-speaking world. Willa's part in this was recognized, as also her part in the nurturing and encouragement of the adult students who came to study at Newbattle when Edwin was warden there. The obituary recognized her 'novels and other work' and her study of the Scottish ballads, but it ended with a reference to 'her own memoirs, *Belonging*, in which, characteristically, she considered her own life almost wholly in terms of the partnership with her husband'. *The Orcadian* of 29 May gave much more information about Willa's Shetland ancestry, her achievements as a first-class honours student at the University of St Andrews in the early years of the century, and her position, when she met Edwin, as vice principal and lecturer at Gipsy Hill Teachers Training College in London—a significant achievement at a time when women were still fighting to obtain voting rights. Their joint translation work, on Kafka and other German-speaking European writers, was given less prominence, however, being described as 'bread-and-butter labours'. There was no recognition, as there would be today, of Willa's principal role in such translation activity, which was seen only as something that took time away from her 'outspoken novels *Imagined Corners* and *Mrs Ritchie*, as well as that brilliant exposé of Scottish religiosity and respectability, *Mrs Grundy in Scotland*'. At least her creative work was recognized in this account, even if *Belonging* was given the last word, being described, in Willa's own words, as the tale of 'a pair of ingenuous people who fell in love and went journeying together through life, blundering by good luck in the right directions so that we came to a lasting wholeness and joy in each other.'

No obituary, nor perhaps any biography, can hope to catch the complexity of a life, and in this case the complexity of two lives, sometimes intertwined, sometimes separate from each other. Perhaps Willa's memoir was indeed written, as she herself suggested, by her 'Unconscious', and perhaps that Unconscious self was making sure that her time with Edwin was already written into his life as poet, for *The Story and the Fable* and its updated version *An Autobiography* are both, as was Wordsworth's *The Prelude*, essentially the story of the growth of a poet's mind, and Willa played a significant part in that story. Edwin was to call his marriage 'the most fortunate event in my life', saying that, 'if my wife had not encouraged me it is unlikely that I would have taken the plunge myself' in order to escape from the limitations and the traumas of his Glasgow life. Equally important, in Edwin's growth as a poet in his early years, was his friendship with John Holms, described by Edwin as 'the most remarkable man I ever met', and as his 'chief friend in

London and for many years afterwards'. Holms was the person who taught Edwin 'to see things with my own eyes', and encouraged his early attempts at poetry in Dresden. If Willa could not accommodate him, it was because his presence, and his influence on Edwin, made her feel unfairly marginalized, when so much of her love for Edwin had to do with their experience of 'belonging' together.

Edwin and Willa were complex and creative individuals, although their creativity took different routes. Willa's loss of literary activity from the late 1930s to the 1950s was mostly as a result of constant ill health, much of it deriving from her wish to have a child at a comparatively late age, followed by the difficult birth of her son, and a lack of proper healthcare afterwards. Nor did her heavy smoking help, so common with 'independent' women at the time. Willa did not, as some commentators have suggested, give up her own ambitions as a writer in order to allow her poet husband to develop his. Her lively letters to friends as well as her more troubled private diaries show how much she wanted recognition of her own, but she knew that her talents were of a different nature from those of Edwin. These talents were the powers that brought her, in a brave old age, the recognition she deserved with her own interpretation of the ballads and her lively account of the people and places she and Edwin met in their various travels throughout their life together. More recently, there has been a proper recognition of the central part she played in the couple's German-language translation work, as well as a major critical assessment of her debut novel *Imagined Corners*.

The Muirs' joint story is a story of Scotland, England, and Europe, at critical points in the history of the twentieth century, a history of spiritual crisis, war, and dispossession. It is also the story of an outstandingly clever young woman's struggle to find a place where she could be both a wife and mother, and also recognized as an individual writer in a society that was still predominantly patriarchal. Her companion's story is the story of a young man who overcame a lack of schooling, and the shock of moving from agrarian Orkney to an industrialized Glasgow, to express the traumas of modernity as well as what is humanly timeless, in a poetry that is still read and valued today. Their story has left an enduring social, political, and artistic record of what it was to live in the twentieth century, and how much it meant to share it with a loving partner.

Appendix

Translations by Willa and Edwin Muir, by author in chronological order, with acknowledgements to Peter Butter, *Edwin Muir: Man and Poet* (Edinburgh: Oliver and Boyd, 1966). Titles marked *translated by Willa Muir alone. RW.

Asch/Ash, Sholem. *Three Cities*, trans. by Willa and Edwin Muir (London: Victor Gollancz, 1933); (New York: Putnam, 1933).
Salvation, trans. by Willa and Edwin Muir (London: Victor Gollancz:1934); (New York, Putnam, 1934).
Mottke the Thief, trans. by Edwin and Willa Muir (London: Victor Gollancz, 1935); (New York: Putnam, 1935).
The Calf of Paper, trans. by Edwin and Willa Muir (London: Victor Gollancz, 1936); pbd. in U.S. as *The War Goes On*, trans. by Willa and Edwin Muir (New York: Putnam, 1936).

Broch, Hermann. 'The Proposal. Chapter from a Novel by Hermann Broch', trans. by Edwin and Willa Muir, *The Modern Scot* 3:2 (Aug. 1932) 98–103 (from *The Sleepwalkers*).
The Sleepwalkers: A Trilogy (*The Romantic, The Anarchist, The Realist*), trans. by Willa and Edwin Muir (London: Martin Secker, 1932); (Boston: Little, Brown, 1932).
The Unknown Quantity, trans. by Willa and Edwin Muir (London: Collins, 1935); (New York: Viking Press, 1925).
'A Passing Cloud', trans. by Willa Muir. *The Modern Scot* 4 (1934) 302–12.

Burckhardt, Carl Jacob. *Richelieu and His Age: His Rise to Power*, abridged and trans. by Edwin and Willa Muir (London: Allen & Unwin, 1940); (New York: OUP, 1940).

Carossa, Hans. *'A Roumanian Diary'*, trans. by Agnes Neill Scott (London: Martin Secker, 1930); New York: Knopf, 1930).
**A Childhood*, trans by Agnes Neill Scott (London: Martin Secker, 1930); (New York: Cape and Smith, 1932).
**Boyhood and Youth*, trans. by Agnes Neill Scott (London: Martin Secker, 1931); (New York: Warren and Putnam, 1932).
**Doctor Gion*, trans. by Agnes Neill Scott (London: Martin Secker, 1933); (New York: Ballon, 1933).

Feuchtwanger, Lion. *Jew Süss*, trans. by Willa and Edwin Muir (London: Martin Secker, 1926); pbd. in US as *Power* (New York: Viking Press, 1926).
The Ugly Duchess, trans. by Willa and Edwin Muir (London: Martin Secker, 1927); (New York: Viking Press, 1928).
Two Anglo-Saxon Plays: The Oil Islands; Warren Hastings, trans. by Willa and Edwin Muir (New York: Viking Press, 1928); (London: Martin Secker, 1929).
Success: Three Years in the Life of a Province, trans. by Willa and Edwin Muir (London: Martin Secker, 1930); (New York: Viking Press, 1930).
Josephus trans. by Willa and Edwin Muir (London: Martin Secker, 1932); (New York: Viking Press, 1932).

The Jew of Rome, trans. by Edwin and Willa Muir (London Hutchinson & Co., 1935); (New York: Viking Press, 1936).
The False Nero, trans. by Edwin and Willa Muir (London: Hutchinson & Co., 1937). pbd. in US as *The Pretender* (New York, 1937).
*Paris Gazette, 'trans. by Willa and Edwin Muir' (New York: Viking Press, 1940).
Glaeser, Ernst. *Class of 1902*, trans. by Willa and Edwin Muir (London: Martin Secker, 1929).
Harsányi, Zsolt de. *Through a Woman's Eyes*, trans. by Willa Muir and Edwin Muir (New York: Putnam, 1940), pbd. in UK as *Through the Eyes of a Woman* (Routledge, 1941).
Lover of Life, trans. from the Hungarian by Paul Tabor in collaboration with Willa and Edwin Muir. (New York: Putnam, 1942).
Hauptmann, Gerhart. *Dramatic Works*, vol. VII, trans. by Edwin and Willa Muir (London: Martin Secker, 1925); (New York: Huebsch, 1925), contains *Indipohdi, The White Saviour, A Winter Ballad*.
The Island of the Great Mother, trans. by Willa and Edwin Muir, (London: Martin Secker, 1925); (New York: Huebsch, 1925).
Dramatic Works, vol. IX, trans. by Edwin and Willa Muir (London: Martin Secker, 1929); (New York: Huebsch, 1929), contains *Veland* 'trans by Edwin Muir'.
Heuser, Kurt. *The Inner Journey*, trans. by Willa and Edwin Muir (London: Martin Secker, 1932); pbd. in US as *The Journey Inward* (New York: Viking Press, 1932).
Kafka, Franz. 'Aphorisms by Franz Kafka', '(Translated from the German by Willa and Edwin Muir)', brief introduction by Edwin Muir, *The Modern Scot* 3:3 (Oct. 1932) 202–8.
The Castle, trans. by Willa and Edwin Muir, with introductory note by E. Muir v–xii (London: Martin Secker, 1930); (New York: Knopf, 1930).
The Great Wall of China and Other Pieces, trans. by Willa and Edwin Muir (London: Martin Secker, 1930); (New York: Schocken, 1946).
*'First Sorrow', trans. by Willa Muir, *European Quarterly*, I (1934), 46–9.
The Trial, trans. by Willa and Edwin Muir, with introductory note by Edwin Muir vii–xvi (London: Victor Gollancz, 1937); (New York: Knopf, 1937).
America, trans. by Willa and Edwin Muir (London: Routledge & Sons, 1938); (Norfolk: New Directions, 1940).
'From Kafka's Diaries: Excerpts', trans. by Willa and Edwin Muir, *The New Statesman*, XXXI (1941), 321–2.
**'Selections from the Diaries and Notebooks of Franz Kafka', *Orion*, I (1945), 104–15.
Kühnelt-Leddihn, Erik Maria von. *Night Over the East*, trans. and adapted by Edwin and Willa Muir (London: Sheed & Ward, 1936); (New York: OUP, 1936).
Lothar, Ernst. *Little Friend*, trans. by Willa and Edwin Muir (London: Martin Secker, 1933).
The Mills of God, trans. by Willa and Edwin Muir (London: Martin Secker, 1935); pbd. as *The Look of Justice* (New York: Putnam, 1935).
Mann, Heinrich. *The Hill of Lies*, trans. by Edwin and Willa Muir (London: Jarrold Ltd., 1934); (New York: Dutton, 1935).
Neumann, Robert. *The Queen's Doctor: Being the Strange Story of the Rise and Fall of Struensee, Dictator, Lover and Doctor of Medicine*, trans. by Edwin and Willa Muir (London: Victor Gollancz, 1936); (New York: Knopf, 1936).
A Woman Screamed, trans. by Willa and Edwin Muir (London: Cassell and Co., 1938); (New York: Diall, 1938).

Paléologue, Georges Maurice. *The Enigmatic Czar: The Life of Alexander I of Russia*, trans. by Edwin and Willa Muir (London: Hamish Hamilton, 1938); (New York: Harper, 1938).

Reinhardt, E. A. *The Life of Eleanora Duse*, trans. by Willa and Edwin Muir (London: Martin Secker, 1930).

Renn, Ludwig (pseud. of **Arnold Friedrich Vieth von Golssenau**). *War*,
trans. by Willa and Edwin Muir (London: Martin Secker, 1929); (New York: Dodd, Mead, 1929).

After War, trans. by Willa and Edwin Muir (London: Martin Secker, 1931); (New York: Dodd, Mead, 1931).

Winsloe, Christa (Baroness Hatvany). * *The Child Manuela*, trans. by Agnes Neill Scott (New York: Farrar and Rinehart, 1933); (London: Chapman and Hall, 1934).

* *Life Begins*, trans. by Agnes Neill Scott (London: Chapman and Hall, 1935); pbd. in US as *Girls Alone* (New York: Farrar and Rinehart, 1936).

Bibliography

Allan, Kirsty. *The Life and Work of Willa Muir, 1890–1955* (PhD research repository, University of St Andrews, 1997).

Anonymous review of *Poor Tom*, *The Modern Scot*, 3.3 Autumn 1932.

Barker, George. 'Coming to London', *London Magazine*, vol. 3, no. 1, January 1956.

Bold, Allan. *MacDiarmid: Christopher Murray Grieve: A Critical Biography* (London: John Murray, 1988).

Bradbrook, Bohuslava. *Karel Čapek: In Pursuit of Truth, Tolerance, and Trust* (Brighton: Sussex Academic Press, 1998).

Bradbrook, Bohuslava. *The Liberating Beauty of Little Things: Decision, Adversity & Reckoning in a Refugee's Journey from Prague to Cambridge* (Brighton: The Alpha Press, 2000).

Bradshaw, David, ed. *Virginia Woolf: Selected Essays* (Oxford: Oxford University Press, 2008).

Broch, Hermann. *Die Briefe, Gesammelte Werke 8* (Zurich; Rhein-Verlag 1950–1961).

Broch, Hermann. *Die Unbekannte Grösse und Frühe Schriften. M den Briefen an Willa Muir* (Zurich: Rhein-Verlag, 1950–1961).

Broch, Hermann. *The Sleepwalkers*, trans. by Edwin and Willa Muir (Berkeley, California: Northpoint Press, 1985).

Brown. George Mackay, ed. and intro. *Edwin Muir: Selected Prose* (London: John Murray, 1987).

Butter, Peter H. *Edwin Muir*. Writers and Critics Series (Edinburgh: Oliver & Boyd, 1962).

Butter, Peter H. *Edwin Muir: Man and Poet* (Edinburgh: Oliver & Boyd, 1966).

Butter, P. H., ed. *Selected Letters of Edwin Muir* (London: The Hogarth Press, 1974).

Butter, Peter, ed. *The Complete Poems of Edwin Muir. An Annotated Edition* (Aberdeen: The Association for Scottish Literary Studies, 1991).

Carossa, Hans. *Eine Kindheit*, Insel Taschenbuch (Leipzig: Insel Verlag, 1922).

Carossa, Hans. *A Childhood*, trans. by Agnes Neill Scott (London: Martin Secker, 1930).

Carswell, Catherine. 'The Grundy Women', *Spectator*, 22 May 1936.

Christianson, Aileen. *Moving in Circles: Willa Muir's Writings* (Edinburgh: Word Power Books, 2007).

Closs, August, ed. *Harrap Anthology of German Poetry* (London: Harrap, 1957).

Cruickshank, Helen B. *Octobiography* (Montrose: Standard Press, 1976).

Fergusson, Maggie. *George Mackay Brown: The Life* (London: John Murray, 2006).

Gaskill, Howard. 'Edwin Muir in Hellerau', *Scottish Literary Journal*, vol. 11, no. 1, May 1984.

Gaskill, P. H. 'Edwin Muir's Friend in Hellerau: Iwar von Lücken, *German Life and Letters*, vol. 32, issue 2, January 1979.

Gibb, Andrew Dewar. *Scotland in Eclipse* (London: Humphrey Toulmin, 1930).

Gibbon, Lewis Grassic. *A Scots Quair* trilogy (Edinburgh: Canongate Classics, 1995).

Golby, J. M. *Culture and Society in Britain 1850–1890* (Oxford: Oxford University Press, 1986).

Grierson, Herbert, ed. *The Poems of John Donne* (London: Oxford University Press, 1933).

Grieve, C. M. 'Foreword', *Northern Numbers* (London & Edinburgh: T. N. Foulis, 1920).
Grieve, C. M. 'The Chapbook Programme', *Scottish Chapbook* 1.1, August 1922.
Grieve, C. M. 'Edwin Muir', *Contemporary Scottish Studies* (London: Leonard Parsons, 1926).
Grieve, C. M. *Contemporary Scottish Studies* (London: Leonard Parsons, 1926).
Guggenheim, Peggy. *Out of This Century: Confessions of an Art Addict* (1946). (London: Deutsch, 2005).
Gunn, Neil M. Review of Muir's *Scott and Scotland*, *Scots Magazine* 26, October 1936.
Gunn, Neil M. *Scots Magazine*, 2 May 1943.
Hall, Michael. 'Newbattle Abbey, Lothian', *Country Life*, 8 July 1993.
Hamilton, Charles H. '*The Freeman*, 1920-1924', *Modern Age*, Winter 1987.
Hargreaves, Neil Kevin. 'An "experiment in the wilderness": Newbattle Abbey College and the idea of residential adult education in Scotland 1931-1955', *History of Education*, 3 April 2009.
Heaney, Seamus. 'The Impact of Translation', *Yale Review*, Autumn 1987.
Heaney, Seamus. *Finders Keepers. Selected Prose 1971-2001* (London: Faber and Faber, 2002).
Hendry, Joy, ed. *On Edwin Muir: Chapman 49*, Summer 1987.
Hendry, Joy, ed. *Peerie Willa Muir: Chapman 71*, Winter 1992-93.
Hubble, Mary. 'Among the Immortals: memories of Edwin and Willa Muir', *Cambridgeshire Life*, October 1990.
Jamieson, Morley. 'Recollections', University of Edinburgh Centre for Research Collections.
Janouch, Gustav. *Conversations with Kafka* (New York: New Directions Paperback, 2012).
Joll, James. *Europe Since 1870* (Harmondsworth: Penguin Books, 1983).
Kafka, Franz. *The Castle*, trans. by Edwin and Willa Muir (London: Martin Secker, 1930).
Kafka, Franz. *America*, trans. by Edwin and Willa Muir (London: Routledge, 1938).
Law, Jonathan. 'John Ferrar Holms: The Greatest Writer Never to Have Actually Written Anything', in *The Dabbler* blog, 4 May 2015. http://thedabbler.co.uk/2015/05/john-ferrar-holmes-the-greatest-writer-never-to-have-actually-written-anything/
Lawrence, D. H. *The Rainbow* (Harmondsworth: Penguin Books, 1961).
Lawrence, D. H. *The Letters of D. H. Lawrence*, ed. by James Boulton (Cambridge: Cambridge University Press, 1979-2000).
Lindsay, Maurice. *Francis George Scott and the Scottish Renaissance* (Edinburgh: Paul Harris Publishing, 1980).
MacDiarmid, Hugh. *The Islands of Scotland* (London: Batsford, 1939).
MacDiarmid, Hugh. *Complete Poems* 1920-1976, vol. 1 (London: Martin Brian & O'Keeffe, 1976).
MacLachlan, C. J. M. and D. S. Robb, eds. *Edwin Muir: Centenary Assessments* (Aberdeen: Association for Scottish Literature Studies, 1990).
Manson, John, ed. *Dear Grieve: Letters to Hugh MacDiarmid (C. M. Grieve)* (Glasgow: Kennedy & Boyd, 2011).
McCleery, Alistair, ed. *Landscape and Light: Essays of Neil M. Gunn* (Aberdeen: Aberdeen University Press, 1987).
McCulloch, Margery Palmer, ed. *Modernism and Nationalism: Source Documents for the Scottish Renaissance* (Glasgow: Association for Scottish Literary Studies, 2004).
McCulloch, Margery Palmer. 'Edwin and Willa Muir: Scottish, European and Gender Journeys, 1918-69', in *Edinburgh History of Scottish Literature, vol. 3, Modern Transformations*, ed. by Thomas Owen Clancy, Susan Manning, and Murray Pittock (Edinburgh: Edinburgh University Press, 2007).

Moncrieff, George Scott. 'Counterblasts to Knox', *New Statesman*, 27 June 1936.
Montgomery, William. Review of *Living with Ballads*, *Scottish Studies*, 9, 1965.
Moore, Edward. *We Moderns: Enigmas and Guesses* (London: George Allen & Unwin, 1918).
Muir, Edwin. 'Impressions of Prague, *Freeman*, 10 May 1922.
Muir, Edwin. 'At Salzburg', *The Freeman*, vol. VIII, 19 September 1923.
Muir, Edwin. 'Hugo von Hofmannsthal', *The Freeman*, October 1923.
Muir, Edwin. *Latitudes* (New York: B. W. Huebsch, 1924).
Muir, Edwin. 'The Poetry of Hölderlin', *The Saturday Review of Literature*, 3 January 1925.
Muir, Edwin. 'Scottish Renaissance', *Saturday Review of Literature* (NY), II, 17 October 1925.
Muir, Edwin. *The Estate of Poetry* (London: Hogarth Press, 1926).
Muir, Edwin. *Transition: Essays on Contemporary Literature* (London: Hogarth Press, 1926).
Muir, Edwin. *The Marionette* (London: Hogarth Press, 1927).
Muir, Edwin. 'Verse', *Nation and Athenaeum*, XL, 22 January 1927.
Muir, Edwin. *John Knox: Portrait of a Calvinist* (London: Jonathan Cape, 1929).
Muir, Edwin. *The Three Brothers* (London: Heinemann, 1931).
Muir, Edwin. *Poor Tom* (London: J. M. Dent & Sons, 1932).
Muir, Edwin. *Scottish Journey* (1935: Edinburgh: Mainstream Publishing, 1979).
Muir, Edwin. *Scott and Scotland* (1936: Edinburgh: Polygon, 1982).
Muir, Edwin. *The Story and the Fable* (London: George Harrop & Co, 1940).
Muir, Edwin. 'Yesterday's Mirror', *Scots Magazine* XXXIII, September 1940.
Muir, Edwin. *Essays on Literature and Society* (London: Hogarth Press, 1949).
Muir, Edwin. *An Autobiography* (1954: London: Methuen & Co, Ltd, University Paperbacks, 1968).
Muir, Edwin. *The Complete Poems of Edwin Muir. An Annotated Edition*, ed. by Peter Butter (Aberdeen: The Association for Scottish Literary Studies, 1991).
Muir, Edwin and Francis George Scott: A Conversation', *The Freeman*, 19 December 1923.
Muir, Willa. *Women: An Inquiry* (London: Hogarth Press, 1925).
Muir, Willa. *Mrs Grundy in Scotland*, Voice of Scotland Series (London: Routledge, 1936).
Muir, Willa. 'Women in Scotland', *The Left Review*, 1936.
Muir, Willa. *Living with Ballads* (London: The Hogarth Press, 1965).
Muir, Willa. *Belonging* (London: Hogarth Press, 1968).
Muir, Willa. *Imagined Corners* (1935: Edinburgh: Canongate Classics, 1987).
Muir, Willa. *Willa Muir: Imagined Selves*, ed. and intro. by Kirsty Allen (Edinburgh: Canongate Classics, 1996). Contains *Imagined Corners, Mrs Ritchie, Mrs Grundy in Scotland, Women: An Inquiry,* 'Women in Scotland'.
Pocock, Simon. *The British Council in Italy: An Early History (1938–58)* (British Council, 1965).
Power, William. *Should Auld Acquaintance: An Autobiography* (London: George Harrap, 1937).
Rilke, Rainer Maria. *Sämtliche Werke* I (Frankfurt am Main, 1955).
Sheldon, Sayre Phillips. 'A Cambridge Literary Footnote: First Performance of "The Antiphon"', *Harvard Review* 15, Fall 1998. http://www.jstor.org/stable/27561155. Accessed 28.02.2018.
Spencer, Herbert. *Principles of Biology* vol. II (London: Williams and Norgate, 1867).
Spencer, Herbert. *Principles of Sociology* vol. I (London: Williams and Norgate, 1876).

Thomson, George Malcolm. *Caledonia or The Future of the Scots* (London: Kegan Paul, Trench, Trubner & Co, 1927).

Tobrmanová-Kühnová, Šarka, ed. and transl. *Believe in People: The Essential Karel Čapek* (London: Faber, 2010).

Tucholsky, Kurt. Blurb from German edition of Franz Kafka, *Der Verschollene* (Frankfurt am Main: Fischer Taschenbuch Verlag, 1993).

Wood, H. Harvey. BBC typescript for talk on Edwin Muir, 31 August 1969, University of Glasgow Library, Archives & Special Collections.

Young, Douglas. '"He sailed strange seas of thought". My Scottish Diary', *News Chronicle*, 9 January 1959.

Young, James D. 'A Socialist's-eye View of Edwin Muir', *Chapman* 49, Summer 1987.

Young, James D. 'Hugh MacDiarmid, the Muirs and Grassic Gibbon', *Cencrastus* 65, 2,000.

Index

A
Abbotsford 150–151
Adam Smith, Janet 139, 165–166, 329–330
Allen, Bill 225–226, 232–233
Allen, Kirsty 2
Anderson, Wilhelmina *see* Muir, Willa
anti-Semitism 61–63, 149, 170–174
Aragon, Louis 212–213
Asch, Shalom 139–140
Athenaeum 23
Auden, W. H. 246–247
Austrian culture 60–63

B
Balcon, Jill 329–330
Barke, James 167–168, 200, 262–264
Barker, George 138–139, 146–148, 170–172
Barnes, Djuna 78–79, 273–274, 282–283, 286–288, 299–300
BBC 96–97, 170–172, 290, 291–292, 315–316, 320–321
Beerbohm, Max 307–308
Belloc, Hilaire 113
Beneš, Edvard 207–208, 235–236
Bennett, Arnold 181
Bergonzi, Bernard 257–258, 262–264
Berlin 29, 45–46
Bloomsbury 18, 20–21
Bollingen Foundation 288, 296–297, 305–306, 313
Bookman, The 146–147
Bosdêt, Mary 305–308, 330
Boston, MA 279
Bottrall, Ronald 251–254
Bowen, Elizabeth 234–235
Bradbrook, Bohuslava 293–294
Bradbrook, Muriel 293–294
Brecht, Bertolt 218
Bristol University 297–298
British Council 204–208, 216–218, 221–222, 225–226, 243, 251–253
Broch, Hermann 1–2, 131, 134, 139, 166–167, 173, 184f, 288
  The Death of Vigil/Der Tod des Vergil 189–190
  leaving Austria 170–172
  The Sleepwalkers/Die Schlafwandler 119–120, 132–133, 184–189, 214–217, 241–242
Brod, Max 170, 176–180
Brooks, Van Wyck 26, 64–65
Brown, George Mackay 7–8, 257–258, 260–262, 261f, 291–292, 299–300, 324–326, 329–332
Buchan, David 321–322
Buchan, John 197–198
Budapest, P.E.N. congress (1932) 132–133, 188
Bunyan, John 179
Burns, Robert 134–135, 151, 162–163
Butter, Peter 2, 248, 315–316, 325–326

C
Cairns, David 207–208, 328–329
Calvinism 161, 172, 179, 248–249, 295–296, 322–323
Cambridge 243
Cambridge, MA 278–279
Cambridge University 294, 296–297, 299–300
Čapek, Josef 32–35, 96–97
Čapek, Karel 32–36, 45–46, 96–97, 172, 198–199, 293–294
Carossa, Hans 115, 119, 180–184
Carswell, Catherine 1–2, 18, 101, 129–131, 134–135, 139, 160–161, 167–168
Carswell, Donald 1–2, 129–131, 134–135, 139, 201–202
Chamberlain, Neville 193
Chandler, Raymond 194–195
Chelsea 316–320
Chesterton, G. K. 16–17
Chiari, Joseph 222–223, 271
Chicago 287–288
Chisholm, Lilias 332–333
Chodak, Alexis Gregorievitch 22–23
Christianson, Aileen 2
Church, Richard 214–215, 321
Church Farm 331–333
Close, Reginald 231–232
Coleman, Emily 147–149
Collins, Sir Godfrey 149
Cologne 218–220
communism 7–8, 161, 200, 212–213, 295–296
Cortot, Alfred 80–81
Criterion, The 92, 129–130, 146–147
Cronin, A. J. 129–130

Crosbie, William 211–212
Crowborough 110–114, 134–135
Cruickshank, Helen 1–2, 129–132, 140–141, 149, 209, 269–270
Cunninghame Graham, R. B. 129–130
Cursiter, Stanley 149–150, 204–205, 211–212, 273–274, 291–292, 303–305
Czechoslavakia 29–31, 36, 38–39
   Communist 'Putsch' (1948) 235–238
   German invasion and occupation 173–174, 226–227
   Munich Agreement and 193
   Soviet occupation 220–222

D
Daiches, David 294
Day Lewis, Cecil 308–309
De la Mare, Walter 197–198
Dent 139–140, 146–147, 168–169, 214–215
Dial, The 51, 64–65, 68
Dick, Kay 329–330
Dobrée, Bonamy 195, 197–198
Donne, John 120–121
Dormansland 105
Douglas, Dorothy 203
Douglas, Norman 80–81
Dresden 39–42, 52–53
Dubrovnik, P.E.N. congress (1933) 142
Dunbar, William 262–264
Dymant, Dora 213–214, 216–217

E
Edinburgh
   Edinburgh Festival 269–270
   P.E.N. congress (1934) 129–130, 149
   Scottish Allied/International Houses 206–208
Eliot, T. S. 1–2, 6, 7, 69–70, 90, 120–121, 139, 169–170, 197–198, 204–205, 209, 273–274, 288, 294–295, 299–300, 302–303, 305, 319–321
   criticism 91–92, 94, 146–147, 251
   and Djuna Barnes 277–278, 286–288
   play 269–270
   poetry 93–94
Eluard, Paul 212–213
European Quarterly 146–147

F
Faber and Faber 214–215, 240, 258–259, 305
Fabre, Jean Henri 35
Faulkner, William 146–147
Feuchtwanger, Lion 1–2, 74–75, 105–106, 112–113, 115, 142, 176, 181
Florence 56–57

Fontaine 212–213
Forster, E. M. 243
Forte dei Marmi 55–56, 59–60
Fouchet, Max-Pol 212–213
Fraser, G. S. 262–264
Freeman, The 26, 36–37, 42–43, 46–47, 57–59, 64–65
French culture 59
French Resistance 212–213
Frost, Robert 278–279, 296–297
Fry, Roger 75

G
Gascoyne, David 138
Gaulle, General Charles de 206–207
Geddes, Patrick 101–103
George, Stefan 47–48
Germany 29
   culture 59
   inflation (1923) 53
   occupation of the Ruhr (1923) 53
   P.E.N. Club 142
   and tourists 42–43
Gibb, Andrew Dewar 151–152, 161
Gibbon, Lewis Grassic 106–107, 139, 155–157, 160–161, 262–264
Gibbs, Sir Philip 149–150
Giotto 179
Glaeser, Ernst 115, 181
Glasgow 6–7, 19–20, 39, 151–153
Glasgow Guilds Group 11–12, 14–15, 25–26
Goebbels, Joseph 75
Goethe, Johann Wolfgang von 41–42, 47–48, 88–89
Gollancz 137–140, 145, 149–150, 170–172
Goodsir Smith, Sydney 211–212
Gordon, Anna 322–323
Gordon, Donald 262–264
Graham, Cuthbert 329–330
Graham, W. S. 262
Graves, Robert 93
Gray, Alexander 211–212
Gray, Norah Nelson 103–104
Greene, Graham 246–247
Greenhill, Lord 272–273
Grierson, Flora 95–96, 136, 266, 311–312, 322–323
Grierson, Herbert 207–208, 211–212
Grieve, Christopher *see* MacDiarmid, Hugh
Grieve, Valda 165–166
Grigson, Geoffrey 138, 146–147
Guggenheim, Peggy 77–79, 117–118, 147–148, 281–282

INDEX

Gunn, Neil M. 163–164, 167–168, 211–212, 214–217

H
Hall, John 258–259, 298–299, 305, 309
Hamburger, Michael 312, 319–320
Hammerskjöld, Dag 299–300
Hampstead 134–138, 243
Hardy, Forsyth 321–322
Harman, Mark 178–180
Harvard University 272–273, 280–282
Hauptmann, Gerhard 1–2, 66–67, 82, 102–103, 115, 175–176
Heaney, Seamus 7–8, 240, 248
Heine, Heinrich 7, 47–48, 88–89
Heinemann 51–52, 145, 146–147, 149–150, 159
Hellerau 44–46, 52–55
Henryson, Robert 299–300, 331–332
Higham, David 310–312
Hind, Archie 257–258, 324–325
Hinks, Roger 243–244, 252–253
Hofmannsthal, Hugo von 47–48, 50–51, 57–58, 61–62, 88–89, 312
Hogarth Press 70–73, 75–76, 85, 90, 99, 100, 258–259, 262, 296–297, 310–311, 327–329
Hölderlin, Friedrich 47–50, 88, 146–147, 159, 248–250
Holloway, John 290
Holms, John 15, 21, 39, 43–44, 46–47, 51–53, 77–79, 81–82, 85–87, 90, 97–98, 139, 214–215, 334–335
    death 147–148
    disliked by Willa 21–22, 43, 55, 76–77, 268
    in Dresden 41–43
    in Italy 55–56
    in St Tropez 76–77
    and Peggy Guggenheim 117–118
Hough, Graham 294–295
Hudson, Stephen *see* Schiff, Sydney
Huebsch, Benjamin W. 64–67, 75–76, 81–82, 90, 175–176
Hungary 133–134
Huxley, Aldous 23, 69–70, 92–94, 170–172
Huxley, Julian 101

I
Irwin, David 321–322

J
Jaeger, Werner 165–166
Jamieson, Flora 210–211
Jamieson, Morley 210–214, 216–217
Jaques-Dalcroze, Émile 44–45

Jennings, Dorothy 41–42, 53, 55, 76–77, 117–118
Jennings, Elizabeth 321, 329–330
Johnson, R. Brimley 101
Joyce, James 93–95, 187–188, 307–308

K
Kafka, Franz 1–2, 36, 131, 170, 189–190, 213–214, 221, 269, 302–303, 333–334
    America/Der Verschollene 177, 179–180
    Great Wall of China, and Other Pieces 139–140, 177
    The Castle/Das Schloss 36, 115–116, 176–179
    The Penal Settlement, Tales and Short Pieces 177, 228–229, 234–235
    The Trial 168–172, 177
Kelsall, Moultrie 200
Kemp, Robert 211–212, 321–322
Kennedy Fraser, Marjory 11
Kennedy Fraser, Patuffa 11
Kerr, Philip, Marquis of Lothian 255, 257
Kerr, Roderick Watson 134–135
King, Sir Frederic Truby 109
King, Jessie M. 103–104
Kingsmill, Hugh 15–17, 21, 78–79, 97–98, 139, 147–148, 165–166
Knights, Lionel C. 300–301, 331–332
Knox, John 95–96, 110–111, 248–249
Kokoschka, Oskar 48
Krapp, Gerda 51–52, 54–56, 65–66, 268
Kukiel, General Marian 206–207
Kundera, Milan 184

L
Lavrin, Janko 23, 26, 139, 146–147
Lawrence, D. H. 18, 93–94, 106–107, 176, 248–249, 302–303
Lawrence and Wishart 166–167
Leavis, F. R. 281–282
Lee, Vernon 176
Left Review 167–168
Lehfeldt, Sylvia 305–306, 319–320
Lehmann, John 203, 308–309
Levin, Harry 281–282
Lewis, Wyndham 69–70, 92
Lindsay, Maurice 211–212
Linklater, Eric 153–154, 193, 204–205, 211–212
Lissitzky, El 45–46
Listener, The 137–139, 146–147, 159–160, 170–172, 202–203, 296–297
Litchfield, Mary 76–77, 160–161, 194–195, 197–198, 200–201
Litvinov, Maxim 18
Lloyd, Roger B. 183–184

Lochhead, Marion 269–270
London 22; *see also* Bloomsbury; Chelsea; Hampstead
London Mercury 159–160
Lothar, Ernst 139–140
Low, Barbara 18–19
Low, Ivy 18
Lowell, Robert 287–288
Lubbock, Percy 139–140
Lucca, Feast of the Black Christ 59–60
Lücken, Iwar von 47–48, 88, 92–93
Lunn, Hugh Kingsmill *see* Kingsmill, Hugh
Luther, Martin 319–320
Luxembourg, Rosa 152–153

M

MacCaig, Norman 198–199, 298–299
McCance, William 72–73
MacColl, Ewen 309–310
MacDiarmid, Hugh (Christopher Grieve) 7–8, 49, 51, 71–72, 129–131, 139, 151, 167–168, 198–199
  British Security Service surveillance 200
  feud with Edwin 161–163, 166–167, 211–212, 262–264
  'Meanings in Scotland' series 155–158
Macdonald, Frances 103–104
Macdonald, Margaret 103–104
MacEwen, David 163–164
McIsaac, Nigel 211–212, 269–270
Mackenzie, Compton 160–161
MacLean, Sorley 211–212
MacLeish, Archibald 280–281, 285
Macmurray, John 271, 319–320
MacNeice, Louis 146–147, 308–309
McNeill, Florence (Floss) Marian 73–75, 104, 122–123, 140–141, 269–270
McNicol, Bessie 103–104
Mann, Thomas 142
Mansfield, Katherine 23, 69–70, 80
Marinetti, Filippo Tommaso 149
Marsden, Dora 100–101
Marwick, Ernest 290–292, 305–307, 315–316, 321, 324–326, 329–331
Marwick, Janette 305–307, 315–316
Masaryk, Jan 236–237
Masaryk, T. G. 32–33, 35, 38, 207–208, 223–224
Mason, Arthur 80–81, 112
Mason, Mary 80–81, 112
Mays, Spike 332–333
Meadowcroft 330–332
Mencken, H. L. 26
Menton 77, 79–81, 116–117
Miller, Karl 281–282, 284–285

Minervini, Laura 243–244
Mitchell, James Leslie *see* Grassic Gibbon, Lewis
Mitchison, Naomi 129–130
Mitrinović, Dmitri 23
Modern Scot, The 122–123, 130–131, 139–141, 146–147, 163–164
Modersohn-Becker, Paula 103–104
Montgomery, William 322–323
Montrose 4, 12–13, 70–71, 73
Moore, Edward *see* Muir, Edwin
Mozart, Wolfgang Amadeus 57–58, 60, 64, 166–167
Muir, Edwin 1–2, 14*f*
  'After a Hypothetical War' 296
  'Ancient Song, An' 90
  'Annunciation, The' 250–251, 295–296
  appearance 11
  approach to creative writing 69–70, 75–76, 120, 247–248
  Autobiography, An 2, 36, 78, 244, 295, 329, 334
  'Ballad of the Black Douglas, The' 85–87
  'Ballad of the Flood' 43, 86–87, 97–98
  ballads 85–87
  'Birthday, A' 216–217
  British Council work 204–208, 216–218, 221–222, 225–226, 243
  British Security Service surveillance 200
  'Childhood' 51–52, 88
  Chorus of the Newly Dead 51, 65–66, 72–73, 85, 90–92
  as a clerk 10–12, 16, 22
  Collected Poems 299–300, 305–309
  'Confirmation, The' 215–216
  as critic 7, 71, 85, 92, 146–147
  dreams 56–57, 169–170
  Dundee Food Office, work at 197–198, 201
  early years 3, 5–7, 15, 200
  education, lack of 197–198
  Estate of Poetry, The (Harvard University lectures) 285–286, 296–297, 305–306
  First Poems 46–47, 51, 56, 85, 86–90
  Gerda in love with 54–55, 268
  'Good Town, The' 240–241
  and Greek mythology 168–169, 214–215, 240–241, 294–296
  'Helmet, The' 241–242
  Home Guard service 195
  honorary doctorates 230–231, 299–300
  'Horses, The' 51–52, 68, 88, 296
  'Houses' 88–89
  ill-health 22–23, 201–202, 270–271, 296–301
  'Incarnate One, The' 295–296

incarnation theme 247–248
'Interrogation, The' 240
John Know: Portrait of a Calvinist 95–96, 110–111
Journeys and Places 168–169
Labyrinth, The 7–8, 240, 251–252
'Labyrinth, The' 240–241, 248
'Last War, The' 298–299
Latitudes 7, 63–64, 66–67, 86–87, 92–93
lecturing style and public speaking 17–18, 224–225, 285, 286
'Lost Land, The' 88–89
Marionette, The 75–76, 81–82, 85, 95–96
marriage proposal 14–15
meeting Willa 10–11
'Myth, The' 216–217
Narrow Place, The (poetry) 214–215
nervous breakdown (1948) 243
'North and South' article (1922) 46–47, 54–55, 59
not Scottish 71–72, 131, 163–164
novels 6, 75–76, 95–96
obituaries 302–305
One Foot in Eden 248–249, 251, 258–259, 294–296, 302–303
personality 22, 25–26, 138, 194–195, 208–209
poetry 1–2, 5–8, 43, 46–47, 51–53, 65–66, 85–86, 131, 258–259, 298–299
Poor Tom 6, 95–96, 139–140
psychoanalysis 7, 25, 46–47, 85–86
'Question to my Love, A' 88–89
recordings of poems 282, 284–285
'Refugees, The' 1–2, 214–215
'Refugees Born for a Land Unknown, The' 309
as religious 247–251
'Return of Odysseus, The' 214–215
'Return of the Greeks, The' 216–217
'Rider Victory, The' 216–217
'River, The' 214–215
Scott and Scotland ('Meanings in Scotland' project) 155–156, 158, 159–164
Scottish Journey 149–153
Six Poems 95–96, 136
and socialism 7, 71–72, 80, 152–155, 161, 262–264
Story and the Fable, The (autobiography) 2–3, 5–6, 38, 196–197, 216–217, 248
Structure of the Novel, The 95–96
study contrasted with Willa's 141
teaching at Charles University, Prague 224–226, 239–240
Three Brothers, The 95–96, 119–120, 139–140
'To J.F.H.' 214–216

Transition 7, 70–71, 93–96
translations 66–67, 70–71, 75, 105–106, 115, 119, 132–133, 137–138, 175–182, 184–190
Variations on a Time Theme 146–147
Voyage, The 216–217
'Wayside Station, The' 201, 214–215
We Moderns 3, 10, 16–17, 26, 68–69, 93
Muir, Gavin 108, 119, 124–126, 134–136, 198–200, 205, 210–211, 227–228, 243, 267–268, 291–292, 305–306, 315–318, 323–324, 330–333
deafness 233–234, 267, 291–293
knocked down by oil tanker 143–144
marriage to Dorothy 309–310, 312–313
at Montessori school 116–117
moving to Swaffham Prior 314–315
musical ability 199, 205, 267–268, 291–292
at St Andrews schools 164–165, 205
at St Andrews University 227
Muir, Jimmie 25–26
Muir, Lizzie *see* Thorburn family
Muir, Willa 1–2, 13*f*, 327*f*
approach to creative writing 69–70, 75–76, 120, 247–248
arthritis 262, 296–297, 306–307, 323–324
Belonging (autobiography) 2–3, 319, 325–330
'Čapek Brothers at Home in Prague, The' 96–97
civil list pension 305–306
diary 228–230, 232–236, 264–265, 269
and domestic staff 72, 124–126, 134–135, 143–144, 146, 172–173, 223–224, 234, 245–246
dreams 229–230, 269
early years 3–5, 12–13
engagement to rugby player 13–14
essays 96–97
as headmistress of Day Continuation School 23–24
ill-health 22–23, 114–115, 124–126, 146, 157–158, 172–173, 194–195, 203–204, 245–246, 271–272, 296–297, 316–318
Imagined Corners (Montrose novel) 2–4, 75–76, 82, 85, 104, 119–124, 188
as 'kept woman' 68
Living with Ballads 313–319, 321–323
Marmaduke Journal (childrearing) 108–110
marriage, others' perception of her 320–321
marriage and loss of job 17
marriage as belonging 21–22, 247–248
marriage proposal 14–15
meeting Edwin 10–11
'Metamorphosis' 229

Muir, Willa (*Continued*)
  miscarriage 73–75, 104
  Mrs Grundy in Scotland ('Meanings in Scotland' project) 155–156, 158, 159–161
  Mrs Ritchie 101–102, 140–141
  Mrs Muttoe and the Top Storey (unpubd) 143, 170
  'Nativity' 99
  Noah's Ark play (unrealized) 97–98
  novels 75–76
  on mortality 264–265
  obituaries 333–334
  personality 22, 54–55, 116–117, 139, 194–195, 211–212, 260–264
  pregnancy and childbirth 104–108
  Shetland roots 4
  study contrasted with Edwin's 141
  teaching at Hellerau International School 45–46
  teaching at New Park School 197–198, 201–202
  'This Lopsided Life' 310–312
  'To Edwin absent' 232
  translations 3–4, 66–67, 70–71, 75, 82, 85, 105–106, 112–113, 115, 132–133, 175–181, 184–190, 234–235
  translations, solo 104, 115, 119, 175–176, 180–184, 268–269
  university education 4–5, 12–14
  'Usurpers, The' (unpubd) 265–266
  'Woman in Prague, A' 96–97
  Women: An Inquiry 3, 70–71, 74, 99–102, 121
Munich Agreement 172, 193
Murry, Middleton 23
Mussolini, Benvenuto 80–81

N
Nation, The 51–52, 64–65, 68, 70–71, 85, 90, 129–130
National Trust 257
Nazis 32–33, 142, 149
Neill, A. S. 1–2, 44–46, 53, 64–65, 67, 71–72, 107, 269–270, 312–313, 319–320
Neilson, Francis 64–65
Neilson, Francis Swift 64–65
Neuberger, Dr Fritz 48
Neustätter, Dr Otto and Frau 44–46, 55
New Age, The 3, 10, 23, 36–37, 46–47, 85–86
New Alliance, The 214–215, 246–247
New Apocalypse movement 262–264
Newbattle Abbey 253–255, 256*f*, 257–260, 271, 272, 324–325
Newbery, Fra 103–104
New Criticism 281–282

New English Weekly, The 146–147, 159–160
Newman, Lyn 328–329
Newtongrange 264
New York 277–278, 286–287
Nietzsche, Friedrich 1–3, 7, 11–12, 15, 26, 47–48
Niven, Barbara 211–212
Nock, Albert Jay 64–65

O
O'Brien, Joe 246–247
Observer, The 296–297
Oeser, Drury 165–167, 173–174
Oeser, Oscar 165–167
Orage, Alfred Richard 3, 16–17, 23, 25, 46–47, 129, 137–138
Orkney Islands 5–8, 49–50, 144–145, 153–154, 260–261, 291–292
Ould, Herman 226
Outlook 163–164, 168

P
Parker, Agnes Millar 72–73
Parsons, Ian 300–301
Pasley, Malcolm 177–179
Pearn, Pollinger & Higham Ltd 310–311
Pearson, Hesketh 165–166
P.E.N. International 113, 129–134, 142, 149, 226, 232
Penn 71–73
Playfair, Nigel 34–35
Plunket Society 109
Poetry Scotland 211–212
Poincaré, Henri 53
Porpoise Press 134–135
Pound, Ezra 23
Power, William 16–17, 131, 149, 158
Prager Quartet 165–166
Prague 26, 30–31, 30*f*, 32, 36–37, 39, 96–97, 216–218, 219*f*, 221–224
  Charles University 224–226
  theatres 33
Priestley, J. B. 149–150
Pritchett, V. S. 246–247
Proust, Marcel 44, 184–185, 307–308

R
Raeburn, Sir Henry 151
Raine, Kathleen 1–2, 91–92, 272–274, 288, 290, 292–293, 302–303, 305–306, 309–310, 314, 315–320, 327–328
Ramsay, Mary 210–211
Ramsden, Sir Eugene 206–207
Read, Herbert 92, 170–172, 319–320

Renn, Ludwig 112–113, 115, 181
Revilliod, Olga 207–208
Rheinhardt, Emil Alphons 116
Richards, I. A. 281–282, 287–288
Rilke, Rainer Maria 88–89, 103–104, 115
Ritchie, T. R. 211–212
Ritchie, W. D. 272–273
Robertson, Ritchie 179–180
Robeson, Paul 80–81
robots 34–35
Romanticism 49
Rome 243–246
   British Institute 243–244, 246–247, 251, 252–254
Ross, Ethel 314–315
Routledge 155–156, 157–158, 166–167, 170–172
Ruskin, John 102–103

S
St Andrews 12–13, 153–155, 159, 163–167, 170–172, 195, 197–198, 225–226, 332–333
St Tropez 74–79
Salzburg 57–58, 60–62
Salzburg Festival 57–58
Samson Press 136
Saunders, Cyril 218
Saurat, Denis 16–17, 19–20, 68–70, 129–131, 139, 197–198
Schiff, Sydney 65–66, 68–70, 81–82, 85, 90–93, 124, 140–141, 170–173, 184–185, 302
Schiff, Violet 68–70, 81–82, 99–101, 245–246, 302, 307–308
Schocken 234–235
Schönberg, Arnold 59
Scotland 35–36, 69–71
   anti-conscription protest 198–199
   ballad and folksong revival 321–322
   Irish immigrants 151–152
   literary revival 71, 129–131, 134–135, 146–147, 161–163
   nationalism 152–153, 161
   Scots language and poetry 71–72, 86–87, 129–130, 162–164, 211–212
   travel writing 150–153
Scotsman, The 23–25, 154–155, 159–160, 170–172, 303–305
Scott, Agnes Neill *see* Muir, Willa
Scott, Alexander 321–322
Scott, Francis George 19–20, 56, 57*f*, 58–59, 71, 76–77, 129, 165–168, 194–195
Scott, Lovey *see* Chisholm, Lilias
Scott, Tom 200, 257–258, 262–264, 273–274, 313–314, 324–325, 331–332
Scott, Sir Walter 134–135, 150, 163–164

Scottish Centre of International P.E.N. 129–130, 149, 264
Scottish Chapbook, The 71
Scottish Literary Renaissance 71
Scottish Nation 71, 129
Scottish National Party 74–75, 152–153, 161, 198–199
Scottish Standard, The 163–164
Scott-Moncrieff, Ann 217
Scott Moncrieff, Charles Kenneth 184–185
Scott Moncrieff, George 160–161, 246–247
Secker 74–75, 112–113, 116, 137, 139–141, 176–177, 181, 234–235
Selver, Paul 32, 34–35
Shaw, George Bernard 113, 151
Shelmerdine, Joan M. 95–96, 136, 266
Sherek, Henry 269–270
Sholokhov, Mikhail 146–147
Sitwell, Edith 23, 93, 99, 131, 308–309
Smallwood, Nora 308–309
Sonntagberg 64–67
Soukup, Catriona 208, 224
Soukup, Lumir 207–209, 221, 222–224, 236–240, 243–244, 266, 284–285, 306
Špála, Václav 34–35, 96–97
Spanish Civil War 168–169
Spanish flu 22–23
Spectator, The 139–140, 146–147
Spencer, Herbert 102–103 n. 9
Spender, Stephen 138, 146–147, 168–169, 197–198, 209, 250, 319–320
Spengler, Oswald 146–147
Steiner, Rudolf 60
Stern, Isaac 269–270
Stevenson, Robert Louis 80
Stobo, Mrs ('Mam') 10, 12
Stobo, Emily 4–5, 10, 12
Strauss, Richard 57–58
Strong, L. A. G. 183–184
Summerhill School 44
Swaffham Prior 290–293, 319–320
Sweeney, Jack 282, 284–285

T
Talich, Václav 224
Tate, Allen 319–320
Taylor, Rachel Annand 129–130
Tessenow, Heinrich 44–45
Thirteen Club 166–167
Thomas, Dylan 138
Thomson, George Malcolm 129–130, 134–135, 139, 151–152, 161
Thomson, J. Arthur 101–103

Thorburn family (George. Lizzie, Ethel, & Irene) 25–26, 80, 110–111, 113–114, 118–119, 124–126, 137–138, 144, 157–158, 264–265
Toller, Ernst 134, 142, 149
Tonge, John 166–168
Toynbee, Philip 329–330
Trakl, Georg 47–48
Tucholsky, Kurt 180

U
Untermeyer, Jean Starr 189–190
Untermeyer, Louis 66–67
Urquhart, Fred 194–195, 197–198, 200–201

V
Vaerting, Mathias 101–103
Vaerting, Mathilde 101–103
Van Dusens 286–287
Vienna 62–64
Vočadlo, Prof. Otakar 239–240, 293–294

W
Wagner, Richard 64
Wander Vogel movement 52–53
Warner, Rex 246–247
Waugh, Alec 78–79
Weisskopf, Victor 288–289

Wells, H. G. 142
West, Rebecca 101, 131, 139–140
Whyte, James 130–132, 139–140, 153–154, 159, 163–168
Wilbur, Charles 279–280
Wilbur, Richard 279–280, 282–283
Williams, Orlo 92
Wilson, Edmund 282–284
Wilson, Elena 283–284
Wood, H. Harvey 204–205, 208–209, 224–225
Woods, Wendy 198–199
Woolf, Leonard 65–66, 70–73, 85, 90–92, 94–95, 100, 202–203
Woolf, Virginia 72–73, 90, 93, 99, 101, 202–203, 310–311
Wordsworth, William 88, 92–93
World War II 195
   aftermath 218–221, 219f, 219f

Y
Young, Douglas 161, 198–199, 201, 211–212, 246–247, 303–305
Young, James D. 262–264

Z
Zrzavy, Jan 34–35, 96–97
Zurich, P.E.N. congress (1947) 232